Honda Civic
Service and Repair Manual

A K Legg LAE MIMI and Mike Stubblefield

(3199-224)

Models covered

Honda Civic models with SOHC engines, including special/limited editions
1.3 litre (1343 cc), 1.5 litre (1493 cc) and 1.6 litre SOHC (1590 cc)

Does not cover 1.6 litre DOHC engine (1595 cc)
Does not cover UK-built 5-door models, nor revised range introduced from March 1995

© Haynes Group Limited 1996

A book in the **Haynes Service and Repair Manual Series**

ISBN **978 0 85733 691 0**

British Library Cataloguing in Publication Data
A catalogue record for this book is available from the British Library.

Haynes Group Limited
Haynes North America, Inc

www.haynes.com

Contents

LIVING WITH YOUR HONDA CIVIC

Roadside Repairs

Weekly Checks

MAINTENANCE

Contents

REPAIRS AND OVERHAUL

Engine and Associated Systems

Transmission

Brakes and Suspension

Body equipment

Wiring Diagrams

REFERENCE

Index

The Honda Civic is available in two-door coupe, hatchback, four-door saloon and two-door convertible body styles.

The transversely mounted in-line four-cylinder engine used in these models is equipped with a carburettor on 1.3 litre models and electronic fuel injection on all other models.

The engine drives the front wheels through either a five-speed manual or a four-speed automatic transmission via independent driveshafts.

Independent suspension, featuring coil spring/shock absorber units, is used on all four wheels. The rack-and-pinion steering unit is mounted behind the engine and on some models it is power-assisted.

The brakes are disc at the front and either discs or drums at the rear, with power assistance standard.

Provided that regular servicing is carried out in accordance with the manufacturer's recommendations, the Honda Civic should prove reliable and economical. Most items requiring frequent attention are easily accessible.

Your Honda Civic Manual

The aim of this manual is to help you get the best value from your vehicle. It can do so in several ways. It can help you decide what work must be done (even should you choose to get it done by a garage), provide information on routine maintenance and servicing, and give a logical course of action and diagnosis when random faults occur. However, it is hoped that you will use the manual by tackling the work yourself. On simpler jobs, it may even be quicker than booking the car into a garage and going there twice, to leave and collect it. Perhaps most important, a lot of money can be saved by avoiding the costs a garage must charge to cover its labour and overheads.

The manual has drawings and descriptions to show the function of the various components, so that their layout can be understood. Then the tasks are described and photographed in a clear step-by-step sequence.

Honda Civic "Bali" 3-door

Honda Civic ESi 4-door

The Honda Civic Team

Haynes manuals are produced by dedicated and enthusiastic people working in close co-operation. The team responsible for the creation of this book included:

Authors	Andy Legg Mike Stubblefield
Sub-editors	Carole Turk
Editor & Page Make-up	Bob Jex
Workshop manager	Paul Buckland
Photo Scans	John Martin Paul Tanswell
Cover illustration & Line Art	Roger Healing
Wiring diagrams	Matthew Marke

We hope the book will help you to get the maximum enjoyment from your car. By carrying out routine maintenance as described you will ensure your car's reliability and preserve its resale value.

Acknowledgements

We are grateful to the Champion Spark Plug Company, who supplied the illustrations of various spark plug conditions. Technical writers who contributed to this project include Rob Maddox, Mark Ryan and Larry Warren.

We take great pride in the accuracy of information given in this manual, but vehicle manufacturers make alterations and design changes during the production run of a particular vehicle of which they do not inform us. No liability can be accepted by the authors or publishers for loss, damage or injury caused by any errors in, or omissions from, the information given.

Project vehicles

Vehicles used in the preparation of this manual, and which appear in many of the photographic sequences, include a Honda Civic VEi and a Honda Civic LSi.

Working on your car can be dangerous. This page shows just some of the potential risks and hazards, with the aim of creating a safety-conscious attitude.

General hazards

Scalding

• Don't remove the radiator or expansion tank cap while the engine is hot.
• Engine oil, automatic transmission fluid or power steering fluid may also be dangerously hot if the engine has recently been running.

Burning

• Beware of burns from the exhaust system and from any part of the engine. Brake discs and drums can also be extremely hot immediately after use.

Crushing

• When working under or near a raised vehicle, always supplement the jack with axle stands, or use drive-on ramps. *Never venture under a car which is only supported by a jack.*
• Take care if loosening or tightening high-torque nuts when the vehicle is on stands. Initial loosening and final tightening should be done with the wheels on the ground.

Fire

• Fuel is highly flammable; fuel vapour is explosive.
• Don't let fuel spill onto a hot engine.
• Do not smoke or allow naked lights (including pilot lights) anywhere near a vehicle being worked on. Also beware of creating sparks (electrically or by use of tools).
• Fuel vapour is heavier than air, so don't work on the fuel system with the vehicle over an inspection pit.
• Another cause of fire is an electrical overload or short-circuit. Take care when repairing or modifying the vehicle wiring.
• Keep a fire extinguisher handy, of a type suitable for use on fuel and electrical fires.

Electric shock

• Ignition HT voltage can be dangerous, especially to people with heart problems or a pacemaker. Don't work on or near the ignition system with the engine running or the ignition switched on.

• Mains voltage is also dangerous. Make sure that any mains-operated equipment is correctly earthed. Mains power points should be protected by a residual current device (RCD) circuit breaker.

Fume or gas intoxication

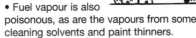

• Exhaust fumes are poisonous; they often contain carbon monoxide, which is rapidly fatal if inhaled. Never run the engine in a confined space such as a garage with the doors shut.
• Fuel vapour is also poisonous, as are the vapours from some cleaning solvents and paint thinners.

Poisonous or irritant substances

• Avoid skin contact with battery acid and with any fuel, fluid or lubricant, especially antifreeze, brake hydraulic fluid and Diesel fuel. Don't syphon them by mouth. If such a substance is swallowed or gets into the eyes, seek medical advice.
• Prolonged contact with used engine oil can cause skin cancer. Wear gloves or use a barrier cream if necessary. Change out of oil-soaked clothes and do not keep oily rags in your pocket.
• Air conditioning refrigerant forms a poisonous gas if exposed to a naked flame (including a cigarette). It can also cause skin burns on contact.

Asbestos

• Asbestos dust can cause cancer if inhaled or swallowed. Asbestos may be found in gaskets and in brake and clutch linings. When dealing with such components it is safest to assume that they contain asbestos.

Special hazards

Hydrofluoric acid

• This extremely corrosive acid is formed when certain types of synthetic rubber, found in some O-rings, oil seals, fuel hoses etc, are exposed to temperatures above 400°C. The rubber changes into a charred or sticky substance containing the acid. *Once formed, the acid remains dangerous for years. If it gets onto the skin, it may be necessary to amputate the limb concerned.*
• When dealing with a vehicle which has suffered a fire, or with components salvaged from such a vehicle, wear protective gloves and discard them after use.

The battery

• Batteries contain sulphuric acid, which attacks clothing, eyes and skin. Take care when topping-up or carrying the battery.
• The hydrogen gas given off by the battery is highly explosive. Never cause a spark or allow a naked light nearby. Be careful when connecting and disconnecting battery chargers or jump leads.

Air bags

• Air bags can cause injury if they go off accidentally. Take care when removing the steering wheel and/or facia. Special storage instructions may apply.

Diesel injection equipment

• Diesel injection pumps supply fuel at very high pressure. Take care when working on the fuel injectors and fuel pipes.

⚠️ *Warning: Never expose the hands, face or any other part of the body to injector spray; the fuel can penetrate the skin with potentially fatal results.*

Remember...

DO

• Do use eye protection when using power tools, and when working under the vehicle.

• Do wear gloves or use barrier cream to protect your hands when necessary.

• Do get someone to check periodically that all is well when working alone on the vehicle.

• Do keep loose clothing and long hair well out of the way of moving mechanical parts.

• Do remove rings, wristwatch etc, before working on the vehicle – especially the electrical system.

• Do ensure that any lifting or jacking equipment has a safe working load rating adequate for the job.

DON'T

• Don't attempt to lift a heavy component which may be beyond your capability – get assistance.

• Don't rush to finish a job, or take unverified short cuts.

• Don't use ill-fitting tools which may slip and cause injury.

• Don't leave tools or parts lying around where someone can trip over them. Mop up oil and fuel spills at once.

• Don't allow children or pets to play in or near a vehicle being worked on.

The following pages are intended to help in dealing with common roadside emergencies and breakdowns. You will find more detailed fault finding information at the back of the manual, and repair information in the main chapters.

If your car won't start and the starter motor doesn't turn

☐ If it's a model with automatic transmission, make sure the selector is in 'P' or 'N'.
☐ Open the bonnet and make sure that the battery terminals are clean and tight.
☐ Switch on the headlights and try to start the engine. If the headlights go very dim when you're trying to start, the battery is probably flat. Get out of trouble by jump starting (see next page) using a friend's car.

If your car won't start even though the starter motor turns as normal

☐ Is there fuel in the tank?
☐ Is there moisture on electrical components under the bonnet? Switch off the ignition, then wipe off any obvious dampness with a dry cloth. Spray a water-repellent aerosol product (WD-40 or equivalent) on ignition and fuel system electrical connectors like those shown in the photos. Pay special attention to the ignition coil wiring connector and HT leads.

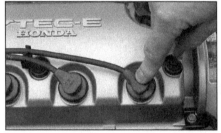

A Check that the spark plug HT leads are securely connected by pushing them home.

B The map sensor wiring plug may cause problems if not connected securely.

C Check all engine wiring plugs for security.

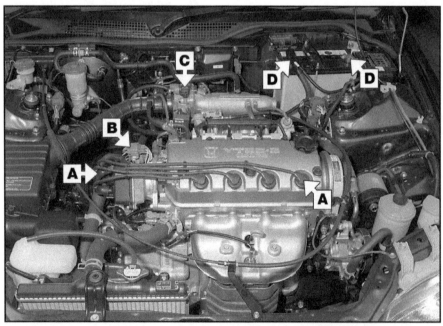

Check that electrical connections are secure (with the ignition switched off) and spray them with a water dispersant spray like WD40 if you suspect a problem due to damp

D Check the security and condition of the battery connections.

Jump starting

 HAYNES HiNT *Jump starting will get you out of trouble, but you must correct whatever made the battery go flat in the first place. There are three possibilities:*

1 *The battery has been drained by repeated attempts to start, or by leaving the lights on.*

2 *The charging system is not working properly (alternator drivebelt slack or broken, alternator wiring fault or alternator itself faulty).*

3 *The battery itself is at fault (electrolyte low, or battery worn out).*

When jump-starting a car using a booster battery, observe the following precautions:

✔ Before connecting the booster battery, make sure that the ignition is switched off.

✔ Ensure that all electrical equipment (lights, heater, wipers, etc) is switched off.

✔ Make sure that the booster battery is the same voltage as the discharged one in the vehicle.

✔ If the battery is being jump-started from the battery in another vehicle, the two vehcles MUST NOT TOUCH each other.

✔ Make sure that the transmission is in neutral (or PARK, in the case of automatic transmission).

1 Connect one end of the red jump lead to the positive (+) terminal of the flat battery

2 Connect the other end of the red lead to the positive (+) terminal of the booster battery.

3 Connect one end of the black jump lead to the negative (-) terminal of the booster battery

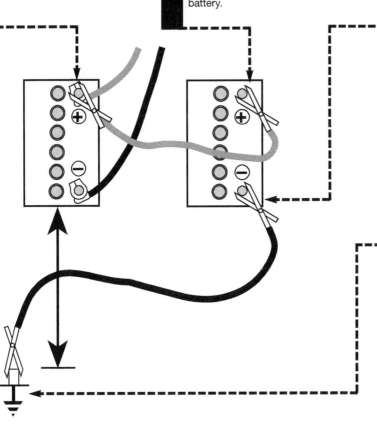

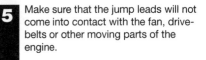

4 Connect the other end of the black jump lead to a bolt or bracket on the engine block, well away from the battery, on the vehicle to be started.

5 Make sure that the jump leads will not come into contact with the fan, drivebelts or other moving parts of the engine.

6 Start the engine using the booster battery, then with the engine running at idle speed, disconnect the jump leads in the reverse order of connection.

Wheel changing

Some of the details shown here will vary according to model. For instance, the location of the spare wheel and jack is not the same on all cars. However, the basic principles apply to all vehicles.

Warning: Do not change a wheel in a situation where you risk being hit by other traffic. On busy roads, try to stop in a lay-by or a gateway. Be wary of passing traffic while changing the wheel – it is easy to become distracted by the job in hand.

Preparation

☐ When a puncture occurs, stop as soon as it is safe to do so.

☐ Park on firm level ground, if possible, and well out of the way of other traffic.

☐ Use hazard warning lights if necessary.

☐ If you have one, use a warning triangle to alert other drivers of your presence.

☐ Apply the handbrake and engage first or reverse gear (or Park on models with automatic transmission.

☐ Chock the wheel diagonally opposite the one being removed – a couple of large stones will do for this.

☐ If the ground is soft, use a flat piece of wood to spread the load under the jack

Changing the wheel

1 The spare wheel, jack and tools are located in the rear luggage compartment.

2 Unscrew the retainer to remove the spare wheel.

3 Unscrew the jack to remove it from its bracket.

4 Loosen the wheel nuts slightly using the wheelbrace.

5 Locate the jack head in the jacking point nearest the wheel to be changed. Turn the jack handle to raise the car until the wheel is just clear of the ground. Unscrew the wheel nuts and remove the wheel.

6 Fit the spare wheel and tighten the nuts firmly by hand, then lower the car and fully tighten the nuts using the wheelbrace.

Finally...

☐ Remove the wheel chocks.

☐ Stow the jack and tools in the correct locations in the car.

☐ Check the tyre pressure on the wheel just fitted. If it is low, or if you don't have a pressure gauge with you, drive slowly to the nearest garage and inflate the tyre to the right pressure.

☐ Have the damaged tyre or wheel repaired as soon as possible.

Identifying leaks

Puddles on the garage floor or drive, or obvious wetness under the bonnet or underneath the car, suggest a leak that needs investigating. It can sometimes be difficult to decide where the leak is coming from, especially if the engine bay is very dirty already. Leaking oil or fluid can also be blown rearwards by the passage of air under the car, giving a false impression of where the problem lies.

 Warning: Most automotive oils and fluids are poisonous. Wash them off skin, and change out of contaminated clothing, without delay.

 HAYNES HINT *The smell of a fluid leaking from the car may provide a clue to what's leaking. Some fluids are distinctively coloured. It may help to clean the car and to park it over some clean paper as an aid to locating the source of the leak. Remember that some leaks may only occur while the engine is running.*

Sump oil

Engine oil may leak from the drain plug...

Oil from filter

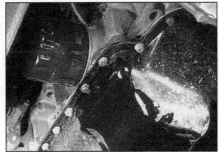

...or from the base of the oil filter.

Gearbox oil

Gearbox oil can leak from the seals at the inboard ends of the driveshafts.

Antifreeze

Leaking antifreeze often leaves a crystalline deposit like this.

Brake fluid

A leak occurring at a wheel is almost certainly brake fluid.

Power steering fluid

Power steering fluid may leak from the pipe connectors on the steering rack.

Towing

When all else fails, you may find yourself having to get a tow home – or of course you may be helping somebody else. Long-distance recovery should only be done by a garage or breakdown service. For shorter distances, DIY towing using another car is easy enough, but observe the following points:

☐ Use a proper tow-rope – they are not expensive. The vehicle being towed must display an 'ON TOW' sign in its rear window.
☐ Always turn the ignition key to the 'on' position when the vehicle is being towed, so that the steering lock is released, and that the direction indicator and brake lights will work.
☐ Only attach the tow-rope to the towing eyes provided.
☐ Before being towed, release the handbrake and select neutral on the transmission.

☐ Note that greater-than-usual pedal pressure will be required to operate the brakes, since the vacuum servo unit is only operational with the engine running.
☐ On models with power steering, greater-than-usual steering effort will also be required.
☐ The driver of the car being towed must keep the tow-rope taut at all times to avoid snatching.
☐ Make sure that both drivers know the route before setting off.
☐ Only drive at moderate speeds and keep the distance towed to a minimum. Drive smoothly and allow plenty of time for slowing down at junctions.
☐ On models with automatic transmission, special precautions apply. If in doubt, do not tow, or transmission damage may result.

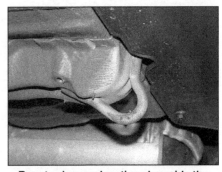

Rear towing eye location alongside the silencer box on the Civic

Introduction

There are some very simple checks which need only take a few minutes to carry out, but which could save you a lot of inconvenience and expense.

These "Weekly checks" require no great skill or special tools, and the small amount of time they take to perform could prove to be very well spent, for example;

☐ Keeping an eye on tyre condition and pressures, will not only help to stop them wearing out prematurely, but could also save your life.

☐ Many breakdowns are caused by electrical problems. Battery-related faults are particularly common, and a quick check on a regular basis will often prevent the majority of these.

☐ If your car develops a brake fluid leak, the first time you might know about it is when your brakes don't work properly. Checking the level regularly will give advance warning of this kind of problem.

☐ If the oil or coolant levels run low, the cost of repairing any engine damage will be far greater than fixing the leak, for example.

Underbonnet check points

◀ **1.5 litre VTEC-E**

A *Engine oil level dipstick*
B *Engine oil filler cap*
C *Coolant expansion tank*
D *Brake fluid reservoir*
E *Clutch fluid reservoir*
F *Screen washer fluid reservoir*
G *Battery*

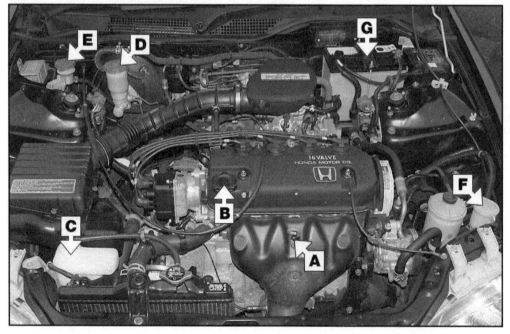

◀ **1.5 litre (D15B2)**

A *Engine oil level dipstick*
B *Engine oil filler cap*
C *Coolant expansion tank*
D *Brake fluid reservoir*
E *Clutch fluid reservoir*
F *Screen washer fluid reservoir*
G *Battery*

Engine oil level

Before you start

✔ Make sure that your car is on level ground.
✔ Check the oil level before the car is driven, or at least 5 minutes after the engine has been switched off.

HAYNES HiNT *If the oil is checked immediately after driving the vehicle, some of the oil will remain in the upper engine components, resulting in an inaccurate reading on the dipstick!*

The correct oil

Modern engines place great demands on their oil. It is very important that the correct oil for your car is used (See "Lubricants, fluids and tyre pressures").

Car Care

● If you have to add oil frequently, you should check whether you have any oil leaks. Place some clean paper under the car overnight, and check for stains in the morning. If there are no leaks, the engine may be burning oil *(see "Fault Finding")*.

● Always maintain the level between the upper and lower dipstick marks (see photo 3). If the level is too low severe engine damage may occur. Oil seal failure may result if the engine is overfilled by adding too much oil.

1 The dipstick top is located on the front of the engine (see *"Underbonnet check points"* on page 0•10 for exact location). Withdraw the dipstick.

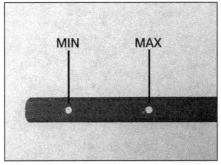

3 Note the oil level on the end of the dipstick, which should be between the upper ("MAX") mark and lower ("MIN") mark. Approximately 1.0 litre of oil will raise the level from the lower mark to the upper mark.

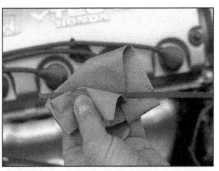

2 Using a clean rag or paper towel remove all oil from the dipstick. Insert the clean dipstick into the tube as far as it will go, then withdraw it again.

4 Oil is added through the filler cap. Unscrew the cap and top-up the level; a funnel may help to reduce spillage. Add the oil slowly, checking the level on the dipstick often. Don't overfill (see *"Car Care" left*).

Coolant level

Warning: DO NOT attempt to remove the expansion tank pressure cap when the engine is hot, as there is a very great risk of scalding. Do not leave open containers of coolant about, as it is poisonous.

Car Care

● With a sealed-type cooling system, adding coolant should not be necessary on a regular basis. If frequent topping-up is required, it is likely there is a leak. Check the radiator, all hoses and joint faces for signs of staining or wetness, and rectify as necessary.

● It is important that antifreeze is used in the cooling system all year round, not just during the winter months. Don't top-up with water alone, as the antifreeze will become too diluted.

1 The coolant level varies with engine temperature. When cold, the coolant level should be between the "MAX" and "MIN" marks on the expansion tank. When hot, the level may rise above the "MAX" mark. If topping up is necessary, **wait until the engine is cold**. Carefully remove the tank cap.

2 Also check the coolant level in the radiator - particularly if there is little or no coolant in the expansion tank. Turn the radiator pressure cap anti-clockwise until it reaches the first stop. Once any pressure is released, push the cap down, turn it anti-clockwise to the second stop and lift it off.

3 Where necessary, add a mixture of water and antifreeze to the radiator until the level reaches the cap contact surface then refit and tighten the cap. Add a mixture of water and antifreeze to the expansion tank until the level reaches the "MAX" mark then refit the cap.

Brake and clutch fluid levels

Warning:
● Brake fluid can harm your eyes and damage painted surfaces, so use extreme caution when handling and pouring it.
● Do not use fluid that has been standing open for some time, as it absorbs moisture from the air, which can cause a dangerous loss of braking effectiveness.

● *The fluid level in the brake reservoir will drop slightly as the brake pads wear down, but the fluid must never be allowed to drop below the "MIN" mark.*

Before you start
● Make sure the car is parked on level ground.
● ABS-equipped models should be driven for a few minutes to equalise the fluid in the system before checking the fluid level in the reservoirs. If the level rises significantly above the "MAX" mark, have the system checked by a dealer because this could indicate a malfunction in the ABS system.

Safety First!
● If the reservoir requires repeated topping-up this is an indication of a fluid leak somewhere in the system, which should be investigated immediately.
● If a leak is suspected, the car should not be driven until the braking system has been checked. Never take any risks where brakes are concerned.

1 The brake master cylinder fluid reservoir is mounted on the front of the brake servo unit on the bulkhead - the brake fluid level should be between the "MIN" and "MAX" marks. Models with an Anti-lock Brake System (ABS) also have a reservoir for the ABS modulator located on the right-hand side of the engine compartment.

2 The clutch master cylinder fluid reservoir is located in the right-hand rear corner of the engine.

3 If topping-up is necessary, wipe clean the exterior of the reservoir, then unscrew the cap.

4 Pour fresh hydraulic fluid carefully into the reservoir. Refit and tighten the cap on completion.

Screen washer fluid level

Screenwash additives not only keep the winscreen clean during foul weather, they also prevent the washer system freezing in cold weather - which is when you are likely to need it most. Don't top up using plain water as the screenwash will become too diluted, and will freeze during cold weather.

Caution: On no account use coolant antifreeze in the washer system - this could discolour or damage paintwork.

1 The windscreen washer fluid reservoir is located at the front left-hand side of the engine compartment. There are no level markings as such; if filling is thought to be necessary, peel back the filler cap.

2 When topping-up the reservoir, a screenwash additive should be added in the quantities recommended on the bottle. Continue filling until fluid can be seen in the filler neck.

Wiper blades

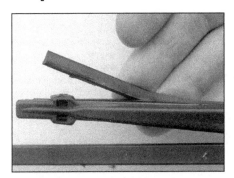 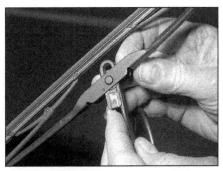 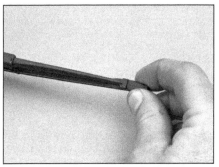

1 Check the condition of the wiper blades; if they are cracked or show any signs of deterioration, or if the glass swept area is smeared, renew them. For maximum clarity of vision, wiper blades should be renewed annually, as a matter of course.

2 To remove a windscreen wiper blade, pull the arm fully away from the glass until it locks. Swivel the blade through 90°, press the locking tab with your fingers, and slide the blade out of the arm's hooked end.

3 Squeeze the blade tabs, then pull the insert out of the metal frame and remove it.

Bulbs and fuses

✔ Check all external lights and the horn. Refer to the appropriate Sections of Chapter 12 for details if any of the circuits are found to be inoperative.

✔ Visually check all accessible wiring connectors, harnesses and retaining clips for security, and for signs of chafing or damage.

 HAYNES HiNT *If you need to check your brake lights and indicators unaided, back up to a wall or garage door and operate the lights. The reflected light should show if they are working properly.*

1 If a single indicator light, brake light or headlight has failed, it is likely that a bulb has blown and will need to be replaced - access to the rear light bulbs is gained by removing the plastic covers in the luggage area. Refer to Chapter 12 for details. If both brake lights have failed, it is possible that the brake light switch built into the brake pedal has failed. Refer to Chapter 9 for details.

2 If more than one indicator light or headlight has failed it is likely that either a fuse has blown or that there is a fault in the circuit (see *"Electrical fault-finding"* in Chapter 12). The fuses are mounted in two locations - inside the vehicle under the facia behind a cover . . .

3 . . . and in the rear corner of the engine compartment.

4 To replace a blown fuse, simply prise it out. Fit a new fuse of the same rating, available from car accessory shops. It is important that you find the reason that the fuse blew - a complete checking procedure is given in Chapter 12.

Tyre condition and pressure

It is very important that tyres are in good condition, and at the correct pressure - having a tyre failure at any speed is highly dangerous. Tyre wear is influenced by driving style - harsh braking and acceleration, or fast cornering, will all produce more rapid tyre wear. As a general rule, the front tyres wear out faster than the rears. Interchanging the tyres from front to rear ("rotating" the tyres) may result in more even wear. However, if this is completely effective, you may have the expense of replacing all four tyres at once! Remove any nails or stones embedded in the tread before they penetrate the tyre to cause deflation. If removal of a nail does reveal that the tyre has been punctured, refit the nail so that its point of penetration is marked. Then immediately change the wheel, and have the tyre repaired by a tyre dealer.

Regularly check the tyres for damage in the form of cuts or bulges, especially in the sidewalls. Periodically remove the wheels, and clean any dirt or mud from the inside and outside surfaces. Examine the wheel rims for signs of rusting, corrosion or other damage. Light alloy wheels are easily damaged by "kerbing" whilst parking; steel wheels may also become dented or buckled. A new wheel is very often the only way to overcome severe damage.

New tyres should be balanced when they are fitted, but it may become necessary to re-balance them as they wear, or if the balance weights fitted to the wheel rim should fall off. Unbalanced tyres will wear more quickly, as will the steering and suspension components. Wheel imbalance is normally signified by vibration, particularly at a certain speed (typically around 50 mph). If this vibration is felt only through the steering, then it is likely that just the front wheels need balancing. If, however, the vibration is felt through the whole car, the rear wheels could be out of balance. Wheel balancing should be carried out by a tyre dealer or garage.

1 Tread Depth - visual check
The original tyres have tread wear safety bands (B), which will appear when the tread depth reaches approximately 1.6 mm. The band positions are indicated by a triangular mark on the tyre sidewall (A).

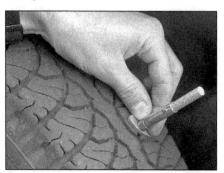

2 Tread Depth - manual check
Alternatively, tread wear can be monitored with a simple, inexpensive device known as a tread depth indicator gauge.

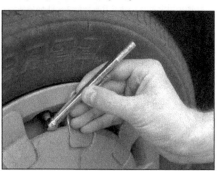

3 Tyre Pressure Check
Check the tyre pressures regularly with the tyres cold. Do not adjust the tyre pressures immediately after the vehicle has been used, or an inaccurate setting will result.

Tyre tread wear patterns

Shoulder Wear

Underinflation (wear on both sides)
Under-inflation will cause overheating of the tyre, because the tyre will flex too much, and the tread will not sit correctly on the road surface. This will cause a loss of grip and excessive wear, not to mention the danger of sudden tyre failure due to heat build-up.
Check and adjust pressures
Incorrect wheel camber (wear on one side)
Repair or renew suspension parts
Hard cornering
Reduce speed!

Centre Wear

Overinflation
Over-inflation will cause rapid wear of the centre part of the tyre tread, coupled with reduced grip, harsher ride, and the danger of shock damage occurring in the tyre casing.
Check and adjust pressures

If you sometimes have to inflate your car's tyres to the higher pressures specified for maximum load or sustained high speed, don't forget to reduce the pressures to normal afterwards.

Uneven Wear

Front tyres may wear unevenly as a result of wheel misalignment. Most tyre dealers and garages can check and adjust the wheel alignment (or "tracking") for a modest charge.
Incorrect camber or castor
Repair or renew suspension parts
Malfunctioning suspension
Repair or renew suspension parts
Unbalanced wheel
Balance tyres
Incorrect toe setting
Adjust front wheel alignment
Note: The feathered edge of the tread which typifies toe wear is best checked by feel.

Battery

Caution: *Before carrying out any work on the vehicle battery, read the precautions given in "Safety first" at the start of this manual.*

✔ Make sure that the battery tray is in good condition, and that the clamp is tight. Corrosion on the tray, retaining clamp and the battery itself can be removed with a solution of water and baking soda. Thoroughly rinse all cleaned areas with water. Any metal parts damaged by corrosion should be covered with a zinc-based primer, then painted.

✔ Periodically (approximately every three months), check the charge condition of the battery as described in Chapter 5.

✔ If the battery is flat, and you need to jump start your vehicle, see **Roadside Repairs**.

1 The battery is located in the left-hand rear corner of the engine compartment and is secured with a clamp. The exterior of the battery should be inspected periodically for damage such as a cracked case or cover. Also check the tightness of the clamp nuts (arrowed).

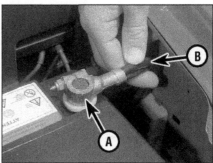

2 Check the tightness of battery clamps (A) to ensure good electrical connections. You should not be able to move them. Also check each cable (B) for cracks and frayed conductors.

HAYNES HiNT

Battery corrosion can be kept to a minimum by applying a layer of petroleum jelly to the clamps and terminals after they are reconnected.

3 If corrosion (white, fluffy deposits) is evident, remove the cables from the battery terminals, clean them with a small wire brush, then refit them. Automotive stores sell a useful tool for cleaning the battery post...

4 ...as well as the battery cable clamps

Lubricants and fluids

Engine . . . . Multigrade engine oil, viscosity SAE 10W/40 to
20W/50, to API SG/CD or better

Cooling system . . . . Ethylene glycol-based antifreeze and soft water

Manual gearbox . . . . Engine oil, viscosity 10W/30 or 10W/40,
to API grade SF or SG

Automatic transmission . . . . Dexron type II automatic transmission fluid (ATF)

Brake hydraulic system . . . . Universal Brake/clutch hydraulic fluid to
SAE J1703 or DOT 4

Power steering . . . . Honda power steering fluid or equivalent (not ATF)

Tyre pressures

Refer to the information label on the driver's door jamb for the tyre pressure applicable to your model.

Chapter 1
Routine maintenance and servicing

Contents

Degrees of difficulty

Easy, suitable for novice with little experience	**Fairly easy,** suitable for beginner with some experience	**Fairly difficult,** suitable for competent DIY mechanic 	**Difficult,** suitable for experienced DIY mechanic	**Very difficult,** suitable for expert DIY or professional

Lubricants and fluids
Refer to the end of "Weekly checks"

Capacities
Engine oil (including filter) . . . . 3.3 litres
Automatic transmission (drain and refill):
    Except 6-position selector model . . . . 2.7 litres
    6-position selector model . . . . 2.4 litres
Manual transmission . . . . 1.8 litres
Coolant . . . . 4.4 litres

Ignition system
Spark plug type (all models) . . . . Champion RN9YCC4
Electrode gap . . . . 1.1 mm

Accessory drivebelt deflection
Power steering pump:
    New belt . . . . 6.0 to 9.0 mm
    Old belt . . . . 8.0 to 12.0 mm
Alternator:
    Without air conditioning:
        New belt . . . . 5.5 mm to 8.0 mm
        Old belt . . . . 7.0 mm to 10.5 mm
    With air conditioning:
        New belt . . . . 5.0 mm to 7.0 mm
        Old belt . . . . 6.5 mm to 10.5 mm

Brakes
Disc brake pad lining thickness (minimum) . . . . 1.6 mm
Drum brake shoe lining thickness (minimum) . . . . 2.0 mm
Handbrake adjustment . . . . 6 to 10 clicks

Idle speed
D13B2 engine . . . . 800 ± 50 rpm
D15Z1 engine . . . . 700 ± 50 rpm
D15B2 engine . . . . 810 ± 50 rpm
D15B7 engine . . . . 750 ± 50 rpm
D16Z6 engine . . . . 750 ± 50 rpm
With IAC (or EACV) valve disconnected (for adjusting):
    Except D15B2 engine . . . . 420 ± 50 rpm
    D15B2 engine . . . . 625 ± 50 rpm

Idle mixture CO content
Carburettor engine:
    With catalytic converter . . . . 0.5 % maximum
    Without catalytic converter . . . . 1.0 % maximum
Fuel injection engines:
    With catalytic converter . . . . 0.1 % maximum
    Without catalytic converter . . . . 1.0 ± 1.0 % maximum

General
Valve clearances (engine cold):
    Inlet . . . . 0.18 to 0.22 mm (0.007 to 0.009 in)
    Exhaust . . . . 0.023 to 0.27 mm (0.009 to 0.011 in)
Accelerator cable deflection (side-to-side) . . . . 10.0 to 12.0 mm
Engine oil filter type (1.3 and 1.6 litre engines) . . . . Champion F208
Air filter type (1.5 litre engines) . . . . Champion U646
Wiper blade type (driver's side) . . . . Champion X-5103
Wiper blade type (passenger's side) . . . . Champion X-4803

Torque wrench settings

	Nm	lbf ft
Automatic transmission drain plug	49	36
Manual transmission drain plug	39	29
Manual transmission filler plug	45	33
Fuel filter:		
Banjo bolt	15	11
Banjo nut	22	16
Spark plugs	18	13
Wheel nuts	109	80

The maintenance intervals in this manual are provided with the assumption that you will be carrying out the work yourself. These are the minimum maintenance intervals recommended by the manufacturer for vehicles driven daily. If you wish to keep your vehicle in peak condition at all times, you may wish to perform some of these procedures more often. We encourage frequent maintenance, because it enhances the efficiency, performance and resale value of your vehicle.

If the vehicle is driven in dusty areas, used to tow a trailer, or driven frequently at slow speeds (idling in traffic) or on short journeys, more frequent maintenance intervals are recommended.

When the vehicle is new, it should be serviced by a factory-authorised dealer service department, in order to preserve the factory warranty.

Every 250 miles or weekly
☐ Refer to *"Weekly checks"*

Every 6000 miles (10 000 km) or 12 months - whichever comes first
All the items in "Weekly checks", plus the following:
☐ Check the power steering fluid level (Section 3)
☐ Check the automatic transmission fluid level (Section 4)
☐ Change the engine oil and oil filter (Section 5)
☐ Check the front disc brake pads (Section 6)

Every 12 000 miles (20 000 km) or 12 months - whichever comes first
All the items listed above, plus the following:
☐ Inspect and renew, if necessary, all underbonnet hoses (Section 7)
☐ Rotate the tyres (Section 8)
☐ Renew the air filter - models without a catalytic converter (Section 9)
☐ Check and renew, if necessary, the spark plugs - models without a catalytic converter (Section 10)
☐ Inspect the suspension and steering components (Section 11)
☐ Inspect the exhaust system (Section 12)
☐ Check and adjust, if necessary, the engine idle speed (Section 13)

Every 24 000 miles (40 000 km) or 2 years - whichever comes first
All the items listed above, plus the following:
☐ Check and adjust, if necessary, the engine drivebelts (Section 14)
☐ Check the cooling system (Section 15)
☐ Renew the air filter - models with a catalytic converter (Section 9)
☐ Check and renew, if necessary, the spark plugs - models with a catalytic converter (Section 10)
☐ Inspect and renew, if necessary, the HT leads, distributor cap and rotor (Section 16)
☐ Check and adjust the valve clearances (Section 17)
☐ Inspect the fuel system (Section 18)
☐ Check the manual transmission lubricant level (Section 19)
☐ Check the driveshaft gaiters(Section 20)
☐ Check and, if necessary, renew the PCV valve (Section 21)
☐ Check the operation of the accelerator linkage (Section 22)
☐ Renew the fuel filter (Section 23)
☐ Brake fluid renewal (Section 24)

Every 36 000 miles (60 000 km) or 3 years - whichever comes first
All the items listed above, plus the following:
☐ Renew the automatic transmission fluid (Section 25)
☐ Renew the manual transmission oil (Section 26)

Every 48 000 miles (80 000 km) or 4 years - whichever comes first
All the items listed above, plus the following:
☐ Service the cooling system (drain, flush and refill) (Section 27)
☐ ABS high pressure hose renewal (Section 28)

Every 60 000 miles (50 000 km) or 5 years - whichever comes first
All the items listed above, plus the following:
☐ Renew timing belt (Section 29)
☐ Inspect the evaporative emissions control system (Section 30)
☐ Check the operation of the Exhaust Gas Recirculation (EGR) system (Section 31)

Underbonnet view of a Honda Civic VEi (D15Z1 engine)

1 Headlight dim-dip unit
2 Clutch master cylinder reservoir
3 Brake master cylinder reservoir
4 Fuel filter
5 Battery
6 Fuse box
7 Engine oil filler cap
8 Power steering fluid reservoir
9 Windscreen washer fluid
   reservoir filler cap
10 Power steering pump
11 Spark plug locations
12 Engine oil dipstick
13 Ignition HT leads
14 Radiator filler cap
15 Radiator top hose
16 Radiator
17 Coolant reservoir
18 Distributor cap
19 Air filter housing

Underbonnet view of a Honda Civic LSi (D15B2 engine)

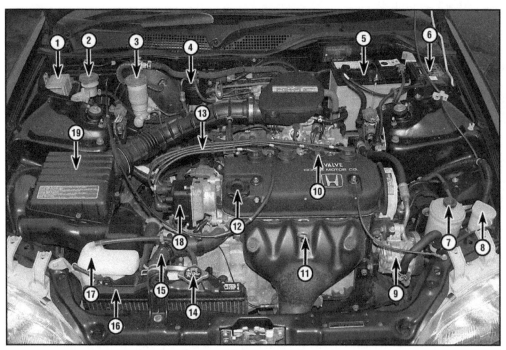

1 Headlight dim-dip unit
2 Clutch master cylinder reservoir
3 Brake master cylinder reservoir
4 Fuel filter
5 Battery
6 Fuse box
7 Power steering fluid reservoir
8 Windscreen washer fluid
   reservoir filler cap
9 Power steering pump
10 Spark plug locations
11 Engine oil dipstick
12 Engine oil filler cap
13 Ignition HT leads
14 Radiator filler cap
15 Radiator top hose
16 Radiator
17 Coolant reservoir
18 Distributor cap
19 Air filter housing

Front underbody view (typical)

1 Radiator drain plug
2 Front brake caliper
3 Outer driveshaft gaiter
4 Engine oil drain plug
5 Exhaust pipe
6 Transmission drain plug
7 Driveshaft

Rear underbody view (typical)

1 Exhaust system mounting
2 Silencer
3 Shock absorber and spring assembly
4 Exhaust pipe
5 Fuel tank
6 Handbrake cable
7 Hydraulic brake hose

Maintenance procedures

1 Introduction

General information

1 This Chapter is designed to help the home mechanic maintain his/her vehicle for safety, economy, long life and peak performance.

2 The Chapter contains a master maintenance schedule, followed by Sections dealing specifically with each task in the schedule. Visual checks, adjustments, component renewal and other helpful items are included. Refer to the accompanying illustrations of the engine compartment and the underside of the vehicle for the locations of the various components.

3 Servicing your vehicle in accordance with the mileage/time maintenance schedule and the following Sections will provide a planned maintenance programme, which should result in a long and reliable service life. This is a comprehensive plan, so maintaining some items but not others at the specified service intervals, will not produce the same results.

4 As you service your vehicle, you will discover that many of the procedures can - and should - be grouped together, because of the particular procedure being performed, or because of the close proximity of two otherwise-unrelated components to one another. For example, if the vehicle is raised for any reason, the exhaust can be inspected at the same time as the suspension and steering components.

5 The first step in this maintenance programme is to prepare yourself before the actual work begins. Read through all the Sections relevant to the work to be carried out, then make a list and gather together all the parts and tools required. If a problem is encountered, seek advice from a parts specialist, or a dealer service department.

2 Intensive maintenance

1 If, from the time the vehicle is new, the routine maintenance schedule is followed closely, and frequent checks are made of fluid levels and high-wear items, as suggested throughout this manual, the engine will be kept in relatively good running condition, and the need for additional work will be minimised.

2 It is possible that there will be times when the engine is running poorly due to the lack of regular maintenance. This is even more likely if a used vehicle, which has not received regular and frequent maintenance checks, is purchased. In such cases, additional work may need to be carried out, outside of the regular maintenance intervals.

3 If engine wear is suspected, a compression test will provide valuable information regarding the overall performance of the main internal components. Such a test can be used as a basis to decide on the extent of the work to be carried out. If, for example, a compression test indicates serious internal engine wear, conventional maintenance as described in this Chapter will not greatly improve the performance of the engine, and may prove a waste of time and money, unless extensive overhaul work is carried out first.

4 The following series of operations are those most often required to improve the performance of a generally poor-running engine:

Primary operations

a) Clean, inspect and test the battery (see "Weekly checks").

b) Check all the engine-related fluids (see "Weekly checks").

c) Check the condition and tension of the auxiliary drivebelt (Section 14).

d) Renew the spark plugs (Section 10).

e) Inspect the distributor cap and HT leads - as applicable (Section 16).

f) Check the condition of the air cleaner filter element, and renew if necessary (Section 9).

g) Renew the fuel filter (Section 23).

h) Check the condition of all hoses, and check for fluid leaks (Section 7).

i) Check the idle speed and mixture settings - as applicable (Section 13).

5 If the above operations do not prove fully effective, carry out the following secondary operations:

Secondary operations

a) Check the charging system (Chapter 5A).

b) Check the ignition system (Chapter 5B).

c) Check the fuel system (Chapter 4).

d) Renew the distributor cap and rotor arm - as applicable (Chapter 5B).

f) Renew the ignition HT leads - as applicable (Section 16).

6000 Mile / 12 Month Service

3 Power steering fluid level check

1 The power steering system relies on fluid which may, over time, require replenishing.

2 The fluid reservoir for the power steering pump is located on the inner wing panel near the left front of the engine compartment.

3 For the check, the front wheels should be pointed straight ahead and the engine should be off. The fluid level should be checked cold.

4 On all models, the reservoir is translucent plastic and the fluid level can be checked visually **(see illustration)**.

5 If additional fluid is required, remove the filler cap and pour the specified type directly into the reservoir **(see illustrations)**.

6 If the reservoir requires frequent fluid additions, all power steering hoses, hose connections, the power steering pump and the steering gear should be carefully checked for leaks.

3.4 Power steering fluid level should be between "UPPER" and "LOWER" marks

3.5a Remove the filler cap from the power steering fluid reservoir . . .

3.5b . . . and top up the fluid

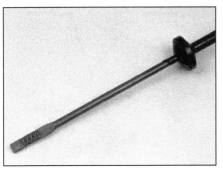

4.5 The automatic transmission fluid level should be in dipstick cross-hatched area

4 Automatic transmission fluid level check

1 The level of the automatic transmission fluid should be carefully maintained. Low fluid level can lead to slipping or loss of drive, while overfilling can cause foaming, loss of fluid and transmission damage.
2 The transmission fluid level should only be checked on level ground within one minute of the engine being shut off.
3 Remove the dipstick - it's located down low on the front of the transmission (in the passenger's side of the engine compartment). Check the level of the fluid on the dipstick and note its condition.
4 Wipe the fluid from the dipstick with a clean rag and reinsert it.
5 Pull the dipstick out again and note the fluid level **(see illustration)**. The level should be between the upper and lower marks on the dipstick. If the level is low, add the specified automatic transmission fluid through the dipstick opening with a funnel.
6 Add just enough of the specified fluid to fill the transmission to the proper level. It takes about one pint to raise the level from the lower mark to the upper mark, so add the fluid a little at a time and keep checking the level until it is correct.
7 The condition of the fluid should also be checked along with the level. If the fluid at the end of the dipstick is black or a dark reddish brown colour, or if it emits a burned smell, the fluid should be changed (see Section 27). If you are in doubt about the condition of the fluid, purchase some new fluid and compare the two for colour and smell.

5 Engine oil and oil filter renewal

1 Frequent oil changes are the best preventive maintenance the home mechanic can give the engine, because ageing oil becomes diluted and contaminated, which leads to premature engine wear.
2 Make sure you have all the necessary tools

before you begin this procedure. You should also have plenty of rags or newspapers handy for mopping up any spills.
3 Access to the underside of the vehicle is greatly improved if the vehicle can be lifted on a hoist, driven onto ramps or supported by axle stands (see 'Jacking and Vehicle Support').

⚠ **Warning: Do not work under a vehicle which is supported only by a hydraulic or scissors-type jack.**

4 If this is your first oil change, get under the vehicle and familiarise yourself with the locations of the oil drain plug and the oil filter. The engine and exhaust components will be warm during the actual work, so try to anticipate any potential problems before the engine and accessories are hot.
5 Park the vehicle on a level spot. Start the engine and allow it to reach its normal operating temperature. Warm oil and sludge will flow out more easily. Turn off the engine when it's warmed up. Remove the filler cap from the valve cover.
6 Raise the vehicle and support it on axle stands (see 'Jacking and Vehicle Support').

⚠ **Warning: Never get beneath the vehicle when it is supported only by a jack. The jack provided with your vehicle is designed solely for raising the vehicle to remove and renew the wheels. Always use axle stands to support the vehicle when it becomes necessary to place your body underneath the vehicle.**

7 Being careful not to touch the hot exhaust components, place the drain pan under the drain plug in the bottom of the pan and remove the plug **(see illustration)**. You may want to wear gloves while unscrewing the plug the final few turns if the engine is hot.
8 Allow the old oil to drain into the pan. It may be necessary to move the pan further under the engine as the oil flow slows to a trickle. Inspect the old oil for the presence of metal shavings and chips.
9 After all the oil has drained, wipe off the drain plug with a clean rag. Even minute metal particles clinging to the plug would immediately contaminate the new oil.

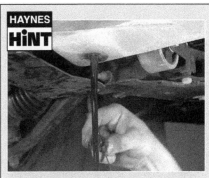

As the drain plug releases from the threads, move it away sharply so the stream of oil issuing from the sump runs into the container, not up your sleeve!

10 Clean the area around the drain plug opening, refit the plug and tighten it securely, but do not strip the threads.
11 Move the drain pan into position under the oil filter.
12 Loosen the oil filter **(see illustration)** by turning it anti-clockwise with a filter removing tool. Any standard filter removing tool will work. Sometimes the oil filter is screwed on so tightly that it cannot be loosened. If this situation occurs, punch a metal bar or long screwdriver directly through the side of the canister and use it as a T-bar to turn the filter. Be prepared for oil to spurt out of the canister as it is punctured. Once the filter is loose, use your hands to unscrew it from the block. Just as the filter is detached from the block, immediately tilt the open end up to prevent the oil inside the filter from spilling out.

⚠ **Warning: The exhaust system may still be hot, so be careful.**

13 With a clean rag, wipe off the mounting surface on the block. If a residue of old oil is allowed to remain, it will smoke when the block is heated up. Also make sure that none of the old gasket remains stuck to the mounting surface. It can be removed with a scraper if necessary.
14 Compare the old filter with the new one to make sure they are the same type. Smear

5.7 Removing the oil drain plug

5.12 The oil filter may be on very tight and will require a strap wrench for removal

5.14 Lubricate the new oil filter gasket with clean engine oil before fitting

some clean engine oil on the rubber gasket of the new filter and screw it into place **(see illustration)**. Because overtightening the filter will damage the gasket, do not use a tool to tighten the filter. Tighten it by hand until the gasket contacts the seating surface. Then seat the filter by giving it an additional 3/4-turn.

15 Remove all tools, rags, etc. from under the vehicle, being careful not to spill the oil in the drain pan, then lower the vehicle.

16 Add new oil to the engine through the oil filler cap in the valve cover. Use a funnel, if necessary, to prevent oil from spilling onto the top of the engine. Pour three quarts of fresh oil into the engine. Wait a few minutes to allow the oil to drain into the pan, then check the level on the oil dipstick (see Section 4 if necessary). If the oil level is at or near the upper hole on the dipstick, refit the filler cap hand tight, start the engine and allow the new oil to circulate.

17 Allow the engine to run for about a minute. While the engine is running, look under the vehicle and check for leaks at the sump drain plug and around the oil filter. If either is leaking, stop the engine and tighten the plug or filter.

18 Wait a few minutes to allow the oil to trickle down into the pan, then recheck the level on the dipstick and, if necessary, add enough oil to bring the level to the upper hole.

19 During the first few trips after an oil change, make it a point to check frequently for leaks and correct oil level.

20 The old oil drained from the engine cannot be re-used in its present state and should be discarded After the oil has cooled, it can be drained into a suitable container (capped plastic jugs, topped bottles, milk cartons, etc.) for transport to a suitable disposal site

Note: It is antisocial and illegal to dump oil down the drain. To find the location of your local oil recycling bank, call this number free.

0800 66 33 66

6 Brake check

Note: *For detailed photographs of the brake system, refer to Chapter 9.*

1 In addition to the specified intervals, the brakes should be inspected every time the wheels are removed or whenever a defect is suspected. Any of the following symptoms could indicate a potential brake system defect: The vehicle pulls to one side when the brake pedal is depressed; the brakes make squealing or dragging noises when applied; brake travel is excessive; the pedal pulsates; brake fluid leaks, usually onto the inside of the tyre or wheel.

2 The disc brake pads have built-in wear indicators which should make a high pitched squealing or scraping noise when they are worn to the renewal point. When you hear this noise, renew the pads immediately or expensive damage to the discs can result.

3 Loosen the wheel nuts.

4 Raise the vehicle and place it securely on axle stands.

5 Remove the wheels (see *"Jacking and Vehicle Support"* at the rear of this book, or your owner's manual, if necessary).

Disc brakes

Note: *All models covered by this manual have front disc brakes. Some models are also equipped with disc brakes at the rear.*

6 There are two pads - an outer and an inner - in each caliper. The pads are visible through an inspection hole in each caliper **(see Haynes Hint).**

7 Check the pad thickness by looking at each end of the caliper and through the inspection hole in the caliper body. If the lining material is less than the specified thickness (see this Chapter's Specifications), renew the pads. **Note:** *Keep in mind that the lining material is riveted or bonded to a metal backing plate and the metal portion is not included in this measurement.*

HAYNES HINT

The amount of brake pad material remaining can be checked by looking through the opening in the caliper or at the ends of the pads

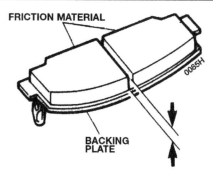

6.9 If the exact pad thickness is required, remove the pads and measure the remaining friction material

8 If it is difficult to determine the exact thickness of the remaining pad material by the above method, or if you are at all concerned about the condition of the pads, remove the caliper(s), then remove the pads from the calipers for further inspection (see Chapter 9).

9 Once the pads are removed from the calipers, clean them with brake cleaner and re-measure them with a ruler or a vernier caliper **(see illustration)**.

10 Measure the disc thickness with a micrometer to make sure that it still has service life remaining. If any disc is thinner than the specified minimum thickness, renew it (see Chapter 9). Even if the disc has service life remaining, check its condition. Look for scoring, gouging and burned spots. If these conditions exist, remove the disc and have it resurfaced (see Chapter 9).

11 Before refitting the wheels, check all brake lines and hoses for damage, wear, deformation, cracks, corrosion, leakage, bends and twists, particularly in the vicinity of the rubber hoses at the calipers. Check the clamps for tightness and the connections for leakage. Make sure all hoses and lines are clear of sharp edges, moving parts and the exhaust system. If any of the above conditions are noted, repair, re-route or renew the lines and/or fittings as necessary (see Chapter 9).

Rear drum brakes

12 Refer to Chapter 9 and remove the rear brake drums.

 Warning: Brake dust produced by lining wear and deposited on brake components may contain asbestos, which is hazardous to your health. DO NOT blow it out with compressed air and DO NOT inhale it! DO NOT use fuel or petroleum-based solvents to remove the dust. Brake system cleaner should be used to flush the dust into a drain pan. After the brake components are wiped clean, dispose of the contaminated rag(s) and cleaner in a covered and labelled container. Try to use non-asbestos renewal parts whenever possible.

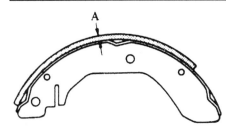

6.13 If lining is bonded to shoe, measure lining thickness from outer surface to metal shoe (A); if lining is riveted, measure from lining outer surface to rivet head

13 Note the thickness of the lining material on the rear brake shoes **(see illustration)** and look for signs of contamination by brake fluid and grease. If the lining material is within 2.0 mm of the recessed rivets or metal shoes, renew the brake shoes with new ones. The shoes should also be replaced if they are cracked, glazed (shiny lining surfaces) or contaminated with brake fluid or grease. See Chapter 9 for the renewal procedure.

14 Check the shoe return and hold-down springs and the adjusting mechanism to make sure they're installed correctly and in good condition. Deteriorated springs, if not replaced, could allow the linings to drag and wear out.

15 Check the wheel cylinders for leakage by carefully peeling back the rubber boots. If brake fluid is noted behind the boots, the wheel cylinders must be replaced (see Chapter 9).

16 Check the drums for cracks, score marks, deep scratches and hard spots, which will appear as small discoloured areas. If imperfections cannot be removed with emery cloth, the drums must be resurfaced by an automotive machine shop (see Chapter 9 for more detailed information).

17 Refer to Chapter 9 and refit the brake drums.

18 Refit the wheels and snug the wheel nuts finger tight.

19 Remove the axle stands and lower the car.

20 Tighten the wheel nuts to the torque listed in this Chapter's Specifications.

Brake servo check

21 Sit in the driver's seat and perform the following sequence of tests.

22 With the engine stopped, depress the brake pedal several times - the travel distance should not change.

23 With the brake fully depressed, start the engine - the pedal should move down a little when the engine starts.

24 Depress the brake, stop the engine and hold the pedal in for about 30 seconds - the pedal should neither sink nor rise.

25 Restart the engine, run it for about a minute and turn it off. Then firmly depress the brake several times - the pedal travel should decrease with each application.

26 If your brakes do not operate as described above when the preceding tests are performed, the brake servo is either in need of repair or has failed. Refer to Chapter 9 for the removal procedure.

Handbrake

27 Slowly pull up on the handbrake and count the number of clicks you hear until the handle is up as far as it will go. The adjustment is correct if you hear the specified number of clicks (see this Chapter's Specifications). If you hear more or fewer clicks, it's time to adjust the handbrake (see Chapter 9).

28 An alternative method of checking the handbrake is to park the vehicle on a steep hill with the handbrake set and the transmission in Neutral. If the handbrake cannot prevent the vehicle from rolling, it is in need of adjustment (see Chapter 9).

12 000 Mile / 12 Month Service

7 Underbonnet hose check and renewal

Warning: Renewal of air conditioning hoses must be left to a dealer service department or air conditioning specialist who have the equipment to depressurise the system safely.

General

1 High temperatures in the engine compartment can cause the detoerioration of the rubber and plastic hoses used for engine, accessory and emission systems operation. Periodic inspection should be made for cracks, loose clamps, material hardening and leaks.

2 Information specific to the cooling system hoses can be found in Section 15.

3 Some, but not all, hoses are secured to the fittings with clamps. Where clamps are used, check to be sure they haven't lost their tension, allowing the hose to leak. If clamps aren't used, make sure the hose has not expanded and/or hardened where it slips over the fitting, allowing it to leak.

Vacuum hoses

4 It's quite common for vacuum hoses, especially those in the emissions system, to be colour coded or identified by coloured stripes moulded into them. Various systems require hoses with different wall thicknesses, collapse resistance and temperature resistance. When replacing hoses, be sure the new ones are made of the same material.

5 Often the only effective way to check a hose is to remove it from the vehicle. If more than one hose is removed, be sure to label the hoses and fittings to ensure correct refitting.

6 When checking vacuum hoses, be sure to include any plastic T-fittings in the check. Inspect the fittings for cracks and the hose where it fits over the fitting for distortion, which could cause leakage.

7 A small piece of vacuum hose (1/4-inch inside diameter) can be used as a stethoscope

A leak in the cooling system will usually show up as white or rust-coloured deposits on the area adjoining the leak

to detect vacuum leaks. Hold one end of the hose to your ear and probe around vacuum hoses and fittings, listening for the "hissing" sound characteristic of a vacuum leak.

Warning: When probing with the vacuum hose stethoscope, be very careful not to come into contact with moving engine components such as the drivebelts, cooling fan, etc.

Fuel hose

Warning: Fuel is extremely flammable, so take extra precautions when you work on any part of the fuel system. Don't smoke or allow naked flames or bare light bulbs near the work area, and don't work in a garage where a natural gas-type appliance (such as a water heater or clothes dryer) with a pilot light is present. Since fuel is carcinogenic, wear rubber gloves when there's a possibility of being exposed to fuel, and, if you spill any fuel on your skin, rinse it off immediately with soap and water. Mop up any spills immediately and do not store fuel-soaked rags where they could ignite. The fuel system is under constant pressure, so, if any fuel lines are to be disconnected, the fuel pressure in the system must be relieved first (see Chapter 4 for more information). When working on the fuel system, wear safety glasses and have a fire extinguisher on hand.

8 Check all rubber fuel lines for deterioration and chafing. Check especially for cracks in areas where the hose bends and just before fittings, such as where a hose attaches to the fuel filter.

9 When replacing hose, use only hose that is designed for your fuel injection system.

Metal lines

10 Sections of metal line are often used for fuel line between the fuel pump and fuel injection unit. Check carefully to be sure the line has not been bent or crimped and that cracks have not started in the line.

11 If a section of metal fuel line must be replaced, only seamless steel tubing should be used, since copper and aluminium tubing don't have the strength necessary to withstand normal engine vibration.

12 Check the metal brake lines where they enter the master cylinder and brake proportioning unit (if used) for cracks in the lines or loose fittings. Any sign of brake fluid leakage calls for an immediate thorough inspection of the brake system.

8 Tyre rotation

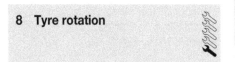

1 The tyres should be rotated at the specified intervals and whenever uneven wear is noticed. Since the vehicle will be raised and the tyres removed anyway, check the brakes (see Section 6) at this time.

2 Radial tyres must be rotated in a specific pattern **(see illustration)**.

3 Refer to the information in *"Jacking and Vehicle Support"* at the rear of this manual for the proper procedures to follow when raising the vehicle and changing a tyre. If the brakes are to be checked, do not apply the handbrake as stated. Make sure the tyres are blocked to prevent the vehicle from rolling.

4 Preferably, the entire vehicle should be raised at the same time. This can be done on a hoist or by jacking up each corner and then lowering the vehicle onto axle stands placed

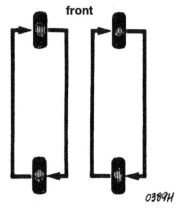

8.2 The recommended tyre rotation pattern for these models

9.2 Remove the air cleaner cover screws with a socket

under the frame rails. Always use four axle stands and make sure the vehicle is firmly supported (see *'Jacking and Vehicle Support'*).

5 After rotation, check and adjust the tyre pressures as necessary and be sure to check the wheel nut tightness.

6 For further information on the wheels and tyres, refer to Chapter 10.

9 Air filter renewal

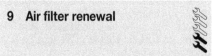

1 At the specified intervals, the air filter should be replaced with a new one.

Fuel injection models

2 Loosen the air cleaner cover screws **(see illustration)**.

3 Lift the cover up.

4 Lift the air filter element out of the housing and wipe out the inside of the air cleaner housing with a clean rag **(see illustration)**.

5 While the air cleaner cover is off, be careful not to drop anything down into the air cleaner.

6 Place the new filter in the air cleaner housing. Make sure it seats properly in the lower half of the housing.

7 Refit the air cleaner cover and tighten the screws securely.

Carburettor models

8 Unscrew and remove the wing nut and washer, then lift the cover off the air cleaner.

9 Lift the air filter element out of the body and wipe out the inside with a clean rag.

10 Place the new element in the body making sure it seats correctly on the base.

11 Refit the cover, position the washer and tighten the wing nut.

10 Spark plug check and renewal

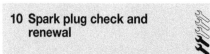

1 The correct functioning of the spark plugs is vital for the correct running and efficiency of the engine. It is essential that the plugs fitted are appropriate for the engine (the suitable type is specified at the beginning of this Chapter). If this type is used, and the engine is in good

9.4 Move the cover out of the way and remove the filter

condition, the spark plugs should not need attention between scheduled replacement intervals. Spark plug cleaning is rarely necessary, and should not be attempted unless specialised equipment is available, as damage can easily be caused to the firing ends.

2 If the marks on the original-equipment spark plug (HT) leads cannot be seen, mark the leads "1" to "4", to correspond to the cylinder the lead serves (No 1 cylinder is at the transmission end of the engine). Pull the leads from the plugs by gripping the end fitting, not the lead, otherwise the lead connection may be fractured **(see illustration)**.

3 It is advisable to remove the dirt from the spark plug recesses using a clean brush, vacuum cleaner or compressed air before removing the plugs, to prevent dirt dropping into the cylinders.

4 Unscrew the plugs using a spark plug spanner, suitable box spanner or a deep socket and extension bar **(see illustrations)**.

10.2 When disconnecting the HT leads, pull only on the boot

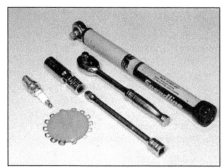

10.4a Tools required for spark plug removal, gap adjustment and refitting

10.4b An extension will be required when removing or refitting the spark plugs

10.8 Measuring the spark plug gap with a wire gauge

10.9 Measuring the spark plug gap with a feeler blade

Keep the socket aligned with the spark plug - if it is forcibly moved to one side, the ceramic insulator may be broken off. As each plug is removed, examine it as follows.

5 Examination of the spark plugs will give a good indication of the condition of the engine. If the insulator nose of the spark plug is clean and white, with no deposits, this is indicative of a weak mixture or too hot a plug (a hot plug transfers heat away from the electrode slowly, a cold plug transfers heat away quickly).

6 If the tip and insulator nose are covered with hard black-looking deposits, then this is indicative that the mixture is too rich. Should the plug be black and oily, then it is likely that the engine is fairly worn, as well as the mixture being too rich.

7 If the insulator nose is covered with light tan to greyish-brown deposits, then the mixture is correct and it is likely that the engine is in good condition.

8 The spark plug electrode gap is of great importance as, if it is too large or too small, the size of the spark and its efficiency will be seriously impaired. The gap should be set to the value given in the Specifications at the beginning of this Chapter **(see illustration)**.

It is very often difficult to insert spark plugs into their holes without cross-threading them. To avoid this possibility, fit a short length of 5/16 inch internal diameter rubber hose over the end of the spark plug. The flexible hose acts as a universal joint to help align the plug with the plug hole. Should the plug begin to cross-thread, the hose will slip on the spark plug, preventing thread damage to the cylinder head.

9 To set the gap, measure it with a feeler blade, and then bend the outer plug electrode until the correct gap is achieved **(see illustration)**. The centre electrode should never be bent, as this may crack the insulator and cause plug failure, if nothing worse. If using feeler blades, the gap is correct when the appropriate-size blade is a firm sliding fit.

10 Special spark plug electrode gap adjusting tools are available from most motor accessory shops, or from some spark plug manufacturers.

11 Before fitting the spark plugs, check that the threaded connector sleeves are tight, and that the plug exterior surfaces and threads are clean **(see Haynes Hint)**.

12 Remove the rubber hose (if used), and tighten the plug to the specified torque using the spark plug socket and a torque wrench. Refit the other plugs in the same manner.

13 Connect the HT leads in the correct order, and refit any parts removed for access.

11 Steering and suspension check

Note: For detailed illustrations of the steering and suspension components, see Chapter 10.

With the wheels on the ground

1 With the vehicle stopped and the front wheels pointing straight ahead, rock the steering wheel gently back and forth. If freeplay is excessive, a front wheel bearing, main shaft yoke, intermediate shaft yoke, lower arm balljoint or steering system joint is worn or the steering gear is out of adjustment, loose on its mounts or broken. Refer to Chapter 10 for the appropriate repair procedure.

2 Other symptoms, such as excessive vehicle body movement over rough roads, swaying (leaning) around corners and binding as the steering wheel is turned, may indicate faulty steering and/or suspension components.

3 Check the shock absorbers by pushing down and releasing the vehicle several times at each corner. If the vehicle does not come back to a level position within one or two bounces, the shocks/struts are worn and

must be replaced. When bouncing the vehicle up and down, listen for squeaks and noises from the suspension components. Additional information can be found in Chapter 10.

4 If the car looks canted to one side or down at one corner, try to level it by rocking it down. If this doesn't work, look for bad springs or worn or loose suspension parts.

Under the vehicle

5 Raise the vehicle with a floor jack and support it securely on axle stands. See *"Jacking and Vehicle Support"* at the rear of this book for the proper jacking points.

6 Check the tyres for irregular wear patterns and proper inflation (see *Weekly Checks*).

7 Inspect the universal joint between the steering shaft and the steering gear housing. Check the steering gear housing for grease leakage or oozing. Make sure that the dust seals and boots are not damaged and that the boot clamps are not loose. Check the steering linkage for looseness or damage. Check the track rod ends for excessive play. Look for loose bolts, broken or disconnected parts and deteriorated rubber bushes on all suspension and steering components. While an assistant turns the steering wheel from side to side, check the steering components for free movement, chafing and binding. If the steering components do not seem to be reacting with the movement of the steering wheel, try to determine where the slack is located.

8 Check the balljoints for wear by levering between each balljoint and lower control arm **(see illustration)** to ensure that the balljoint

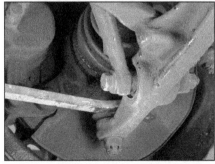

11.8 Lever between the balljoint and the lower control arm to check for movement indicating balljoint wear

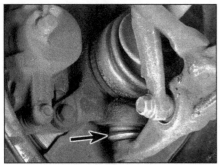

11.9 Push on the balljoint gaiter (arrowed) to check for tears and grease leaks

13.11a Idle adjusting screw (arrowed) on multi-point fuel injection models

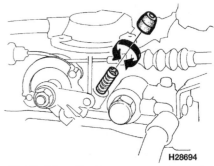

13.11b Idle adjusting screw on dual-point fuel injection models

has no play. If any balljoint does have play, renew it. Refer to Chapter 10 for the front balljoint renewal procedure.

9 Inspect the balljoint boots for tears and leaking grease **(see illustration)**. Renew the boots with new ones if they are damaged (see Chapter 10).

12 Exhaust system check

1 With the engine cold (at least three hours after the vehicle has been driven), check the complete exhaust system from its starting point at the engine to the end of the tailpipe. This should be done on a hoist where unrestricted access is available.
2 Check the pipes and connections for evidence of leaks, severe corrosion or damage. Make sure that all brackets and hangers are in good condition and tight.
3 At the same time, inspect the underside of the body for holes, corrosion, open seams, etc. which may allow exhaust gases to enter the passenger compartment. Seal all body openings with silicone sealant or body putty.
4 Rattles and other noises can often be traced to the exhaust system, especially the mounts and hangers. Try to move the pipes, silencer and catalytic converter. If the components can come in contact with the body or suspension parts, secure the exhaust system with new mounts.

13 Idle speed check and adjustment

1 Engine idle speed is the speed of the engine when no accelerator pedal pressure is applied, as when stopped at a traffic light. This speed is critical to the performance of the engine itself, as well as many subsystems.

Check

2 Set the handbrake firmly and block the wheels to prevent the vehicle from rolling. Place the transmission in Neutral (manual gearbox) or Park (automatic transmission).
3 Start the engine and allow it to warm up to normal operating temperature (the cooling fan should come on at least twice).
4 Stop the engine. Hook up a hand-held tachometer and an exhaust gas analyser (CO meter) in accordance with its manufacturer's instructions.
5 Start the engine. Make sure all accessories are turned off and the transmission is in Neutral (manual transmission) or Park (automatic transmission).

5 Check the running condition of the engine by inspecting inside the end of the tailpipe. The exhaust deposits here are an indication of engine state-of-tune. If the pipe is black and sooty or coated with white deposits, the engine is in need of a tune-up, including a thorough fuel system inspection.

6 Note the idle speed rpm on the tachometer and compare it to that given in the Specifications.

Adjustment

Carburettor engines

7 If the idle speed is too low or too high, turn the throttle stop screw on the rear of the carburettor as necessary.
8 To check the idle mixture (exhaust gas CO level), run the engine at idle speed and check the CO reading on the meter.
9 If adjustment is required where necessary remove the tamperproof cap, then turn the adjustment screw on the rear of the carburettor as necessary. Recheck and if necessary adjust the idle speed.

Fuel injection engines

10 If the idle speed is too low or too high, disconnect the electrical connector from the Idle Air Control (IAC) valve (see Chapter 4 - this valve is also referred to as the EACV).
11 Turn the screw to obtain the specified idle speed **(see illustrations)**.
12 Plug in the electrical connector to the IAC valve and remove the 7.5 amp BACK UP fuse from the underbonnet fuse block for ten seconds. This will clear any trouble codes from the ECM's memory.
13 Turn on the engine and let it idle for one minute, then recheck the idle speed.
14 Turn off the engine and disconnect the tachometer.

24 000 Mile / 2 Year Service

14 Drivebelt check, adjustment and renewal

Check

1 The alternator and air conditioning compressor drivebelts are either V-belts or V-ribbed belts. Sometimes referred to as "fan" belts, the drivebelts are located at the left end of the engine. The good condition and proper adjustment of the alternator belt is critical to

the operation of the engine. Because of their composition and the high stresses to which they are subjected, drivebelts stretch and deteriorate as they get older. They must therefore be periodically inspected.
2 The number of belts used on a particular vehicle depends on the accessories installed **(see illustration)**.
3 With the engine off, open the bonnet and locate the drivebelts at the left end of the engine. With a torch, check each belt: On V-belts, check for cracks and separation of the belt plies **(see illustration)**. On V-ribbed belts,

14.2 A typical drivebelt layout

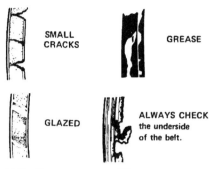

14.3a Here are some of the more common problems associated with drivebelts

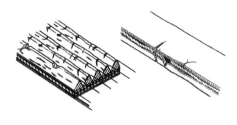

14.3b Check V-ribbed belts for signs of wear like these - renew the belt if worn

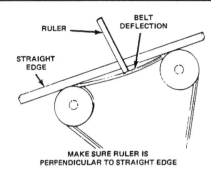

MAKE SURE RULER IS PERPENDICULAR TO STRAIGHT EDGE

14.4 Measuring drivebelt deflection with a straightedge and ruler

check for separation of the adhesive rubber on both sides of the core, core separation from the belt side, a severed core, separation of the ribs from the adhesive rubber, cracking or separation of the ribs, and torn or worn ribs or cracks in the inner ridges of the ribs (see illustration). On both belt types, check for fraying and glazing, which gives the belt a shiny appearance. Both sides of the belt should be inspected, which means you will have to twist the belt to check the underside. Use your fingers to feel the belt where you can't see it. If any of the above conditions are evident, renew the belt (go to paragraph 8).

4 The tightness of each belt is checked by pushing on it at a distance halfway between the pulleys (see illustration). Apply firm thumb pressure and see how much the belt moves down (deflects). Refer to the Specifications at the beginning of this Chapter for the amount of deflection allowed in each belt.

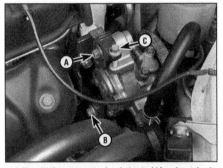

14.7a Adjustment pinch bolt (A), pivot bolt (B) and adjustment bolt (C) clockwise

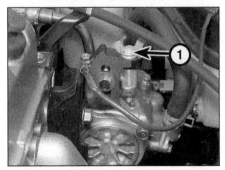

14.7b A wing bolt (1) is fitted to some models instead of the adjustment bolt

Adjustment

5 If adjustment is necessary, it is done by moving the belt-driven accessory (ie the power steering pump) on the bracket.
6 For some components, there will be an adjusting bolt and a pivot bolt. Both must be loosened slightly to enable you to move the component. After the two bolts have been loosened, move the component away from the engine (to tighten the belt) or toward the engine (to loosen the belt). After adjustment, tighten the bolts securely.
7 On other components, loosen the pivot bolt and locknut on the adjusting bolt. Turn the adjuster to tension the belt (see illustrations).

Renewal

8 To renew a belt, follow the above procedures for drivebelt adjustment but slip the belt off the crankshaft pulley and remove it. If you are replacing the alternator belt, you might have to remove another belt first because of the way they are arranged on the crankshaft pulley. Because of this and because belts tend to wear out more or less together, it is a good idea to renew both belts at the same time. Mark each belt and its appropriate pulley groove so the renewal belts can be installed in their proper positions. On some models, it may be necessary to remove the two left engine mount bolts to provide sufficient clearance for removal of the air conditioner compressor drivebelt.
9 Take the old belts to the parts store in order to make a direct comparison for length, width and design.
10 After replacing a V-ribbed drivebelt, make sure it fits properly in the ribbed grooves in the pulleys (see illustration). It is essential that the belt be properly centred.
11 Adjust the belt(s) in accordance with the procedure outlined above.

CORRECT   WRONG   WRONG

14.10 When refitting the V-ribbed belt, make sure it is centred on the pulley - it must not overlap either edge of the pulley

15 Cooling system check

1 Many major engine failures can be attributed to a faulty cooling system. If the vehicle is equipped with an automatic transmission, the cooling system also cools the transmission fluid and thus plays an important role in prolonging transmission life.
2 The cooling system should be checked with the engine cold. Do this before the vehicle is driven for the day or after the engine has been shut off for at least three hours.
3 Remove the radiator cap by turning it to the left until it reaches a stop. If you hear a hissing sound (indicating there is still pressure in the system), wait until it stops. Now press down on the cap with the palm of your hand and continue turning to the left until the cap can be removed. Thoroughly clean the cap, inside and out, with clean water. Also clean the filler neck on the radiator. All traces of corrosion should be removed. The coolant inside the radiator should be relatively transparent. If it's rust coloured, the system should be drained and refilled (see Section 27). If the coolant level isn't up to the top, add additional antifreeze/coolant mixture .
4 Carefully check the large upper and lower radiator hoses along with the smaller diameter heater hoses which run from the engine to the bulkhead. Inspect each hose along its entire length, replacing any hose which is cracked, swollen or shows signs of deterioration. Cracks may become more apparent if the hose is squeezed (see illustration). Regardless of condition, it's a good idea to renew hoses with new ones every two years.
5 Make sure that all hose connections are tight. A leak in the cooling system will usually show up as white or rust coloured deposits on the areas adjoining the leak. If wire-type clamps are used at the ends of the hoses, it may be a good idea to renew them with more secure screw-type clamps.
6 Use compressed air or a soft brush to remove bugs, leaves, etc. from the front of the radiator or air conditioning condenser. Be careful not to damage the delicate cooling fins or cut yourself on them.

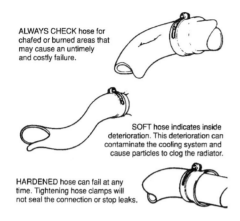

ALWAYS CHECK hose for chafed or burned areas that may cause an untimely and costly failure.

SOFT hose indicates inside deterioration. This deterioration can contaminate the cooling system and cause particles to clog the radiator.

HARDENED hose can fail at any time. Tightening hose clamps will not seal the connection or stop leaks.

SWOLLEN hose or oil soaked ends indicate danger and possible failure from oil or grease contamination. Squeeze the hose to locate cracks and breaks that cause leaks.

15.4 To prevent the inconvenience of a blown radiator or heater hose, inspect them carefully as shown here

7 Every other inspection, or at the first indication of cooling system problems, have the cap and system pressure tested. If you don't have a pressure tester, most garages will do this for a minimal charge.

16 HT leads, distributor cap and rotor check and renewal

1 The HT leads should be checked whenever new spark plugs are installed.
2 Begin this procedure by making a visual check of the HT leads while the engine is running. In a darkened garage (make sure there is ventilation) start the engine and observe each plug HT lead. Be careful not to come into contact with any moving engine parts. If there is a break in the wire, you will see arcing or a small spark at the damaged area. If arcing is noticed, make a note to obtain new wires, then allow the engine to cool and check the distributor cap and rotor.
3 The HT leads should be inspected one at a time to prevent mixing up the order, which is essential for correct engine operation. Each original plug wire should be numbered to help identify its location. If the number is illegible, a piece of tape can be marked with the correct number and wrapped around the plug wire.
4 Disconnect the plug wire from the spark plug. A removal tool can be used for this purpose or you can grasp the rubber boot, twist the boot half a turn and pull the boot free. Do not pull on the wire itself.
5 Check inside the boot for corrosion, which will look like a white crusty powder.
6 Push the wire and boot back onto the end of the spark plug. It should fit tightly onto the end of the plug. If not, remove the wire and

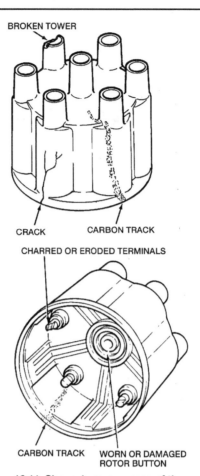

BROKEN TOWER

CRACK   CARBON TRACK

CHARRED OR ERODED TERMINALS

CARBON TRACK   WORN OR DAMAGED ROTOR BUTTON

16.11 Shown here are some of the common defects to look for when inspecting the distributor cap (if in doubt about its condition, fit a new one)

use pliers to crimp the metal connector inside the wire boot until the fit is snug.
7 Using a clean rag, wipe the entire length of the wire to remove built-up dirt and grease. Once the wire is clean, check for burns, cracks and other damage. Do not bend the wire sharply, as the conductor might break.
8 Disconnect the wire from the distributor. Again, pull only on the rubber boot. Check for corrosion and a tight fit. Renew the wire in the distributor.
9 Inspect the remaining HT leads, making sure that each one is securely fastened at the distributor and spark plug when the check is complete.
10 If new HT leads are required, purchase a set for your specific engine model. Pre-cut wire sets with the boots already installed are available. Remove and renew the wires one at a time to avoid mix-ups in the firing order.
11 Detach the distributor cap by removing the three cap retaining bolts. Look inside it for cracks, carbon tracks and worn, burned or loose contacts (see illustration).
12 Remove the retaining screw and pull the rotor off the distributor shaft. It may be necessary to use a small screwdriver to gently prise off the rotor and examine it for cracks

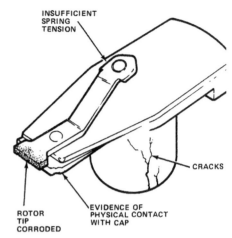

INSUFFICIENT SPRING TENSION

CRACKS

ROTOR TIP CORRODED

EVIDENCE OF PHYSICAL CONTACT WITH CAP

16.12 The rotor arm should be checked for wear and corrosion as indicated here (if in doubt about its condition, buy a new one)

and carbon tracks (see illustration). Renew the cap and rotor if any damage or defects are noted.
13 It is common practice to refit a new cap and rotor whenever new HT leads are installed, but if you wish to continue using the old cap, check the resistance between the HT leads and the cap first. If the indicated resistance is more than 30 000 ohms per lead, renew the cap and/or wires.
14 When refitting a new cap, remove the wires from the old cap one at a time and attach them to the new cap in the exact same location - do not simultaneously remove all the wires from the old cap or firing order mix-ups may occur.

17 Valve clearance check and adjustment

1 The valve clearances must be checked and adjusted with the engine cold.
2 Place the number one piston (closest to the drivebelt end of the engine) at Top Dead Centre (TDC) on the compression stroke. This is accomplished by rotating the crankshaft pulley clockwise until the timing pointer on the block lines up with the TDC mark on the front pulley (see illustration). The distributor rotor

17.2 Timing marks on the crankshaft pulley and timing cover

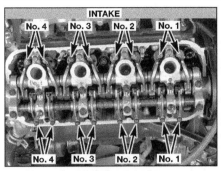

17.4 Valve layout

17.5 Adjusting a valve clearance using a ring spanner and screwdriver

should be pointing toward the number one spark plug wire terminal on the distributor cap. If it isn't, rotate the engine one complete turn and realign the marks.

3 Remove the valve cover (see Chapter 2A)

4 With the engine in this position, the number one cylinder valve adjustment can be checked and adjusted **(see illustration)**.

5 Start with the inlet valve clearance. Insert a feeler blade of the correct thickness (see this Chapter's Specifications) between the valve stem and the rocker arm **(see illustration)**. Withdraw it; you should feel a slight tension. If there's a heavy tension, loosen the adjuster nut and back off the adjuster screw. Tighten the adjuster screw until you can feel a slight tension on the feeler blade as you withdraw it.

6 Hold the adjuster screw with a screwdriver (to keep it from turning) and tighten the locknut. Recheck the clearance to make sure it hasn't changed. Repeat the procedure in this paragraph and the previous paragraph on the other inlet valve, then on the two exhaust valves.

7 Rotate the crankshaft pulley 180° anti-clockwise (the camshaft pulley will turn 90°) until the number three cylinder is at TDC. With the number three cylinder at TDC, the UP mark on the camshaft sprocket should be at the exhaust side (nine O'clock position) and the distributor rotor should point at the number three spark plug wire terminal. Check and adjust the number three cylinder valves.

8 Rotate the crankshaft pulley 180° anti-clockwise until the number four cylinder is at TDC. With the number four cylinder at TDC, the UP mark on the camshaft sprocket should

be pointed straight down. The distributor rotor should point at the number four spark plug wire terminal. Check and adjust the number four cylinder valves.

9 Rotate the crankshaft pulley 180° anti-clockwise to bring the number two cylinder to TDC. The UP mark on the camshaft sprocket should be on the inlet side (three o'clock position). The distributor rotor should point at the number two spark plug wire. Check and adjust the number two cylinder valves.

10 Refit the valve cover.

18 Fuel system check

Note: Refer to the warning on the dangers of working on the fuel system, given in Section 4, before starting.

1 If you smell fuel while driving or after the vehicle has been sitting in the sun, inspect the fuel system immediately.

2 Remove the fuel filler cap and inspect it for damage and corrosion. The gasket should have an unbroken sealing imprint. If the gasket is damaged or corroded, remove it and refit a new one.

3 Inspect the fuel feed and return lines for cracks. All fuel line connections must be tight.

⚠ *Warning: It is necessary to relieve the fuel system pressure before servicing fuel system components. The correct procedure for fuel system pressure relief is outlined in Chapter 4.*

4 Since some components of the fuel system - the fuel tank and part of the fuel feed and return lines, for example - are underneath the vehicle, they can be inspected more easily with the vehicle raised on a hoist. If that's not possible, raise the vehicle and support it securely on axle stands.

5 With the vehicle raised and safely supported, inspect the fuel tank and filler neck for punctures, cracks and other damage. The connection between the filler neck and the tank is particularly critical. Sometimes a rubber filler neck will leak because of loose clamps or deteriorated rubber. These are problems a home mechanic can usually rectify.

⚠ *Warning: Do not, under any circumstances, try to repair a fuel tank (except rubber components). A welding torch or any naked flame can easily cause fuel vapours inside the tank to explode.*

6 Carefully check all rubber hoses and metal lines leading away from the fuel tank. Check for loose connections, deteriorated hoses, crimped lines and other damage. Carefully inspect the lines from the tank to the fuel injection system. Repair or renew damaged sections as necessary.

19 Manual transmission lubricant level check

1 The manual transmission does not have a dipstick. To check the fluid level, where necessary raise the vehicle and support it securely on axle stands. The check/fill plug is on the right side of the transmission housing **(see illustration)**. Remove it. If the lubricant level is correct, it should be up to the lower edge of the hole.

2 If the transmission needs more lubricant (if the level is not up to the hole), use a funnel to add more **(see illustrations)**. Stop filling the transmission when the lubricant begins to run out the hole.

3 Refit the plug and tighten it securely. Drive the vehicle a short distance, then check for leaks.

19.1 The transmission check/fill plug is on the right-hand side of the transmission

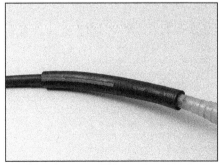

19.2a Use two different size pieces of hose to make an adapter on the funnel . . .

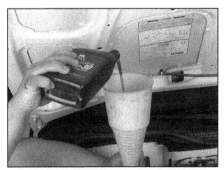

19.2b . . . so that you can easily add lubricant to the transmission from above

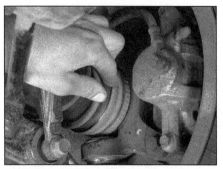

20.2 Flex the driveshaft gaiters by hand to check for tears, cracks and leaking grease

20 Driveshaft gaiter check

The driveshaft gaiters are very important because they prevent dirt, water and foreign material from entering and damaging the constant velocity (CV) joints. Oil and grease can cause the gaiter material to deteriorate prematurely, so it's a good idea to wash the gaiters with soap and water.

Inspect the gaiters for tears and cracks as well as loose clamps **(see illustration)**. If there is any evidence of cracks or leaking grease, they must be replaced (see Chapter 8).

21 Positive Crankcase Ventilation (PCV) valve check and renewal

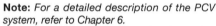

Note: *For a detailed description of the PCV system, refer to Chapter 6.*
1 The PCV valve is in a breather hose that connects the crankcase and inlet manifold.

Check

2 With the engine idling at normal operating temperature, gently squeeze shut the PCV hose located at the top of the engine with a pair of pliers, using a rag to protect the surface of the hose **(see illustration)**.
3 If the PCV valve is operating properly, it will make a clicking sound when the hose is pinched shut. If it doesn't, renew the valve.

Renewal

4 The PCV valve is located in the inlet manifold - below the fuel injector rail on multipoint fuel injection systems **(see illustration)**. Detach the hose and remove the valve, noting its installed position and direction.
5 Refitting is the reversal of removal.

22 Accelerator linkage inspection

1 Inspect the accelerator cable, pedal and lever for damage and missing parts and for binding and interference.

21.2 Squeeze the PCV hose gently and listen for a clicking sound from the valve

21.4 The PCV valve (arrowed) is located in the intake manifold - to remove, simply pull it out of the rubber grommet

2 Lubricate the various linkage pivot points with engine oil.
3 Push on the accelerator cable with your fingers to check the deflection. Compare the measurement with those found in this Chapter's Specifications. If the deflection is incorrect, loosen the locknut and turn the adjusting nut as necessary to adjust the tension.
4 Tighten the locknut.

23 Fuel filter renewal

Note: Refer to the warning on the dangers of working on the fuel system, given in Section 4, before starting.
1 This job should be done with the engine cold (after sitting at least three hours).

Carburettor models

2 There are two fuel filters - one is located in the engine compartment and the other beneath the rear of the car on the left-hand side of the fuel tank. To renew the engine compartment filter remove the air cleaner where necessary then place cloth rags beneath the filter to catch spilled fuel or alternatively use hose clamps to clamp the inlet and outlet hoses. Note which way round the filter is fitted then loosen the clips, disconnect the hoses and remove the filter. Fit the new filter using a reversal of the removal procedure but making sure that the filter is fitted the correct way round.
3 To renew the other filter chock the front

wheels then jack up the rear of the car and support on axle stands (see 'Jacking and Vehicle Support').
4 Depress the tab and remove the filter from its mounting bracket. Use hose clamps to clamp the inlet and outlet hoses, then loosen the clips and detach the filter - be prepared for some fuel spillage. Fit the new filter using a reversal of the removal procedure

Fuel injection models

4 The fuel filter is located on the bulkhead in the engine compartment.
5 Relieve the fuel system pressure as described in Chapter 4.
6 Place cloth rags around and under the filter. Remove the banjo bolt, unscrew the threaded fitting, remove the clamp bolt and lift the filter from the engine compartment **(see illustrations)**.
Note: *If available, use a flare-nut spanner when disconnecting the fuel line fitting at the filter.*

23.6a Use a flare nut spanner, if available, to disconnect the fuel line . . .

23.6b . . . unscrew the banjo bolt (it isn't necessary to remove the small service port bolt in the centre of the banjo bolt) . . .

23.6c . . . then use a socket and extension to remove the filter clamp bolt

7 Refitting is the reverse of removal. Use new sealing washers on either side of the banjo fitting and tighten the banjo bolt to the torque listed in this Chapter's Specifications. Tighten the threaded line fitting securely. Start the engine and check for leaks.

24 Brake fluid renewal

Warning: Brake fluid can harm your eyes and damage painted surfaces, so take care when handling and pouring it. Do not use fluid that has been standing open for some time, as it absorbs moisture from the air. Excess moisture can cause a loss of braking effectiveness.

1 The procedure is similar to that for the bleeding of the hydraulic system as described in Chapter 9, except that the brake fluid reservoir should be emptied by siphoning, using a clean poultry baster or similar before starting, and allowance should be made for the old fluid to be expelled when bleeding a section of the circuit.

2 Working as described in Chapter 9, open the first bleed screw in the sequence, and pump the brake pedal gently until nearly all the old fluid has been emptied from the master cylinder reservoir. Top-up to the "MAX" level with new fluid, and continue pumping until only the new fluid remains in the reservoir, and new fluid can be seen emerging from the bleed screw **(see Haynes Hint)**. Tighten the screw, and top the reservoir level up to the "MAX" level line.

3 Work through all the remaining bleed screws in the sequence until new fluid can be seen at all of them. Be careful to keep the master cylinder reservoir topped-up to above the "MIN" level at all times, or air may enter the system and greatly increase the length of the task.

4 When the operation is complete, check that all bleed screws are securely tightened, and that their dust caps are refitted.

5 Wash off all traces of spilt fluid, and recheck the master cylinder reservoir fluid level.

6 Check the operation of the brakes before taking the car on the road.

> **HAYNES HiNT** *Old hydraulic fluid is invariably much darker in colour than new fluid, making it easy to distinguish the two.*

36 000 Mile / 3 Year Service

25 Automatic transmission fluid change

1 At the specified time intervals, the automatic transmission fluid should be drained and replaced.

2 Before beginning work, purchase the specified transmission fluid (see *"Weekly checks"* at the front of this Chapter).

3 Other tools necessary for this job include axle stands to support the vehicle in a raised position, a 3/8-inch drive ratchet and extension, a drain pan capable of holding at least eight pints, newspapers and clean rags.

4 The fluid should be drained immediately after the vehicle has been driven. Hot fluid is more effective than cold fluid at removing built-up sediment.

Warning: The fluid may be very hot, and there is a risk of scalding - wear gloves.

5 After the vehicle has been driven to warm up the fluid, raise it and place it on axle stands for access to the transmission and differential drain plugs.

6 Move the necessary equipment under the vehicle, being careful not to touch any of the hot exhaust components.

7 Place the drain pan under the drain plug in the transmission and remove the drain plug with the ratchet - it's located on the right (passenger's) side of the transmission, near the bottom **(see illustration)**. Be sure the drain pan is in position, as fluid will come out with some force. Once the fluid is drained, clean the drain plug and refit it securely.

8 Lower the vehicle.

9 With the engine switched off pull out the dipstick, then add new fluid to the transmission through the dipstick hole (see *"Weekly checks"* for the recommended fluid type and capacity). Use a funnel to prevent spills. It is best to add a little fluid at a time, continually checking the level with the dipstick. Allow the fluid time to drain into the pan.

10 Start the engine and gearchange the selector into all positions from P through 2, then gearchange into P and apply the handbrake.

11 Turn off the engine and check the fluid level. Add fluid to bring the level into the cross-hatched area on the dipstick.

26 Manual transmission lubricant change

1 Remove the drain plug and drain the lubricant into a drain pan **(see illustration)**.

2 Refit the drain plug securely.

3 Add new lubricant until it begins to run out of the filler hole. See *"Weekly checks"* for the specified lubricant type.

25.7 Unscrewing the automatic transmission drain plug

26.1 Unscrewing the manual transmission drain plug

48 000 Mile / 4 Year Service

27 Cooling system servicing (draining, flushing and refilling)

 Warning: Do not allow antifreeze to come in contact with your skin or painted surfaces of the vehicle. Rinse off spills immediately with plenty of water. Antifreeze is highly toxic if ingested. Never leave antifreeze lying around in an open container or in puddles on the floor; children and pets are attracted by it's sweet smell and may drink it. Check with local authorities about disposing of used antifreeze. Many communities have collection centres which will see that antifreeze is disposed of safely.

Wait until the engine has completely cooled before beginning this procedure.

1 Periodically, the cooling system should be drained, flushed and refilled to replenish the antifreeze mixture and prevent formation of rust and corrosion, which can impair the performance of the cooling system and cause engine damage. When the cooling system is serviced, all hoses and the radiator cap should be checked and replaced if necessary.

Draining

2 Apply the handbrake and block the wheels. If the vehicle has just been driven, wait several hours to allow the engine to cool down before beginning this procedure.
3 Once the engine is completely cool, remove the radiator cap.
4 Move a large container under the radiator drain fitting to catch the coolant. Then open the drain fitting (a pair of pliers may be required to turn it) **(see illustration)**.
5 After the coolant stops flowing out of the radiator, move the container under the engine block drain plugs on the engine **(see illustrations)**. Loosen the plug and allow the coolant in the block to drain.
6 While the coolant is draining, check the condition of the radiator hoses, heater hoses and clamps.
7 Renew any damaged clamps or hoses.

Flushing

8 Once the system is drained, flush the radiator with fresh water from a garden hose until water runs clear at the drain. The flushing

27.4 Remove a cover for access to drain fitting on the base of the radiator (arrowed)

27.5b The coolant drain plug on the rear of the block (arrowed) is near the oil filter

action of the water will remove sediments from the radiator but will not remove rust and scale from the engine and cooling tube surfaces.
9 These deposits can be removed by the chemical action of a cleaner. Follow the procedure outlined in the manufacturer's instructions. If the radiator is severely corroded, damaged or leaking, it should be removed (see Chapter 3) and taken to a radiator garage.
10 Remove the overflow hose from the coolant recovery reservoir. Drain the reservoir and flush it with clean water, then reconnect the hose.

Refilling

11 Close and tighten the radiator drain. Refit and tighten the block drain plugs.
12 Place the heater temperature control in the maximum heat position.
13 Loosen the air bleed bolt, located on the top of the thermostat housing **(see illustration)**.
14 Slowly add new coolant (a 50/50 mixture

27.5a Location of the coolant drain plug (arrowed) on the front of the engine block

27.13 The air bleed bolt (arrowed) is on the thermostat housing

of water and antifreeze) to the radiator until a steady, bubble-free stream flows from the air bleed bolt, then tighten the bolt securely. Add coolant to the reservoir until the level is at the upper mark.
15 Leave the radiator cap off and run the engine in a well-ventilated area until the thermostat opens (coolant will begin flowing through the radiator and the upper radiator hose will become hot).
16 Turn the engine off and let it cool. Add more coolant mixture to bring the level back up to the lip on the radiator filler neck.
17 Squeeze the upper radiator hose to expel air, then add more coolant mixture if necessary. Refit the radiator cap.
18 Start the engine, allow it to reach normal operating temperature and check for leaks.

28 ABS high pressure hose renewal

Refer to Chapter 9 for details.

60 000 Mile / 5 Year Service

29 Timing belt renewal

Refer to Chapter 2A.

30 Evaporative emissions control system check

1 The function of the Fuel Evaporative Emission Control (EVAP) system is to store fuel vapours from the fuel tank in a charcoal canister until they can be routed to the inlet manifold where they mix with incoming air before being burned in the cylinder combustion chambers.

2 The most common symptom of a faulty evaporative emissions system is a strong fuel odour in the engine compartment. If a fuel odour is detected, inspect the charcoal canister, located on the bulkhead in the engine compartment, and the hoses attached to it **(see illustration)**.

3 The evaporative emissions control system is explained in more detail in Chapter 6.

30.2 The charcoal canister (arrowed) is mounted on the bulkhead - check the hoses and connections for damage

31 Exhaust Gas Recirculation (EGR) system check

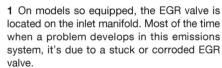

1 On models so equipped, the EGR valve is located on the inlet manifold. Most of the time when a problem develops in this emissions system, it's due to a stuck or corroded EGR valve.

2 With the engine cold to prevent burns, push

31.2 Reach up under the EGR valve and press on the diaphragm (make sure the valve is cool when you do this)

on the EGR valve diaphragm. Using moderate pressure, you should be able to press the diaphragm up-and-down within the housing **(see illustration)**.

3 If the diaphragm doesn't move or moves only with much effort, renew the EGR valve with a new one. If in doubt about the condition of the valve, compare the free movement of your EGR valve with a new valve.

4 Refer to Chapter 6 for more information on the EGR system.

Chapter 2 Part A:
Engine in-car repair procedures

Contents

Degrees of difficulty

Easy, suitable for novice with little experience	Fairly easy, suitable for beginner with some experience	Fairly difficult, suitable for competent DIY mechanic	Difficult, suitable for experienced DIY mechanic	Very difficult, suitable for expert DIY or professional

Specifications

General

Firing order	1-3-4-2
Number one cylinder location	Timing belt end
Designation:	
1343 cc engine	D13B2
1493 cc engine	D15Z1, D15B2 and D15B7
1590 cc engine	D16Z6
Bore	
All engines	75.00 mm
Stroke	
1343 cc engine	76.00 mm
1493 cc engine	84.50 mm
1590 cc engine	90.00 mm
Compression ratio	
1343 cc engine	9.0 : 1
1493 cc engine	9.2 : 1 (non-VTEC) or 9.3 : 1 (VTEC)
1590 cc engine	9.1 : 1 (non-VTEC) or 9.2 : 1 (VTEC)

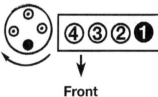

Front

Camshaft

Endfloat	
Standard	0.05 to 0.15 mm
Maximum	0.5 mm
Runout	
Standard	0.03 mm
Maximum	0.04 mm
Journal oil clearance	
Standard	0.05 to 0.089 mm
Maximum	0.15 mm

Oil pump

Rotor-to-cover clearance	0.03 to 0.08 mm
Tooth tip clearance	0.02 to 0.14 mm
Outer rotor-to-pump body clearance	0.10 to 0.18 mm

Torque wrench settings

	Nm	lbf ft
Air bleed bolt	10	7
Camshaft bearing cap bolts		
6 mm bolts	12	9
8 mm bolts	22	16
Catalytic converter-to-exhaust manifold nuts	34	25
Camshaft sprocket bolt	37	27
Crankshaft pulley bolt	182	134
Cylinder head bolts		
First step	30	22
Second step		
D15Z1 and D16Z6	73	53
D13B2, D15B2 and D16B7	65	47
Driveplate-to-crankshaft bolts	73	54
Inlet manifold bolts	23	17
Exhaust manifold-to-cylinder head nuts	31	23
Exhaust manifold-to-exhaust pipe nuts	54	40
Exhaust pipe-to-catalytic converter nuts	34	25
Exhaust manifold cover bolts	22	16
Flywheel-to-crankshaft bolts	118	87
Oxygen sensor	45	33
Oil pressure switch	18	13
Sump drain plug	45	33
Sump-to-engine bolts	14	10
Oil pump pick-up tube to pump housing nuts	23	17
Oil pump screen-to-main bearing cap	11	8
Oil pump housing-to-block bolts	11	8
Oil pump cover-to-housing	7	5
Rear main oil seal housing bolts	12	9
Timing belt cover bolts	10	7
Timing belt tensioner bolt	45	33
Valve cover bolts	10	7
VTEC lock-up solenoid bolts	12	9
Water pump bolts	12	9

1 General information

This Part of Chapter 2 is devoted to in-car repair procedures for 1.3 litre, 1.5 litre and 1.6 litre, four cylinder engines. All information concerning engine removal and refitting and engine block and cylinder head overhaul can be found in Part B of this Chapter.

There are four different versions of engines covered in this manual. All engines are Single Overhead Camshaft (SOHC), with either a 2 valves per cylinder (8V) or a 4 valves per cylinder (16V) version.

There are two versions of the VTEC (Variable Valve Timing and Lift Electronic Control) engine available in models covered by this manual. For more information on VTEC engines see Section 5 of this Chapter.

Engines covered: **Engine code:**
1343 cc SOHC   D13B2
1493 cc SOHC (VTEC-E)   D15Z1
1493 cc SOHC   D15B2 and D15B7
1590 cc SOHC (VTEC)   D16Z6

The following repair procedures are based on the assumption that the engine is installed in the vehicle. If the engine has been removed from the vehicle and mounted on a stand, many of the steps outlined in this Part of Chapter 2 will not apply.

The Specifications included in this Part of Chapter 2 apply only to the procedures contained in this chapter. Chapter 2B contains the Specifications necessary for cylinder head and engine block overhauling.

It is a compact and lightweight engine with an aluminium alloy block (with steel cylinder liners) and an aluminium alloy cylinder head. The engine rotates anticlockwise when viewed from the left-hand (timing) end of the engine. The crankshaft rides in a single carriage unit that houses the renewable insert-type main bearings, with the number four bearing (the thrust bearing) assigned the additional task of controlling crankshaft endfloat.

The pistons have two compression rings and one oil control ring. The semi-floating gudgeon pins are press fitted into the small end of the connecting rod. The connecting rod big ends are also equipped with renewable insert-type plain bearings.

The engine is liquid-cooled, utilising a centrifugal impeller-type pump, driven by a belt, to circulate coolant around the cylinders and combustion chambers and through the inlet manifold.

Lubrication is handled by a rotor-type oil pump mounted on the front of the engine under the timing belt cover. It is driven by the balance shaft belt. The oil is filtered continuously by a cartridge-type filter mounted on the radiator side of the engine.

2 Repair operations possible with the engine in the vehicle

Clean the engine compartment and the exterior of the engine with some type of degreaser before any work is done. It will make the job easier and help keep dirt out of the internal areas of the engine.

Depending on the components involved, it may be helpful to remove the bonnet to improve access to the engine as repairs are performed (refer to Chapter 11 if necessary). Cover the wings to prevent damage to the paint. Special pads are available, but an old bedspread or blanket will also work.

If vacuum, exhaust, oil or coolant leaks develop, indicating a need for gasket or seal renewal, the repairs can generally be made with the engine in the vehicle. The inlet and exhaust manifold gaskets, sump gasket, crankshaft oil seals and cylinder head gasket are all accessible with the engine in place.

Exterior engine components, such as the inlet and exhaust manifolds, the sump, the water pump, the starter motor, the alternator, the distributor and the fuel system components can be removed for repair with the engine in place.

Since the cylinder head can be removed without removing the engine, camshaft and valve component servicing can also be

3.10 Mark the distributor housing beneath the number one spark plug lead terminal

3.11 Align the mark in the flywheel/driveplate with the notch in the pointer

accomplished with the engine in the vehicle. Renewal of the timing belt and sprockets is also possible with the engine in the vehicle.

In extreme cases caused by a lack of necessary equipment, repair or renewal of piston rings, pistons, connecting rods and big-end bearings is possible with the engine in the vehicle. However, this practice is not recommended because of the cleaning and preparation work that must be done to the components involved.

3 Top Dead Centre (TDC) for number one piston - locating

Note: *The following procedure is based on the assumption that the HT leads and distributor are correctly installed. If you are trying to locate TDC to refit the distributor correctly, piston position must be determined by feeling for compression at the number one spark plug hole, then aligning the ignition timing marks.*

1 Top Dead Centre (TDC) is the highest point in the cylinder that each piston reaches as it travels up-and-down when the crankshaft turns. Each piston reaches TDC on the compression stroke and again on the exhaust stroke, but TDC generally refers to piston position on the compression stroke.

2 Positioning the piston(s) at TDC is an essential part of many procedures such as camshaft and timing belt/sprocket removal and distributor removal.

3 Before beginning this procedure, be sure to place the transmission in Neutral and apply the handbrake or block the rear wheels.

4 Disable the ignition system by detaching the two pin and 8 pin connectors at the distributor (see Chapter 5).

5 Disable the fuel system (see Chapter 4).

6 Remove the spark plugs (see Chapter 1).

7 In order to bring any piston to TDC, the crankshaft must be turned using one of the methods outlined below. When looking at the front (left) of the engine, normal crankshaft rotation is anticlockwise.

a) *The preferred method is to turn the crankshaft with a socket and ratchet attached to the bolt threaded into the front of the crankshaft.*

b) *A remote starter switch, which may save some time, can also be used. Follow the instructions included with the switch. Once the piston is close to TDC, use a socket and ratchet as described in the previous paragraph.*

c) *If an assistant is available to turn the ignition switch to the Start position in short bursts, you can get the piston close to TDC without a remote starter switch. Make sure your assistant is out of the vehicle, away from the ignition switch, then use a socket and ratchet as described in Paragraph a) to complete the procedure.*

8 Note the position of the terminal for the number one spark plug HT lead on the distributor cap. If the terminal isn't marked, follow the plug HT lead from the number one cylinder spark plug to the cap.

9 Detach the cap from the distributor and set it aside (see Chapter 1 if necessary).

10 Mark the distributor cover directly under the rotor terminal **(see illustration)** for the number 1 cylinder.

11 Remove the plug from the bellhousing and locate the timing marks inside the bellhousing access hole. You'll see the timing increments directly next to the timing pointer. Turn the crankshaft until the TDC mark (zero) on the flywheel/driveplate is aligned with the groove in the pointer **(see illustration)**.

12 Look at the distributor rotor - it should be pointing directly at the mark you made on the distributor body (cover). If the rotor is 180° off, the number one piston is at TDC on the exhaust stroke.

13 To get the piston to TDC on the compression stroke, turn the crankshaft one complete turn (360°) clockwise. The rotor should now be pointing at the mark on the distributor.

14 When the rotor is pointing at the number one spark plug HT lead terminal in the distributor cap and the ignition timing marks are aligned, the number one piston is at TDC on the compression stroke.

15 After the number one piston has been positioned at TDC on the compression stroke, TDC for any of the remaining pistons can be located by turning the crankshaft and following the firing order. Mark the remaining

spark plug HT lead terminal locations on the distributor body just like you did for the number one terminal, then number the marks to correspond with the cylinder numbers. As you turn the crankshaft, the rotor will also turn. When it's pointing directly at one of the marks on the distributor, the piston for that particular cylinder is at TDC on the compression stroke.

4 Valve cover - removal and refitting

Removal

1 Detach the cable from the negative battery terminal.

Caution: If the radio in your car is equipped with an anti-theft system, make sure you have the correct activation code before disconnecting the battery.

2 Remove the distributor cap and HT leads from their cylinder head and valve cover connections (see Chapter 1). Be sure to mark each HT lead for correct refitting.

3 Mark and detach any hoses or wires from the throttle body (fuel injection models), carburettor (carburettor models) or valve cover that will interfere with the removal of the valve cover.

4 Disconnect the vacuum hose from the PCV valve.

5 Wipe off the valve cover thoroughly to prevent debris from falling onto the exposed cylinder head or camshaft/valve train assembly.

6 Remove the valve cover nuts **(see illustration)**.

7 Carefully lift off the valve cover and gasket. If the gasket is stuck to the cylinder head, tap it with a rubber mallet to break the seal. Do not prise between the cover and cylinder head or you'll damage the gasket mating surfaces.

Refitting

8 Remove the old gasket and clean the mating surfaces of the cylinder head and the valve cover **(see illustration)**. Clean the surfaces with a rag soaked in lacquer thinner or acetone.

4.6 Remove the valve cover nuts (arrowed) and sealing grommets

4.8 Check the gasket and renew it if it has been damaged or has developed a leak

9 Apply beads of RTV sealant to the corners where the cylinder head mates with the rocker arm assembly. Wait five minutes or so and let the RTV "set-up" (slightly harden).

10 Fit a new rubber gasket into the valve cover. Refit the moulded rubber gasket onto the cover by pushing it into the slot that circles the valve cover perimeter. Refit the valve cover, sealing grommets and nuts and

tighten them to the torque listed in this Chapter's Specifications. **Note:** *Make sure the RTV sealant has slightly hardened before refitting the valve cover. If the weather is damp and cold, the sealant will take some extra time to harden.*

11 The rest of refitting is the reverse of removal.

5 VTEC systems - description and component check

Description

1 The **VTEC** system (**V**ariable Valve **T**iming and Lift **E**lectronic **C**ontrol) is used on several displacement engines across the entire Honda line of cars. The Civic models uses two different methods of varying valve timing.

2 The differences between the base engines and their VTEC counterparts is strictly in the components and operation of the valve train. The engine short block, oiling and cooling

5.2a Models with VTEC engines have "VTEC" moulded into the valve cover

systems are identical, as are all attached components. Models equipped with VTEC engines can be distinguished by the letters "VTEC" moulded into the top of the valve cover **(see illustrations)**.

3 The engine management computer has the ability to alter valve lift and timing through the use of different camshaft inlet valve lobes. The computer turns the system ON or OFF, depending on sensor input.

4 The following are used on both systems to determine VTEC operation:

> Engine speed (rpm)
> Vehicle speed (mph)
> Throttle position sensor (TPS)
> Engine load measured by Manifold Absolute Pressure (MAP) sensor
> Coolant temperature

5 The components and method of operation are slightly different between the 1.5 litre VTEC-E and 1.6 litre VTEC systems. The following describes the differences in the way the two systems operate.

1.5 litre VTEC-E

6 The camshaft has different primary and secondary inlet valve lobe profiles (lift and duration specifications).

7 At low speeds, the secondary valve operates on its own camshaft lobe, which has very low lift and duration (compared to the primary valve). The opening is intended to be just enough to keep atomised fuel from

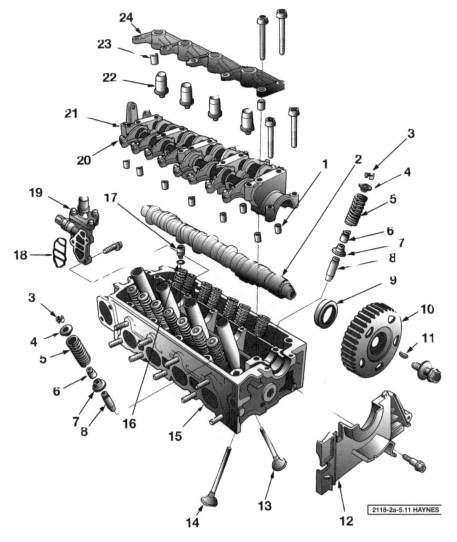

5.2b Typical VTEC cylinder head and related components

1 Dowel pin	13 Exhaust valve
2 Camshaft	14 Intake valve
3 Valve collets	15 Cylinder head
4 Valve spring retainer	16 O-ring
5 Intake valve spring	17 Oil control orifice
6 Valve seal	18 O-ring
7 Valve spring seat	19 Spool valve
8 Valve guide	20 Adjusting screws
9 Oil seal	21 Rocker arm assembly
10 Cam pulley	22 Lost motion assembly
11 Key	23 Dowel pin
12 Timing belt backplate	24 Lost motion assembly holder

2118-2a-5.11 HAYNES

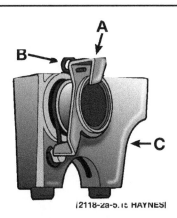

**5.15 Timing plate synchronising assembly
(D15Z1 only)**

A Timing plate   C Cam holder
B Return spring

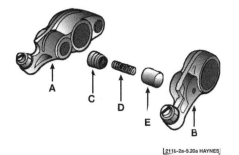

**5.20a Rocker arms and synchronising
assembly (D15Z1 only)**

A Primary rocker arm
B Secondary rocker arm
C Timing piston
D Timing spring
E Synchronising piston

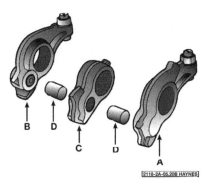

**5.20b Rocker arms and synchronising
assembly (D16Z6 only)**

A Primary rocker arm
B Secondary rocker arm
C Mid rocker arm
D Synchronising piston

building up, "puddling", at the valve head. This limited valve operation provides good low end torque and responsiveness.

8 When performance is needed, the secondary rocker arm is locked together (through the use of an electrically controlled, hydraulic system), with the primary rocker arm. **Note:** *The secondary rocker arms no longer contact its own camshaft lobe, until the system is disengaged.* When activated both valves open to the full lift and duration of the primary camshaft lobe, increasing performance at higher rpm's.

1.6 litre VTEC

9 The camshaft used in this system has identical primary and secondary inlet lobes and has an additional third lobe and rocker arm placed between the primary and secondary. This third, or "Mid", lobe has larger lift and longer duration than the primary and secondary camshaft lobes.

10 During low speed operation both inlet valves operate on their own cam lobes, but both camshaft lobes have the same specifications for lift and duration (unlike the 1.5 litre VTEC-E). As performance is required, the primary and secondary rocker arms are both locked to the Mid rocker arm through the use of an electrically controlled, hydraulic system. Both inlet valves now operate on the Mid inlet camshaft lobe. **Note:** *The primary and secondary rocker arms no longer contact their respective camshaft lobes until the Mid rocker arm is disengaged.* This provides good torque at both low and high speeds by using the camshaft lobe profile that most matches driving needs at any given speed and load.

Component check

**Lost motion assembly
(1.6 litre VTEC only)**

11 The lost motion assemblies (4 required) are held in place by the assembly holder **(see illustration 5.2b)**.
12 Unbolt and remove the lost motion assembly holder.

13 Remove the individual lost motion assemblies from the holder.
14 Test each motion assembly by pushing the plunger with your finger. If the assembly doesn't move smoothly, renew it.

**Timing plate, collar and return spring
(1.5 litre VTEC-E only)**

15 The timing plate and return spring **(see illustration)** are assembled to the camshaft holder on the inlet rocker shaft (4 required). **Note:** *As shown in the illustration, the collar used with the return spring and timing plate has a shoulder to hold the spring.*
16 Inspect the spring, making sure the spring is connected to the camshaft holder and timing plate.
17 Look for signs of scoring, broken parts or overheating (discoloration, bluish colour).
18 Renew parts as necessary.
19 Reassemble as shown **(see illustration 5.15)**.

Synchronising assembly

20 Once the rocker arm assemblies have been removed and disassembled (see Section 6), separate the rocker arms and synchronising components **(see illustrations)**.
1.5 litre VTEC-E components:
a) Primary rocker arm
b) Secondary rocker arm
c) Timing piston
d) Timing spring
e) Synchronising piston
1.6 litre VTEC components:
a) Primary rocker arm
b) Secondary rocker arm
c) Mid rocker arm
d) Synchronising piston
21 Where applicable, inspect the timing spring. Be sure it's not broken or collapsed. Renew if necessary.
22 Inspect all other parts (rocker arms and synchronising pistons) for wear, galling, scoring or signs of overheating (bluish in colour). Renew any parts necessary.
23 Reassembly is the reverse of removal.

Note: *Reassemble and hold together (rubber bands work well) each cylinders components before trying to assemble them on the rocker arm shaft* (see Section 6).
VTEC lock-up control solenoid valve
Note 1: *A problem in the VTEC solenoid valve circuit will turn on the Malfunction Indicator Lamp (MIL) and set a diagnostic trouble code (DTC) 21.*
Note 2: *A problem in the VTEC pressure switch circuit will turn on the Malfunction Indicator Lamp (MIL) and set a diagnostic trouble code 22.*
24 The lock-up VTEC solenoid valve **(see illustration)** is located on the left rear of the cylinder head (bulkhead side of head).
25 Check for continuity between the computer (ECM) pin connector D6 and body earth (see Chapter 6).
26 Check the continuity between the VTEC solenoid harness connector and ECM pin connection A4. There should be continuity, if not, repair the open in the harness to ECM.
27 Check for continuity between the VTEC solenoid wiring harness connector and earth. There should not be continuity, if there is, repair the short between the ECM and VTEC solenoid connector.
28 Check for continuity between the VTEC solenoid valve connector and earth. There

5.24 Location of VTEC solenoid valve assembly (arrowed) bolted to the left rear (bulkhead side) of cylinder head

should be 14 to 30 ohms, if not renew VTEC solenoid valve.

29 With the ignition off, check for continuity between the two oil pressure switch terminals on the VTEC solenoid connector. There should be continuity, if not, renew the oil pressure switch.

30 Turn the ignition on and check for voltage between oil pressure switch harness blue/black wire and earth. There should be approximately 12-volts, if not, inspect for an open or short to earth in the blue/black wire between the connector and the ECM.

31 With the ignition still in the On position, measure the voltage across the blue/black and brown/black terminals of the oil pressure switch harness. **Note:** *On some models the brown/black wire may be a solid black wire. There should be approximately 12-volts, if not, repair the open in the brown/black wire.*

32 Check for continuity between the blue/black terminal of the oil pressure switch harness and ECM pin connector D6. There should be continuity, if not, repair the open in the blue/black wire to the ECM.

Oil control orifice
Refer to Section 6 this Chapter for inspection details.

Primary rocker arm
Refer to Section 6 this Chapter for inspection details.

Secondary rocker arm
Refer to Section 6 of this Chapter for inspection details.

Mid rocker arm (1.6 litre VTEC only)
Refer to Section 6 of this Chapter for inspection details.

Mid camshaft lobe (1.6 litre VTEC only)
Refer to Section 12 of this Chapter for inspection details.

---

6 Rocker arm assembly - removal, inspection and refitting

Note 1: *The camshaft bearing caps are removed together with the rocker arm assembly. To prevent the opposite end (transmission end) of the camshaft from popping up (from timing belt tension) after the assembly is removed, have an assistant hold the opposite end of the camshaft down, then fit the bearing cap on that end to hold it in place until reassembly (if the timing belt remains installed).*

Note 2: *While the camshaft bearing caps are off, inspect them, as well as the camshaft bearing journals, as described in Section 12.*

Removal

1 Remove the valve cover (see Section 4).
2 Position the number one piston at Top Dead Centre (see Section 3).
3 Have an assistant hold-down the transmission end of the camshaft, then loosen the camshaft bearing cap bolts 1/4-turn at a time, in the correct order, until the spring pressure is relieved.

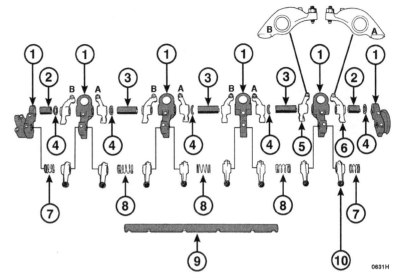

6.6a An exploded view of the rocker arms and shafts (non-VTEC engines)

1 Camshaft holder	4 Wave washer	7 Spring	9 Exhaust rocker shaft
2 Intake rocker shaft	5 Intake rocker arm (B)	8 Spring	10 Exhaust rocker arm
3 Intake rocker shaft	6 Intake rocker arm (A)		

4 Lift the rocker arms and shaft assembly from the cylinder head.

Oil control orifice (VTEC engines only)

5 Pull the orifice from the cylinder head **(see illustration 5.11)**.

Inspection

6 If you wish to dismantle and inspect the rocker arm assembly, (a good idea as long as you have them off), remove the retaining bolts and slip the rocker arms, springs and bearing caps off the shafts **(see illustrations)**.

Caution: On VTEC engines, it is a good idea to bundle the inlet rocker arms together, as shown in the illustration (rubber bands work well). Mark the relationship of the shafts to the bearing caps and keep the parts in order, they must be reassembled in the same positions they were removed from.

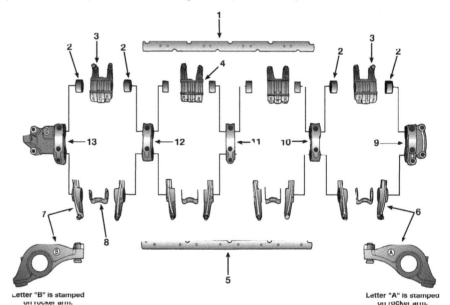

Letter "B" is stamped on rocker arm.
Letter "A" is stamped on rocker arm.

6.6b An exploded view of the rocker arms and shafts (VTEC engines)

1 Intake rocker shaft	6 Exhaust rocker arm (A)	10 Camshaft holder number 2
2 Collar	7 Exhaust rocker arm (B)	11 Camshaft holder number 3
3 Intake rocker arm assembly	8 Rocker shaft spring	12 Camshaft holder number 4
4 Rubber band	9 Camshaft holder number 1	13 Camshaft holder number 5
5 Exhaust rocker shaft		

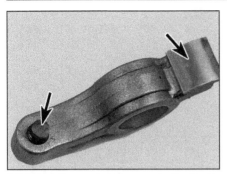

6.7 Check the contact face and adjuster tip for damage or wear (arrowed)

6.12a TIGHTENING sequence for rocker arm assembly bolts - non-VTEC engines

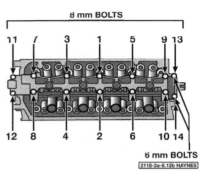

6.12b TIGHTENING sequence for rocker arm assembly bolts - VTEC engines

7 Thoroughly clean the parts and inspect them for wear and damage. Check the rocker arm faces that contact the camshaft and the rocker arm tips **(see illustration)**. **Note:** *The 1.5 litre VTEC (D15B7) engine has roller rocker arms. In addition to the normal checks, be sure that the roller tip spins freely and has no rough spots.* Check the surfaces of the shafts that the rocker arms ride on, as well as the bearing surfaces inside the rocker arms, for scoring and excessive wear. Renew any parts that are damaged or excessively worn. Also, make sure the oil holes in the shafts are not plugged.
8 Clean the orifice so there are no obstructions and oil flows freely through the orifice.

Refitting

9 Lubricate all components with assembly oil or engine oil and reassemble the shafts. When refitting the rocker arms, shafts and springs, note the markings and the difference between the left and right side parts.
10 On VTEC engines. renew the O-ring on the oil control orifice, then fit the orifice in the cylinder head.
11 Coat the cam lobes and journals with camshaft refitting lubricant. Apply silicone sealant to the cylinder head contact surfaces of bearing caps 1 and 6 and refit the rocker arm assembly.
12 Tighten the camshaft bearing cap bolts a little at a time, in the proper sequence **(see illustrations)** to the torque listed in this Chapter's Specifications.
13 The remainder of refitting is the reverse of removal. Adjust the valve clearance, if necessary (see Chapter 1).
14 Run the engine and check for oil leaks and proper operation.

7 Valve springs, retainers and seals - renewal

Note: *Broken valve springs and defective valve stem seals can be replaced without removing the cylinder head. Two special tools and a compressed air source are normally required to perform this operation, so read*

through this Section carefully and hire or buy the tools before beginning the job. If compressed air isn't available, a length of nylon rope can be used to keep the valves from falling into the cylinder during this procedure.
1 Refer to Section 4 and remove the valve cover.
2 Remove the spark plug from the cylinder that has the defective component. If all of the valve stem seals are being replaced, all of the spark plugs should be removed.
3 Turn the crankshaft until the piston in the affected cylinder is at top dead centre on the compression stroke (refer to Section 3 for instructions). If you're replacing all of the valve stem seals, begin with cylinder number one and work on the valves for one cylinder at a time. Move from cylinder-to-cylinder following the firing order sequence (see this Chapter's Specifications).
4 Remove the rocker arms and shafts (see Section 6).
5 Thread an adapter into the spark plug hole and connect an air hose from a compressed air source to it **(see illustration)**. Most motor factors can supply the air hose adapter. **Note:** *Many cylinder compression gauges utilise a screw-in fitting that may work with your air hose quick-disconnect fitting.*
6 Apply compressed air to the cylinder.

⚠ **Warning: The piston may be forced down by compressed air, causing the crankshaft to turn suddenly. If the spanner used when positioning the number one piston**

at TDC is still attached to the bolt in the crankshaft nose, it could cause damage or injury when the crankshaft moves.

7 The valves should be held in place by the air pressure. If the valve faces or seats are in poor condition, leaks may prevent air pressure from retaining the valves - refer to the alternative procedure below.
8 If you don't have access to compressed air, an alternative method can be used. Position the piston at a point about 45° before TDC on the compression stroke, then feed a long piece of nylon rope through the spark plug hole until it fills the combustion chamber. Be sure to leave the end of the rope hanging out of the engine so it can be removed easily. Use a large ratchet and socket to rotate the crankshaft in the normal direction of rotation (anticlockwise) until slight resistance is felt.
9 Place rags into the cylinder head holes around the valves to prevent parts and tools from falling into the engine, then use a valve spring compressor to compress the spring **(see illustration)**.
10 Remove the collets with small needle-nose pliers or a magnet.
11 Remove the spring retainer, shield and valve spring, then remove the umbrella type guide seal. **Note:** *If air pressure fails to hold the valve in the closed position during this operation, the valve face or seat is probably damaged. If so, the cylinder head will have to be removed for additional repair operations.*
12 Wrap a rubber band or tape around the top of the valve stem so the valve won't fall into the

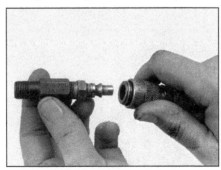

7.5 This is what the air hose adapter that threads into the spark plug hole looks like

7.9 Use a valve spring compressor to compress the springs, then remove the collets with needle-nose pliers

combustion chamber, then release the air pressure. **Note:** *If a rope was used instead of air pressure, turn the crankshaft slightly in the direction opposite normal rotation.*

13 Inspect the valve stem for damage. Rotate the valve in the guide and check the end for eccentric movement, which would indicate that the valve is bent.

14 Move the valve up-and-down in the guide and make sure it doesn't bind. If the valve stem binds, either the valve is bent or the guide is damaged. In either case, the head will have to be removed for repair.

15 Re-apply air pressure to the cylinder to retain the valve in the closed position, then remove the tape or rubber band from the valve stem. If a rope was used instead of air pressure, rotate the crankshaft in the normal direction of rotation until slight resistance is felt.

16 Lubricate the valve stem with engine oil and fit a new guide seal. **Note:** *The valve stem seals are colour coded; white for the inlet valves and black for the exhaust valves.*

17 Refit the spring(s) in position over the valve. Place the end of the spring with the closely wound coils toward the cylinder head.

18 Refit the valve spring retainer. Compress the valve spring and carefully position the collets in the groove. Apply a small dab of grease to the inside of each collet to hold it in place.

19 Remove the pressure from the spring tool and make sure the collets are seated.

20 Disconnect the air hose and remove the adapter from the spark plug hole. If a rope was used in place of air pressure, pull it out of the cylinder.

21 Refer to Section 6 and refit the rocker arm assembly.

22 Refit the valve cover (see Section 4).

23 Refit the spark plug(s) and hook up the HT lead(s).

24 Start and run the engine, then check for oil leaks and unusual sounds coming from the valve cover area.

8 Inlet manifold - removal and refitting

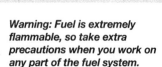

⚠ **Warning: Fuel is extremely flammable, so take extra precautions when you work on any part of the fuel system.**
Don't smoke or allow naked flames or bare light bulbs near the work area, and don't work in a garage where a natural gas-type appliance (such as a water heater or clothes dryer) with a pilot light is present. If you spill any fuel on your skin, rinse it off immediately with soap and water.

Removal

1 Detach the cable from the negative battery terminal.
Caution: If the radio in your car is equipped with an anti-theft system, make

8.4 Disconnect all hoses and attached items from the intake manifold (arrowed)

sure you have the correct activation code before disconnecting the battery.

2 Drain the cooling system (see Chapter 1).

3 Remove the inlet air ducts from the air cleaner assembly (see Chapter 4).

4 Clearly label and detach the vacuum lines and electrical connectors which will interfere with removal of the manifold **(see illustration)**. If necessary remove the components from the inlet manifold (ie the inlet air temperature sensor) with reference to Chapter 4.

5 Detach the accelerator cable from the throttle lever.

6 Remove the coolant hoses from the inlet manifold.

7 Disconnect the fuel feed and return lines at the fuel rail (multipoint injection), throttle body (dual point injection) or carburettor - if required remove the throttle housing or carburettor (see Chapter 4).

8 Working under the engine compartment, remove the brace that supports the inlet manifold **(see illustration)**.

9 Remove the thermostat housing assembly from the inlet manifold **(see illustration)**.

10 Remove the inlet manifold bolts and remove the manifold from the engine **(see illustration)**.

Refitting

11 Clean the manifold nuts with solvent and dry them with compressed air, if available.

12 Check the mating surfaces of the manifold for flatness with a precision straightedge and feeler blades. Refer to this Chapter's Specifications for the warpage limit.

8.9 Remove the bolts (arrowed) from the thermostat assembly. The third bolt is near the EGR valve (hidden from view)

8.8 Remove the bolts (arrowed) and remove the brace from the intake manifold

13 Inspect the manifold for cracks and distortion. If the manifold is cracked or warped, renew it or see if it can be resurfaced at a specialist machine shop.

14 Check carefully for any stripped or broken inlet manifold bolts/studs. Renew any defective bolts with new parts.

15 Using a scraper, remove all traces of old gasket material from the cylinder head and manifold mating surfaces. Clean the surfaces with lacquer thinner or acetone.

16 Refit the inlet manifold with a new gasket and tighten the bolts finger-tight. Starting at the centre and working out in both directions, tighten the bolts in a criss-cross pattern until the torque listed in this Chapter's Specifications is reached.

17 The remainder of the refitting procedure is the reverse of removal. Refer to Chapter 1 and refill the cooling system.

9 Exhaust manifold - removal and refitting

Removal

1 Disconnect the battery cable from the negative battery terminal.
Caution: If the radio in your car is equipped with an anti-theft system, make sure you have the correct activation code before disconnecting the battery.

2 Raise the front of the vehicle and support it securely on axle stands (see '*Jacking and*

8.10 Remove the nuts from the intake manifold (arrowed). The nut on the far right, below the EGR casting, is hidden

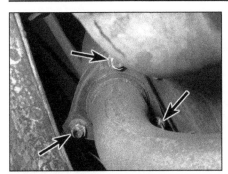

9.2 Remove the flange nuts (arrowed) and lower the exhaust pipe

9.3 Heat shield mounting bolts (arrowed)

9.4 Exhaust manifold mounting nuts (arrowed)

Vehicle Support'). Detach the exhaust pipe **(see illustration)** from the exhaust manifold (see Chapter 4). Apply penetrating oil to the fastener threads if they are difficult to remove.
3 Remove the heat shield from the exhaust manifold **(see illustration)**. Be sure to soak the bolts and nuts with penetrating oil before attempting to remove them from the manifold.
4 Remove the exhaust manifold nuts **(see illustration)** and detach the exhaust manifold from the cylinder head. **Note**: *Be sure to remove the bolts from the lower brace located near the flange of the exhaust manifold.*

Refitting

5 Discard the old gasket and use a scraper to clean the gasket mating surfaces on the manifold and head, then clean the surfaces with a rag soaked in lacquer thinner or acetone.

6 Place the exhaust manifold in position on the cylinder head and refit the nuts. Starting at the centre, tighten the nuts in a criss-cross pattern to the torque listed in this Chapter's Specifications.
7 The rest of refitting is the reverse of removal.
8 Start the engine and check for exhaust leaks between the manifold and the cylinder head and between the manifold and the exhaust pipe.

10 Timing belt and sprockets - removal, inspection and refitting

Removal

1 Disconnect the battery negative cable.

2 Place blocks behind the rear wheels and set the handbrake.
3 Loosen the wheel nuts on the left front wheel and raise the front of the vehicle. Support the front of the vehicle on axle stands (see *'Jacking and Vehicle Support'*).
4 Remove the left front wheel for easier access to the end of the crankshaft.
5 Support the engine with a trolley jack. Place a wood block between the jack pad and the sump to avoid damaging the pan.
6 Remove the left engine mount (Section 18).
7 Remove the spark plugs and drivebelts (see Chapter 1).
8 Position the number one piston at Top Dead Centre (see Section 3).
9 Remove the valve cover (see Section 4) and remove the upper timing belt cover **(see illustration)**.

10.9 Timing belt and related components

1 *Upper timing belt cover*
2 *Washer*
3 *Timing belt*
4 *Camshaft sprocket*
5 *Woodruff key*
6 *Belt tensioner*
7 *Crankshaft sprocket*
8 *Alternator drivebelt*
9 *Crankshaft drivebelt pulley*
10 *Lower timing belt cover*
11 *Timing belt tensioner adjustment bolt*

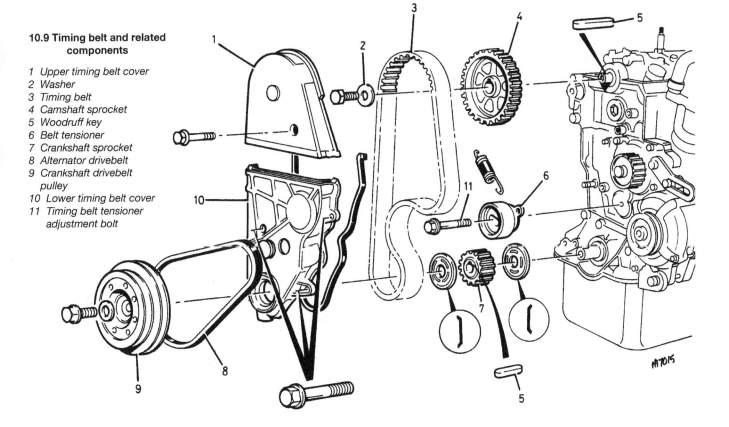

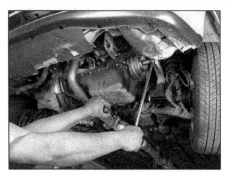

10.13 Loosen the crankshaft bolt using a long bar and socket

10.15 Remove the water pump pulley bolts (arrowed), then slip off the pulley

10.17 Direction of rotation arrow and sprocket alignment marks (arrowed)

10.18a Location of the timing belt tensioner bolt (arrowed)

10.18b Remove the outer belt guide - curved outer edge faces away from belt

10.18c Don't remove the crankshaft sprocket unless renewing the oil seal

10.18d Slide off the inner belt guide; curved edge faces away from timing belt

10.20 Check the belt tensioner pulley for roughness, play and freedom of movement

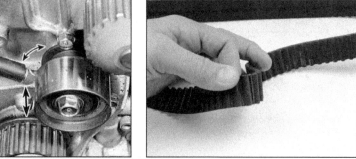

10.21a Carefully inspect the timing belt for wear or damage

10 Remove the alternator and bracket (see Chapter 5).

11 Unbolt the power steering pump without disconnecting the hoses and set it aside (see Chapter 10).

12 On air conditioned models, unbolt the compressor and set it aside **without disconnecting the refrigerant hoses** (Chapter 3).

13 Remove the flywheel inspection cover. Keep the crankshaft pulley from turning, have an assistant hold a large screwdriver wedged in the ring gear teeth on the flywheel, and loosen the pulley-to-crankshaft bolt with a socket and breaker bar **(see illustration)**.

14 Slip the pulley off the crankshaft.

15 Remove the bolts and detach the water pump pulley **(see illustration)**.

16 Remove the lower timing belt cover.

17 If you intend to reuse the timing belt, use white paint or chalk to make match marks to align the sprockets with the belt and an arrow to

indicate direction of rotation **(see illustration)**.

18 Loosen the timing belt tensioner bolt **(see illustration)**. Push on the tensioner to release the tension on the belt, then retighten the bolt. Remove the outer belt guide **(see illustration)** and slip the belt off. Note the way the belt guide is facing for proper refitting. If you're replacing the crankshaft oil seal, slip the sprocket and inner belt guide off the crankshaft **(see illustrations)**.

19 If you're renewing the camshaft or camshaft oil seal, slip a large screwdriver through the camshaft sprocket to keep it from rotating and remove the bolt, then pull off the sprocket. Also remove the Woodruff key.

Inspection

20 Rotate the belt tensioner pulley by hand and move it from side-to-side, checking for play and rough rotation **(see illustration)**. Renew it if roughness or play is detected.

21 Check the timing belt for wear (especially on the thrust side of the teeth), cracks, splits, fraying and oil contamination **(see illustrations)**. Renew the belt if any of these conditions are

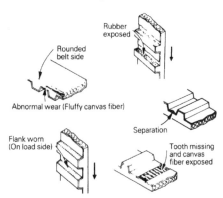

10.21b Timing belt conditions

10.23 Camshaft sprocket alignment marks

10.25 Routing of timing belt through the water pump and belt tensioner

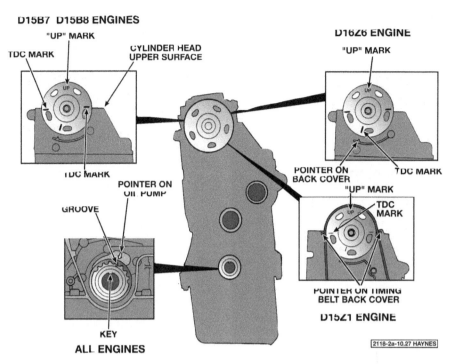

D15B7 D15B8 ENGINES

"UP" MARK
TDC MARK
CYLINDER HEAD UPPER SURFACE

D16Z6 ENGINE
"UP" MARK

TDC MARK
POINTER ON OIL PUMP
GROOVE

POINTER ON BACK COVER TDC MARK

"UP" MARK
TDC MARK

POINTER ON TIMING BELT BACK COVER

D15Z1 ENGINE

KEY
ALL ENGINES

10.27 Timing mark alignment details for all engines

noted. **Note:** *Unless the engine has very low mileage, it's common practice to renew the timing belt with a new one every time it's removed. Don't refit the original belt unless it's in like-new condition. Never refit a belt in questionable condition.*

Refitting

22 If you removed the sprockets, refit them. Do not forget the Woodruff key for the camshaft sprocket and the inner belt guide for the crankshaft sprocket (you can leave the outer guide off for now). Tighten the camshaft sprocket bolt to the torque listed in this Chapter's specifications.
23 Before refitting the timing belt, make sure the dot or "UP" mark on the camshaft sprocket is at the top. The two index marks must be in line with the cylinder head surface - use a straight-edge or ruler if necessary to check this **(see illustration).**
24 Temporarily refit the crankshaft pulley and bolt and turn the crankshaft (if it was disturbed) until the timing marks on the crankshaft sprocket and the pointer on the oil pump are aligned **(see illustration 10.27).**
25 Refit the timing belt **(see illustration)** with slight tension between the sprockets on the front (radiator) side. With the belt tensioner bolt loose, rotate the crankshaft anti-clockwise for a distance of three teeth on the camshaft sprocket. This puts tension on the belt.
26 Tighten the belt tensioner bolt.
27 Carefully turn the crankshaft through two revolutions and recheck the timing marks and camshaft sprocket index marks for proper alignment **(see illustration).** If the crankshaft binds or seems to hit something, do not force

it, as the valves may be hitting the pistons. If this happens, valve timing is incorrect. Remove the belt and repeat the refitting procedure and verify that the refitting is correct.
28 Refit the remaining parts in the reverse order of removal.
29 Run the engine and check for proper operation.

11 Crankshaft front oil seal - renewal

1 Remove the drivebelts (see Chapter 1).
2 Remove the crankshaft pulley.
3 Remove the timing belt (see Section 10).
4 Remove the crankshaft sprocket from the crankshaft **(see illustration 10.18c)**, then remove the inner belt guide.
5 Carefully prise the seal out of the oil pump housing with a seal removal tool or a screwdriver. Don't scratch the seal bore or damage the crankshaft in the process (if the crankshaft is damaged, the new seal will end up leaking).
6 Clean the bore in the oil pump housing and coat the outer edge of the new seal with engine oil or multi-purpose grease. Using a socket with an outside diameter slightly smaller than the outside diameter of the seal, drive the seal into place with a hammer. If a socket is not available, a section of a large diameter pipe will work. Check the seal after refitting to be sure the spring did not pop out.
7 Refit the inner belt guide and the crankshaft sprocket. Refit the timing belt (Section 10).

8 Lubricate the sleeve of the crankshaft pulley with engine oil or multi-purpose grease, then refit the crankshaft pulley. The remainder of refitting is the reverse of removal.
9 Run the engine and check for leaks.

12 Camshaft - removal, inspection and refitting

Endfloat and runout check

1 To check camshaft endfloat:
a) *Fit the camshaft, and secure with the caps.*
b) *Mount a dial indicator on the head* **(see illustration).**
c) *Using a large screwdriver as a lever at the opposite end, move the camshaft forward-and-backward and note the dial indicator reading.*

12.1 To check camshaft endfloat, set a dial indicator like this, with the gauge plunger touching the nose of the camshaft

TOOL TIP

Using a home-made tool to retain the camshaft sprocket whilst the sprocket retaining bolt is tightened

12.8 Lift the camshaft from the cylinder head

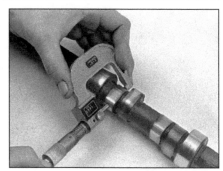

12.10 Measure the camshaft lobe heights with a micrometer

d) *Compare the reading with the endfloat listed in this Chapter's Specifications.*
e) *If the indicated reading is higher, either the camshaft or the head is worn. Renew parts as necessary.*

2 To check camshaft runout:
a) *Support the camshaft with a pair of V-blocks and set up a dial indicator with the plunger resting against the centre bearing journal on the camshaft.*
b) *Rotate the camshaft and note the indicated runout.*
c) *Compare the results to the specified camshaft runout.*
d) *If the indicated runout exceeds the specified runout, renew the camshaft.*

Removal

3 Remove the valve cover (see Section 4).
4 Set the engine at TDC for cylinder number one (see Section 3).
5 Remove the distributor (see Chapter 5).
6 If it necessary to separate the sprocket from the camshaft, remove the camshaft sprocket bolt. **Note:** *Prevent the camshaft from turning by inserting a screwdriver through one of the holes in the sprocket (also see Tool Tip).*
7 Remove the rocker arm assembly (see Section 6). If the camshaft bearing caps must be removed from the assembly and they don't have numbers on them, number them before removal. Be sure to put the marks on the same ends of all the caps to prevent incorrect orientation of the caps during refitting.
8 Lift out the camshaft **(see illustration)**, wipe it off with a clean rag, remove the camshaft seal and set the camshaft aside.

Inspection

9 Check the camshaft bearing journals and caps for scoring and signs of wear. If they are worn, renew the cylinder head with a new or rebuilt unit. Check the oil clearance of each camshaft journal with Plastigage, comparing your readings with this Chapter's Specifications. **Note:** *For instructions on the use of Plastigage, see Chapter 2, Part B, Sections 23 and 25.* If the oil clearance of any of the journals is out of specification, renew the camshaft.

10 Check the cam lobes for wear:
a) *Check the toe and ramp areas of each cam lobe for score marks and uneven wear. Also check for flaking and pitting.*
b) *If there's wear on the toe or the ramp, renew the camshaft, but first try to find the cause of the wear. Look for abrasive substances in the oil and inspect the oil pump and oil passages for blockage. Lobe wear is usually caused by inadequate lubrication or dirty oil.*
c) *Using a micrometer, measure the cam lobe height* **(see illustration)**. *If the lobe wear is greater than listed in this Chapter's Specifications, renew the camshaft.*

11 Inspect the rocker arms for wear, scoring and pitting of the contact surfaces.
12 If any of the conditions described above are noted, the cylinder head is probably getting insufficient lubrication or dirty oil, so make sure you track down the cause of this problem (low oil level, low oil pump capacity, clogged oil passage, etc.) before refitting a new head, camshaft or rocker arms.

Refitting

13 Thoroughly clean the camshaft, the bearing surfaces in the head and caps and the rocker arms. Remove all sludge and dirt. Wipe off all components with a clean, lint-free cloth.
14 Lubricate the camshaft bearing surfaces in the head and the bearing journals and lobes on the camshaft with camshaft assembly oil or moly-base grease **(see illustration)**.

12.14 Be sure to apply grease to the cam lobes and bearing journals before refitting

Caution: Failure to adequately lubricate the camshaft and related components can cause serious damage to bearing and friction surfaces during the first few seconds after engine start-up, when the oil pressure is low or non-existent.

15 Carefully lower the camshaft into position. Using an appropriate sized deep socket or section of pipe, fit a new camshaft seal with the open (spring) side facing in.
16 Fit the rocker arm assembly (Section 6).
17 Rotate the camshaft as necessary and fit the camshaft sprocket with the "UP" mark stamped on the camshaft sprocket at the twelve o'clock position **(see illustration 10.23)**.
18 Refit the timing belt and related components as described in Section 10.
Caution: if the crankshaft position was disturbed, be sure to realign the crankshaft sprocket before refitting the timing belt (see illustration 10.27).
19 Remove the spark plugs and rotate the crankshaft by hand to make sure the valve timing is correct. After two revolutions, the timing marks on the sprockets should still be aligned. If they're not, remove the timing belt and set all the timing marks again.
Caution: If you feel resistance while rotating the crankshaft, stop immediately!
20 The remainder of refitting is the reversal of removal.

13 Cylinder head -
removal and refitting

Warning: Allow the engine to cool completely before beginning this procedure.

Removal

1 Position the number one piston at Top Dead Centre (see Section 3).
2 Disconnect the negative cable from the battery.
Caution: The radio in your car is equipped with an anti-theft system, refer to the information at the rear of this manual before detaching the battery cable.

13.9a If the cylinder head sticks to the block, prise between the power steering pump bracket and the engine block

13.9b Lift the cylinder head with the intake and exhaust manifolds attached

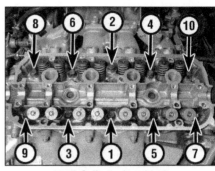

13.16 Cylinder head bolt TIGHTENING sequence

3 Drain the cooling system and remove the spark plugs (see Chapter 1).

4 Remove the inlet manifold brace and exhaust manifold flange bolts. **Note:** *You may wish to detach the inlet manifold (see Section 8) and/or exhaust manifold (see Section 9), rather than removing it with the cylinder head, to make the cylinder head easier to handle.*

5 Remove the valve cover (see Section 4).

6 Remove the distributor (see Chapter 5), including the cap and HT leads.

7 Remove the timing belt (see Section 10), rocker arm assembly (see Section 6) and the camshaft (see Section 12).

8 Loosen the head bolts in 1/4-turn increments until they can be removed by hand. Work in a pattern that's the reverse of the tightening sequence **(see illustration 13.16)** to avoid warping the head. Note where each bolt goes so it can be returned to the same location on refitting.

9 Lift the head off the engine **(see illustrations)**. If resistance is felt, don't prise between the head and block gasket mating surfaces - damage to the mating surfaces will result. Instead, prise between the power steering pump bracket and the engine block. Set the head on blocks of wood to prevent damage to the gasket sealing surfaces.

10 Cylinder head dismantling and inspection are covered in Chapter 2B. It's a good idea to have the head checked for warpage, even if you're just replacing the gasket.

Refitting

11 The mating surfaces of the cylinder head and block must be perfectly clean when the head is installed.

12 Use a gasket scraper to remove all traces of carbon and old gasket material, then clean the mating surfaces with lacquer thinner or acetone. If there's oil on the mating surfaces when the head is installed, the gasket may not seal correctly and leaks may develop. When working on the block, block the cylinders with clean rags to keep out debris. Use a vacuum cleaner to remove material that falls into the cylinders. Since the head and block are made of aluminium, aggressive scraping can cause damage. Be extra careful not to nick or gouge the mating surfaces with the scraper.

13 Check the block and head mating surfaces for nicks, deep scratches and other damage. If damage is slight, it can be removed with a file; if it's excessive, machining may be the only alternative.

14 Use a tap of the correct size to chase the threads in the head bolt holes. Mount each head bolt in a vice and run a die down the threads to remove corrosion and restore the threads. Dirt, corrosion, sealant and damaged threads will affect torque readings.

15 Place a new gasket on the block. Check to see if there are any markings (such as "TOP") on the gasket that say how it is to be installed. Those marks must face UP. Also, apply sealant to the edges of the timing chain cover where it mates with the engine block. Set the cylinder head in position.

16 Lubricate the threads and the seats of the cylinder head bolts with clean engine oil, then refit them. They must be tightened in a specific sequence **(see illustration)**, in two stages and to the torque listed in this Chapter's Specifications.

17 Attach the camshaft sprocket to the camshaft and fit the timing belt (Section 10).

18 Refit the remaining parts in the reverse order of removal.

19 Be sure to refill the cooling system and check all fluid levels.

20 Rotate the crankshaft clockwise slowly by hand through two complete revolutions. **Caution: If you feel any resistance while turning the engine over, stop and re-check the camshaft timing. The valves may be hitting the pistons.**

21 Start the engine and check the ignition timing (see Chapter 1).

22 Run the engine until normal operating temperature is reached. Check for leaks and proper operation.

14 Sump - removal and refitting

Removal

1 Warm up the engine, then drain the oil and renew the oil filter (see Chapter 1).

2 Detach the cable from the negative battery terminal.

Caution: If the radio in your vehicle is equipped with an anti-theft system, make sure you have the correct activation code before disconnecting the battery.

3 Raise the vehicle and support it on axle stands (see 'Jacking and Vehicle Support').

4 Remove the bolts securing the sump to the engine block **(see illustration)**.

5 Tap on the sump with a soft-face hammer to break the gasket seal, then detach the sump from the engine. Do not prise between the block and sump mating surfaces.

6 Using a gasket scraper, remove all traces of old gasket and/or sealant from the engine block and sump. Remove the seals from each end of the engine block or sump. Clean the mating surfaces with lacquer thinner or acetone. Make sure the threaded bolt holes in the block are clean.

Refitting

7 Clean the sump with solvent and dry it thoroughly. Check the gasket flanges for distortion, particularly around the bolt holes. If necessary, place the pan on a wood block and use a hammer to flatten and restore the gasket surfaces.

8 Apply a 3.0 mm wide bead of RTV sealant to the sump gasket surfaces. Make sure the sealant is applied to the inside edge of the bolt holes.

9 Carefully place the sump in position.

10 Fit the bolts and tighten them in small increments to the specified torque. Start with

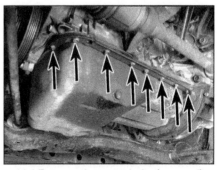

14.4 Remove the sump bolts (arrowed) from the sump

15.3 Remove the oil pick-up tube bolts (arrowed) from the oil pump and main bearing cap bridge

the bolts closest to the centre of the pan and work out in a spiral pattern. Don't overtighten them or leakage may occur.

11 Add oil (see Chapter 1), run the engine and check for oil leaks.

15 Oil pump - removal, inspection and refitting

Removal

1 Remove the timing belt (see Section 10).
2 Remove the sump (see Section 14).
3 Remove the oil pick-up tube and screen from the pump housing and the main bearing cap bridge **(see illustration)**.
4 Remove the bolts from the oil pump housing and separate the assembly from the engine **(see illustration)**.

15.5 Remove the oil pump cover screws (arrowed)

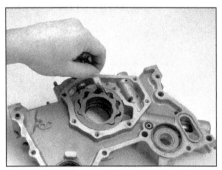

15.6b Use a feeler blade to check the tooth-tip clearance

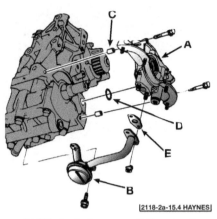

[2118-2a-15.4 HAYNES]

15.4 Typical oil pump refitting details

    A Oil pump assembly
    B Oil screen/pick-up tube
    C Alignment dowel pin
    D O-ring
    E Gasket

5 Remove the screws and dismantle the oil pump **(see illustration)**. You may need to use an impact screwdriver to loosen the pump cover screws without stripping the heads.

Inspection

6 Check the clearances on the oil pump rotors **(see illustrations)**. Compare your measurements to the figures listed in this Chapter's Specifications. Renew the pump if any of the measurements are outside of the specified limits.
7 Remove the pressure relief valve plug and

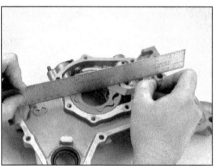

15.6a Use a feeler blade and straight-edge to check the rotor-to-cover clearance

15.6c Use a feeler blade to check the outer rotor-to-pump body clearance

extract the spring and pressure relief valve plunger from the pump housing. Check the spring for distortion and the relief valve plunger for scoring. Renew parts as necessary.
8 Fit the pump rotors. Pack the spaces between the rotors with petroleum jelly (this will help prime the pump).
9 Apply thread-locking compound to the pump cover screws, fit the cover and tighten the screws to the torque listed in this Chapter's Specifications. Fit the oil pressure relief valve and spring assembly. Use a new sealing washer on the plug and tighten the plug securely.

Refitting

10 Apply a thin coat of RTV sealant to the pump housing-to-block sealing surface and a new O-ring in the pump housing. Refit the pump housing to the engine block and tighten the bolts to the torque listed in this Chapter's Specifications.
11 Refit the oil pick-up tube and screen, using a new gasket. Tighten the bolts to the torque listed in this Chapter's Specifications.
12 Refit the sump (see Section 14).
13 Remainder of refitting is the reverse of removal. Add the specified type and quantity of oil and coolant (see Chapter 1), run the engine and check for leaks.

16 Flywheel/driveplate - removal and refitting

Removal

1 Raise the vehicle and support it securely on axle stands (see 'Jacking and Vehicle Support'), then refer to Chapter 7 and remove the transmission.
2 Remove the pressure plate and clutch disc (see Chapter 8) (manual transmission vehicles). Now is a good time to check/renew the clutch components and pilot bearing.
3 Remove the bolts that secure the flywheel/driveplate to the crankshaft **(see illustration)**. If the crankshaft turns, remove the starter (see Chapter 5) and wedge a screwdriver in the ring gear teeth (manual transmission models), or insert a long punch

16.3 Remove the flywheel/driveplate bolts (arrowed) from the crankshaft

17.4a Carefully prise the oil seal out with a removal tool or a screwdriver

17.4b Lubricate journal and seal lip with grease and carefully work the seal on

through one of the holes in the driveplate and allow it to rest against a projection on the engine block (automatic transmission models).

4 Remove the flywheel/driveplate from the crankshaft. Since the flywheel is heavy, be sure to support it while removing the last bolt.

5 Clean the flywheel to remove grease and oil. Inspect the surface for cracks, rivet grooves, burned areas and score marks. Light scoring can be removed with emery cloth. Check for cracked and broken ring gear teeth. Lay the flywheel on a flat surface and use a straightedge to check for warpage.

6 Clean and inspect the mating surfaces of the flywheel/driveplate and the crankshaft. If the rear main oil seal is leaking, renew it before refitting the flywheel/driveplate (see Section 17).

Refitting

7 Position the flywheel/driveplate against the crankshaft. Note that some engines have an alignment dowel or staggered bolt holes to ensure correct refitting. Before refitting the bolts, remove any locking compound from the threads of the crankshaft holes, using the correct-size tap, if available. Apply thread-locking compound to the threads of the bolts.

 HAYNES HiNT *If a tap is not available, cut two slots into the threads of an old flywheel bolt and use the bolt to remove the locking compound from the threads.*

8 Prevent the flywheel/driveplate from turning by using one of the methods described in paragraph 3. Using a crossing pattern, tighten the bolts to the torque listed in this Chapter's Specifications.

9 The remainder of refitting is the reverse of the removal procedure.

---

17 Rear main oil seal - renewal

1 The transmission must be removed from the vehicle for this procedure (see Chapter 7).

2 Remove the flywheel/driveplate (see Section 16).

3 Before removing the seal, it is very important that the clearance between the seal and the outside edge of the retainer is checked. Use a small ruler or vernier calipers and record the distance. The new seal must not be driven in past this measurement (see Chapter 2B).

4 The seal can be replaced without removing the sump or seal retainer. Use a screwdriver and a rag to carefully prise the seal out of the housing **(see illustration)**. Use the rag to be sure no nicks are made in the crankshaft seal surface. Apply a film of clean oil to the crankshaft seal journal and the lip of the new seal and carefully tap the seal into place **(see illustration)**. The lip is stiff so carefully work it onto the seal journal of the crankshaft with a smooth object like the end of a socket

extension. Tap the seal into the retainer with a seal driver. If a seal driver isn't available, a large socket or piece of pipe, with an outside diameter slightly smaller than that of the seal, can be used. Don't rush it or you may damage the seal. **Note:** *Removal of the oil seal retainer and renewal of the seal are covered in Chapter 2B.*

5 The remaining steps are the reversal of removal.

6 Run the engine and check for oil leaks.

---

18 Engine mountings -
check and renewal

1 Engine mountings seldom require attention, but broken or deteriorated mountings should be replaced immediately or the added strain placed on the driveline components may cause damage or wear.

Check

2 During the check, the engine must be raised slightly to remove the weight from the mountings.

3 Raise the vehicle and support it securely on axle stands, then position a jack under the engine sump. Place a large wood block between the jack head and the sump, then carefully raise the engine just enough to take the weight off the mountings.

⚠️ *Warning: DO NOT place any part of your body under the engine when it's supported only by a jack!*

4 Check the mounting insulators to see if the rubber is cracked, hardened or separated from the metal plates. Sometimes the rubber will split right down the centre.

5 Check for relative movement between the mounting plates and the engine or frame (use a large screwdriver or crowbar to attempt to move the mountings). If movement is noted, lower the engine and tighten the mounting fasteners.

6 Rubber preservative should be applied to the insulators to slow deterioration.

18.9a Left side engine mount and mounting bolt (arrowed)

18.9b Front engine mount and mounting bolt (arrowed)

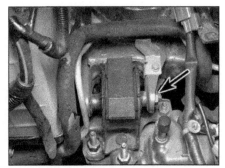

18.9c Right side engine mount and mounting bolt (arrowed)

Renewal

7 Disconnect the battery negative cable. *Caution: The radio in your car is equipped with an anti-theft system, refer to the information at the rear of this manual before detaching the battery cable.*

8 Raise the vehicle and support it securely on axle stands (if not already done). Support the engine as described in paragraph 3.

9 Remove the fasteners, raise the engine with the jack and detach the mounting from the frame bracket and engine.

10 Fit the new mounting, making sure it is correctly positioned in its bracket **(see illustrations)**. Refit the fasteners and tighten them securely.

Chapter 2 Part B:
Engine removal and overhaul procedures

Contents

Degrees of difficulty

Easy, suitable for novice with little experience	**Fairly easy,** suitable for beginner with some experience	**Fairly difficult,** suitable for competent DIY mechanic	**Difficult,** suitable for experienced DIY mechanic	**Very difficult,** suitable for expert DIY or professional

Specifications

General

Cylinder compression pressure
  Standard . . . . 185 psi
  Minimum:
    Except D15Z1 and D16Z6 . . . . 135 psi
    D15Z1 and D16Z6 . . . . 165 psi
  Maximum variation between cylinders . . . . 28 psi
Oil pressure (hot)
  At idle . . . . 10 psi
  At 3000 rpm . . . . 50 psi

Engine block

Cylinder bore . . . . 75.00 to 75.02 mm
  Service limit . . . . 75.07 mm
Cylinder taper limit . . . . 0.05 mm
Cylinder out-of-round limit . . . . 0.05 mm
Block deck warpage . . . . 0.07 mm
  Service limit . . . . 0.10 mm

Pistons and rings

Piston diameter . . . . 74.980 to 74.990 mm
  Service limit . . . . 74.970 mm minimum
Piston to cylinder wall clearance . . . . 0.010 to 0.040 mm
  Service limit . . . . 0.05 mm

Pistons and rings (continued)

Ring groove clearance
  Top compression ring
    D15Z1 .... 0.035 to 0.060 mm
      Service limit .... 0.13 mm maximum
    All others .... 0.030 to 0.060 mm
      Service limit .... 0.13 mm maximum
  Second compression ring
    D15Z1 .... 0.030 to 0.060 mm
      Service limit .... 0.13 mm maximum
    All others .... 0.030 to 0.055 mm
      Service limit .... 0.13 mm maximum
Ring end gap
  Top compression ring .... 0.15 to 0.30 mm
    Service limit .... 0.60 mm maximum
  Second compression ring .... 0.30 to 0.45 mm
    Service limit .... 0.70 mm maximum
  Oil control ring
    D15Z1 and D16Z6 .... 0.20 to 0.50 mm
      Service limit .... 0.80 mm maximum
    D13B2, D15B2 and D15B7 .... 0.20 to 0.80 mm
      Service limit .... 0.90 mm maximum
Crankshaft and connecting rods
Endfloat
  Standard .... 0.10 to 0.35 mm
  Service limit .... 0.45 mm maximum
Main bearing journals
  Diameter
    D16Z6 .... 54.976 to 55.000 mm
    All others .... 44.976 to 45.000 mm
  Taper
    Standard .... 0.0025 mm
    Service limit .... 0.005 mm maximum
  Out-of-round
    Standard .... 0.0025 mm
    Service limit .... 0.005 mm maximum
  Runout
    Standard .... 0.03 mm
    Service limit .... 0.04 mm maximum
Main bearing oil clearance
  Journals no. 1 and 5 .... 0.018 to 0.036 mm
    Service limit .... 0.05 mm maximum
  Journals no. 2, 3 and 4 .... 0.024 to 0.042 mm
    Service limit .... 0.05 mm maximum
Connecting rod journal
  Diameter
    D13B2 .... 39.976 to 40.000 mm
    D15Z1, D15B2 and D15B7 .... 41.976 to 42.000 mm
    D16Z6 .... 44.976 to 45.000 mm
  Taper
    Standard .... 0.0025 mm
    Service limit .... 0.005 mm maximum
  Out-of-round
    Standard .... 0.0025 mm
    Service limit .... 0.005 mm maximum
  Runout
    Standard .... 0.03 mm
    Service limit .... 0.04 mm maximum
Connecting big-end bearing oil clearance
  Standard .... 0.020 to 0.038 mm
  Service limit .... 0.05 mm maximum
Connecting rod side clearance (endfloat)
  Standard .... 0.15 to 0.30 mm
  Service limit .... 0.40 mm maximum

Cylinder head and valves

Head warpage limits
  Minimum allowable before regrinding . . . . 0.05 mm
  Service limit . . . . 0.2 mm
Head warpage at manifold surfaces . . . . 0.15 mm
Valve seat angle . . . . 45°
Valve face angle . . . . 45°
Valve margin width
  Inlet . . . . 0.85 to 1.15 mm
    Service limit . . . . 1.60 mm minimum
  Exhaust . . . . 1.25 to 1.55 mm
    Service limit . . . . 2.00 mm minimum
Valve stem diameter
  Inlet . . . . 5.450 to 5.490 mm
    Service limit . . . . 5.450 mm minimum
  Exhaust . . . . 5.450 to 5.460 mm
    Service limit . . . . 5.420 mm minimum
Valve guide inside diameter
  Inlet . . . . 5.51 to 5.53 mm
    Service limit . . . . 5.55 mm maximum
  Exhaust . . . . 5.51 to 5.53 mm
    Service limit . . . . 5.55 mm
Valve stem-to-guide clearance
  D16Z6
    Inlet . . . . 0.02 to 0.05 mm
      Service limit . . . . 0.08 mm maximum
    Exhaust . . . . 0.05 to 0.08 mm
      Service limit . . . . 0.12 mm maximum
  All others
    Inlet . . . . 0.02 to 0.05 mm
      Service limit . . . . 0.08 mm maximum
    Exhaust . . . . 0.05 to 0.08 mm
      Service limit . . . . 0.12 mm maximum
Valve stem fitted height
  D13B2, D15B2 and D15B7
    Inlet . . . . 46.985 to 47.455 mm
      Service limit . . . . 47.705 mm maximum
    Exhaust . . . . 48.965 to 49.435 mm
      Service limit . . . . 49.685 mm maximum
  D15Z1 and D16Z6
    Inlet . . . . 53.165 to 53.635 mm
      Service limit . . . . 53.885 mm maximum
    Exhaust . . . . 53.165 to 53.635 mm
      Service limit . . . . 53.885 mm maximum
Valve spring free length
  D13B2
    Inlet . . . . 47.97 mm
    Exhaust . . . . 49.19 mm
  D15B2
    Inlet . . . . 48.58 mm
    Exhaust . . . . 49.19 mm
  D15B7
    Inlet . . . . 51.90 mm
    Exhaust . . . . 55.28 mm
  D15Z1
    Inlet . . . . 54.78 mm
    Exhaust . . . . 58.23 mm
  D16Z6
    Inlet . . . . 57.97 mm
    Exhaust . . . . 58.41 mm

Torque wrench settings

	Nm	lbf ft
Main bearing cap bolts		
D16Z6	52	38
All others	45	33
Connecting big-end bearing cap nuts	31	23

Refer to Part A Specifications for additional torque figures

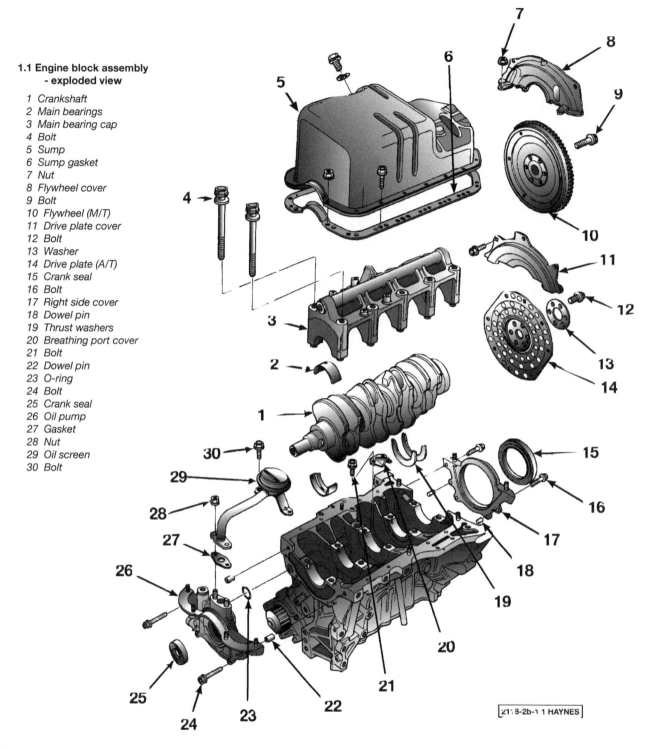

1.1 Engine block assembly - exploded view

1 Crankshaft
2 Main bearings
3 Main bearing cap
4 Bolt
5 Sump
6 Sump gasket
7 Nut
8 Flywheel cover
9 Bolt
10 Flywheel (M/T)
11 Drive plate cover
12 Bolt
13 Washer
14 Drive plate (A/T)
15 Crank seal
16 Bolt
17 Right side cover
18 Dowel pin
19 Thrust washers
20 Breathing port cover
21 Bolt
22 Dowel pin
23 O-ring
24 Bolt
25 Crank seal
26 Oil pump
27 Gasket
28 Nut
29 Oil screen
30 Bolt

z1\ 8-2b-1 1 HAYNES

1 General information

Included in this portion of Chapter 2 are the general overhaul procedures for the cylinder head(s), cylinder block and internal engine components **(see illustration)**.

The information ranges from advice concerning preparation for an overhaul and the purchase of renewal parts to detailed, step-by-step procedures covering removal and refitting of internal engine components and the inspection of parts.

The following Sections have been written based on the assumption the engine has been removed from the car. For information concerning in-car engine repair, as well as removal and refitting of the external components necessary for the overhaul, see Part A of this Chapter.

The Specifications included in this Part are only those necessary for the inspection and overhaul procedures which follow. Refer to Part A for additional Specifications.

2 Engine overhaul - general information

It is not always easy to determine when, or if, an engine should be completely overhauled, as a number of factors must be considered.

High mileage is not necessarily an indication an overhaul is needed, while low mileage does not preclude the need for an overhaul. Frequency of servicing is probably the most important consideration. An engine that has had regular and frequent oil and filter changes, as well as other required maintenance, will most likely give many thousands of miles of reliable service. Conversely, a neglected engine may require an overhaul very early in its life.

Excessive oil consumption is an indication that piston rings, valve seals and/or valve guides are in need of attention. Make sure oil leaks are not responsible before deciding the rings and/or guides are bad. Perform a cylinder compression check to determine the extent of the work required (see Section 3).

Remove the oil pressure sending unit (see illustration) and check the oil pressure with a gauge fitted in its place. Compare the results to this Chapter's Specifications. As a general rule, engines should have 10 psi of oil pressure for every 1,000 rpm. If the pressure is extremely low, the bearings and/or oil pump are probably worn out.

Loss of power, rough running, knocking or metallic engine noises, excessive valve train noise and high fuel consumption rates may also point to the need for an overhaul, especially if they're all present at the same time. If a complete tune-up doesn't remedy the situation, major mechanical work is the only solution.

An engine overhaul involves restoring the internal parts to the specifications of a new engine. During an overhaul, the piston rings are replaced and the cylinder walls are reconditioned (rebored and/or honed). If a rebore is done by a specialist machine shop, new oversize pistons will also be fitted. The main bearings, connecting big-end bearings and camshaft bearings are generally replaced with new ones and, if necessary, the crankshaft may be reground to restore the journals. The engine block may need a "line bore" to straighten the crankshaft main journals and connecting rods sometimes need to be "resized". All this machining is to properly fit bearings and give correct oil clearances, to ensure long engine life. These services can only be done by a well equipped machine shop.

Generally, the valves are serviced as well, since they are usually in less-than-perfect condition at this point. While the engine is being overhauled, other components, such as the starter and alternator, can be rebuilt as well. The end result should be a like-new engine that will give many trouble free miles. **Note:** *Critical cooling system components such as the hoses, drivebelts, thermostat and water pump MUST be replaced with new parts when an engine is overhauled. The radiator should be checked carefully to ensure it isn't clogged or leaking* (see Chapter 3).

Before beginning the engine overhaul, read through the entire chapter to familiarise yourself with the scope and requirements of the job. Overhauling an engine isn't particularly difficult, if you follow all of the instructions carefully, have the necessary tools and equipment and pay close attention to all specifications; however, it can be time consuming. Plan on the car being tied up for a minimum of two weeks, especially if parts must be taken to an engine reconditioning machine shop for repair or reconditioning. Check on availability of parts and make sure any necessary special tools and equipment are obtained in advance. Most work can be done with typical hand tools, although a number of precision measuring tools are required for inspecting parts to determine if they must be replaced. Often a machine shop will handle the inspection of parts and offer advice concerning reconditioning and renewal. **Note:** *Always wait until the engine has been completely disassembled and all components, especially the engine block, have been inspected before deciding what service and repair operations must be performed by an engine overhaul specialist. Since the block's condition will be the major factor to consider when determining whether to overhaul the original engine or buy a rebuilt one, never purchase parts or have machine work done on other components until the block has been thoroughly inspected. As a general rule, time is the primary cost of an overhaul, so it doesn't pay to refit worn or substandard parts.*

As a final note, to ensure maximum life and minimum trouble from a rebuilt engine, everything must be assembled with care in a spotlessly clean environment.

3 Cylinder compression check

1 A compression check will tell you what mechanical condition the upper end (pistons, rings, valves, head gaskets) of the engine is in. Specifically, it can tell you if the compression is down due to leakage caused by worn piston rings, defective valves and seats or a blown head gasket. **Note:** *The engine must be at normal operating temperature and the battery must be fully charged for this check.*

2 Begin by cleaning the area round the spark plugs before you remove them. Compressed air should be used, if available, otherwise a small brush or even a bicycle pump will work. The idea is to prevent dirt from getting into the cylinders as the compression check is done.

3 Remove all of the spark plugs from the engine (see Chapter 1).

4 Block the throttle wide open.

5 On fuel injection models disable the fuel system by removing the fuel pump fuse (see Chapter 4).

6 Disable the ignition system by detaching the 2 pin and 8 pin connectors at the distributor (see Chapter 5).

7 Fit the compression gauge in the number one (timing end) spark plug hole (see illustration).

8 Crank the engine over at least seven compression strokes and watch the gauge. The compression should build up quickly in a healthy engine. Low compression on the first stroke, followed by gradually increasing pressure on successive strokes, indicates worn piston rings. A low compression reading on the first stroke, which doesn't build up during successive strokes, indicates leaking valves or a blown head gasket (a cracked head could also be the cause). Deposits on the undersides of the valve heads can also cause low compression. Record the highest gauge reading obtained.

9 Repeat the procedure for the remaining cylinders and compare the results to this Chapter's Specifications.

10 If the readings are below normal, add some engine oil (about three squirts from a plunger-type oil can) to each cylinder, through the spark plug hole, and repeat the test.

11 If the compression increases significantly after the oil is added, the piston rings are definitely worn. If the compression doesn't increase significantly, the leakage is occurring at the valves or head gasket. Leakage past the valves may be caused by burned valve seats and/or faces or warped, cracked or bent valves.

2.4 The oil pressure sending unit is located directly above the oil filter

3.7 A compression gauge with a threaded fitting for the spark plug hole is preferred

12 If two adjacent cylinders have equally low compression, there's a strong possibility the head gasket between them is blown. The appearance of coolant in the combustion chambers or the crankcase would verify this condition.

13 If one cylinder is about 20% lower than the others, and the engine has a slightly rough idle, a worn exhaust lobe on the camshaft could be the cause.

14 If compression is way down or varies greatly between cylinders, it would be a good idea to have a leak-down test performed by a garage. This test will pinpoint exactly where the leakage is occurring and how severe it is.

4 Vacuum gauge diagnostic checks

1 A vacuum gauge provides valuable information about what is going on in the engine at a low cost. You can check for worn rings or cylinder walls, leaking head or inlet manifold gaskets, incorrect carburettor adjustments, restricted exhaust, stuck or burned valves, weak valve springs, improper ignition or valve timing and ignition problems.

2 Unfortunately, vacuum gauge readings are easy to misinterpret, so they should be used in conjunction with other tests to confirm the diagnosis.

3 Both the absolute readings and the rate of needle movement are important for accurate interpretation. Most gauges measure vacuum in inches of mercury (in-Hg). The following references to vacuum assume the diagnosis is being performed at sea level. As elevation increases (or atmospheric pressure decreases), the reading will decrease. For every 1,000 foot increase in elevation above approximately 2000 feet, the gauge readings will decrease about one inch of mercury.

4 Connect the vacuum gauge directly to inlet manifold vacuum, not to ported (throttle body) vacuum. Be sure no hoses are left disconnected during the test or false readings will result.

5 Before you begin the test, allow the engine to warm up completely. Block the wheels and apply the handbrake. Start the engine and allow it to run at normal idle speed.

 Warning: Carefully inspect the fan blades for cracks or damage before starting the engine. Keep your hands and the vacuum gauge clear of the fan and do not stand in front of the vehicle or in line with the fan when the engine is running.

6 Read the vacuum gauge; an average, healthy engine should normally produce about 17 to 22 inches of vacuum with a fairly steady needle. Refer to the following vacuum gauge readings and what they indicate about the engine's condition:

a) *A low steady reading usually indicates a leaking gasket between the inlet manifold and carburettor or throttle body, a leaky vacuum hose, late ignition timing or incorrect camshaft timing. Check ignition timing with a timing light and eliminate all other possible causes, utilising the tests provided in this Chapter before you remove the timing cover to check the timing marks.*

b) *If the reading is three to eight inches below normal and it fluctuates at that low reading, suspect an inlet manifold gasket leak at an inlet port or a faulty fuel injector.*

c) *If the needle has regular drops of about two-to-four inches at a steady rate, the valves are probably leaking. Perform a compression check or leak-down test to confirm this.*

d) *An irregular drop or down-flick of the needle can be caused by a sticking valve or an ignition misfire. Perform a compression check or leak-down test and read the spark plugs.*

e) *A rapid vibration of about four in.-Hg vibration at idle combined with exhaust smoke indicates worn valve guides. Perform a leak-down test to confirm this. If the rapid vibration occurs with an increase in engine speed, check for a leaking inlet manifold gasket or head gasket, weak valve springs, burned valves or ignition misfire.*

f) *A slight fluctuation, say one inch up and down, may mean ignition problems. Check all the usual tune-up items and, if necessary, run the engine on an ignition analyser.*

g) *If there is a large fluctuation, perform a compression or leak-down test to look for a weak or dead cylinder or a blown head gasket.*

h) *If the needle moves slowly through a wide range, check for a clogged PCV system, incorrect idle fuel mixture, carburettor/throttle body or inlet manifold gasket leaks.*

i) *Check for a slow return after revving the engine by quickly snapping the throttle open until the engine reaches about 2,500 rpm and let it shut. Normally the reading should drop to near zero, rise above normal idle reading (about 5 in.-Hg over) and then return to the previous idle reading. If the vacuum returns slowly and doesn't peak when the throttle is snapped shut, the rings may be worn. If there is a long delay, look for a restricted exhaust system (often the silencer or catalytic converter). An easy way to check this is to temporarily disconnect the exhaust ahead of the suspected part and redo the test.*

5 Engine removal - methods and precautions

1 If you've decided the engine must be removed for overhaul or major repair work, several preliminary steps should be taken.

2 Locating a suitable place to work is extremely important. Adequate work space, along with storage space for the car, will be needed. If a shop or garage isn't available, at the very least a flat, level, clean work surface made of concrete or asphalt is required.

3 Cleaning the engine compartment and engine before beginning the removal procedure will help keep tools clean and organised.

4 An engine hoist or A-frame will also be necessary. Make sure the equipment is rated in excess of the combined weight of the engine and its accessories. Safety is of primary importance, considering the potential hazards involved in lifting the engine out of the car.

5 If the engine is being removed by a novice, a helper should be available. Advice and aid from someone more experienced would also be helpful. There are many instances when one person cannot simultaneously perform all of the operations required when lifting the engine out of the car.

6 Plan the operation ahead of time. Arrange for or obtain all of the tools and equipment you'll need prior to beginning the job. Some of the equipment necessary to perform engine removal and refitting safely and with relative ease are (in addition to an engine hoist) a heavy duty floor jack, complete sets of spanners and sockets as described in the front of this manual, wooden blocks and plenty of rags and cleaning solvent for mopping up spilled oil, coolant and fuel. If the hoist must be rented, be sure to arrange for it in advance and perform all of the operations possible without it beforehand. This will save you money and time.

7 Plan for the car to be out of use for quite a while. A machine shop will be required to perform some of the work which the do-it-yourselfer can't accomplish without special equipment. These shops often have a busy schedule, so it would be a good idea to consult them before removing the engine in order to accurately estimate the amount of time required to overhaul or repair components that may need work.

8 Always be extremely careful when removing and refitting the engine. Serious injury can result from careless actions. Plan ahead, take your time and a job of this nature, although major, can be accomplished successfully.

6 Engine - removal and refitting

Note: *This Section describes the engine removal and refitting procedure for fuel injection models. The procedure for carburettor models is similar - refer to Chapter 4 for more details.*

> ⚠️ **Warning: Refer to the warnings given in Chapter 4 when disconnecting components of the fuel system.**

Note 1: *Read through the following steps carefully and familiarise yourself with the procedure before beginning work. Also at this point it may be helpful to use a penetrating fluid or spray on nuts and bolts that may be difficult to remove, such as exhaust manifolds, bellhousing, engine mounts, etc.*

Note 2: *The engine and transmission are usually removed together, as a single unit. It is possible to remove the engine while leaving the transmission intact. This method saves time disconnecting the transmission but it is not recommended because of the difficulty aligning the transmission and the engine when refitting.*

Removal

1 Refer to Chapter 4 and relieve the fuel system pressure.

2 Disconnect the negative battery cable. *Caution: If the radio in your car is equipped with an anti-theft system, make sure you have the correct activation code before disconnecting the battery.*

3 Cover the wings and cowl and remove the bonnet (see Chapter 11). Special pads are available to protect the wings, but an old bedspread or blanket will also work.

4 Remove the air cleaner assembly (see Chapter 4), and the air inlet duct.

5 Disconnect the charcoal canister hose from the throttle body (see Chapter 6).

6 Label the vacuum lines, emissions system hoses, electrical connectors, earth straps and fuel lines to ensure correct refitting, then detach them. Pieces of masking tape with numbers or letters written on them work well. If there's any

possibility of confusion, make a sketch of the engine compartment and clearly label the lines, hoses and wires.

7 Label and detach all coolant hoses from the engine.

8 Remove the coolant reservoir, cooling fan, shroud and radiator (see Chapter 3).

9 Remove the drivebelt(s) and idler, if applicable (see Chapter 1).

10 Disconnect the fuel lines running from the engine to the chassis (see Chapter 4). Plug or cap all open fittings and lines.

11 Disconnect the accelerator linkage (and cruise control cable, if applicable) from the engine (see Chapters 4 and 7).

12 Unbolt the power steering pump and set it aside (see Chapter 10). Leave the lines/hoses attached and make sure the pump is kept in an upright position in the engine compartment.

13 Unbolt the air conditioning compressor (see Chapter 3) and set it aside. Do not disconnect the hoses.

14 Unbolt the alternator and mounting strap and set it aside (see Chapter 5).

15 Raise the car and support it on axle stands (see 'Jacking and Vehicle Support'). Drain the cooling system (see Chapter 1).

16 Drain the engine oil and remove the filter (see Chapter 1).

17 Remove the starter (see Chapter 5).

18 Remove the splash shields from the wheel wells and the underside of the engine compartment (see Chapter 11).

Automatic transmission models

19 Remove the throttle control cable from the transmission. Also, disconnect the speed sensor, lock-up control solenoid and linkage from the transmission (see Chapter 7B).

20 Remove the inspection cover from the transmission bellhousing, which will give access to the torque converter.

21 Remove the transmission cooler lines.

22 Remove the crankshaft pulley and fit the bolt. Use a socket and a long extension bar or ratchet to rotate the engine to position the torque converter bolts for removal. Remove the torque converter-to-driveplate bolts.

All models

23 Disconnect the exhaust system from the engine (see Chapter 4).

24 Support the transmission with a jack

(preferably a transmission jack). If you're not using a transmission jack, position a wood block on the jack head to prevent damage to the transmission.

25 Attach an engine sling or a length of chain to the lifting brackets on the engine **(see illustration)**.

26 Roll the hoist into position and connect the sling to it. Take up the slack in the sling or chain, but don't lift the engine

> ⚠️ **Warning: DO NOT place any part of your body under the engine when it's supported only by a hoist or other lifting device.**

27 Remove the driveshaft(s) (see Chapter 8).

28 If you're working on a model equipped with a manual transmission, unbolt the clutch slave cylinder (don't disconnect the hydraulic line) and position it out of the way (see Chapter 8).

29 Remove the centre crossmember from the underside of the engine compartment to make easy access to the engine mounts.

30 Remove the engine mount-to-chassis bolts **(see illustration)**.

31 Recheck to be sure nothing is still connecting the engine to the car. Disconnect anything still remaining.

32 Raise the engine slightly to disengage the mounts. Also, slightly raise the jack supporting the transmission. Slowly raise the engine/transmission assembly out of the engine compartment, turning it sideways, as necessary, for clearance. Check carefully to make sure nothing is left attached as the hoist is raised **(see illustration)**.

33 Lower the engine/transmission assembly to the earth and support it with wood blocks. Remove the clutch and flywheel or driveplate and mount the engine on an engine stand.

34 Separate the transmission from the engine at this time (see Chapter 7).

Refitting

35 Check the engine and transmission mounts. If they're worn or damaged, renew them.

36 If you're working on a manual transmission model, fit the clutch and pressure plate (see Chapter 8). Now is a good time to fit a new clutch. Apply a dab of high-temperature grease to the input shaft.

6.25 Attach the hoist chain to fixtures (arrowed) found mounted to the engine

6.30 Location of the rear engine mount bolt (arrowed) and engine mount

6.32 Engine/transmission assembly being removed from the vehicle

37 Attach the transmission to the engine. *Caution: DO NOT use the bolts to force the transmission and engine together. If you're working on an automatic transmission model, take great care when refitting the torque converter, following the procedure outlined in Chapter 7B. Line up the holes in the engine mounts with the frame and refit the bolts, tightening them securely.*
38 Attach a chain hoist to the engine/transmission assembly and lower the assembly into the engine compartment.
39 The rest of refitting is a reversal of removal.
40 Add coolant, oil, power steering and transmission fluid as needed (see Chapter 1).
41 Run the engine and check for leaks and proper operation of all accessories, then refit the bonnet and test drive the car.
42 If the air conditioning system was discharged, have it evacuated, recharged and leak tested by the shop that discharged it.

7 Engine overhauling alternatives

The home mechanic is faced with a number of options when overhauling an engine. The decision to renew the engine block, piston/connecting rod assemblies and crankshaft depends on a number of factors, with the number one consideration being the condition of the block. Other considerations are cost, access to machine shop facilities, parts availability, time required to complete the project and prior mechanical experience.

Some of the rebuilding alternatives include:
Note: *The costs of alternatives described in this Section can vary, depending upon quality of parts, machine work required and the necessary tools and equipment to correctly do the work. Many parts stores carry complete (long and short block) assemblies in addition to individual repair parts. Consult the local parts store on price and availability to make the final repair/renew decision.*

Individual parts - If the inspection procedures reveal the engine block and most engine components are in reusable condition, purchasing individual parts may be the most economical alternative. The block, crankshaft and piston/connecting rod assemblies should all be inspected carefully. Even if the block shows little wear, the cylinder bores should be surface honed.

Short block - A short block consists of an engine block with a crankshaft and piston/connecting rod assemblies already fitted. All new bearings are fitted and all clearances will be correct. The existing camshaft, valve train components, cylinder head(s) and external parts can be bolted to the short block with little or no machine shop work necessary.

Complete block - A complete block consists of a short block plus an oil pump, sump, cylinder head, valve cover, camshaft and valve train components, timing sprockets

and belt. All components are fitted with new bearings, seals and gaskets incorporated throughout. The refitting of manifolds and external parts is all that's necessary.

Give careful thought to which alternative is best for you and discuss it with local engine reconditioning specialists, spare parts dealers and experienced overhaul specialists before ordering or purchasing new parts.

8 Engine overhaul - dismantling sequence

1 It's much easier to dismantle and work on the engine if it's mounted on a portable engine stand. A stand can often be hired quite cheaply. Before it's mounted on a stand, the flywheel/driveplate should be removed from the engine.
2 If a stand isn't available, it's possible to dismantle the engine with it blocked up on the floor. Be extra careful not to tip or drop the engine when working without a stand.
3 If you're going to obtain an overhauled engine, all external components must come off first, to be transferred to the new engine, just as they will if you're doing a complete engine overhaul yourself. These include:

Alternator and brackets
Power steering pump and brackets
Emissions control components
Distributor, HT leads and spark plugs
Thermostat and housing cover
Water pump bypass pipe
Fuel injection or carburettor components
Inlet/exhaust manifolds
Oil filter
Engine mounts
Clutch and flywheel or driveplate

Note: *When removing the external components from the engine, pay close attention to details that may be helpful or important during refitting. Note the fitted position of gaskets, seals, spacers, pins, brackets, washers, bolts, wiring and other small items.*
4 If you're obtaining a short block, which consists of the engine block, crankshaft, pistons and connecting rods all assembled, then the cylinder head(s), sump and oil pump will have to be removed as well.
5 If you're planning a complete overhaul, the engine must be disassembled and the internal components removed in the following order :

Inlet and exhaust manifolds
Valve cover
Timing belt covers and bolts
Timing belt and sprockets
Rocker arm assembly and camshaft
Cylinder head
Water pump
Sump
Oil pick-up tube
Oil pump
Piston/connecting rod assemblies
Rear main oil seal retainer
Crankshaft and main bearings

6 Before beginning the dismantling and overhaul procedures, make sure the following items are available. Also, refer to *Engine overhaul - reassembly sequence* for a list of tools and materials needed for engine reassembly.

Common hand tools
Small cardboard boxes or plastic bags for storing parts
Gasket scraper
Ridge reamer
Vibration damper puller
Micrometers
Telescoping gauges
Dial indicator set
Valve spring compressor
Cylinder surfacing hone
Piston ring groove cleaning tool
Electric drill motor
Tap and die set
Wire brushes
Oil gallery brushes
Cleaning solvent

9 Cylinder head - dismantling

Note: *New and overhauled cylinder heads may be available at from engine reconditioning specialists. Due to the fact that some specialised tools are necessary for the dismantling and inspection procedures, and overhaul parts aren't always readily available, it may be more practical and economical for the home mechanic to purchase overhauled head(s) rather than taking the time to dismantle, inspect and recondition the original(s).*
1 Cylinder head dismantling involves removal of the inlet and exhaust valves and related components. The rocker arm assemblies and camshaft(s) must be removed before beginning the cylinder head dismantling procedure (see Part A of this Chapter). Label the parts or store them separately so they can be refitted in their original locations.
2 Before the valves are removed, arrange to label and store them, along with their related components, so they can be kept separate and refitted in their original locations **(see illustration).**

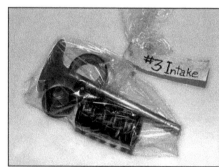

9.2 A small labelled plastic bag can be used to store the valve components

9.3 Compress the valve springs then remove the collets from the valve stem with a magnet or small needle-nose pliers

9.4 Deburring the edge of the stem end and the area around the top of the collet groove with a file or whetstone

3 Compress the springs on the first valve with a spring compressor and remove the collets **(see illustration)**. Carefully release the valve spring compressor and remove the retainer, the spring and the spring seat (if used).
4 Pull the valve out of the head, then remove the oil seal from the guide. If the valve binds in the guide (won't pull through), push it back into the head and deburr the area around the stem and the collet groove with a fine file or whetstone **(see illustration)**.
5 Repeat the procedure for the remaining valves. Remember to keep all the parts for each valve together so they can be refitted in the same locations. **Note:** *On VTEC engines only, remember to remove the Oil Control Orifice and O-ring from the cylinder head (see Chapter 2A).*
6 Once the valves and related components have been removed and stored in an organised manner, the head should be thoroughly cleaned and inspected. If a complete engine overhaul is being done, finish the engine dismantling procedures before beginning the cylinder head cleaning and inspection process.

10 Cylinder head - cleaning and inspection

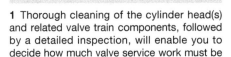

1 Thorough cleaning of the cylinder head(s) and related valve train components, followed by a detailed inspection, will enable you to decide how much valve service work must be

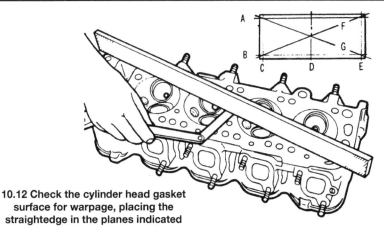

10.12 Check the cylinder head gasket surface for warpage, placing the straightedge in the planes indicated

done during the engine overhaul. **Note:** *If the engine was severely overheated, the cylinder head is probably warped.*

Cleaning

2 Scrape all traces of old gasket material and sealant off the head gasket, inlet manifold and exhaust manifold mating surfaces. Be very careful not to gouge the cylinder head. Special gasket removal solvents that soften gaskets and make removal much easier are available at motor factors.
3 Remove all built-up scale from the coolant passages.
4 Run a stiff wire brush through the various holes to remove deposits that may have formed in them.
5 Run an appropriate size tap into each of the threaded holes to remove corrosion and thread sealant that may be present. If compressed air is available, use it to clear the holes of debris produced by this operation.

 Warning: Wear eye protection when using compressed air!

6 Clean the camshaft bearing cap bolt threads with a wire brush.
7 Clean the cylinder head with solvent and dry it thoroughly. Compressed air will speed the drying process and ensure that all holes and recessed areas are clean. **Note:** *Decarbonizing chemicals are available and may prove very useful when cleaning cylinder heads and valve train components. They're very caustic and should be used with caution. Be sure to follow the instructions on the container.*
8 Clean the rocker arms and bearing caps with solvent and dry them thoroughly (do not mix them up during the cleaning process). Compressed air will speed the drying process and can be used to clean out the oil passages.
9 Clean all the valve springs, spring seats, collets and retainers with solvent and dry them thoroughly. Work on the components from one valve at a time to avoid mixing up the parts.
10 Scrape off any heavy deposits that may have formed on the valves, then use an

electric drill wire brush to remove deposits from the valve heads and stems. Again, make sure the valves do not get mixed up.

Inspection

Note: *Be sure to perform all of the following inspection procedures before concluding specialist work is required. Make a list of the items that need attention.*

Cylinder head

11 Inspect the head very carefully for cracks, evidence of coolant leakage and other damage. If cracks are found, check with a specialist concerning repair. If repair isn't possible, a new cylinder head should be obtained.
12 Using a straightedge and feeler blade, check the head gasket mating surface for warpage **(see illustration)**. Try to slip a feeler gauge equal in thickness to the specified warpage limit under the straightedge. If the warpage exceeds the limit in this Chapter's Specifications, it can be resurfaced at a machine shop.
13 Examine the valve seats in each of the combustion chambers. If they're pitted, cracked or burned, the head will require valve service that's beyond the scope of the home mechanic.
14 Check the valve stem-to-guide clearance by measuring the lateral movement of the valve stem with a dial indicator attached securely to the head **(see illustration)**. The valve must be in the guide and approximately 1/16-inch off the seat. The total valve stem

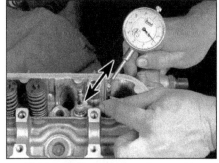

10.14 A dial indicator can be used to determine valve stem-to-guide clearance - move the stem as shown

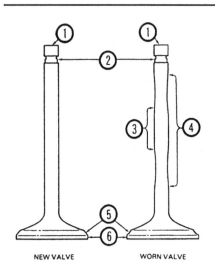

10.15 Check for valve wear
at the points shown here

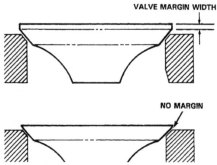

10.16 The margin width on each valve must
be as specified (if no margin exists, the
valve cannot be reused)

movement indicated by the gauge needle must be divided by two to obtain the actual clearance. After this is done, if there's still some doubt regarding the condition of the valve guides, they should be checked by a specialist (the cost should be minimal).

Valves

15 Carefully inspect each valve face for uneven wear, deformation, cracks, pits and burned areas. Check the valve stem for scuffing and scoring and the neck for cracks. Rotate the valve and check for any obvious indication that it's bent. Look for pits and excessive wear on the end of the stem **(see illustration)**. The presence of any of these conditions indicates the need for valve service by an engine reconditioning specialist.

16 Measure the margin width on each valve **(see illustration)**. Any valve with a margin narrower than specified in this Chapter's Specifications will have to be replaced with a new one.

Valve components

17 Check each valve spring for wear (on the ends) and pits. Measure the free length and compare it to this Chapter's Specifications **(see illustration)**. Any springs that are shorter than specified have sagged and shouldn't be

reused. The tension of all springs should be checked with a special fixture before deciding they're suitable for use in a rebuilt engine (take the springs to an automotive engineering specialist for this check).

18 Stand each spring on a flat surface and check it for squareness with a carpenters square **(see illustration)**. If any of the springs are distorted or sagged, renew all of them with new parts.

19 Check the spring retainers and collets for obvious wear and cracks. Any questionable parts should be replaced with new ones, as extensive damage will occur if they fail during engine operation.

20 If the inspection process indicates the valve components are in generally poor condition and worn beyond the limits specified, which is usually the case in an engine that's being overhauled, reassemble the valves in the cylinder head and refer to Section 11 for valve servicing recommendations.

11 Valves - servicing

1 Because of the complex nature of the job and the special tools and equipment needed, servicing of the valves, the valve seats and the valve guides should be done by a professional.

2 The home mechanic can remove and dismantle the head, do the initial cleaning and

inspection, then reassemble and deliver it to an engine overhaul specialist for the actual service work. Doing the inspection will enable you to see what condition the head and valve components are in and will ensure that you know what work and new parts are required.

3 The engine overhaul specialist will remove the valves and springs, recondition or renew the valves and valve seats, recondition the valve guides, check and renew the valve springs, rotators, spring retainers and collets (as necessary), renew the valve seals with new ones, reassemble the valve components and make sure the fitted height is correct. The cylinder head gasket surface will also be resurfaced if it's warped.

4 After the overhaul work has been performed, the head will be in like new condition. When the head is returned, be sure to clean it again before refitting on the engine to remove any metal particles and abrasive grit that may still be present from the valve service or head resurfacing operations. Use compressed air, if available, to blow out all the oil holes and passages.

12 Cylinder head - reassembly

1 Regardless of whether or not the head was sent to an engine overhaul specialist, make sure it's clean before beginning reassembly.

2 If the head was sent out for valve servicing, the valves and related components will already be in place. Begin the reassembly procedure with paragraph 8.

3 Refit the spring seats before the valve seals.

4 Refit new seals on each of the valve guides. Using a hammer and a deep socket or seal refitting tool of the correct diameter, gently tap each seal into place until it's completely seated on the guide **(see illustration)**. Don't twist the seals during refitting or they won't seal properly on the stems. **Note:** *The valve stem seals are colour coded; white for the inlet valves and black for the exhaust valves.*

5 Beginning at one end of the head, lubricate and refit the first valve. Apply moly-base grease or clean engine oil to the valve stem.

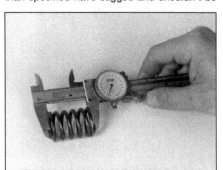

10.17 Measure the free length of each
valve spring with a dial or vernier caliper

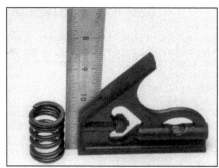

10.18 Check each valve spring for
squareness

12.4 Fitting valve guide seals

HAYNES HiNT

Apply a small dab of grease to each collet as shown here before refitting - it will hold them in place on the valve stem as the spring is released

6 Position the valve springs (and shims, if used) over the valves. Place the end of the valve spring with the closely wound coils toward the cylinder head. Compress the springs with a valve spring compressor and carefully refit the collets in the groove, then slowly release the compressor and make sure the collets seat properly **(see Haynes Hint)**.
7 Repeat the procedure for the remaining valves. Be sure to return the components to their original locations - don't mix them up!
8 Check the fitted valve stem height (dimension L) with a vernier or dial caliper **(see illustration)**. If the head was sent out for service work, the fitted height should be correct (but don't automatically assume it is). The measurement is taken from the spring seat to the top of the valve stem. If the height is greater than listed in this Chapter's Specifications, shims can be added under the springs to correct it.
Caution: Do not, under any circumstances, shim the springs to the point where the fitted height is less than specified.
9 Apply camshaft assembly oil or moly-base grease to the rocker arm faces, the camshaft and the rocker shafts, then refit the camshaft, rocker arms and shafts (refer to Chapter 2A).

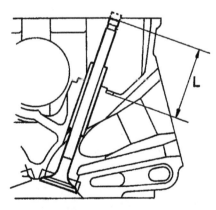

12.8 Be sure to check the valve stem installed height (the distance from the spring seat to the top of the valve stem)

13 Pistons and connecting rods - removal

Note: *Prior to removing the piston/connecting rod assemblies, remove the cylinder head, the sump and the oil pump by referring to the appropriate Sections in Chapter 2, Part A.*
1 Use your fingernail to feel if a ridge has formed at the upper limit of ring travel (about 1/4-inch down from the top of each cylinder). If carbon deposits or cylinder wear have produced ridges, they must be completely removed with a special tool **(see illustration)**. Follow the manufacturer's instructions provided with the tool. Failure to remove the ridges before attempting to remove the piston/connecting rod assemblies may result in piston breakage.
2 After the cylinder ridges have been removed, turn the engine upside-down so the crankshaft is facing up.
3 Before the connecting rods are removed, check the connecting rod side clearance (endfloat) with feeler blades. Slide them between the first connecting rod and the crankshaft throw until the play is removed **(see illustration)**. The endfloat is equal to the thickness of the feeler blade(s). If the endfloat exceeds the service limit, new connecting rods will be required. If new rods (or a new crankshaft) are fitted, the endfloat may fall under the minimum listed in this Chapter's Specifications (if it does, the rods will have to be machined to restore it - consult an engine

overhaul specialist for advice if necessary). Repeat the procedure for the remaining connecting rods.
4 Check the connecting rods and caps for identification marks. If they aren't plainly marked, use a small centre-punch to make the appropriate number of indentations on each rod and cap (1, 2, 3, etc., depending on the cylinder they're associated with) **(see illustration)**. **Note:** *Don't confuse the rod journal size designation number already stamped on the rod as the cylinder identification number.*
5 Loosen each of the connecting rod cap nuts 1/2-turn at a time until they can be removed by hand. Remove the number one connecting rod cap and bearing insert. Don't drop the bearing insert out of the cap.
6 Slip a short length of plastic or rubber hose over each connecting rod cap bolt to protect the crankshaft journal and cylinder wall as the piston is removed **(see illustration)**.
7 Remove the bearing insert and push the connecting rod/piston assembly out through the top of the engine. Use a wooden or plastic hammer handle to push on the upper bearing surface in the connecting rod. If resistance is felt, double-check to make sure all of the ridge was removed from the cylinder.
8 Repeat the procedure for the remaining cylinders.
9 After removal, reassemble the connecting rod caps and bearing inserts in their respective connecting rods and refit the cap nuts finger tight. Leaving the old bearing inserts in place until reassembly will help

13.1 A ridge reamer is required to remove the ridge from the top of each cylinder - do this before removing the pistons!

13.4 Mark each connecting rod and its bearing cap (arrowed)

13.3 Check the connecting rod side clearance (endfloat) with a feeler blade

13.6 Slip sections of rubber or plastic hose over the rod bolts

prevent the connecting big-end bearing surfaces from being accidentally damaged.

10 Don't separate the pistons from the connecting rods (see Section 18).

14 Crankshaft - removal

Note: *It's assumed the flywheel or driveplate, crankshaft vibration damper, timing belt, sump, oil pump and piston/connecting rod assemblies have already been removed. The rear main oil seal housing must be unbolted and separated from the block before proceeding with crankshaft removal.*

1 Before the crankshaft is removed, check the endfloat. Mount a dial indicator with the stem in line with the crankshaft and touching one of the crank throws.

2 Push the crankshaft all the way to the rear and zero the dial indicator. Next, prise the crankshaft to the front as far as possible and check the reading on the dial indicator. The distance it moves is the endfloat. If it's greater than specified in this Chapter, check the crankshaft thrust surfaces for wear. If no wear is evident, new main bearings should correct the endfloat.

3 If a dial indicator isn't available, feeler blades can be used. Gently prise or push the crankshaft all the way to the front of the engine. Slip feeler blades between the crankshaft and the front face of the thrust main bearing to determine the clearance.

4 Loosen the main bearing cap bridge bolts by 1/4-turn at a time each, until they can be removed by hand. **Note:** *Use the opposite order of the tightening sequence. Note if any stud bolts are used and make sure they're returned to their original locations when the crankshaft is refitted.*

5 Gently tap the bridge with a soft-face hammer, then separate the assembly from the engine block. If necessary, use a large screwdriver as a lever to remove the bridge. Try not to drop the bearing inserts if they come out with the bridge.

6 Carefully lift the crankshaft out of the engine. It may be a good idea to have an assistant available, since the crankshaft is heavy. With the bearing inserts in place in the engine block and main bearing caps, return the caps to their respective locations on the engine block and tighten the bolts finger tight.

15 Engine block - cleaning

1 Remove the main bearing caps and separate the bearing inserts from the caps and the engine block. Tag the bearings, indicating which cylinder they were removed from and whether they were in the cap or the block, then set them aside.

15.4a A hammer and a large punch can be used to remove the core plugs

2 Using a gasket scraper, remove all traces of gasket material from the engine block. Be very careful not to nick or gouge the gasket sealing surfaces.

3 Remove all of the covers and threaded oil gallery plugs from the block. The plugs are usually very tight - they may have to be drilled out and the holes re-tapped. Use new plugs when the engine is reassembled.

4 Remove the core plugs from the engine block. To do this, knock one side of the plug into the block with a hammer and a punch, then grasp them with large pliers and pull them out **(see illustrations).**

5 If the engine is extremely dirty, it should be taken to an engine specialist to be cleaned.

6 After the block is returned, clean all oil holes and oil galleries one more time. Brushes specifically designed for this purpose are available at most motor factors. Flush the passages with warm water until the water runs clear, dry the block thoroughly and wipe all machined surfaces with a light, rust preventive oil. If you have access to compressed air, use it to speed the drying process and blow out all the oil holes and galleries.

⚠️ *Warning: Wear eye protection when using compressed air!*

HAYNES HINT *An alternative is to inject aerosol-applied water-dispersant lubricant into each hole, using the long spout supplied. Wear eye protection when cleaning out holes this way!*

15.8 All bolt holes in the block should be cleaned and restored with a tap

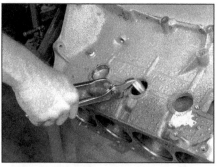

15.4b Pull the core plugs from the block with pliers

7 If the block is not extremely dirty or sludged up, you can do an adequate cleaning job with hot soapy water and a stiff brush. Take plenty of time and do a thorough job. Regardless of the cleaning method used, be sure to clean all oil holes and galleries very thoroughly, dry the block completely and coat all machined surfaces with light oil.

8 The threaded holes in the block must be clean to ensure accurate torque readings during reassembly. Run the proper size tap into each of the holes to remove rust, corrosion, thread sealant or sludge and restore damaged threads **(see illustration)**. If possible, use compressed air to clear the holes of debris produced by this operation. Now is a good time to clean the threads on the head bolts and the main bearing cap bolts as well.

9 Fit the main bearing caps and tighten the bolts finger tight.

10 After coating the sealing surfaces of the new core plugs with a suitable sealant, fit them in the engine block **(see illustration)**. Make sure they're driven in straight and seated properly or leakage could result. Special tools are available for this purpose, but a large socket, with an outside diameter that will just slip into the core plug, a 1/2-inch drive extension and a hammer will work just as well.

11 Apply non-hardening sealant to the new oil gallery plugs and thread them into the holes in the block. Make sure they're tightened securely.

12 If the engine isn't going to be reassembled right away, cover it with a large plastic bag to keep it clean.

15.10 A large socket on an extension can be used to drive in the new core plugs

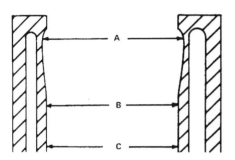

16.4a Measure the diameter of each cylinder just under the wear ridge (A), at the centre (B) and at the bottom (C)

16.4b The ability to "feel" when the telescoping gauge is at the correct point will be developed over time

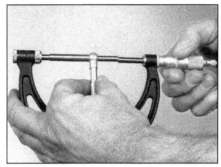

16.4c The gauge is then measured with a micrometer to determine the bore size

16 Engine block - inspection

1 Before the block is inspected, it should be cleaned as described in Section 15.

2 Visually check the block for cracks, rust and corrosion. Look for stripped threads in the threaded holes. It's also a good idea to have the block checked for hidden cracks by an engine overhaul specialist that has the special equipment to do this type of work. If defects are found, have the block repaired, if possible, or replaced.

3 Check the cylinder bores for scuffing and scoring.

4 Measure the diameter of each cylinder at the top (just under the ridge area), centre and bottom of the cylinder bore, parallel to the crankshaft axis **(see illustrations)**. **Note:** *These measurements should not be made with the block mounted on an engine stand - the cylinders will be distorted and the measurements will be inaccurate.*

5 Next, measure each cylinder's diameter at the same three locations across the crankshaft axis. Compare the results to this Chapter's Specifications.

6 If the required precision measuring tools aren't available, the piston-to-cylinder clearances can be obtained, though not quite as accurately, using feeler blades.

7 To check the clearance, select a feeler blade and slip it into the cylinder along with

the matching piston. The piston must be positioned exactly as it normally would be. The feeler blade must be between the piston and cylinder on one of the thrust faces (90° to the gudgeon pin bore).

8 The piston should slip through the cylinder (with the feeler blade in place) with moderate pressure.

9 If it falls through or slides through easily, the clearance is excessive and a new piston will be required. If the piston binds at the lower end of the cylinder and is loose toward the top, the cylinder is tapered. If tight spots are encountered as the piston/feeler blade is rotated in the cylinder, the cylinder is out-of-round.

10 Repeat the procedure for the remaining pistons and cylinders.

11 If the cylinder walls are badly scuffed or scored, or if they're out-of-round or tapered beyond the limits given in this Chapter's Specifications, have the engine block rebored and honed at an automotive machine shop. If a rebore is done, oversize pistons and rings will be required.

12 Using a precision straightedge and feeler blade, check the block surface that mates with the cylinder head for distortion **(see illustrations)**.

13 If the cylinders are in reasonably good condition and not worn to the outside of the limits, and if the piston-to-cylinder clearances can be maintained properly, they don't have to be rebored. Honing is all that's necessary (see Section 17).

17 Cylinder honing

1 Prior to engine reassembly, the cylinder bores must be honed so the new piston rings will seat correctly and provide the best possible combustion chamber seal. **Note:** *If you don't have the tools or don't want to tackle the honing operation, most engine overhaul specialists will do it for a reasonable fee.*

2 Before honing the cylinders, fit the main bearing caps and bridge and tighten the bolts to the specified torque.

3 Two types of cylinder hones are commonly available - the flex hone or "bottle-brush" type and the more traditional surfacing hone with spring-loaded stones. Both will do the job, but for the less experienced mechanic the "bottle brush" hone will probably be easier to use. You'll also need some honing oil (paraffin will work if honing oil isn't available), rags and an electric drill motor. Proceed as follows:

a) *Mount the hone in the drill motor, compress the stones and slip it into the first cylinder* **(see illustration)**. *Be sure to wear safety goggles or a face shield!*

b) *Lubricate the cylinder with plenty of honing oil, turn on the drill and move the hone up-and-down in the cylinder at a pace that will produce a fine crosshatch pattern on the cylinder walls. Ideally, the crosshatch lines should intersect at*

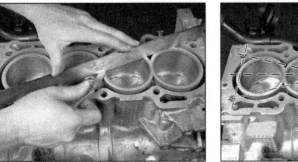

16.12a Check the block deck with a precision straightedge and feeler blades

16.12b Lay the straightedge across the block, diagonally and from end-to-end

17.3a A spring-loaded, stone-edged hone is the most common type of cylinder hone

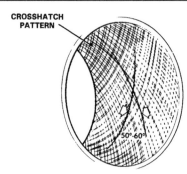

17.3b Cylinder honing crosshatch pattern with the lines intersecting at a 60° angle

approximately a 60° angle **(see illustration)**. Be sure to use plenty of lubricant and don't take off any more material than is absolutely necessary to produce the desired finish. **Note:** Piston ring manufacturers may specify a smaller crosshatch angle than the traditional 60° - read and follow any instructions included with the new rings.

c) Don't withdraw the hone from the cylinder while it's running. Instead, shut off the drill and continue moving the hone up-and-down in the cylinder until it comes to a complete stop, then compress the stones and withdraw the hone. If you're using a "bottle brush" type hone, stop the drill motor, then turn the chuck in the normal direction of rotation while withdrawing the hone from the cylinder.

d) Wipe the oil out of the cylinder and repeat the procedure for the remaining cylinders.

4 After the honing job is complete, chamfer the top edges of the cylinder bores with a small file so the rings won't catch when the pistons are fitted. Be very careful not to nick the cylinder walls with the end of the file.

5 The entire engine block must be washed again very thoroughly with warm, soapy water to remove all traces of the abrasive grit produced during the honing operation. **Note:** The bores can be considered clean when a lint-free white cloth - dampened with clean engine oil - used to wipe them out doesn't pick-up any more honing residue, which will show up as grey areas on the cloth. Be sure to run a brush through all oil holes and galleries and flush them with running water.

6 After rinsing, dry the block and apply a coat of light rust preventive oil to all machined surfaces. Wrap the block in a plastic bag to keep it clean and set it aside until reassembly.

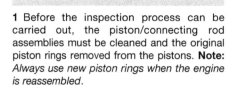

18 Pistons and connecting rods - inspection

1 Before the inspection process can be carried out, the piston/connecting rod assemblies must be cleaned and the original piston rings removed from the pistons. **Note:** Always use new piston rings when the engine is reassembled.

2 Using a piston ring expander tool, carefully remove the rings from the pistons. Be careful not to nick or gouge the pistons in the process.

3 Scrape all traces of carbon from the top of the piston. A hand held wire brush or a piece of fine emery cloth can be used once the majority of the deposits have been scraped away. Do not, under any circumstances, use a wire brush mounted in a drill motor to remove deposits from the pistons. The piston material is soft and may be eroded away by the wire brush.

4 Use a piston ring groove cleaning tool to remove carbon deposits from the ring grooves. If a tool isn't available, a piece broken off the old ring will do the job. Be very careful to remove only the carbon deposits - don't remove any metal and do not nick or scratch the sides of the ring grooves **(see illustrations)**.

5 Once the deposits have been removed, clean the piston/rod assemblies with solvent and dry them with compressed air (if available).

 Warning: Wear eye protection. Make sure the oil return holes in the back of the ring grooves are clear.

6 If the pistons and cylinder walls aren't damaged or worn excessively, and if the engine block isn't rebored, new pistons won't be necessary. Normal piston wear appears as even vertical wear on the piston thrust surfaces and slight looseness of the top ring in its groove. New piston rings, however,

should always be used when an engine is overhauled.

7 Carefully inspect each piston for cracks around the skirt, at the pin bosses and at the ring lands.

8 Look for scoring and scuffing on the thrust faces of the skirt, holes in the piston crown and burned areas at the edge of the crown. If the skirt is scored or scuffed, the engine may have been suffering from overheating and/or abnormal combustion, which caused excessively high operating temperatures. The cooling and lubrication systems should be checked thoroughly. A hole in the piston crown is an indication that abnormal combustion (pre-ignition) was occurring. Burned areas at the edge of the piston crown are usually evidence of pre-ignition (detonation). If any of the above problems exist, the causes must be corrected or the damage will occur again. The causes may include inlet air leaks, incorrect fuel/air mixture, low octane fuel, ignition timing and EGR system malfunctions.

9 Corrosion of the piston, in the form of small pits, indicates coolant is leaking into the combustion chamber and/or the crankcase. Again, the cause must be corrected or the problem may persist in the overhauled engine.

10 Measure the piston ring side clearance by laying a new piston ring in each ring groove and slipping a feeler blade in beside it **(see illustration)**. Check the clearance at three or four locations around each groove. Use the correct ring for each groove - they are different. If the side clearance is greater than specified, new pistons will have to be used.

11 Check the piston-to-bore clearance by measuring the bore (see Section 16) and the piston diameter. Make sure the pistons and bores are correctly matched. Measure the piston across the skirt, at a 90° angle to the gudgeon pin **(see illustration)** below the axis of the gudgeon pin.

12 Subtract the piston diameter from the bore diameter to obtain the clearance. If it's greater than listed in this Chapter's Specifications, the block will have to be rebored and new pistons and rings fitted.

13 Check the piston-to-rod clearance by twisting the piston and rod in opposite directions. Any noticeable play indicates excessive wear,

18.4a The piston ring grooves can be cleaned with a special tool, as shown . . .

18.4b . . . or a section of a broken ring

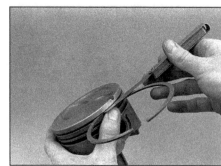

18.10 Check the ring side clearance with a feeler gauge at several points

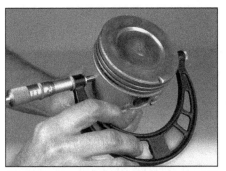

18.11 Measure the piston diameter at a 90° angle to the gudgeon pin and below it

19.1 Oil holes should be chamfered so sharp edges don't scratch new bearings

19.2 Use a wire or plastic bristle brush to clean the oil passages in the crankshaft

which must be corrected. The piston/connecting rod assemblies should be taken to an engine overhaul specialist to have the pistons and rods re-sized and new pins fitted.

14 If the pistons must be removed from the connecting rods for any reason, they should be taken to an engine overhaul specialist. While they are there have the connecting rods checked for bend and twist, since engine overhaul specialists have special equipment for this purpose. **Note:** *Unless new pistons and/or connecting rods must be fitted, do not dismantle the pistons and connecting rods.*

15 Check the connecting rods for cracks and other damage. Temporarily remove the rod caps, lift out the old bearing inserts, wipe the rod and cap bearing surfaces clean and inspect them for nicks, gouges and scratches. After checking the rods, renew the old bearings, slip the caps into place and tighten the nuts finger tight. **Note:** *If the engine is being overhauled because of a connecting rod knock, be sure to fit new rods.*

19 Crankshaft - inspection

1 Remove all burrs from the crankshaft oil holes with a stone, file or scraper **(see illustration)**.
2 Clean the crankshaft with solvent and dry it with compressed air (if available). Be sure to clean the oil holes with a stiff brush **(see illustration)** and flush them with solvent..

 Warning: Wear eye protection when using compressed air.

3 Check the main and connecting big end bearing journals for uneven wear, scoring, pits and cracks.
4 Rub a copper coin across each journal several times **(see illustration)**. If a journal picks up copper from the coin, it's too rough and must be reground.
5 Check the rest of the crankshaft for cracks and other damage. If necessary take it to an engine overhaul specialist.
6 Using a micrometer, measure the diameter of the main and connecting rod journals and compare the results to this Chapter's Specifications **(see illustration)**. By measuring the

19.4 Rubbing a coin lengthways on each journal will reveal its condition

diameter at a number of points around each journal's circumference, you'll be able to determine whether or not the journal is out-of-round. Take the measurement at each end of the journal, near the crank throws, to determine if the journal is tapered.
7 If the crankshaft journals are damaged, tapered, out-of-round or worn beyond the limits given in the Specifications, have the crankshaft reground by an engine specialist. Be sure to use the correct size bearing inserts if the crankshaft is reconditioned.
8 Check the oil seal journals at each end of the crankshaft for wear and damage. If the seal has worn a groove in the journal, or if it's nicked or scratched **(see illustration)**, the new seal may leak when the engine is reassembled. In some cases, an engine overhaul specialist may be able to repair the journal by pressing on a thin sleeve. If repair isn't feasible, a new or different crankshaft should be fitted.

19.8 If the seals have worn grooves in the crankshaft journals, the new seals will leak

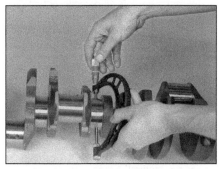

19.6 Measure the diameter of each crankshaft journal at several points

9 Refer to Section 20 and examine the main and big-end bearing inserts.

20 Main and connecting big-end bearings - inspection

1 Even though the main and connecting big-end bearings should be renewed during the engine overhaul, the old bearings should be retained for close examination, as they may reveal valuable information about the condition of the engine **(see illustration)**.

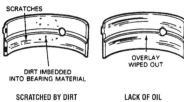

20.1 Typical bearing failures

2 Bearing failure occurs because of lack of lubrication, the presence of dirt or other foreign particles, overloading the engine and corrosion. Regardless of the cause of bearing failure, it must be corrected before the engine is re-assembled to prevent it from happening again.

3 When examining the bearings, remove them from the engine block, the main bearing caps, the connecting rods and the rod caps and lay them out on a clean surface in the same general position as their location in the engine. This will enable you to match any bearing problems with the corresponding crankshaft journal.

4 Dirt and other foreign particles get into the engine in a variety of ways. It may be left in the engine during assembly, or it may pass through filters or the PCV system. It may get into the oil, and from there into the bearings. Metal chips from machining operations and normal engine wear are often present. Abrasives are sometimes left in engine components after reconditioning, especially when parts aren't thoroughly cleaned using the proper cleaning methods. Whatever the source, these foreign objects often end up embedded in the soft bearing material and are easily recognised. Large particles will not embed in the bearing and will score or gouge the bearing and journal. The best prevention for this cause of bearing failure is to clean all parts thoroughly and keep everything spotlessly clean during engine assembly. Frequent and regular engine oil and filter changes are also recommended.

5 Lack of lubrication (or lubrication breakdown) has a number of interrelated causes. Excessive heat (which thins the oil), overloading (which squeezes the oil from the bearing face) and oil leakage or throw off (from excessive bearing clearances, worn oil pump or high engine speeds) all contribute to lubrication breakdown. Blocked oil passages, which usually are the result of misaligned oil holes in a bearing shell, will also oil starve a bearing and destroy it. When lack of lubrication is the cause of bearing failure, the bearing material is wiped or extruded from the steel backing of the bearing. Temperatures may increase to the point where the steel backing turns blue from overheating.

6 Driving habits can have a definite effect on bearing life. Full throttle, low speed operation (lugging the engine) puts very high loads on bearings, which tends to squeeze out the oil film. These loads cause the bearings to flex, which produces fine cracks in the bearing face (fatigue failure). Eventually the bearing material will loosen in pieces and tear away from the steel backing. Short trip driving leads to corrosion of bearings because insufficient engine heat is produced to drive off the condensed water and corrosive gases. These products collect in the engine oil, forming acid and sludge. As the oil is carried to the engine bearings, the acid attacks and corrodes the bearing material.

7 Incorrect bearing refitting during engine assembly will lead to bearing failure as well. Tight fitting bearings leave insufficient oil clearance and will result in oil starvation. Dirt or foreign particles trapped behind a bearing insert result in high spots on the bearing which lead to failure.

21 Engine overhaul - reassembly sequence

1 Before beginning engine reassembly, make sure you have all the necessary new parts, gaskets and seals as well as the following items on hand:

> Common hand tools
> Torque wrench (1/2-inch drive)
> Piston ring refitting tool
> Piston ring compressor
> Short lengths of rubber or plastic hose to fit over connecting rod bolts
> Plastigage
> Feeler blades
> Fine-tooth file
> New engine oil
> Engine assembly oil or moly-base grease
> Gasket sealant
> Thread locking compound

2 To save time and avoid problems, engine reassembly must be done in the following general order:

> Crankshaft and main bearings
> Rear main oil seal and retainer
> Piston/connecting rod assemblies
> Oil pump and oil pump pick-up
> Sump
> Cylinder head
> Camshaft and rocker arm assembly
> Water pump
> Timing belt and sprockets
> Inlet and exhaust manifolds
> Timing belt covers
> Valve cover
> Flywheel/driveplate

22 Piston rings - refitting

1 Before refitting the new piston rings, the ring end gaps must be checked. It's assumed the piston ring side clearance has been checked and verified correct (see Section 18).

2 Lay out the piston/connecting rod assemblies and the new ring sets so the ring sets will be matched with the same piston and cylinder during the end gap measurement and engine assembly.

3 Insert the top (number one) ring into the first cylinder and square it up with the cylinder walls by pushing it in with the top of the piston **(see illustration)**. The ring should be near the bottom of the cylinder, at the lower limit of ring travel.

4 To measure the end gap, slip feeler blades between the ends of the ring until a gauge equal to the gap width is found **(see illustration)**. The feeler blade should slide between the ring ends with a slight amount of drag. Compare the measurement to this Chapter's Specifications. If the gap is larger or smaller than specified, double-check to make sure you have the correct rings before proceeding.

5 If the gap is too small, it must be enlarged or the ring ends may come in contact with each other during engine operation, which can cause serious engine damage. The end gap can be increased by filing the ring ends very carefully with a fine file. Mount the file in a vice equipped with soft jaws, slip the ring over the file with the ends contacting the file teeth and slowly move the ring to remove material from the ends. When performing this operation, file only from the outside in.

6 Excess end gap isn't critical unless it's greater than 0.040-inch. Again, double-check to make sure you have the correct rings for the engine.

7 Repeat the procedure for each ring that will be fitted in the first cylinder and for each ring in the remaining cylinders. Remember to keep rings, pistons and cylinders matched up.

8 Once the ring end gaps have been checked/corrected, the rings can be fitted on the pistons.

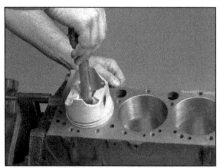

22.3 Pushing the ring down the bore with the top of a piston

22.4 With the ring square in the cylinder, measure the end gap with a feeler blade

22.9a Refitting the spacer/expander in the oil control ring groove

22.9b DO NOT use a piston ring refitting tool when refitting the oil ring side rails

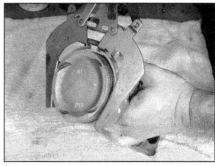

22.12 Refitting the compression rings with a ring expander - the ring mark faces up

	A or I	B or II	C or III	D or IIII
1 or I	Pink	Pink/yellow	Yellow	Yellow/green
2 or II	Pink/yellow	Yellow	Yellow/green	Green
3 or III	Yellow	Yellow/green	Green	Green/brown
4 or IIII	Green	Green	Green/brown	Brown
5 or IIIII	Green/brown	Green/brown	Brown	Brown/black
6 or IIIIII	Brown	Brown	Brown/black	Black

23.5a Main bearing selection chart for original sized crankshaft diameters. The numbers (vertical column) are stamped onto the crankshaft and the horizontal letters are stamped onto the engine block

9 The oil control ring (lowest one on the piston) is usually fitted first. It's composed of three separate components. Slip the spacer/expander into the groove **(see illustration)**. If an anti-rotation tang is used, make sure it's inserted into the drilled hole in the ring groove. Next, fit the lower side rail. Don't use a piston ring refitting tool on the oil ring side rails, as they may be damaged. Instead, place one end of the side rail into the groove between the spacer/expander and the ring land, hold it firmly in place and slide a finger around the piston while pushing the rail into the groove **(see illustration)**. Next, fit the upper side rail in the same manner.

10 After the three oil ring components have been fitted, check to make sure both the upper and lower side rails can be turned smoothly in the ring groove.

11 The number two (middle) ring is fitted next. It's usually stamped with a mark, which must face up, toward the top of the piston. **Note:** *Always follow the instructions printed on the ring package or box - different manufacturers may require different approaches. Don't mix up the top and middle rings, as they have different cross-sections.*

12 Use a piston ring refitting tool and make sure the identification mark is facing the top of the piston, then slip the ring into the middle groove on the piston **(see illustration)**. Don't expand the ring any more than necessary to slide it over the piston.

13 Fit the number one (top) ring in the same manner. Make sure the mark is facing up. Be careful not to confuse the number one and number two rings.

14 Repeat the procedure for the remaining pistons and rings.

23 Crankshaft - refitting and main bearing oil clearance check

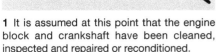

1 It is assumed at this point that the engine block and crankshaft have been cleaned, inspected and repaired or reconditioned.
2 Position the engine with the bottom facing up.
3 Remove the main bearing cap bridge assembly (if not already done) and make sure

the original bearings are not in place in the block and bridge assembly.
4 If they are still in place, remove the original bearing inserts from the block and the main bearing caps. Wipe the bearing surfaces of the block and caps with a clean, lint-free cloth. They must be kept spotlessly clean.

Main bearing oil clearance check

Note: *Don't touch the faces of the new bearing inserts with your fingers. Oil and acids from your skin can etch the bearings.*
5 Clean the backs of the new main bearing inserts and lay one in each main bearing saddle in the block. If one of the bearing inserts from each set has a large groove in it, make sure the grooved insert is fitted in the block. Lay the other bearing from each set in the corresponding main bearing cap. Make sure the tab on the bearing insert fits into the recess in the block or cap. **Note:** *If the crankshaft has been reground, use a set of undersize bearings from the local motor factors. If the crankshaft is original and the bearings will be renewed, use the following chart and illustrations to match the correct bearings* **(see illustrations)**. *Caution: If the codes on the crankshaft are not visible, do not scrub then with a wire brush or scraper. Use only solvent or detergent.*

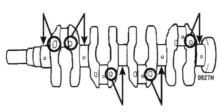

23.5b The crankshaft journal designations are stamped onto the crankshaft

6 The flanged thrustwashers must be fitted in the number four cap and saddle (counting from the front of the engine) **(see illustration)**.
7 Clean the faces of the bearings in the block and the crankshaft main bearing journals with a clean, lint-free cloth.
8 Check or clean the oil holes in the crankshaft, as any dirt here can go only one way - straight through the new bearings.
9 Once you're certain the crankshaft is clean, carefully lay it in position in the main bearings.

23.5c The crankcase journal designations are stamped onto the engine block

23.6 Location of number four thrust bearings (arrowed). Grooved sides face OUT

23.11 Lay the Plastigage strips on the main bearing journals, parallel to the crankshaft

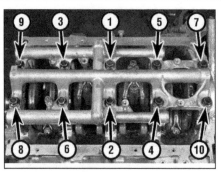

23.13 Main bearing cap bridge assembly TIGHTENING sequence

23.15 Compare the width of the crushed Plastigage to the scale on the envelope

10 Before the crankshaft can be permanently fitted, the main bearing oil clearance must be checked.
11 Cut several pieces of the appropriate size Plastigage (they should be slightly shorter than the width of the main bearings) and place one piece on each crankshaft main bearing journal, parallel with the journal axis **(see illustration)**.
12 Clean the faces of the bearings in the main bearing cap bridge assembly and fit the assembly. Don't disturb the Plastigage.
13 Starting with the centre bolts and working out toward the ends, tighten the main bearing cap bridge assembly, in three steps, to the torque figure listed in this Chapter's Specifications **(see illustration)**. Don't rotate the crankshaft at any time during this operation.
14 Remove the bolts and carefully lift off the main bearing cap bridge assembly. Keep them in order. Don't disturb the Plastigage or rotate the crankshaft. If any of the main bearing caps are difficult to remove, tap them gently from side-to-side with a soft-face mallet to loosen them.
15 Compare the width of the crushed Plastigage on each journal to the scale printed on the Plastigage envelope to obtain the main bearing oil clearance **(see illustration)**. Check the Specifications at the beginning of this Chapter to make sure it's correct.
16 If the clearance is not as specified, the bearing inserts may be the wrong size (which means different ones will be required). Before deciding different inserts are needed, make sure no dirt or oil was between the bearing inserts and the caps or block when the

clearance was measured. If the Plastigage was wider at one end than the other, the journal may be tapered (see Section 19).
17 Carefully scrape all traces of the Plastigage material off the main bearing journals and/or the bearing faces. Use your fingernail or the edge of a credit card - don't nick or scratch the bearing faces.

Final crankshaft refitting

18 Carefully lift the crankshaft out.
19 Clean the bearing faces in the block, then apply a thin, uniform layer of moly-base grease or engine assembly oil to each of the bearing surfaces. Be sure to coat the thrust faces as well as the journal face of the thrust bearing.
20 Make sure the crankshaft journals are clean, then lay the crankshaft back in place in the block.
21 Clean the faces of the bearings in the caps, then apply lubricant to them.
22 Fit the main bearing cap bridge assembly.
23 Fit the bolts.
24 Tighten all main bearing cap bolts to the specified torque, starting with the centre main and working out toward the ends **(see illustration 23.13)**.
25 Rotate the crankshaft a number of times by hand to check for any obvious binding.
26 The final step is to check the crankshaft endfloat with feeler blades or a dial indicator (Section 14). The endfloat should be correct if the crankshaft thrust faces aren't worn or damaged and new bearings have been fitted.
27 Refer to Section 24 and fit the new rear main oil seal.

24 Rear main oil seal - refitting

Note: *The crankshaft must be fitted and the main bearing caps bolted in place before the new seal and retainer assembly can be bolted to the block.*

1 Remove the old seal from the retainer with a hammer and punch by driving it out from the back **(see illustration)**. Be sure to note how far it's recessed into the retainer bore before removing it; the new seal will have to be recessed an equal amount. Be very careful not to scratch or otherwise damage the bore in the retainer or oil leaks could develop.
2 Make sure the retainer is clean, then apply a thin coat of engine oil to the outer edge of the new seal. The seal must be pressed squarely into the retainer bore, so hammering it into place isn't recommended. If you don't have access to a press, sandwich the retainer and seal between two smooth pieces of wood and press the seal into place with the jaws of a large vice. If you do not have a vice big enough, lay the retainer on a workbench and drive the seal into place with a wood block and hammer **(see illustration)**. The piece of wood must be thick enough to distribute the force evenly around the entire circumference of the seal. Work slowly and make sure the seal enters the bore squarely. **Note:** *Using a feeler blade, confirm that the clearance between the seal and the retainer is equal all the way around* **(see illustrations)**.

24.1 Support the retainer on blocks and drive out the old seal with a punch

24.2a Drive the new seal into the retainer with a wood block or a section of pipe

24.2b Check the clearance between the seal and retainer using a feeler gauge

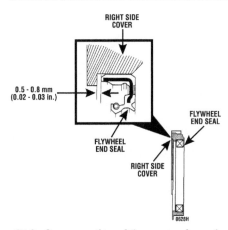

24.2c Cross-section of the rear main seal and the retainer

3 Place a thin coat of RTV sealant to the entire edge of the retainer.

4 Lubricate the seal lips with multi-purpose grease or engine oil before you slip the seal/retainer over the crankshaft and bolt it to the block. Be sure to use a new gasket. **Note:** *Apply a film of RTV sealant to both sides of the gasket before refitting.*

5 Tighten the retainer bolts, a little at a time, to the torque listed in the Chapter 2, Part A Specifications. Trim the gasket flush with the sump gasket surface, being careful not to scratch it.

25 Pistons and connecting rods - refitting and big-end bearing oil clearance check

1 Before refitting the piston/connecting rod assemblies, the cylinder walls must be perfectly clean, the top edge of each cylinder must be chamfered, and the crankshaft must be in place.

2 Remove the cap from the end of the number one connecting rod (check the marks made during removal). Remove the original bearing inserts and wipe the bearing surfaces of the connecting rod and cap with a clean, lint-free cloth. They must be kept spotlessly clean.

	1 or I	2 or II	3 or III	4 or IIII
A or	Red	Pink	Yellow	Green
B or II	Pink	Yellow	Green	Brown
C or III	Yellow	Green	Brown	Black
D or IIII	Green	Brown	Black	Blue

25.3a Big-end bearing selection chart for original sized crankshaft diameters. The letters (vertical column) are stamped onto the crankshaft and the horizontal numbers are stamped onto the connecting rod

Connecting big-end bearing oil clearance check

Note: *Don't touch the faces of the new bearing inserts with your fingers. Oil and acids from your skin can etch the bearings.*

3 Clean the back of the new upper bearing insert, then lay it in place in the connecting rod. Make sure the tab on the bearing fits into the recess in the rod. Don't hammer the bearing insert into place and be very careful not to nick or gouge the bearing face. Don't lubricate the bearing at this time. **Note:** *If the crankshaft has been reground, use a set of undersize bearings from the local motor factors. If the crankshaft is original and the bearings will be renewed, use the following chart and illustrations to match the correct connecting big-end bearings* **(see illustrations). *Caution: If the codes on the crankshaft are not visible, do not scrub them with a wire brush or scraper. Use only solvent or detergent.***

4 Clean the back of the other bearing insert and fit it in the rod cap. Again, make sure the tab on the bearing fits into the recess in the cap **(see illustration)**, and don't apply any lubricant. It's critically important that the mating surfaces of the bearing and connecting rod are perfectly clean and oil free when they're assembled.

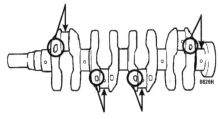

25.3c Crankshaft journal designation for the connecting rod

5 Position the piston ring gaps at intervals around the piston **(see illustration)**. *Caution: DON'T position any ring gap at piston thrust surfaces (90° to gudgeon pin).*

6 Slip a section of plastic or rubber hose over each connecting rod cap bolt.

7 Lubricate the piston and rings with clean engine oil and attach a piston ring compressor to the piston. Leave the skirt protruding about 1/4-inch to guide the piston into the cylinder. The rings must be compressed until they're flush with the piston.

8 Rotate the crankshaft until the number one connecting rod journal is at BDC (bottom dead centre) and apply a coat of engine oil to the cylinder walls.

9 With the mark or notch on top of the piston facing the front of the engine **(see illustration)**, gently insert the piston/connecting rod assembly into the number one cylinder bore and rest the bottom edge of the ring compressor on the engine block.

25.5 Position the ring gaps as shown before refitting the piston/connecting rod assemblies into the engine

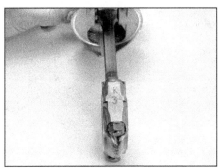

25.3b Connecting rod journal designation

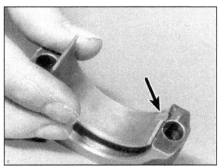

25.4 The tab on the bearing (arrowed) must fit into the recess so the bearing will seat

25.9 Arrow on the piston points toward the front (timing belt end) of the engine

25.11 Drive the piston gently into the cylinder bore with the end of a wooden or plastic hammer handle

25.13 Lay the Plastigage strips on each big-end bearing journal, parallel to the crankshaft centreline

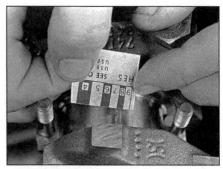

25.17 Measuring the width of the crushed Plastigage to determine the big-end bearing oil clearance

10 Tap the top edge of the ring compressor to make sure it's contacting the block around its entire circumference.

11 Gently tap on the top of the piston with the end of a wooden or plastic hammer handle **(see illustration)** while guiding the end of the connecting rod into place on the crankshaft journal. The piston rings may try to pop out of the ring compressor just before entering the cylinder bore, so keep some pressure on the ring compressor. Work slowly, and if any resistance is felt as the piston enters the cylinder, stop immediately. Find out what's the problem and fix it before proceeding. Do not, for any reason, force the piston into the cylinder - you might break a ring and/or the piston.

12 Once the piston/connecting rod assembly is fitted, the connecting big-end bearing oil clearance must be checked before the rod cap is permanently tightened.

13 Cut a piece of the appropriate size Plastigage slightly shorter than the width of the connecting big-end bearing and lay it in place on the number one connecting rod journal, parallel with the journal axis **(see illustration)**.

14 Clean the connecting rod cap bearing shell face, remove the protective hoses from the rod bolts and fit the rod cap. Make sure the mating mark on the cap is on the same side as the mark on the connecting rod.

15 Fit the nuts and tighten them to the torque listed in this Chapter's Specifications. Work up to it in three steps. **Note:** *Use a thin-wall socket to avoid erroneous torque readings that can result if the socket is wedged between the rod cap and nut. If the socket tends to wedge itself between the nut and the cap, lift up on it slightly until it no longer contacts the cap. Do not rotate the crankshaft at any time during this operation.*

16 Remove the nuts and detach the rod cap, being very careful not to disturb the Plastigage.

17 Compare the width of the crushed Plastigage to the scale printed on the envelope to obtain the oil clearance **(see illustration)**. Compare it to the Specifications to make sure the clearance is correct.

18 If the clearance is not as specified, the bearing shells may be the wrong size (which

means different ones will be required). Before deciding different bearing shells are needed, make sure no dirt or oil was between the shells and the connecting rod or cap when the clearance was measured. Also, recheck the journal diameter. If the Plastigage was wider at one end than the other, the journal may be tapered.

Final connecting rod refitting

19 Carefully scrape all traces of the Plastigage material off the rod journal and/or bearing shell face. Be very careful not to scratch the bearing - use your fingernail or the edge of a credit card.

20 Make sure the bearing shell faces are perfectly clean, then apply a uniform layer of clean moly-base grease or engine assembly oil to both of them. You'll have to push the piston into the cylinder to expose the face of the bearing shell in the connecting rod - be sure to slip the protective hoses over the rod bolts first.

21 Slide the connecting rod back into place on the journal, remove the protective hoses from the rod cap bolts, fit the rod cap and tighten the nuts to the torque listed in this Chapter's Specifications. Again, work up to the torque in three steps. **Note:** *Again, make sure the mating mark on the cap is on the same side as the mark on the connecting rod.*

22 Repeat the entire procedure for the remaining pistons/connecting rods.

23 The important points to remember are:

a) *Keep the backs of the bearing shells and the insides of the connecting rods and caps clean when assembling them.*

b) *Make sure you have the correct piston/rod assembly for each cylinder.*

c) *The arrow or mark on the piston must face the front of the engine.*

d) *Lubricate the cylinder walls with clean oil.*

e) *Lubricate the bearing faces when refitting the rod caps after the oil clearance has been checked.*

24 After all the piston/connecting rod assemblies have been properly fitted, rotate the crankshaft a number of times by hand to check for any obvious binding.

25 As a final step, the connecting rod endfloat must be checked. Refer to Section 13.

26 Compare the measured endfloat to this Chapter's Specifications to make sure it's correct. If it was correct before dismantling and the original crankshaft and rods were refitted, it should still be right. If new rods or a new crankshaft were fitted, the endfloat may be inadequate. If so, the rods will have to be removed and taken to an engine overhaul specialist for machining.

26 Initial start-up after overhaul

 Warning: Have a fire extinguisher handy when starting the engine for the first time.

1 Once the engine has been fitted, double-check the engine oil and coolant levels.

2 With the spark plugs out of the engine and the ignition system disabled, crank the engine until oil pressure registers on the gauge or the light goes out.

3 Refit the spark plugs and connect the plug HT leads.

4 Start the engine. It may take a few moments for the fuel system to build up pressure, but the engine should start without a great deal of effort. **Note:** *If backfiring occurs through the throttle body or carburettor, recheck the valve timing and ignition timing.*

5 After the engine starts, it should be allowed to warm up to normal operating temperature. While the engine is warming up, make a thorough check for fuel, oil and coolant leaks.

6 Switch off the engine and recheck the engine oil and coolant levels.

8 Drive the car easily for the first 500 miles (no sustained high speeds or towing) and keep a constant check on the oil level. It isn't unusual for an engine to use oil during the running-in period.

9 At approximately 500 to 600 miles, change the oil **and** filter.

10 For the next few hundred miles, drive the car normally. Don't pamper or abuse it.

11 After 2000 miles, change the oil and filter again and consider the engine run in.

Chapter 3
Cooling, heating and air conditioning systems

Contents

Degrees of difficulty

Easy, suitable for novice with little experience	**Fairly easy,** suitable for beginner with some experience	**Fairly difficult,** suitable for competent DIY mechanic	**Difficult,** suitable for experienced DIY mechanic	**Very difficult,** suitable for expert DIY or professional

Specifications

General
Coolant capacity	See Chapter 1
Drivebelt tension	See Chapter 1
Radiator pressure cap rating	13.5 to 18.0 psi

Thermostat
Opening temperatures
Starts to open	
D15Z1	80 to 84°C
Except D15Z1	76 to 80°C
Fully open	
D15Z1	95°C
Except D15Z1	90°C

Torque wrench settings
	Nm	lbf ft
Alternator adjustment bracket-to-water pump bolt	45	33
Thermostat housing cover bolts	10	7
Upper radiator hose fitting-to-block bolts	11	8
Water pump-to-block bolts	12	9

1 General information

Engine cooling system

All vehicles covered by this manual employ a pressurised engine cooling system with thermostatically controlled coolant circulation. An impeller-type water pump mounted on the engine block pumps coolant through the engine. The coolant flows around each cylinder and toward the rear of the engine. Cast-in coolant passages direct coolant around the inlet and exhaust ports, near the spark plug areas and in close proximity to the exhaust valve guides.

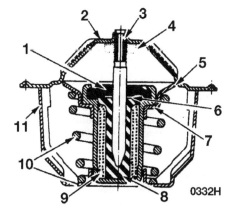

A wax pellet type thermostat controls engine coolant temperature. During warm up, the closed thermostat prevents coolant from circulating through the radiator. As the engine nears normal operating temperature, the thermostat opens and allows hot coolant to travel through the radiator, where it's cooled before returning to the engine **(see illustration)**.

1.2 Pellet type thermostat

1 Flange seal	7 Valve
2 Flange	8 Rubber diaphragm
3 Piston	9 Wax pellet
4 Nut	10 Coil spring
5 Valve seat	11 Frame
6 Teflon seal	

0332H

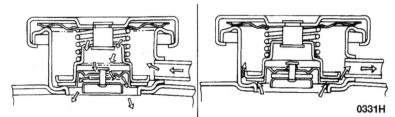

0331H

1.3 Pressure-type radiator cap

The cooling system is sealed by a pressure type radiator cap, which raises the boiling point of the coolant and increases the cooling efficiency of the radiator. If the system pressure exceeds the cap pressure relief value, the excess pressure in the system forces the spring-loaded valve inside the cap off its seat and allows the coolant to escape through the overflow tube into a coolant reservoir. When the system cools the excess coolant is drawn from the reservoir back into the radiator **(see illustration)**.

The coolant reservoir serves as both the point at which fresh coolant is added to the cooling system to maintain the proper fluid level and as a holding tank for hot coolant.

This type of cooling system is known as a closed design because coolant that escapes past the pressure cap is saved and reused.

Heating system

The heating system consists of a blower fan and heater matrix located in the heater box, the hoses connecting the heater matrix to the engine cooling system and the heater/air conditioning control head on the dashboard. Hot engine coolant is circulated through the heater matrix. When the heater mode is activated, a flap door opens to expose the heater box to the passenger compartment. A fan switch on the control head activates the blower motor, which forces air through the matrix, heating the air.

Air conditioning system

The air conditioning system consists of a condenser mounted in front of the radiator, an evaporator mounted adjacent to the heater matrix, a compressor mounted on the engine, a receiver-drier which contains a high pressure relief valve and the plumbing connecting all of the above components.

A blower fan forces the warmer air of the passenger compartment through the evaporator matrix (sort of a radiator-in-reverse), transferring the heat from the air to the refrigerant. The liquid refrigerant boils off into low pressure vapour, taking the heat with it when it leaves the evaporator.

2 Antifreeze -
general information

Warning: Do not allow antifreeze to come in contact with your skin or painted

surfaces of the vehicle. Rinse off spills immediately with plenty of water. Antifreeze is highly toxic if ingested. Never leave antifreeze lying around in an open container or in puddles on the floor; children and pets are attracted by it's sweet smell and may drink it. Check with local authorities about disposing of used antifreeze.

The cooling system should be filled with a water/ethylene glycol based antifreeze solution, which will prevent freezing down to at least -15°C, or lower if local climate requires it. It also provides protection against corrosion and increases the coolant boiling point.

The cooling system should be drained, flushed and refilled at the specified intervals (see Chapter 1). Old or contaminated antifreeze solutions are likely to cause damage and encourage the formation of rust and scale in the system. Use distilled water with the antifreeze.

Before adding antifreeze, check all hose connections, because antifreeze tends to leak through very minute openings. Engines don't normally consume coolant, so if the level goes down, find the cause and correct it.

The exact mixture of antifreeze-to-water which you should use depends on the relative weather conditions. The mixture should contain at least 50-percent antifreeze, but should never contain more than 70-percent antifreeze. Consult the mixture ratio chart on the antifreeze container before adding coolant. Hydrometers are available at most motor factors to test the coolant. Use antifreeze which meets the vehicle manufacturer's specifications.

3 Thermostat -
check and renewal

Warning: Do not remove the radiator cap, drain the coolant or renew the thermostat until the engine has cooled completely. Read the warning at the beginning of Section 2.

Check

1 Before assuming the thermostat is to blame for a cooling system problem, check the coolant level and temperature gauge operation.

2 If the engine seems to be taking a long time to warm up (based on heater output or temperature gauge operation), the thermostat is probably stuck open. Renew the thermostat with a new one.

3 If the engine runs hot, use your hand to check the temperature of the upper radiator hose. If the hose isn't hot, but the engine is, the thermostat is probably stuck closed, preventing the coolant inside the engine from escaping to the radiator. Renew the thermostat. *Caution: Don't drive the car without a thermostat - the computer may stay in open loop and emissions and fuel economy will suffer.*

4 If the upper radiator hose is hot, it means that the coolant is flowing and the thermostat is open. Consult the 'Faultfinding' section at the rear of this manual for cooling system diagnosis.

Renewal

5 Disconnect the cable from the negative battery terminal. *Caution: If the radio in your car is equipped with an anti-theft system, make sure you have the correct activation code before disconnecting the battery.*

6 Drain the cooling system (see Chapter 1). If the coolant is relatively new or in good condition (see Chapter 1), save it and reuse it.

7 Follow the upper radiator hose to the engine to locate the thermostat housing cover.

8 Loosen the hose clamp, then detach the hose from the fitting. If it's stuck, grasp it near the end with a pair of adjustable pliers and twist it to break the seal, then pull it off. If the hose is old or deteriorated, cut it off and fit a new one.

9 If the outer surface of the large fitting that mates with the hose is deteriorated (corroded, pitted, etc.) it may be damaged further by hose removal. If it is, the thermostat housing cover will have to be replaced.

10 Disconnect the engine coolant temperature (ECT) sensor **(see illustration)**, remove the thermostat cover bolts and detach the housing cover. If the cover is stuck, tap it with a soft-face hammer to jar it loose. Be prepared for some coolant to spill as the gasket seal is broken.

3.10 Remove the two cover bolts (arrowed), pull off the cover and remove the thermostat from the housing

3.13 Refit a new rubber seal over the thermostat

3.14 Refit the new thermostat in the housing with the spring towards the engine, and jiggle pin (arrowed) at the top

11 Note how it's fitted - with the jiggle pin up - then remove the thermostat.

12 Remove all traces of old gasket material and/or sealant from the housing and cover.

13 Fit a new rubber gasket over the thermostat (see illustration).

14 Fit the new thermostat in the housing without using sealant. Make sure the jiggle pin, if applicable, is at the top and the spring end is directed into the engine (see illustration).

15 Refit the housing cover and bolts. Tighten the bolts to the specified torque.

16 Reattach the hose and tighten the hose clamp securely. Refit all components that were removed for access.

17 Refill the cooling system (see Chapter 1).

18 Start the engine and allow it to reach normal operating temperature, then check for leaks and proper thermostat operation.

4 Engine cooling fan(s) and circuit - check and component renewal

⚠ *Warning: To avoid possible injury or damage, DO NOT operate the engine with a damaged fan. Do not attempt to repair fan blades - replace a damaged fan with a new one.*

Check

Note: *Models equipped with air conditioning have two complete fan circuits - one for the*

condenser and one for the radiator. The following procedures apply to both.

1 To test a fan motor, disconnect the electrical connector at the motor (see illustrations) and use suitable jumper wires to connect the fan directly to the battery. If the fan still doesn't work, renew the motor.

2 If the motor tests OK, check the fuse and relay (see Chapter 12), the fan switch, the condenser fan relay (mounted at the left front corner of the engine compartment), if applicable, or the wiring which connects the components.

3 To test the radiator fan switch, remove the switch electrical connector (see illustration), and using an ohmmeter check for continuity across the terminals of the switch with the engine cold. The switch should not have

continuity while the coolant is below 87°C. Start the engine and allow the engine to reach normal operating temperature. Stop the engine and check for continuity again. The radiator fan switch should show continuity when the coolant temperature reaches the specified temperature. If the switch fails to show continuity above this temperature, renew it.

4 The air conditioning condenser fan is controlled by the ECM. If the fan fails to operate with the air conditioning On after all other checks have been completed, check for a low refrigerant charge or have the ECM diagnosed by a dealership service department or other qualified repair facility.

Renewal

Note: *This procedure applies to either fan.*

5 Disconnect the battery cable from the negative battery terminal. *Caution: If the radio in your car is equipped with an anti-theft system, make sure you have the correct activation code before disconnecting the battery.*

6 Set the handbrake and block the rear wheels to prevent the car from rolling. Raise the front of the car and support it securely with axle stands (see "*Jacking and Vehicle Support*"). Remove the lower splash guard, if applicable, from under the radiator.

7 Insert a small screwdriver into the connector to lift the lock tab and disconnect the fan wiring.

8 Remove the fan lower mounting bolt(s) (see illustrations).

4.1a Radiator cooling fan motor electrical connector location (arrowed)

4.1b Condenser fan motor electrical connector location (arrowed)

4.3 Engine coolant temperature switch location (arrowed)

4.8a The condenser fan shroud has a single lower retaining bolt (arrowed) . . .

4.8b . . . and the radiator fan shroud has two lower retaining bolts (right bolt shown, other bolt not visible in this photo)

4.9 Upper condenser and radiator fan mounting bolts (arrowed)

4.12 Fan centre nut (top arrow) and one of the motor mounting screws (lower arrow)

9 Unbolt the fan upper brackets **(see illustration)** and the condenser top mountings.
10 Remove the upper radiator support bar (see Section 5).
11 To remove the condenser fan, remove the air conditioning line bracket bolts, push the bracket aside, then carefully lift the fan out of the engine compartment; to remove the radiator fan assembly, simply unbolt it and pull it out. Tilt the radiator forward slightly, then carefully lift the fan out of the engine compartment **(see illustration)**.
12 To detach the fan from the motor, remove the motor shaft nut, then pull the fan blade from the motor shaft **(see illustration)**.
13 To detach the fan motor from the shroud, remove the mounting screws **(see illustration)**.
14 Refitting is the reverse of removal.

5 Radiator - removal and refitting

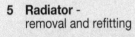

Removal

⚠️ **Warning: Wait until the engine is completely cool before beginning this procedure. Read the warning at the beginning of Section 2.**

1 Disconnect the cable from the negative battery terminal. *Caution: If the radio in your car is equipped with an anti-theft system, make sure you have the correct activation code before disconnecting the battery.*
2 Set the handbrake and block the rear

4.11 To remove the radiator fan assembly, simply unbolt it and pull it out

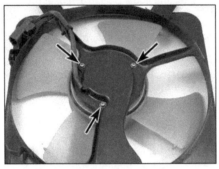

4.13 To detach the condenser fan motor from the shroud, remove screws (arrowed)

wheels. Raise the front of the car and support it securely on axle stands (see "*Jacking and Vehicle Support*"). Remove the splash pan beneath the radiator.
3 Drain the cooling system (see Chapter 1). If the coolant is in good condition, reuse it.

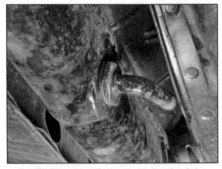

5.4 Fluid cooler lines at the back of the radiator (one pipe shown, other similar)

5.6b . . . .then loosen the hose clamp and detach the lower radiator hose (arrowed)

4 If the car is equipped with an automatic transmission, disconnect the cooler lines from the radiator **(see illustration)**. Use a drip pan to catch spilled fluid and plug the lines and fittings.
5 Disconnect the electrical connector for the cooling fan motor.
6 Loosen the hose clamps, then detach the radiator hoses from the fittings **(see illustrations)**. If they're stuck, grasp each hose near the end with a pair of slip joint pliers and twist it to break the seal, then pull it off - be careful not to damage the radiator fittings! If the hoses are old or deteriorated, cut them off and fit new ones.
7 Remove the engine cooling fan (Section 4).
8 Unbolt and remove the small brackets that attach the upper end of the radiator to the radiator support **(see illustration)**.
9 Carefully lift out the radiator. Don't spill coolant on the car or scratch the paint.
10 Inspect the radiator for leaks and damage. If it needs repair, leave this to a radiator specialist.
11 Flies and dirt can be removed from the radiator by spraying with a garden hose from the back.
12 Check the radiator mounts for deterioration and renew if necessary.

Refitting

13 Refitting is the reverse of the removal procedure. Guide the radiator into the mounts until they seat properly.
14 After refitting, fill the cooling system with the proper mixture of antifreeze and water. Refer to Chapter 1 if necessary.

5.6a Loosen the hose clamp and detach the upper radiator hose (arrowed) . . .

5.8 Remove these bolts (arrowed) and brackets to remove the radiator

15 Start the engine and check for leaks. Allow the engine to reach normal operating temperature, indicated by the upper radiator hose becoming hot. Recheck the coolant level and add more if required.
16 If you're working on an automatic transmission equipped car, check and add fluid as needed.

6 Coolant reservoir - removal and refitting

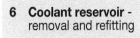

> ⚠ **Warning: The engine must be completely cool before removing the reservoir. Read the warning at the beginning of Section 2.**

Removal

1 The coolant reservoir is mounted adjacent to the radiator in the right front corner of the engine compartment.
2 Trace the overflow hose from the radiator neck to the top of coolant reservoir. Remove the cap with the hose still attached. Lift the reservoir straight up out of the bracket.
3 Pour the coolant into a container.
4 Wash out and inspect the reservoir for cracks and chafing. Examine the reservoir closely. If it's damaged, renew it.

Refitting

5 Refitting is the reverse of removal.

7 Oil cooler - removal and refitting

> ⚠ **Warning: Allow the engine to cool completely before beginning this procedure.**

Removal

1 The oil cooler is mounted between the oil filter and engine block.
2 Remove the oil filter and drain the coolant (see Chapter 1).
3 Detach the two coolant lines from the oil cooler. Be prepared for coolant to escape from the open fittings. Cap or plug the open fittings.
4 Remove the large nut (actually part of the hollow retaining bolt) in the centre of the oil cooler and separate the oil cooler from the engine.

Refitting

5 Refitting is the reverse of removal. Be sure to use a new O-ring between the block and oil cooler (lubricate the O-ring with clean engine oil before refitting). Tighten the coolant hoses securely at the fittings.
6 Fit a new oil filter and change the engine oil (see Chapter 1).

8.3 The weep holes (arrowed) are located on the rear side of the water pump

7 Add coolant and oil as needed.
8 Start the engine and check for oil and coolant leaks.
9 Recheck the coolant and oil levels.

8 Water pump - check

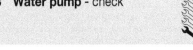

1 A failure in the water pump can cause serious engine damage due to overheating.
2 There are two ways to check the operation of the water pump while it's fitted on the engine. If the pump is defective, it should be renewed.
3 Water pumps are equipped with vent)holes **(see illustration)**. If a failure occurs in the pump seal, coolant will leak from the hole. With the timing belt cover removed, you'll need a torch and small mirror to find the hole on the water pump from underneath to check for leaks.
4 If the water pump shaft bearings fail there may be a howling or shrieking sound at the pump while it's running. Shaft wear can be felt with the timing belt removed if the water pump pulley is rocked up and down. Don't mistake drivebelt slippage, which causes a squealing sound, for water pump bearing failure.

9 Water pump - renewal

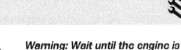

> ⚠ **Warning: Wait until the engine is completely cool before beginning this procedure. Read the warning at the beginning of Section 2.**

1 Disconnect the cable from the negative battery terminal. *Caution: If the radio in your car is equipped with an anti-theft system, make sure you have the correct activation code before disconnecting the battery.*
2 Drain the cooling system (see Chapter 1). If the coolant is relatively new or in good condition, save it and reuse it.
3 Remove the drivebelts (see Chapter 1).

9.6 Remove the water pump bolts (arrowed) and detach the water pump

4 Remove the timing belt (see Chapter 2A).
5 Remove any accessory brackets from the water pump.
6 Remove the bolts **(see illustration)** and detach the water pump from the engine. Note the location of the longer bolt.
7 Clean the bolt threads and the threaded holes in the engine to remove corrosion and sealant.
8 Compare the new pump to the old one to make sure they're identical.
9 Remove all traces of old gasket sealant and O-ring from the engine.
10 Clean the engine and new water pump mating surfaces with lacquer thinner or acetone.
11 Apply a thin layer of RTV sealant to the O-ring groove of the new pump, then carefully set a new O-ring in the groove **(see illustration)**.
12 Carefully attach the pump to the engine and thread the bolts into the holes finger tight.
13 Refit the remaining bolts (if they also hold an accessory bracket in place, be sure to reposition the bracket at this time). Tighten them to the torque listed in this Chapter's Specifications in 1/4-turn increments. Don't overtighten them or the pump may be distorted.
14 Refit all parts removed for access to the pump.
15 Refill and bleed the cooling system and check the drivebelt tension (see Chapter 1). Run the engine and check for leaks.

9.11 Apply a thin layer of RTV sealant to the O-ring groove of the new pump, then carefully set a new O-ring in the groove

10.1 Location of the coolant temperature sending unit (arrowed)

10 Coolant temperature sending unit - check and renewal

⚠ **Warning: Allow the engine to cool completely before beginning this procedure.**

1 The coolant temperature indicator system consists of a temperature gauge mounted in the instrument panel and a coolant temperature sending unit mounted on the engine directly below the distributor **(see illustration)**.
2 If an overheating indication occurs even when the engine is cold, check the wiring between the dash and the sending unit for a short circuit to earth.
3 If the gauge is inoperative, test the circuit by briefly grounding the wire to the sending unit while the ignition is on (engine not running for safety). If the gauge deflects full scale, renew the sending unit.

⚠ **Warning: This car is equipped with electric cooling fans. Stay clear of the fan blades, which can come on even when the engine is not running.**

4 If the gauge doesn't respond in the test outlined in paragraph 3, check for an open circuit in the gauge wiring.
5 If the sending unit must be replaced, simply unscrew it from the engine and quickly fit the replacement. Use sealant on the threads. Make sure the engine is cool before removing the defective sending unit. There will be some coolant loss as the unit is removed, so be prepared to catch it. Check the level after the replacement part has been fitted.

11 Blower motor and circuit - check

1 Check the fuse and all connections in the circuit for looseness and corrosion. Make sure the battery is fully charged.
2 With the transmission in Park, the handbrake securely set, turn the ignition switch On (engine not running).

3 Without disconnecting the blower motor, insert a jumper wire into the backside of the blower motor connector blue/black wire **(see illustration 12.2)** and connect the other end of the jumper wire to earth. If the blower motor runs the fault lies with the blower fan switch, the blower resistors or related wiring.
4 If the motor did not run with the jumper connected to earth, remove the jumper, disconnect the electrical connector at the blower motor and with a voltmeter measure the voltage between the connector blue/white wire and earth. If there is battery voltage present and the motor didn't run at any speed, renew the blower motor. If no battery voltage is present, check the blower motor relay or related wiring (see Chapter 12).
5 The blower resistor assembly is located on the blower motor housing unit case **(see illustration 12.4)**. There are several resistance elements mounted on the resistor board to provide low and medium blower speeds.
6 If the blower motor runs, but one or more speeds are inoperative, remove the blower resistor from the heater case mounting location and visually check for damage. Using an ohmmeter, check the resistor block for continuity between all the terminals. If any of the resistors are open renew the blower resistor assembly.

12 Blower motor - removal and refitting

⚠ **Warning: Most models covered by this manual are equipped with a Supplemental Restraint System (SRS). Always disable the airbag system before working in the vicinity of the SRS unit, steering column or instrument panel to avoid the possibility of accidental deployment of the airbag, which could cause personal injury (see Chapter 12).**

Removal

1 Disconnect the cable from the negative battery terminal. Disable the airbag, if applicable (see Chapter 12). *Caution: If the radio in your*

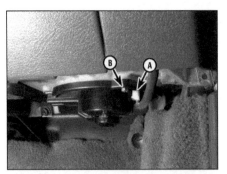

12.2 Disconnect the electrical connector (A) and remove the mounting screws (B) to remove the blower motor

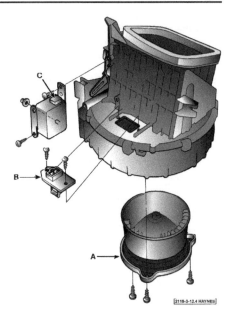

12.4 Blower motor housing and components

a Blower motor
b Blower motor resistor
c Recirculation control motor

car is equipped with an anti-theft system, make sure you have the correct activation code before disconnecting the battery.
2 The blower unit is located under the dash, behind the glovebox **(see illustration)**.
3 Disconnect the electrical connector from the blower motor.
4 Remove the three retaining screws and remove the blower motor **(see illustration)**.
5 If you're replacing the blower motor itself, separate the blower motor from the fan wheel and place the fan on the new blower motor.

Refitting

6 Refitting is the reverse of removal. Check for proper operation.

13 Heater and air conditioning control assembly - removal and refitting

Note: *Refer to the warning at the start of Section 12 before proceeding.*

Removal

1 Disconnect the cable from the negative battery terminal. Disable the airbag, if applicable (see Chapter 12). *Caution: If the radio in your car is equipped with an anti-theft system, make sure you have the correct activation code before disconnecting the battery.*
2 Remove the centre console lower trim (see Chapter 11).
3 Remove the stereo (see Chapter 12).
4 Remove the four heater/air conditioner control assembly mounting screws **(see illustration)**.

13.4 Remove the four screws (arrowed) from the heater/air conditioner control assembly, pull the unit out of the dash

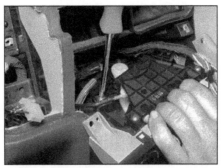

13.5a If the assembly has levers instead of buttons, remove this screw and detach the cable from the upper lever arm . . .

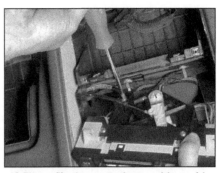

13.5b . . . flip the control assembly upside down and remove this screw to detach the other cable from the lower lever arm

5 Pull out the heater/air conditioner control assembly and disconnect the electrical connector. If the control assembly uses levers instead of buttons, detach the function control and air mix cables **(see illustrations)**.

Refitting

6 Refitting is the reverse of removal.
7 Run the engine and check the operation of the heater and air conditioning system.

---

14 Heater matrix -
removal and refitting

Note: *Refer to the warning at the start of Section 12 before proceeding.*

> ⚠️ **Warning: The air conditioning system is under high pressure. Do not loosen any hose fittings or remove any components until**
after the system has been discharged. Air conditioning refrigerant should be properly discharged at a dealer service department. Always wear eye protection when disconnecting air conditioning system fittings.

Removal

1 If the car is equipped with air conditioning, have the system discharged by a dealer service department. Disconnect the cable from the negative battery terminal. Disable the airbag, if applicable (see Chapter 12). *Caution: If the*

radio in your car is equipped with an anti-theft system, make sure you have the correct activation code before disconnecting the battery.
2 Drain the cooling system (see Chapter 1).
3 Disconnect the heater valve cable **(see illustration)**.
4 Working in the engine compartment, disconnect the heater hoses **(see illustration)** where they enter the bulkhead. Place a drain pan underneath the hoses to catch any coolant that runs out when the hoses are disconnected. Remove the heater unit mounting nut located above the heater hose inlet and outlet tubes. *Caution: Be careful not to damage or bend the fuel lines or brake pipes when removing the nut.*
5 Remove the heater/air conditioner control assembly (see Section 13).
6 Remove the instrument cluster trim panel, the console and the instrument panel (see Chapter 11).
7 On non-air conditioned models, remove the heater duct from between the heater unit and the blower unit. If applicable with air conditioning, remove the evaporator unit (Section 19).
8 Remove the steering column bracket.
9 Remove the wire harness clip from the heater unit, the two nuts retaining the heater unit to the bulkhead and remove the heater unit from the car.
10 Remove the screws from the heater matrix cover and the heater pipe clamp. Lift the heater matrix from the housing **(see illustration)**.

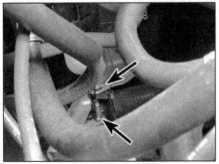

14.3 Prise open this clip (upper arrow) and lift the cable end off the pin (lower arrow) on the heater valve lever arm

14.4 Loosen the two heater hose clamps and disconnect the heater hoses (arrowed) from the heater pipes at the bulkhead

Place a piece of plastic sheeting on the car floor to prevent any coolant spillage from staining the carpet.

Refitting

11 Refitting is the reverse of removal. Be sure to check the operation of the air control flaps. If any parts bind, correct the problem before refitting.

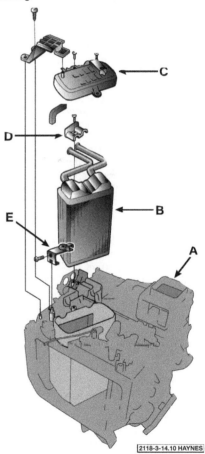

14.10 Heater unit components

A Heater unit	D Pipe clamp
B Heater matrix	E Damper cable arm
C Heater matrix cover	

2118-3-14.10 HAYNES

12 Refill and bleed the cooling system (see Chapter 1), reconnect the battery and run the engine. Check for coolant leaks and proper heater system operation. If applicable with air conditioning, have the system charged by a dealer service department or automotive air conditioning repair facility.

15 Air conditioning and heating system - check and maintenance

Air conditioning system

1 The following maintenance checks should be performed on a regular basis to ensure that the air conditioner continues to operate at peak efficiency.

a) *Inspect the condition of the compressor drivebelt. If it is worn or deteriorated, renew it (see Chapter 1).*
b) *Check the drivebelt tension and, if necessary, adjust it (see Chapter 1).*
c) *Inspect the system hoses. Look for cracks, bubbles, hardening and deterioration. Inspect the hoses and all fittings for oil bubbles or seepage. If there is any evidence of wear, damage or leakage, have the hose(s) replaced by a dealership service department or specialist air conditioning repair facility.*
d) *Inspect the condenser fins for leaves, flies and any other foreign material that may have embedded itself in the fins. Use a "fin comb" or compressed air to remove debris from the condenser.*
e) *Make sure the system has the correct refrigerant charge.*
f) *If you hear water in the dash area or have water dripping on the carpet, slip off the evaporative housing condensation drain tube (located in the lower right forward corner of the housing) and insert a piece of wire into both openings to check for blockage.*

2 It's a good idea to operate the system for about ten minutes at least once a month. This is particularly important during the winter months because long term non-use can cause hardening, and subsequent failure, of the seals. Note that using the Defrost function operates the compressor.

3 Because of the complexity of the air conditioning system and cost of special equipment necessary to capture refrigerant and correctly service air conditioning systems, in-depth troubleshooting and repairs are not covered in this manual. However, simple component renewal procedures are provided in this Chapter.

4 The most common cause of poor cooling is simply a low system refrigerant charge. If a noticeable drop in system cooling ability occurs, a quick check of the system will help you determine whether the refrigerant level is low.

5 With the air conditioning operating inspect

15.5 With the air conditioning system on, inspect the sight glass (right arrow). Do not disconnect the line fittings (lower left arrows). Receiver-drier bracket pinch bolt also arrowed (top left)

the sight glass **(see illustration)**. The sight glass is located on the top of the receiver-drier near the front corner of the engine compartment. If the refrigerant contains bubbles and looks foamy, it's low. Have the system charged by a dealer service department or specialist air conditioning repair facility.

Heating systems

6 If the air coming out of the heater vents is not hot, the problem could stem from any of the following causes:

a) *The thermostat is stuck open, preventing the engine coolant from warming up enough to carry heat to the heater matrix. Renew the thermostat (see Section 3).*
b) *A heater hose is blocked, preventing the flow of coolant through the heater matrix. Feel both heater hoses at the bulkhead. They should be hot. If one of them is cold, there is an obstruction in one of the hoses or in the heater matrix, or the heater control valve is shut. Detach the hoses and reverse flush the heater matrix with a water hose. If the heater matrix is clear but circulation is impeded, remove the two hoses and flush them out with a water hose.*
c) *If flushing fails to remove the blockage from the heater matrix, the matrix must be replaced.*

7 If the blower motor speed does not correspond to the setting selected on the blower switch, the problem could be a bad fuse, circuit, switch, blower motor resistor or motor.

a) *Before checking an inoperative blower motor or circuit, always check the fuse first.*
b) *Using a test light or voltmeter, check the voltage at the motor.*
c) *Pull the heating/air conditioning control assembly (see Section 13) far enough from the dash to verify - with a test light or voltmeter - that current is reaching the blower switch on the control assembly. If the switch is not getting current, troubleshoot the circuit between the battery and the switch.*

d) *Using a test light or voltmeter, verify that the blower motor is getting current. If the blower motor is not getting current, check the circuit between the fuse box and motor, including the blower relay.*

8 If there isn't any air coming out of the vents:

a) *Turn the ignition ON and activate the fan control. Place your ear at the heating/air conditioning register (vent) and listen. Most motors are audible. Can you hear the motor running?*
b) *If you cannot (and have already verified that the blower switch and the blower motor circuit are good), the blower motor itself is probably bad (see Section 11). You can verify the motor's condition by hooking up a fused jumper wire directly between battery positive terminal and the blower motor.*

9 If the carpet under the heater matrix is damp, or if antifreeze vapour or steam is coming through the vents, the heater matrix is leaking. Remove it (see Section 14) and fit a new unit.

16 Air conditioning receiver-drier - removal and refitting

⚠️ *Warning: The air conditioning system is under high pressure. Do not loosen any hose fittings or remove any components until after the system has been discharged. Air conditioning refrigerant should be properly discharged at a dealer service department. Always wear eye protection when disconnecting air conditioning system fittings.*

Removal

1 Have the refrigerant discharged by a dealership service department or specialist air conditioning repair facility.

2 Disconnect the cable from the negative battery terminal. *Caution: If the radio in your car is equipped with an anti-theft system, make sure you have the correct activation code before disconnecting the battery.*

3 Disconnect the refrigerant lines **(see illustration 15.5)** from the receiver-drier and cap the open fittings to prevent dirt and moisture entry.

4 Remove the receiver bracket bolt and lift the receiver-drier out of the car.

Refitting

5 Refitting is the reverse of removal.

6 Have the system evacuated, charged and leak tested by a dealership service department or specialist air conditioning repair facility. If the receiver was replaced, add 1/3 ounce of refrigerant oil.

17 Air conditioning compressor
- removal and refitting

⚠️ **Warning: The air conditioning system is under high pressure. Do not loosen any hose fittings or remove any components until after the system has been discharged. Air conditioning refrigerant should be properly discharged at a dealer service department. Always wear eye protection when disconnecting air conditioning system fittings.**

Note : *The air conditioning compressor is a non-serviceable unit. It must be replaced with a complete unit or rebuilt by an authorised rebuild. The receiver-drier should be replaced whenever the compressor is replaced.*

Removal

1 Have the air conditioning system refrigerant discharged by dealership service department or air conditioning repair facility.
2 Disconnect the cable from the negative battery terminal. *Caution: If the radio in your car is equipped with an anti-theft system, make sure you have the correct activation code before disconnecting the battery.*
3 Set the handbrake, block the rear wheels and raise the front of the car, supporting it securely on axle stands (see *"Jacking and Vehicle Support"*).
4 Remove the drivebelt (see Chapter 1).
5 Remove the power steering pump (see Chapter 10).
6 Remove the cruise control actuator (if applicable).
7 Disconnect the refrigerant lines from the compressor **(see illustration)**. Plug the open fittings to prevent entry of dirt and moisture.
8 Disconnect the compressor clutch wiring harness **(see illustration 17.7)**.
9 Unbolt the compressor **(see illustration)** from the mounting bracket and remove it from the car.
10 The clutch may have to be transferred from the old compressor to the new unit.
11 Here's how to calculate the amount of refrigerant oil for the new compressor:
a) Drain the refrigerant oil from the old compressor through the suction fitting and measure it in ounces or cubic centimetres.
b) Subtract this volume from 4 fluid ounces (120 ml)
c) The difference between these two figures is equal to the amount you should drain from the new compressor.

Refitting

12 Refitting is otherwise the reverse of removal.
13 Have the system evacuated, recharged and leak tested by a dealership service department or specialist air conditioning repair facility.

17.7 Disconnect clutch connector (A), unscrew the refrigerant line fitting nuts (B), and disconnect the lines. Plug open fittings to prevent entry of dirt and moisture

18 Air conditioning condenser -
removal and refitting

Note: *Refer to the warning at the start of Section 17 before proceeding.*

Removal

1 Have the refrigerant discharged by a dealership service department or air conditioning repair facility.
2 Disconnect the cable from the negative battery terminal. *Caution: If the radio in your car is equipped with an anti-theft system, make sure you have the correct activation code before disconnecting the battery.*
3 Disconnect the air conditioning pressure switch electrical connector and the condenser fan electrical connector
4 Disconnect the condenser hose and discharge line from the condenser **(see illustration)**.
5 Remove the condenser brackets **(see illustration)**.
6 Lift the condenser from the car. Try not to damage the condenser fins or the radiator when removing or refitting the condenser.

Refitting

7 Refitting is the reverse of removal. **Note:** *Always renew all O-rings with new ones and lightly lubricate them with refrigerant oil before assembly.*

18.4 Disconnect the condenser line and discharge line attaching bolts (arrowed) from the condenser

17.9 Remove the compressor mounting bolts (arrowed) and lower the compressor out from under the vehicle

8 Have the system evacuated, charged and leak tested by a dealership service department. If a new condenser was fitted, add 2/3-ounce of refrigerant oil.

19 Air conditioning evaporator -
removal and refitting

Note: *Refer to the warning at the start of Section 17 before proceeding.*

⚠️ **Warning: Most models covered by this manual are equipped with a Supplemental Restraint System (SRS), more commonly known as an airbag(s). Always disable the airbag system before working in the vicinity of the SRS unit, steering column or instrument panel to avoid the possibility of accidental deployment of the airbag, which could cause personal injury (see Chapter 12).**

Removal

1 Have the air conditioning system discharged by a dealer service department or automotive air conditioning repair facility.
2 Disconnect the cable from the negative battery terminal. Disable the airbag, if applicable (see Chapter 12). *Caution: If the radio in your car is equipped with an anti-theft system, make sure you have the correct activation code before disconnecting the battery.*

18.5 Remove the condenser bracket bolts (arrowed) and brackets, then disconnect the condenser fan electrical connector

3 Disconnect the receiver line and suction line from the evaporator **(see illustration)**. Plug both lines to prevent the entry of contaminants and moisture into air conditioning system.

4 Remove the glovebox and the glovebox frame (see Chapter 11).

5 Disconnect the connector from the air conditioning thermostat and remove the wiring harness clips from the evaporator housing.

6 Remove the evaporator unit retaining screws and nuts, pull the evaporator unit out far enough to disconnect the drain hose and remove the unit from the car.

7 Remove the screws and clips retaining the evaporator case halves together, remove the air conditioning thermostat and separated the housing.

8 Remove the evaporator matrix from the housing and remove the expansion valve, if necessary.

Refitting

9 Refitting is the reverse of removal.

10 Have the system evacuated, charged and leak tested by a dealer service department or specialist air conditioning repair facility. If a new evaporator was fitted, add 1.5 ounces of refrigerant oil.

19.3 Disconnect refrigerant lines (arrowed) from the evaporator - plug both lines to prevent the entry of contaminants

Chapter 4
Fuel and exhaust systems

Contents

Degrees of difficulty

Easy, suitable for novice with little experience		Fairly easy, suitable for beginner with some experience		Fairly difficult, suitable for competent DIY mechanic	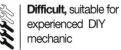	Difficult, suitable for experienced DIY mechanic		Very difficult, suitable for expert DIY or professional	

Specifications

Fuel injection system
Fuel pressure
  With regulator vacuum hose attached . . . . 31 to 38 psi
  With regulator vacuum hose disconnected . . . . 40 to 47 psi
Fuel injector resistance
  Multi-point . . . . 10 to 13 ohms
  Dual-point
    Main . . . . 0.6 to 1.6 ohms
    Auxiliary . . . . 6 to 10 ohms

Carburettor
Type . . . . Keihin 2V (twin choke), with electronic control system
Choke type . . . . Automatic (bi-metallic spring)
Float level . . . . Sight glass

Torque wrench settings

	Nm	lbf ft
Fuel injection service bolt	11	8
Throttle body mounting nuts	22	16
Fuel rail mounting nuts	12	9

1.1a Intake air temperature sensor (dual-point injection system)

1.1b Electronic Air Control Valve (EACV) (dual-point injection system)

2.2 Unscrewing fuel filter service bolt - cover with a rag to catch escaping fuel

1 General information

Fuel injection models

The fuel injection vehicles covered by this manual are equipped with the Programmed Fuel Injection (PGM-FI) system. This system uses timed impulses to sequentially inject the fuel directly into the inlet ports of each cylinder. The injectors are controlled by the Engine Control Module (ECM). The ECM monitors various engine parameters by means of sensors **(see illustrations)** and delivers the exact amount of fuel, in the correct sequence, into the inlet ports.

All models are equipped with an electric fuel pump, mounted in the fuel tank. It is not necessary to remove the fuel tank for access to the fuel pump. The fuel pump and the fuel level sending unit can be removed through the access hole under the rear seat with the fuel tank in the car.

Carburettor models

The carburettor cars covered by this manual are equipped with the Programmed Carburettor (PGM-CARB) Control system. This system uses an electronic control unit (located in the passenger footwell) to control the carburettor settings using various sensors to monitor engine condition. The ECU input devices include the following.

a) Oxygen sensor
b) Vehicle speed sensor
c) MAP sensor
d) Vacuum Switch
e) Ignition coil sensor
f) Air conditioning sensors
g) Coolant (TW) and inlet air (TA) temperature sensors
h) Clutch switch sensor (where applicable)

The ECU controls the following output devices.

a) Electronic Air Control Valve (EACV)
b) Slow Mixture cut-off solenoid valve
c) Air conditioning idle boost solenoid valve
d) Air leak solenoid valve
e) Power valve control solenoid
f) Vacuum control solenoid valve

The Keihin 2V carburettor is a downdraught progressive twin-venturi instrument. At low speeds when the primary throttle is opened moderately, only the primary bore is operational, however at higher speeds both the primary and secondary bores are operational. The secondary bore is brought into operation by a vacuum diaphragm unit.

The choke valve is in the primary bore and is operated by a bi-metallic coil spring.

On models with air conditioning, idle control is accomplished using an idle boost system with its own electronic control unit.

A mechanical diaphragm fuel pump is located on the left-hand end of the cylinder head and is driven by a lever in contact with the camshaft.

All models

The exhaust system consists of an exhaust manifold pipe, exhaust manifold, a catalytic converter, an exhaust pipe and a silencer. Each of these components is replaceable. For further information regarding the catalytic converter, refer to Chapter 6.

2 Fuel pressure relief procedure (fuel injection models)

Note: *Refer to the warning note in Section 1 before proceeding.*

Warning: Many of the procedures in this Chapter require the removal of fuel lines and connections, which may result in some fuel spillage. Before carrying out any operation on the fuel system, refer to the precautions given in "Safety first!" at the beginning of this manual, and follow them implicitly. Petrol is a highly dangerous and volatile liquid, and the precautions necessary when handling it cannot be overstressed.

1 Detach the cable from the negative battery terminal. Unscrew the fuel filler cap to relieve pressure built up in the fuel tank. *Caution: If the stereo in your car is equipped with an anti-theft system, make sure you have the correct activation code before disconnecting the battery.*

2 You'll need two spanners for this procedure - one to loosen the service bolt on the fuel filter and another to hold the special banjo bolt into which the service bolt is installed **(see illustration)**.

3 Place a cloth rag over the service bolt, located on top of the fuel filter.

4 While holding the special banjo bolt, *slowly* loosen the service bolt one complete turn - fuel will begin to flow from the fitting. Allow the pressure to be relieved completely, then remove the bolt and fit a new sealing washer.

5 After all work to the fuel system has been performed, refit the service bolt and tighten it to the torque listed in this Chapter's Specifications.

3 Fuel pump/fuel pressure (fuel injection models) - check

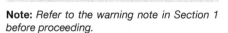

Note: *Refer to the warning note in Section 1 before proceeding.*

Preliminary check

1 If you suspect insufficient fuel delivery, first inspect all fuel lines to ensure that the problem is not simply a leak in a line.

Fuel pump operational check

Note: *On all fuel injection models, the fuel pump is located inside the fuel tank (see Section 4).*

2 Apply the handbrake and have an assistant turn the ignition switch to the ON position while you listen to the fuel pump. You should hear a whirring sound, lasting for a couple of seconds. Start the engine. The whirring sound should now be continuous (although harder to hear with the engine running). If there is no whirring sound, either the fuel pump or the fuel main relay circuit is defective (proceed to paragraph 8).

Pressure check

3 Relieve the fuel pressure (see Section 2).

4 Remove the service bolt from the top of the service fitting located on the fuel filter and attach a fuel pressure gauge, using a special adapter which can be purchased at a tool hire shop or dealer service department

3.4 Fit a fuel pressure gauge on the service port

(see illustration). If you can't locate the proper adapter, you can fabricate one from a bolt and nut (see Tool Tip). If you choose this route, also remove the fitting on the fuel filter that the service bolt screws into.

5 Start the engine and check the pressure on the gauge, comparing your reading with the pressure listed in this Chapter's Specifications. Now, detach the vacuum hose from the fuel pressure regulator. With the engine idling, measure the fuel pressure. It should be as listed in this Chapter's Specifications. Reconnect the vacuum hose.

6 If the fuel pressure is not within specifications, check the following:

a) If the pressure is within specifications when the vacuum hose is connected to the pressure regulator but does not increase when the vacuum hose is disconnected, check for vacuum at the hose. If there is vacuum present, renew the pressure regulator (see Section 14). If there is no vacuum, check the hose for a break or an obstruction.

b) If the pressure is higher than specified, check for a pinched or clogged fuel return hose or pipe. If the return line is not obstructed, renew the fuel pressure regulator (see Section 14).

c) If the pressure is lower than specified:
1) Inspect the fuel filter - make sure it's not clogged.
2) Look for a pinched or clogged fuel hose between the fuel tank and the fuel rail.

Cut the head off a bolt (12 mm diameter/1.25 thread pitch) and drill a hole directly through the centre. Grind the end to form a slight taper and drill a vertical hole to allow system pressure to flow. It is important that the vertical hole is drilled in the correct location. The easiest method is to use the banjo bolt that was removed from the fuel filter and place it directly next to the tool for the correct alignment of the vertical passage for fuel flow.

3) Check the pressure regulator for a malfunction (see Section 14).
4) Look for leaks in the fuel line.

7 If there are no problems with any of the above-listed components, check the fuel pump (see below).

Fuel pump check

8 Remove the rear seat (see Chapter 11).
9 Remove the protective covering from the chassis to expose the fuel pump and fuel level sending unit access cover (see Section 4).
10 If you suspect a problem with the fuel pump, verify the pump actually runs. Have an assistant turn the ignition switch to ON - you should hear a brief whirring noise as the pump comes on and pressurises the system. Have the assistant start the engine. This time you should hear a constant whirring sound from the pump (but it's more difficult to hear with the engine running).
11 If the pump does not come on (makes no sound), proceed to the next step.

12 Disconnect the main fuel pump relay connector and fit a jumper wire between the black/yellow terminal (terminal number 5) and the yellow terminal (terminal number 7) (see illustration).
13 Remove the rear seat (see Chapter 11) and detach the three-pin connector (make sure the ignition switch is turned off before disconnecting the wires) from the fuel pump electrical connector (see illustration).
14 Touch the positive probe of a voltmeter to the yellow wire and the negative probe to the black wire (or a suitable earth) and with the ignition switch ON, verify there is voltage available.
15 If voltage is available, but the fuel pump doesn't run when connected, renew the fuel pump (see Section 5). If no voltage is available, check the main relay (see below).

Main relay check (except dual-point injection)

16 To test the main relay, first remove it from its location next to the fuse panel under the facia.
17 Remove the relay from the connector and verify that there is battery voltage (ignition switch ON) at the black/yellow wire of the connector (opposite terminal number 5) (see illustration).
18 If there is no voltage, check the number 2 fuse. If battery voltage is present, check the relay.
19 Working on the bench, using a pair of jumper wires, connect battery voltage to the no. 6 terminal of the relay, earth the no. 8 terminal, then check for continuity between the no. 5 and no. 7 terminals. If there's no continuity, renew the relay.
20 Connect battery voltage to the no. 5 terminal, earth the no. 2 terminal and verify there's continuity between the no. 1 and no. 3 terminals. If there isn't, renew the relay.
21 Connect battery voltage to the no. 3 terminal, earth the no. 8 terminal. Verify there's continuity between the no. 5 and no. 7 terminals. If there is no continuity, renew the relay. If there is continuity, the relay is OK. Check the wiring harness from the fuses to the relay and the pump.

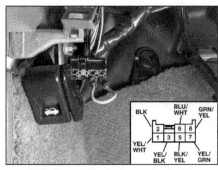

3.12 Connect a jumper wire to the number 5 and 7 terminals of the fuel pump relay

3.13 Check for battery voltage at the fuel pump electrical connector under the rear seat

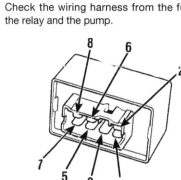

3.17 The main relay is located under the dash in the drivers side corner - refer to the terminal numbers when testing

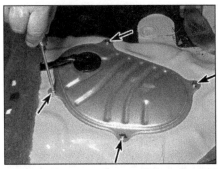

4.4 Remove screws (arrowed) from the fuel pump/fuel level sending unit access cover

4.6 Remove the nuts that retain the fuel pump to the fuel tank

4.7 Lift out the pump. Angle it to avoid damaging pump screen on the bottom

4.8 Remove the blue protective connector from the main electrical connector

4.9 Lift tab on main electrical connector and disconnect it from the fuel pump

4.12 Prise off the retaining clip and detach the filter (sock) from the pump

4 Fuel pump (fuel injection models) - removal and refitting

Note: *Refer to the warning note in Section 1 before proceeding.*

Removal

1 Detach the cable from the negative battery terminal. **Caution: If the stereo in your car is equipped with an anti-theft system, make sure you have the correct activation code before disconnecting the battery.**
2 Relieve the fuel system pressure (see Section 2).
3 Remove the rear seat (see Chapter 11).
4 Remove the bolts that retain the fuel pump access cover **(see illustration)**.
5 Unplug the electrical connector from the fuel pump and detach the fuel lines.
6 Remove the fuel pump assembly retaining nuts **(see illustration)**.
7 Remove the fuel pump from the tank **(see illustration)**.
8 Remove the electrical connector protective cover **(see illustration)**.
9 Remove the electrical connector from the fuel pump **(see illustration)**.
10 Squeeze the hose clamps with a pair of pliers - remove the upper clamp from the hose and slide the lower clamp half-way up the hose, off the fuel pump inlet.
11 Separate the pump from the fuel pump bracket.
12 Remove the sock filter from the end of the pump **(see illustration)**.

Refitting

13 Refitting is the reverse of removal. Be sure to use a new gasket on the cover plate flange.

5 Fuel level sending unit - check and renewal

Note: *Refer to the warning note in Section 1 before proceeding.*

Check

1 Remove the fuel pump/ fuel level sending unit access cover **(see illustration 4.4)**.
2 Position the ohmmeter probes onto the electrical connector terminals and check for resistance **(see illustration)**.
3 First, check the resistance of the sending unit with the fuel tank completely full. The

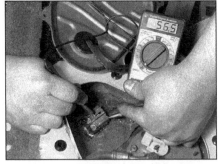

5.2 Measure fuel level sending unit resistance with float raised (full tank) and then with the float near the bottom (empty)

resistance of the sending unit should be about 2 to 5 ohms.
4 Now check the resistance of the unit with the fuel tank almost empty. The resistance should be 150 to 155 ohms.
5 If the readings are incorrect or there is very little change in resistance as the float travels from full to empty, renew the sending unit. **Note:** *The fuel level sending unit can also be checked by removing the unit (see paragraphs 6 to 10). Check the resistance while moving the float from full (arm at highest point of travel) to empty (arm at lowest point of travel)* **(see illustration)**.

Renewal

6 Remove the rear seat (see Chapter 11).
7 Remove the fuel level sending unit/fuel pump access cover **(see illustration 4.3)** and lift the access cover from the floor of the car.

5.5 If necessary, remove the fuel level sending unit and measure the resistance while manually operating the float

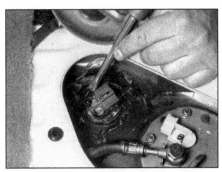

5.8 Use a brass punch to remove the locking ring

8 Use a brass punch and tap on the locking ring **(see illustration)** until the tabs line up with the recess in the housing.

 Warning: A steel punch shouldn't be used, since a spark could cause an explosion.

9 Lift the fuel level sending unit from the tank **(see illustration)**. Be careful not to damage the float arm.
10 Refitting is the reverse of removal. Be sure to use a new gasket under the sealing flange.

6 Fuel lines and fittings - repair and renewal

Note: *Refer to the warning note in Section 1 before proceeding.*
1 Always relieve the fuel pressure on fuel injection models before servicing fuel lines or fittings (see Section 2).
2 The fuel feed, return and vapour lines extend from the fuel tank to the engine compartment. The lines are secured to the underbody with clip and screw assemblies. These lines must be occasionally inspected for leaks, kinks and dents.
3 If evidence of dirt is found in the system or fuel filter during dismantling, the line should be disconnected and blown out. Check the fuel strainer on the fuel gauge sending unit (see Section 5) for damage and deterioration.

Steel tubing

4 If renewal of a fuel line or emission line is

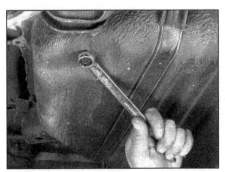

7.4 Loosen the drain plug and drain the fuel into an approved container

5.9 Lift the fuel level sending unit through the access hole

called for, use welded steel tubing to the manufacturer's specifications or equivalent.
5 Don't use copper or aluminium tubing to renew steel tubing. These materials cannot withstand normal car vibration.
6 Because fuel lines used on fuel-injected cars are under high pressure, they require special consideration.
7 Some fuel lines have threaded fittings with O-rings. Any time the fittings are loosened to service or renew components:
   a) Use a holding spanner while loosening and tightening the fittings.
   b) Check all O-rings for cuts, cracks and deterioration. Renew any that appear hardened, worn or damaged.
   c) If the lines are replaced, always use original equipment parts, or parts that meet the original equipment standards specified in this Section.

Flexible hose

 Warning: Use only original equipment renewal hoses or equivalent. Others may fail from the high pressures of this system.

8 Don't route fuel hoses within four inches of any part of the exhaust system or within ten inches of the catalytic converter. Metal lines and rubber hoses must never be allowed to chafe against the frame. A minimum of 1/4-inch clearance must be maintained around a line or hose to prevent contact with the frame.

Removal and refitting

9 First, relieve the fuel pressure on fuel

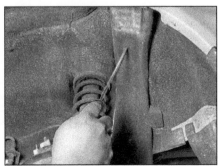

7.7a Remove the screws and separate the upper cover from inside the wheel opening

injection models, with reference to Section 2.
10 Remove all clips attaching the lines to the car body.
11 Detach the clamp(s) that attach the fuel hoses to the metal lines, then pull the hoses off the fitting. Twisting the hoses back and forth will allow them to separate more easily.
12 Refitting is the reverse of removal. Be sure to use new O-rings at the threaded fittings (if applicable).

Repair

13 If rerplacing any fuel line (metal or flexible lines) use only genuine parts. Others may fail from the high pressures of this system.

7 Fuel tank - removal and refitting

Note: *Refer to the warning note in Section 1 before proceeding.*
Note: *The following procedure is much easier to perform if the fuel tank is empty. Some tanks have a drain plug for this purpose. If the tank does not have a drain plug, the fuel can be siphoned from the tank using a siphoning kit, available at most motor factors. NEVER start the siphoning action with your mouth!*

Removal

1 Remove the fuel tank filler cap to relieve fuel tank pressure.
2 Relieve the fuel system pressure (Section 2).
3 Detach the cable from the negative terminal of the battery. *Caution: If the stereo in your car is equipped with an anti-theft system, make sure you have the correct activation code before disconnecting the battery.*
4 If the tank has a drain plug, remove it and drain the fuel into an approved fuel container **(see illustration)**. If it doesn't have a drain plug, siphon the fuel into an approved fuel container, using a siphoning kit (available at most motor factors).
5 Remove the rear seat (see Chapter 11) and disconnect the fuel gauge and fuel pump electrical connectors.
6 Raise the rear of the car and place it on axle stands (see "*Jacking and Vehicle Support*").
7 Remove the splash panels that protect the fuel tank and the fuel lines **(see illustrations)**.

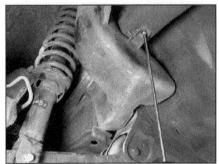

7.7b Remove the lower outer cover

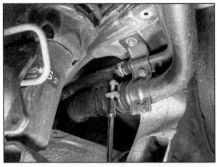

7.7c Finally, remove the tank cover to expose the fuel lines

7.8 Remove the clamp that retains the rubber fuel line to the inlet pipe

7.10 Support the fuel tank and remove the nuts from the strap bolts (arrowed)

8 Label and disconnect the fuel hoses and any brackets that may secure them **(see illustration)**.

9 Support the fuel tank with a trolley jack. Position a wood block between the jack head and the fuel tank to protect the tank.

10 Disconnect both fuel tank retaining straps and pivot them down until they are out of the way **(see illustration)**.

11 Remove the tank from the car.

Refitting

12 Refitting is the reverse of removal.

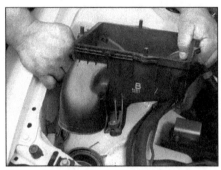

9.4 Remove the bolts (arrowed) . . .

9.5 . . . then lift the air cleaner assembly up and off the fresh air intake duct

8 Fuel tank cleaning and repair - general information

All repairs to the fuel tank or filler neck should be carried out by a professional who has experience in this critical and potentially dangerous work. Even after cleaning and flushing of the fuel system, explosive fumes can remain and ignite during repair of the tank.

If the fuel tank is removed from the car, it should not be placed in an area where sparks or naked flames could ignite the fumes coming out of the tank.

9 Air cleaner assembly - removal and refitting

1 Detach the cable from the negative battery terminal. *Caution: If the stereo in your car is equipped with an anti-theft system, make sure you have the correct activation code before disconnecting the battery.*

2 Remove the air cleaner cover and filter element (see Chapter 1).

Fuel injection models

Removal

3 Remove the clamps that hold the air inlet duct to the air cleaner housing.

4 Remove the bolts that hold the air cleaner housing to the engine compartment (except dual-point) or throttle housing (dual-point) **(see illustration)**.

5 Lift the assembly up and detach it from the fresh air inlet duct, then remove it from the engine compartment **(see illustration)**.

Refitting

6 Refitting is the reverse of removal.

Carburettor models

Removal

7 Disconnect the air inlet duct and hot air hose from the air cleaner body.

8 Unscrew the nuts and remove the filter gauze from the centre of the body.

9 Unscrew the mounting bolt(s) and remove the air cleaner body from the top of the carburettor.

Refitting

10 Refitting is a reversal of removal.

10 Accelerator cable - renewal and adjustment

Renewal

1 Detach the cable from the negative battery terminal. *Caution: If the stereo in your car is equipped with an anti-theft system, make sure you have the correct activation code before disconnecting the battery.*

2 Loosen the locknut and remove the accelerator cable from its bracket **(see illustrations)**.

3 Rotate the throttle shaft bellcrank until the cable is out of its guide groove in the bellcrank and detach the cable from the bellcrank **(see illustrations)**.

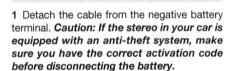

10.2a Hold the adjusting nut while loosening the locknut (multi-point version)

10.2b Accelerator cable and mounting bracket (dual-point version)

10.3a Remove the cable end from the throttle valve (multi-point version)

10.3b Accelerator cable connection to the bellcrank

10.4 Pull the accelerator cable end out and then lift the cable out of the recess (arrowed) in the pedal

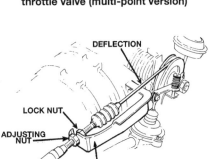

10.7 Lift up the cable to remove the slack, then turn the adjusting nut until it is 1/8-inch from the cable bracket, then tighten the locknut

4 Working underneath the facia, detach the cable from the accelerator pedal **(see illustration)**.
5 Pull the grommet from the bulkhead and pull the cable through the bulkhead from the engine compartment side.
6 Refitting is the reverse of removal.

Adjustment

7 To adjust the cable **(see illustration)**:
 a) *Loosen the adjusting nuts then position the outer cable so that it is possible to move the inner cable up and down under light finger pressure by approximately 10 to 12 mm on fuel injection models or 4 to 10 mm on carburettor models.*
 b) *Tighten the adjusting nuts and recheck the deflection.*
 c) *After you have adjusted the throttle cable, have an assistant help you verify that the throttle valve opens all the way when you depress the accelerator pedal to the floor and that it returns to the idle position when you release the accelerator. Verify the cable operates smoothly. It must not bind or stick.*
 d) *If the car is equipped with an automatic transmission, adjust the transmission Throttle Valve (TV) cable (kickdown cable) (see Chapter 7B).*

11 Fuel injection system - general information

The Programmed Fuel Injection (PGM-FI) system **(see illustration)** consists of three sub-systems: air inlet, electronic control and fuel delivery. The system uses an Engine Control Module (ECM) along with the sensors (coolant temperature sensor, Throttle Position Sensor (TPS), Manifold Absolute Pressure (MAP) sensor etc.) to determine the proper air/fuel ratio under all operating conditions.

The fuel injection system and the emissions control system are closely linked in function and design. For additional information, refer to Chapter 6.

Air inlet system

The air inlet system consists of the air cleaner, the air inlet ducts, the throttle body, the idle control system and the inlet manifold. A resonator in the air inlet tube provides silencing as air is drawn into the system.

The throttle body is a single barrel design, side-draught on multi-point versions and down-draught on dual-point versions. The lower portion of the throttle body is heated by engine coolant to prevent icing in cold weather. The idle adjusting screw is located on the throttle body. A throttle position sensor is attached to the throttle shaft to monitor changes in the throttle opening.

When the engine is idling, the air/fuel ratio is controlled by the idle air control (IAC) system, which consists of the Engine Control Module (ECM), the fast idle thermo valve, the IAC valve and the starting valve. The IAC valve is activated by the ECM depending upon the running conditions of the engine (air conditioning system, power steering, cold and warm running etc.). This valve regulates the amount of airflow past the throttle plate and

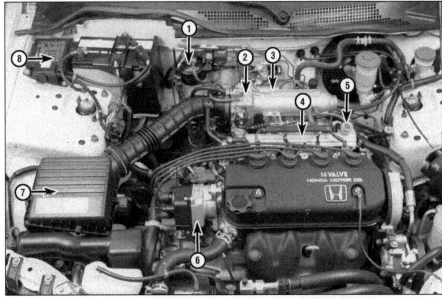

11.1 Typical multi-point fuel injection system components

1 Fuel pressure service fitting
2 Throttle body
3 IAC motor
4 Fuel rail
5 Fuel pressure regulator
6 Distributor
7 Air cleaner housing
8 Fuse and relay control centre

into the inlet manifold. The ECM receives information from the sensors (car speed, coolant temperature, air conditioning, power steering mode etc.) and adjusts the idle according to the demands of the engine and driver. Finally, to prevent rough running after the engine starts, the starting valve is opened during cranking and immediately after starting to provide additional air into the inlet manifold.

Some models are equipped with the Inlet Air Bypass (IAB) system. The IAB system allows the inlet manifold to divert the path of inlet air into the combustion chamber. Two air inlet paths are provided in the inlet manifold to allow the option of the inlet volume most favourable for the particular engine speed. Optimum performance is achieved by switching the valves from either the closed position (for high torque at low RPM) or the open position (for maximum horsepower at high RPM).

Electronic control system

This control and the Engine Control Module (ECM) are explained in detail in Chapter 6.

Fuel delivery system

The fuel delivery system consists of these components: The fuel pump, the pressure regulator, the fuel injectors, the injector resistor and the main relay.

The fuel pump is an in-line, direct drive type. Fuel is drawn through a filter into the pump, flows past the armature through the one-way valve, passes through another filter and is delivered to the injectors. A relief valve prevents excessive pressure build-up by opening in the event of a blockage in the discharge side and allowing fuel to flow from the high to the low pressure side.

The pressure regulator maintains a constant fuel pressure to the injectors. Excess fuel is routed back to the fuel tank through the return line.

The injectors are solenoid-actuated, constant stroke, pintle types consisting of a solenoid, plunger, needle valve and housing. When current is applied to the solenoid coil, the needle valve rises and pressurised fuel fills the injector housing and squirts out the nozzle. The injection quantity is determined by the length of time the valve is open (the length of time during which current is supplied to the solenoid coils).

Because it determines opening and closing intervals - which in turn determines the air-fuel mixture ratio - injector timing must be quite accurate. To attain the best possible injector response, the current rise time, when voltage is being applied to each injector coil, must be as short as possible. The number of windings in the coil has therefore been reduced to lower the inductance in the coil. However, this creates low coil resistance, which could compromise the durability of the coil. The flow of current in the coil is therefore restricted by a resistor installed in the injector wire harness.

The main relay, which is located adjacent to the fuse box, is a direct coupler type which contains the relays for the Engine Control Module power supply and the fuel pump power supply.

12 Fuel injection system - check

Note: *The following procedure is based on the assumption that the fuel pressure is adequate (see Section 3).*

1 Check the earth wire connections on the inlet manifold for tightness. Check all wiring harness connectors that are related to the system. Loose connectors and poor grounds can cause many problems that resemble more serious malfunctions.
2 Check to see that the battery is fully charged, as the control unit and sensors depend on an accurate supply voltage in order to properly meter the fuel.
3 Check the air filter element - a dirty or partially blocked filter will severely impede performance and economy (see Chapter 1).
4 If a blown fuse is found, renew it and see if it blows again. If it does, search for a shorted wire in the harness to the fuel pump.
5 Check the air inlet duct to the inlet manifold for leaks, which will result in a lean mixture. Also check the condition of all vacuum hoses connected to the inlet manifold.
6 Remove the air inlet duct (and cover on dual-point versions) from the throttle body and check for dirt, carbon or other residue build-up inside the throttle body bore. If it's

dirty, clean it with aerosol carburettor cleaner, cloth rags and a toothbrush.
7 The remainder of the system checks can be found in the following Sections.

13 Throttle body (fuel injection system) - check, removal and refitting

Check

1 On the throttle body, locate the vacuum hose that goes to the MAP sensor **(see illustration)**. Detach it from the throttle body and attach a vacuum gauge in its place.
2 Start the engine and warm it to operating temperature (wait until the cooling fan comes on twice). Verify the gauge indicates no vacuum.
3 Open the throttle slightly from idle and verify that the gauge indicates vacuum. If the gauge indicates no vacuum, check the port to make sure it is not clogged. Clean it with aerosol carburettor cleaner if necessary.
4 Stop the engine and verify the accelerator cable and throttle valve operate smoothly without binding or sticking.
5 If the accelerator cable or throttle valve binds or sticks, check for a build-up of sludge on the cable or throttle shaft.
6 If a build-up of sludge is evident, remove it with carburettor cleaner or a similar solvent.
7 If cleaning fails to remedy the problem, renew the throttle body.

Removal

⚠️ *Warning: Wait until the engine is completely cool before beginning this procedure.*

8 Detach the cable from the negative battery terminal. *Caution: If the stereo in your car is equipped with an anti-theft system, make sure you have the correct activation code before disconnecting the battery.*
9 Remove the air duct that connects the air cleaner assembly to the throttle body. On dual-point models also remove the upper cover **(see illustration)**.
10 Unplug the throttle position sensor from the throttle body **(see illustration)**. Also label and detach all vacuum hoses from the throttle body.

13.1 Remove the hose that connects the throttle body to the MAP sensor

13.9 Throttle body upper cover on dual-point models

13.10 Throttle position sensor (dual-point models)

13.13 Remove the four nuts (arrowed) and
separate the throttle body (multi-point)
from the air intake plenum

11 Detach the accelerator cable (Section 10)
and, if applicable, the transmission Throttle
Valve (TV or kickdown) cable (Chapter 7B).
12 Detach the coolant hoses from the throttle
body. Plug the lines to prevent coolant loss.
13 Unscrew the four mounting nuts **(see
illustration)** and remove the throttle body and
gasket. Remove all traces of old gasket
material from the throttle body and air inlet
plenum.

Refitting

14 Refitting is the reverse of removal. Be sure
to use a new gasket. Adjust the accelerator
cable (see Section 10) and, if applicable, the
Throttle Valve (TV) cable (see Chapter 7B).
Check the coolant level and add some, if
necessary (see Chapter 1).

14 Fuel pressure regulator (fuel injection models) - check and renewal

Note: *Refer to the warning note in Section 1
before proceeding.*

Check

1 Relieve the fuel system pressure (see
Section 2) and fit a fuel pressure gauge (see
Section 3). Check for leakage around the
gauge connections when the engine is
started.
2 Follow the vacuum hose from the fuel
pressure regulator to the inlet manifold.

14.3b . . . next, apply vacuum and check
the fuel pressure - the fuel pressure should
fall, then rise, as the vacuum is released

Disconnect the hose from the manifold and fit
a vacuum gauge to the port **(see illustration)**.
Start the engine and make sure vacuum is
present. If the gauge doesn't indicate
vacuum, check the port for an obstruction.
Remove the vacuum gauge and reconnect the
hose.
3 Detach the vacuum hose from the fuel
pressure regulator and connect a hand-held
vacuum pump to the regulator. Start the
engine and read the fuel pressure gauge with
vacuum applied to the pressure regulator and
also with no vacuum applied **(see
illustrations)**. The fuel pressure should
decrease as vacuum increases. Compare
your readings with the values listed in this
Chapter's Specifications.
4 Reconnect the vacuum hose to the
regulator and check the fuel pressure at idle,
comparing your reading with the value listed
in this Chapter's Specifications. Disconnect
the vacuum hose and watch the gauge - the
pressure should jump up to the maximum
specified pressure as soon as the hose is
disconnected. If the pressure doesn't
fluctuate, renew the fuel pressure regulator.
5 If the fuel pressure is low, pinch the fuel
return line shut and watch the gauge **(see
illustration)**. If the pressure doesn't rise, the
fuel pump is defective or there is a restriction
in the fuel feed line. If the pressure rises
sharply, renew the pressure regulator.
6 If the indicated fuel pressure is too high,
stop the engine and relieve the fuel pressure
(see Section 2). Disconnect the fuel return line

14.2 Check for vacuum
at the fuel pressure regulator
vacuum port

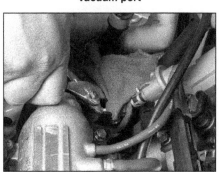

14.5 If the fuel pressure is low, test the
pressure regulator by pinching the fuel
return line as shown

and blow through it to check for a blockage. If
there is no blockage, renew the fuel pressure
regulator.

Renewal

7 Relieve the system fuel pressure (see
Section 2).
8 Detach the cable from the negative battery
terminal. *Caution: If the stereo in your car is
equipped with an anti-theft system, make
sure you have the correct activation code
before disconnecting the battery.*
9 Detach the vacuum hose and fuel hose
from the pressure regulator, then unscrew the
mounting bolts **(see illustration)**.
10 Remove the pressure regulator.
11 Refitting is the reverse of removal. Be sure
to use a new O-ring. Lubricate the O-ring with
a light coat of clean engine oil before refitting.
12 Check for fuel leaks after refitting the
pressure regulator.

15 Fuel injectors - check, removal and refitting

Note: *Refer to the warning note in Section 1
before proceeding.*

Check

1 Start the engine and warm it to its normal
operating temperature.
2 With the engine idling, place an auto
stethoscope against each injector, one at a

14.3a Refit a vacuum pump to the fuel
pressure regulator and check for fuel
pressure without vacuum applied . . .

14.9 Remove the fuel pressure regulator
bolts (arrowed)

15.2 Use a stethoscope or screwdriver to determine if the injectors are working

15.5 Using a special LED test light to confirm injector operation

15.3 Disconnect fuel injector connector and measure resistance of each injector

15.8 Use a small screwdriver to remove the bail from the injector electrical connector

Removal

6 Detach the cable from the negative battery terminal. *Caution: If the stereo in your car is equipped with an anti-theft system, make sure you have the correct activation code before disconnecting the battery.*

7 Relieve the fuel pressure (see Section 2).

Multi-point

8 Unplug the injector connectors **(see illustration)**.

9 Detach the vacuum and fuel return hoses from the fuel pressure regulator (Section 14).

10 Detach any earth cables from the fuel rail.

11 Detach the fuel feed line from the fuel rail.

12 Remove the mounting nuts **(see illustration)** and detach the fuel rail from the injectors.

13 Remove the injector(s) from the bore(s) in the inlet manifold and remove and discard the O-ring, cushion ring and seal ring **(see illustration)**. **Note**: *Whether you're replacing an injector or a leaking O-ring, it's a good idea to remove all the injectors from the fuel rail and renew all the O-rings, seal rings and cushion rings.*

Dual-point

14 Remove the air inlet chamber and disconnect the connector from the injector.

15 Place a cloth rag around the throttle housing, then unscrew the mounting screws, remove the plate and pull out the injector **(see illustration)**.

Refitting

Multi-point

16 Coat the new cushion rings with clean engine oil and slide onto the injectors.

15 Coat the new O-rings with clean engine oil and fit them on the injector(s), then insert each injector into its corresponding bore in the fuel rail.

16 Coat the new seal rings with clean engine oil and press them into the injector bore(s) in the inlet manifold.

17 Fit the injector and fuel rail assembly on the inlet manifold. Tighten the fuel rail mounting nuts to the torque listed in this Chapter's Specifications.

18 The remainder of refitting is the reverse of removal.

time, and listen for a clicking sound, indicating operation **(see illustration)**. If you don't have a stethoscope, place the tip of a screwdriver against the injector and listen through the handle. On multi-point versions, unplug each injector one-at-a-time, note the change in idle speed then reconnect the injector. If the idle speed drop is almost the same for each cylinder, the injectors are operating correctly. If unplugging a particular injector fails to change the idle speed, proceed to the next step. **Note**: *It is necessary to remove the nuts from the wiring harness straps and lift up on the harness rail to make clearance for removal of the connectors from the injectors.*

3 Turn the engine off. Remove the connector from the injector, and measure the resistance between the two terminals of the injector **(see illustration)**.

4 The resistance should be as given in the Specifications. If not, renew the fuel injector.

5 If the resistance is as specified, connect the positive lead of a voltmeter to the injector harness connector positive terminal (yellow/black wire) and the negative lead to a good body earth; or use a special injector harness test light (available at some motor factors) connected to the harness electrical connector **(see illustration)**.

a) *If the battery voltage is present with the ignition On (or if the light flashes when the starter is activated), the injector is receiving proper voltage.*

b) *If there is no voltage, check the wiring harness for damage.*

c) *If the wiring harness is not damaged or shorted, check the wiring between the PGM-FI main relay and the injector(s) for an open or short circuit or a bad connection.*

15.12 Remove the fuel rail mounting nuts (multi-point)

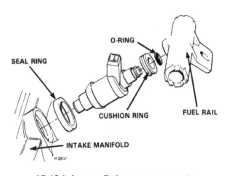

15.13 Injector fitting components (multi-point)

O-RING

SEAL RING

CUSHION RING

FUEL RAIL

INTAKE MANIFOLD

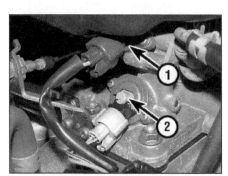

15.15 Primary injector (1) and auxiliary injector (2) (dual-point)

19 After the injector/fuel rail assembly refitting is complete, turn the ignition switch to ON, but don't operate the starter (this activates the fuel pump for about two seconds, which builds up fuel pressure in the fuel lines and the fuel rail). Repeat this about two or three times, then check the fuel lines, rail and injectors for fuel leakage.

Dual-point

20 Coat the new O-ring with clean engine oil and fit it to the injector, then insert it into the throttle housing. Make sure the O-ring is correctly seated by turning the injector slightly either way.
21 Refit the plate and tighten the mounting screws.
22 Reconnect the connector and refit the air inlet chamber.
23 After fitting the injector, turn the ignition switch to ON, but don't operate the starter (this activates the fuel pump for about two seconds, which builds up fuel pressure in the fuel lines and the fuel rail). Repeat this about two or three times, then check the fuel lines, rail and injector for fuel leakage.

16 Idle Air Control (IAC) system - check and component renewal

1 The idle speed is controlled by the IAC valve. This valve changes the amount of air that will bypass into the inlet manifold. The IAC valve is activated by the ECM depending upon the running conditions of the engine (air conditioning system, power steering, cold and warm running etc.). A malfunction in the IAC system will normally set a Code 14 in the self-diagnosis system (see Chapter 6).

Check

2 Apply the handbrake, block the wheels and place the transmission in Neutral (manual) or Park (automatic). Connect a tachometer to the engine according to the manufacturer's instructions. Start the engine and hold the accelerator steady at 3,000 rpm until the coolant fan comes on. Return the engine to idle and disconnect the electrical connector to the IAC valve.

> ⚠ **Warning: Keep hands, loose clothing, etc. away from any moving engine parts while working on a running engine or personal injury may result.**

3 There should be a noticeable reduction in idle speed with the IAC valve disconnected. If there is not the IAC valve is probably defective. If there was a drop in idle with the IAC valve disconnected and an intermittent idle problem still persists, check the wiring harness from the IAC valve to the ECM for poor connections or damaged wires.
4 If a code 14 was indicated by the self-diagnosis system, disconnect the electrical connector from the IAC valve, turn the ignition key ON (engine not running) and measure the voltage between the positive yellow/black terminal of the wiring harness connector and body earth **(see illustration)**. There should be battery voltage. If no voltage is present, check for an open circuit in the yellow/black wire from the IAC valve to the PGM-FI main relay.
5 Using an ohmmeter, measure the resistance of the IAC valve **(see illustration)**. It should be between 8 and 15 ohms. Check for continuity between each terminal of the IAC valve and earth. There should be no continuity. If there is, renew the IAC valve.
6 If the voltage and resistance readings are correct, have the ECM and electrical circuit for the IAC valve diagnosed by a dealer service department or other qualified garage.

Renewal

7 Disconnect the electrical connector from the IAC valve.
8 Remove the two mounting screws from the valve and lift it from the air inlet plenum **(see illustration)**.
9 Refitting is the reverse of removal. Be sure to fit a new O-ring.

17 Carburettor - float level adjustment

1 Position the car on level ground then run the engine to normal operating temperature.
2 Run the engine to 3000 rpm several times then let the engine idle.

3 Where necessary remove the air cleaner for access to the sight glass on the side of the carburettor.
4 Allow the fuel level to stabilise then check that it is between the upper and lower marks in the sight glass. Leave the engine idling while making the check.
5 If adjustment is required, turn the adjustment screw near the fuel inlet on the top of the carburettor cover. Allow the level to stabilise before checking it and only turn the screw 1/8th of a turn every 15 seconds.
6 Fit the air cleaner.

18 Carburettor - removal and refitting

Note: *Refer to the warning note in Section 1 before proceeding.*

Removal

1 Disconnect the battery negative terminal.
2 Unscrew the wing nut and remove the cover from the top of the air cleaner. Lift out the air filter element.
3 Disconnect the air inlet duct and hot air hose from the air cleaner body.
4 Unscrew the nuts and remove the filter gauze from the centre of the body.
5 Unscrew the mounting bolt(s) and remove the air cleaner body from the top of the carburettor.
6 Loosen the nuts and release the accelerator cable from the bracket on the carburettor.
7 Disconnect the accelerator inner cable from the cam on the carburettor.
8 Disconnect the automatic choke wiring plug and the cut-off valve solenoid wiring.
9 Identify all fuel and vacuum hoses for position then disconnect them from the carburettor.
10 Unscrew the four main nuts securing the carburettor to the inlet manifold and carefully lift the carburettor off the mounting studs. Recover the insulating block, rubber ring and gasket.
11 Plug the inlet manifold ports with clean rag to prevent the possible entry of foreign matter.

16.4 Remove the electrical connector from the IAC valve and check for battery voltage

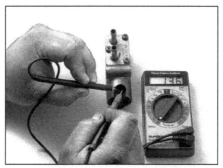

16.5 Check the IAC valve resistance using an ohmmeter

16.8 Remove the screws from the IAC valve

Refitting

12 Refitting is the reverse of the removal procedure, noting the following points.

a) *Ensure that the carburettor and inlet manifold sealing faces are clean. Fit a new gasket and rubber ring as necessary.*

b) *Fit and adjust the accelerator cable with reference to Section 10.*

c) *Check and, if necessary, adjust the idle speed and mixture setting (Chapter 1).*

19 Carburettor - cleaning

Note: *Refer to the warning note in Section 1 before proceeding.*

1 First remove the air cleaner (Section 18).

2 Extract the clip, remove the washer and disconnect the accelerator pump lever from the cover.

3 Identify all hose connections to the cover, then disconnect them.

4 Unscrew and remove the cover-to-main body screws, noting the location of the special screw for the air cleaner.

5 Carefully lift the cover from the main body and remove the gasket. Take care not to damage the float assembly attached to the bottom of the cover.

6 Check the float chamber for signs of sediment and water. Mop up the fuel and wipe clean the interior of the float chamber.

7 Unscrew the jets and power valve one at a time, clean them and fit them in their correct positions.

8 Reassemble the carburettor using a reversal of the dismantling procedure.

20 Fuel pump (carburettor models) - testing, removal and refitting

Note: *Refer to the warning note in Section 1 before proceeding.*

Testing

1 To test the fuel pump on the engine, disconnect the outlet pipe (which leads to the carburettor) from the fuel pump. Hold a wad of rag by the pump outlet while an assistant spins the engine on the starter. *Keep your hands away from the electric cooling fan.* Regular spurts of fuel should be ejected as the engine turns. Be careful not to spill fuel onto hot engine components.

2 The pump can also be tested by removing it. With the pump outlet pipe disconnected but the inlet pipe still connected, hold the wad of rag by the outlet. Operate the pump lever by hand, moving it in and out; if the pump is in a satisfactory condition, the lever should move and return smoothly, and a strong jet of fuel should be ejected.

21.1 Check for any broken or missing rubber mountings

Removal

3 Identify the pump inlet and outlet hoses, and slacken both retaining clips. Place wads of rag beneath the hose unions to catch any fuel, then disconnect both hoses from the pump; plug the hose ends to reduce fuel loss.

4 Progressively unscrew the pump mounting nuts and remove the washers, then remove the pump from the mounting studs. Remove the insulating block.

Refitting

5 Ensure that the pump and cylinder head mating surfaces are clean and dry, then offer up the insulating block and fit the pump to the studs on the cylinder head.

6 Fit the mounting nuts and washers and tighten securely.

7 Fit the hoses and tighten the clips.

21 Exhaust system servicing - general information

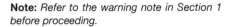 **Warning: Inspection and repair of exhaust system components should be done only after enough time has elapsed after driving the car to allow the system components to cool down completely. Also, when working under the car, make sure it is securely supported on axle stands.**

1 The exhaust system consists of the exhaust manifold(s), the catalytic converter, the silencer, the tailpipe and all connecting pipes, brackets, mountings and clamps. The exhaust system is attached to the body with mounting brackets and rubber mountings **(see illustration)**. If any of the parts are improperly fitted, excessive noise and vibration will be transmitted to the body.

Silencer and pipes

2 Conduct regular inspections of the exhaust system to keep it safe and quiet. Look for any damaged or bent parts, open seams, holes, loose connections, excessive corrosion or other defects which could allow exhaust fumes to enter the car. Also check the

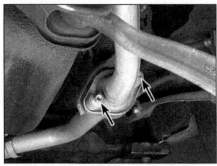

21.7 Remove the bolts (arrowed) from the exhaust pipe flange

catalytic converter when you inspect the exhaust system (see below).

3 If the exhaust system components are extremely corroded or rusted together, welding equipment will probably be required to remove them. The convenient way to accomplish this is to have an exhaust specialist remove the corroded sections. If, however, you want to save money by doing it yourself, simply cut off the old components with a hacksaw.

4 Here are some simple guidelines to follow when repairing the exhaust system:

a) *Work from the back to the front when removing exhaust system components.*

b) *Apply penetrating oil to the exhaust system component mountings to make them easier to remove.*

c) *Use new gaskets, mounting rubbers and clamps when refitting exhaust systems components.*

d) *Apply anti-seize compound to the threads of all exhaust system mountings during reassembly.*

e) *Be sure to allow sufficient clearance between newly fitted parts and all points on the underbody to avoid overheating the floor pan and possibly damaging the interior carpet and insulation. Pay particularly close attention to the catalytic converter and heat shield.*

Catalytic converter

Note: *See Chapter 6 for more information on the catalytic converter.*

 Warning: The converter gets very hot during operation. Make sure it's cooled down before you touch it.

5 Periodically, inspect the heat shield for cracks, dents and loose or missing fasteners.

6 Remove the heat shield and inspect the converter for cracks or other damage.

7 If the converter must be replaced, remove the mounting nuts from the flanges at each end **(see illustration)**, detach the rubber mounts and separate the converter from the exhaust system (you should be able to push the exhaust pipes at each end out of the way to clear the converter studs).

8 Refitting is the reverse of removal. Be sure to use new gaskets.

Chapter 5
Engine electrical systems

Contents

Degrees of difficulty

Easy, suitable for novice with little experience		Fairly easy, suitable for beginner with some experience		Fairly difficult, suitable for competent DIY mechanic		Difficult, suitable for experienced DIY mechanic		Very difficult, suitable for expert DIY or professional	

Specifications

Ignition system

Coil	
Primary resistance	
D13B2	0.5 to 0.7 ohms
D15B2, D15B7, D15Z1 and D16Z6	0.6 to 0.7 ohms
Secondary resistance	
D13B2	14.4 to 21.6 ohms
D15B2, D15B7, D15Z1 and D16Z6	13.2 to 19.8 ohms
Ignition Control Module resistance	1.1 to 3.3 K-ohms
Alternator brush length (minimum)	
Nippondenso	1.5 mm
Mitsubishi	5.0 mm

Ignition timing

D13B2	20° ± 2° BTDC (Red) at idle speed
Except D13B2	16° ± 2° BTDC (Red) at idle speed

1 General information

General information

The engine electrical system consists mainly of the charging and starting systems. Because of their engine-related functions, these components are covered separately from the body electrical devices such as the lights, instruments, etc (which are covered in Chapter 12).

The electrical system is of the 12-volt negative earth type.

The battery is of the low maintenance or "maintenance-free" (sealed for life) type and is charged by the alternator, which is belt-driven from the crankshaft pulley.

The starter motor is of the pre-engaged type incorporating an integral solenoid. On starting, the solenoid moves the drive pinion into engagement with the flywheel ring gear before the starter motor is energised. Once the engine has started, a one-way clutch prevents the motor armature being driven by the engine until the pinion disengages from the flywheel.

Precautions

Further details of the various systems are given in the relevant Sections of this Chapter. While some repair procedures are given, the usual course of action is to renew the component concerned. The owner whose interest extends beyond mere component renewal should obtain a copy of the *"Automobile Electrical & Electronic Systems Manual"*, available from the publishers of this manual.

It is necessary to take extra care when working on the electrical system to avoid damage to semi-conductor devices (diodes and transistors), and to avoid the risk of personal injury. In addition to the precautions given in *"Safety first!"* at the beginning of this manual, observe the following when working on the system:

Always remove rings, watches, etc before working on the electrical system. Even with the battery disconnected, capacitive discharge could occur if a component's live terminal is earthed through a metal object.

This could cause a shock or nasty burn.

Do not reverse the battery connections. Components such as the alternator, electronic control units, or any other components having semi-conductor circuitry could be irreparably damaged.

If the engine is being started using jump leads and a slave battery, connect the batteries *positive-to-positive and negative-to-negative* (see "*Booster battery (jump) starting*"). This also applies when connecting a battery charger.

Never disconnect the battery terminals, the alternator, any electrical wiring or any test instruments when the engine is running.

Do not allow the engine to turn the alternator when the alternator is not connected.

Never "test" for alternator output by "flashing" the output lead to earth.

Never use an ohmmeter of the type incorporating a hand-cranked generator for circuit or continuity testing.

Always ensure that the battery negative lead is disconnected when working on the electrical system.

Before using electric-arc welding equipment on the car, disconnect the battery, alternator and components such as the fuel injection/ignition electronic control unit to protect them from the risk of damage.

The radio/cassette unit fitted as standard equipment by Honda is equipped with a built-in security code to deter thieves. If the power source to the unit is cut, the anti-theft system will activate. Even if the power source is immediately reconnected, the radio/cassette unit will not function until the correct security code has been entered. Therefore, if you do not know the correct security code for the radio/cassette unit do not disconnect the battery negative terminal of the battery or remove the radio/cassette unit from the car. Refer to "Radio/cassette unit anti-theft system precaution" Section at the beginning of this manual for further information.

2 Battery - testing and charging

Standard and low maintenance battery - testing

1 If the car covers a small annual mileage, it is worthwhile checking the specific gravity of the electrolyte every three months to determine the state of charge of the battery. Use a hydrometer to make the check and compare the results with the following table. The temperatures quoted in the table are ambient (air) temperatures. Note that the specific gravity readings assume an electrolyte temperature of 15°C (60°F); for every 10°C (50°F) below 15°C (60°F) subtract 0.007. For every 10°C (50°F) above 15°C (60°F) add 0.007.

	Above 25°C(77°F)	Below 25°C(77°F)
Fully-charged	*1.210 to 1.230*	*1.270 to 1.290*
70% charged	*1.170 to 1.190*	*1.230 to 1.250*
Discharged	*1.050 to 1.070*	*1.110 to 1.130*

2 If the battery condition is suspect, first check the specific gravity of electrolyte in each cell. A variation of 0.040 or more between any cells indicates loss of electrolyte or deterioration of the internal plates.

3 If the specific gravity variation is 0.040 or more, the battery should be renewed. If the cell variation is satisfactory but the battery is discharged, it should be charged as described later in this Section.

Maintenance-free battery - testing

4 In cases where a "sealed for life" maintenance-free battery is fitted, topping-up and testing of the electrolyte in each cell is not possible. The condition of the battery can therefore only be tested using a battery condition indicator or a voltmeter.

5 Certain models may be fitted with a "Delco" type maintenance-free battery, with a built-in charge condition indicator. The indicator is located in the top of the battery casing, and indicates the condition of the battery from its colour. If the indicator shows green, then the battery is in a good state of charge. If the indicator turns darker, eventually to black, then the battery requires charging, as described later in this Section. If the indicator shows clear/yellow, then the electrolyte level in the battery is too low to allow further use, and the battery should be renewed. **Do not** attempt to charge, load or jump start a battery when the indicator shows clear/yellow.

6 If testing the battery using a voltmeter, connect the voltmeter across the battery and compare the result with those given in the Specifications under "charge condition". The test is only accurate if the battery has not been subjected to any kind of charge for the previous six hours. If this is not the case, switch on the headlights for 30 seconds, then wait four to five minutes before testing the battery after switching off the headlights. All other electrical circuits must be switched off, so check that the doors and tailgate are fully shut when making the test.

7 If the voltage reading is less than 12.2 volts, then the battery is discharged, whilst a reading of 12.2 to 12.4 volts indicates a partially discharged condition.

8 If the battery is to be charged, remove it from the car (Section 4) and charge it as described later in this Section.

Standard and low maintenance battery - charging

Note: *The following is intended as a guide only. Always refer to the manufacturer's recommendations (often printed on a label attached to the battery) before charging a battery.*

9 Charge the battery at a rate of 3.5 to 4 amps and continue to charge the battery at this rate until no further rise in specific gravity is noted over a four hour period.

10 Alternatively, a trickle charger charging at the rate of 1.5 amps can safely be used overnight.

11 Specially rapid "boost" charges which are claimed to restore the power of the battery in 1 to 2 hours are not recommended, as they can cause serious damage to the battery plates through overheating.

12 While charging the battery, note that the temperature of the electrolyte should never exceed 37.8°C (100°F).

Maintenance-free battery - charging

Note: *The following is intended as a guide only. Always refer to the manufacturer's recommendations (often printed on a label attached to the battery) before charging a battery.*

13 This battery type takes considerably longer to fully recharge than the standard type, the time taken being dependent on the extent of discharge, but it can take anything up to three days.

14 A constant voltage type charger is required, to be set, when connected, to 13.9 to 14.9 volts with a charger current below 25 amps. Using this method, the battery should be usable within three hours, giving a voltage reading of 12.5 volts, but this is for a partially discharged battery and, as mentioned, full charging can take considerably longer.

15 If the battery is to be charged from a fully discharged state (condition reading less than 12.2 volts), have it recharged by an automotive electrician, as the charge rate is higher and constant supervision during charging is necessary.

3 Battery cables - check and renewal

1 Periodically inspect the entire length of each battery cable for damage, cracked or burned insulation and corrosion. Poor battery cable connections can cause starting problems and decreased engine performance.

2 Check the cable-to-terminal connections at the ends of the cables for cracks, loose wire strands and corrosion. The presence of white, fluffy deposits under the insulation at the cable terminal connection is a sign that the cable is corroded and should be replaced. Check the terminals for distortion, missing mounting bolts and corrosion.

3 When removing the cables, always disconnect the negative cable first and connect it up last or the battery may be shorted by the tool used to loosen the cable clamps. Even if only the positive cable is being replaced, be sure to disconnect the negative cable from the battery first (see

Chapter 1 for further information regarding battery cable removal). *Caution: If the radio in your car is equipped with an anti-theft system, make sure you have the correct activation code before disconnecting the battery.*

4 Disconnect the old cables from the battery, then trace each of them to their opposite ends and detach them from the starter solenoid and earth terminals. Note the routing of each cable to ensure correct refitting.

5 If you are renewing either or both of the old cables, take them with you when buying new cables. It is vitally important that you renew the cables with identical parts. Cables have characteristics that make them easy to identify: positive cables are usually red and larger in cross-section; earth cables are usually black and smaller in cross section.

6 Clean the threads of the solenoid or earth connection with a wire brush to remove rust and corrosion. Apply a light coat of battery terminal corrosion inhibitor, or petroleum jelly, to the threads to prevent future corrosion.

7 Attach the cable to the solenoid or earth connection and tighten the mounting nut/bolt securely.

8 Before connecting a new cable to the battery, make sure that it reaches the battery post without having to be stretched.

9 Connect the positive cable first, followed by the negative cable.

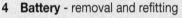

4 Battery - removal and refitting

Note: *On LHD models the battery is located on the right-hand side of the engine compartment, on RHD models it is on the left-hand side.*

Removal

1 Disconnect both cables from the battery terminals. *Caution: Always disconnect the negative cable first and connect it up last or the battery may be shorted by the tool being used to loosen the cable clamps. Caution: If the radio in your car is equipped with an anti-theft system, make sure you have the correct activation code before disconnecting the battery.*

4.2 Remove the two nuts (arrowed) and detach the hold-down clamps

4.3 If available, attach a battery strap and lift the battery straight up

2 Remove the battery hold-down clamp **(see Illustration)**.

3 Lift out the battery. Be careful - it's heavy. **Note:** *Battery straps and handlers* **(see illustration)** *may be available at motor factors. They make it easier to remove and carry the battery.*

4 While the battery is out, remove and inspect the tray for corrosion.

5 If corrosion has leaked down to the battery support, remove the bolts and lift the support out. Clean the deposits from the metal to prevent the support from further oxidation.

6 If you are renewing the battery, make sure you get one that's identical, with the same dimensions, amperage rating, cold cranking rating, etc.

Refitting

7 Refitting is the reverse of removal.

5 Ignition system - general information

 Warning: The transistorised electronic ignition systems used on the models covered by this manual generate considerably higher voltage than conventional systems. Be extra careful when servicing these ignition systems.

The Programmed Ignition (PGM-IG) system provides complete control of the ignition timing by determining the optimum timing using a micro computer in response to engine speed, coolant temperature, throttle position and vacuum pressure in the inlet manifold. These parameters are relayed to the ECM by the TDC/CKP/CYP Sensor, the Throttle Angle Sensor (TPS) on fuel injection models, Coolant Temperature Sensor and MAP Sensor. Ignition timing is altered during warm-up, idling and warm running conditions by the PGM-IG system. This electronic ignition system also consists of the ignition switch, battery, coil, distributor, HT leads and spark plugs.

All distributors are driven by the camshaft. Distributors are advanced and retarded by the Engine Control Module (ECM). All models

employ a crank angle sensor which is located inside the distributor; these distributors must be replaced as a single unit if they become defective. Refer to a dealer parts department or spare parts store for any questions concerning the availability of the distributor parts and assemblies. Testing the TDC/CKP/CYP sensors are covered in Chapter 6.

6 Ignition system - check

 *Warning: Because of the very high voltage generated by the ignition system, extreme care should be taken whenever an operation is performed involving ignition components. This not only includes the coil, ICM and HT leads, but related items connected to the system as well, such as the plug connections, tachometer and any test equipment.*

1 With the ignition switch turned to the "ON" position, confirm that the "Battery" and "Check Engine" lights are on as a basic check for ignition and battery supply to the ECM.

2 Check all ignition wiring connections for tightness, cuts, corrosion or any other signs of a bad connection.

3 Where available, use a calibrated ignition tester to verify that adequate secondary voltage is available to fire each spark plug **(see Illustration)**. A faulty or poor connection at that plug could also result in a misfire. Also, check for carbon deposits inside the spark plug boot.

4 Check for carbon tracking on the coil. If carbon tracking is evident, renew the coil and be sure the secondary wires related to that coil are clean and tight. Excessive wire resistance or faulty connections could cause damage to the coil.

5 Check the distributor cap and rotor for cracks, wear, damage or pitted terminals (see Chapter 1).

6 Using an ohmmeter, check the resistance of the HT leads. Renew any lead with a resistance of more than 25,000 ohms.

6.3 Using a calibrated ignition tester to check an HT lead and spark plug

7.6 Checking the resistance between the coil primary terminals.

7.7 Checking the resistance between coil positive terminal and the HT terminal

7.12 Lift the coil from the distributor

7 Using an ohmmeter, check the primary and secondary resistance of the ignition coil (see Section 7). If an open circuit is found (verified by an infinite reading), renew the coil.

8 Check the Ignition Control Module (ICM) for proper operation (see Section 8).

9 Additional checks should be performed by a dealer service department or garage.

---

7 Ignition coil - check and renewal

Check

1 Make sure the ignition switch is turned OFF for the following checks.

2 Detach the high tension lead from the secondary terminal (coil tower).

3 Remove the distributor cap, rotor and where necessary the cover.

Fuel injection engines

4 Remove the two screws that retain the black/yellow wire (terminal A (+) [round terminal connector] and the white/blue wire (terminal B (-) [square terminal connector]) from the distributor.

Carburettor engines

5 Disconnect the black/white and blue wires from the terminals A and B.

All engines

6 Using an ohmmeter, touch the probes to the primary terminals (A and B) of the coil, measure the primary resistance and compare your reading to the value listed in this Chapter's Specifications **(see illustration)**.

7 Touch the probes to the secondary winding terminal and the positive primary terminal (A) (round terminal connector) **(see illustration)**, measure the secondary resistance and compare your reading to the resistance value listed in this Chapter's Specifications.

8 The figures in the Specifications will vary somewhat with the temperature of the coil. The specified resistance values are for a coil temperature of about 21°C.

9 If the coil fails either check, renew it.

Renewal

10 Detach the cable from the negative terminal of the battery. *Caution: If the radio in your car is equipped with an anti-theft system, make sure you have the activation code before disconnecting the battery.*

11 Remove the distributor cap (Chapter 1) and leak cover (if applicable). Remove the screws and detach the wires from the primary terminals **(see illustration)**.

12 On fuel injection engines, remove the two screws and slide the coil out **(see illustration)**. On carburettor engines remove the rubber caps then unscrew the four screws and slide the coil out of the distributor.

13 Refitting is the reverse of removal.

---

8 Ignition Control Module (ICM) - check and renewal

Check

1 Remove the distributor cap and the ICM cover.

2 Disconnect the wires from the ICM unit.

3 With the ignition key turned ON (engine not running), check for voltage between the black/yellow wire (middle terminal of the ICM unit) and body earth **(see illustration)**. There should be battery voltage.

8.3 Check for battery voltage between the black/yellow wire and body earth

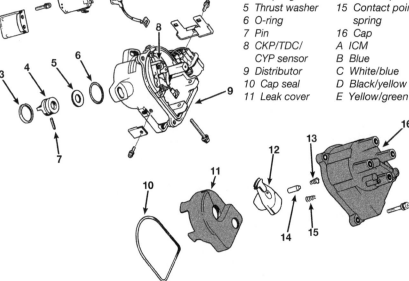

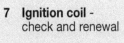
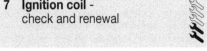

7.11 Exploded view of the distributor assembly (fuel injection models)

1 ICM	12 Rotor
2 Coil	13 Carbon point
3 Pin retainer	spring
4 Coupling	14 Carbon point
5 Thrust washer	15 Contact point
6 O-ring	spring
7 Pin	16 Cap
8 CKP/TDC/	A ICM
CYP sensor	B Blue
9 Distributor	C White/blue
10 Cap seal	D Black/yellow
11 Leak cover	E Yellow/green

8.5 Check for battery voltage on the white/blue wire and body earth

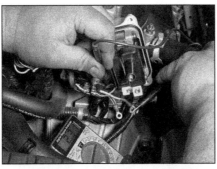

8.7 Check the resistance between the white/blue wire and the blue wire

8.12 Remove the ICM unit straight out from the distributor body

4 If there is no voltage, check the circuit between the black/yellow wire and the ignition switch.

5 With the ignition key turned ON (engine not running), check for voltage between the white/blue wire and body earth **(see illustration)**. There should be battery voltage.

6 If there is no voltage, check the circuit between the corresponding wire and the coil.

7 Check for continuity between the white/blue wire and the blue wire (from offset terminal) on the ICM. There should be between 1.1 to 3.3 K-ohms **(see illustration)**.

8 If the ICM fails either of the above checks, renew it. **Note:** *When refitting the ICM, pack silicone grease in the connector housing.*

Renewal

9 Disconnect the negative battery cable from the battery terminal. *Caution: If the radio in your car is equipped with an anti-theft system, make sure you have the activation code before disconnecting the battery.*

10 Remove the distributor cap and cover from the distributor (see Chapter 1).

11 Remove all the electrical connectors from the ICM unit.

12 Remove the two screws from the ICM body and pull the ICM unit out **(see illustration)**.

13 Refitting is the reverse of removal.

9 Distributor - removal and refitting

Removal

1 Detach the cable from the negative battery terminal. *Caution: If the radio in your car is equipped with an anti-theft system, make sure you have the correct activation code before disconnecting the battery.*

2 Detach any clamps and connectors on the distributor. Mark the wires and hoses so they can be returned to their original locations.

3 Look for a raised number or letter on the distributor cap. This marks the location for the number one cylinder spark plug HT lead terminal. If the cap does not have a mark for the number one terminal, locate the number one spark plug and trace the HT lead back to the terminal on the cap.

4 Remove the distributor cap (see Chapter 1) and turn the engine over until the rotor is pointing toward the number one spark plug HT lead terminal (see Chapter 2A, Section 3).

5 Make a mark on the edge of the distributor base directly below the rotor tip **(see illustration 3.10** in Chapter 2A) and in line with it (if the rotor on your engine has more than one tip, use the centre one for reference). Also, mark the distributor base and the cylinder head to ensure that the distributor is refitted correctly **(see illustration)**.

6 If not already done, unplug the ICM wires. On carburettor models disconnect the vacuum hose.

7 Remove the distributor hold-down bolt(s) and pull out the distributor. *Caution: Do not turn the crankshaft while the distributor is out of the engine, or the alignment marks will be useless.*

Refitting

Note: *If the crankshaft has been moved while the distributor is out, the number one piston must be repositioned at TDC. This can be done by feeling for compression pressure at the number one plug hole as the crankshaft is turned. Once compression is felt, align the ignition timing zero mark with the pointer.*

8 Fit a new O-ring on the distributor housing and smear a little engine oil on it.

9 Insert the distributor into the cylinder head in exactly the same relationship to the head that it was when removed. **Note:** *The lugs on the distributor and the grooves in the camshaft end are offset to eliminate incorrect refitting of the distributor.*

9.5 Make one mark directly underneath the rotor tip and another between the distributor base and the cylinder head

10 Recheck the alignment marks between the distributor base and the cylinder head to verify the distributor is in the same position it was in before removal. Also check the rotor to see if it's aligned with the mark you made on the distributor.

11 Loosely fit the hold-down bolt(s).

12 The remainder of refitting is the reverse of removal. Check the ignition timing and tighten the distributor hold-down bolt(s) securely.

10 Ignition timing - adjustment

1 Start the engine and allow it to reach normal operating temperature.

2 Several special tools may be needed in order to check the ignition timing - on some models an angled spanner will be required to loosen and tighten the distributor mounting bolt **(see illustration)**.

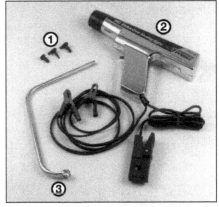

10.2 Tools needed to check and adjust the ignition timing

1 Vacuum plugs - *Vacuum hoses will, in most cases, have to be disconnected and plugged. Moulded plugs are available for this*
2 Inductive pick-up timing light - *Flashes a bright beam of light when the number one spark plug fires. Connect the leads according to the instructions supplied with the light*
3 Distributor spanner - *On some models, the distributor bolt for the distributor is difficult to reach with conventional spanners.*

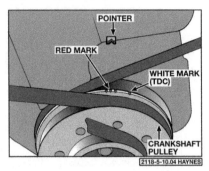

10.4 Be sure when viewing the timing mark on the pulley that you are directly above the pointer aiming the timing light down so as not to create an extreme angle

3 With the ignition off, connect an inductive pick-up timing light in accordance with the manufacturer's instructions. Connect the inductive pick-up lead of the timing light to the number one spark plug HT lead. On all models, number one is the one closest to the timing end of the engine.
4 Locate the timing marks on the front pulley **(see illustration).**

Fuel injection engines

5 Locate the service check connector **(see illustration)**, it is the white/green and brown, two-terminal electrical connector under the dash in the passenger's side corner. With the ignition off, connect the two terminals together with a jumper wire.

Carburettor engines

6 Disconnect the vacuum hose from the vacuum advance diaphragm unit on the distributor and plug it.

All engines

7 With the engine at normal operating temperature, start the engine and point the timing light at the timing pointer.
8 The appropriate mark on the flywheel (refer to this Chapter's Specifications) will appear stationary and be aligned with the pointer if the timing is correct.
9 If an adjustment is required, loosen the three adjusting bolts and rotate the distributor slightly until the timing is correct. Note that the distributor rotor rotates clockwise when viewed from the right-hand end of the engine,

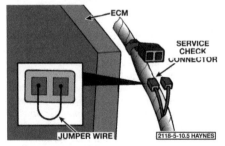

10.5 The service check connector on fuel injection models is located behind the kick-panel next to the ECM

so turning it anticlockwise will advance the ignition timing and turning it clockwise will retard the ignition timing.
10 Tighten the adjusting bolts and recheck the timing.
11 Turn off the engine and remove the timing light. On carburettor engines reconnect the vacuum hose to the vacuum advance diaphragm unit.
12 Renew inspection plug and remove the jumper wire from the service check connector.

11 Charging system - general information and precautions

The charging system includes the alternator, an internal voltage regulator, a charge indicator light, the battery, a fusible link and the wiring between all the components. The charging system supplies electrical power for the ignition system, the lights, the radio, etc. The alternator is driven by a drivebelt at the timing end of the engine.

The alternator control system changes the voltage generated in accordance with driving conditions. Depending upon electric load, car speed, engine coolant temperature, accessories (air conditioning system, radio, cruise control etc.) and the inlet air temperature, the system will adjust the amount of voltage generated, creating less load on the engine.

The purpose of the voltage regulator is to limit the alternator's voltage to a preset value. This prevents power surges, circuit overloads, etc., during peak voltage output.

The charging system doesn't ordinarily require periodic maintenance. However, the drivebelt, battery and wires and connections should be inspected at the intervals outlined in Chapter 1.

The dashboard warning light should come on when the ignition key is turned to On, but it should go off immediately after the engine is started. If it remains on, there is a malfunction in the charging system (see Section 11). Some cars are also equipped with a voltmeter. If the voltmeter indicates abnormally high or low voltage, check the charging system (see Section 11).

Be very careful when making electrical circuit connections to a car equipped with an alternator and note the following:

a) *When reconnecting wires to the alternator from the battery, be sure to note the polarity.*
b) *Before using arc welding equipment to repair any part of the car, disconnect the wires from the alternator and the battery terminals.*
c) *Never start the engine with a battery charger connected.*
d) *Always disconnect both battery leads before using a battery charger.*

e) *The alternator is turned by an engine drivebelt which could cause serious injury if your hands, hair or clothes become entangled in it with the engine running.*
f) *Because the alternator is connected directly to the battery, it could arc or cause a fire if overloaded or shorted out.*
g) *Wrap a plastic bag over the alternator and secure it with rubber bands before steam cleaning the engine.*

12 Charging system - check

1 If a malfunction occurs in the charging circuit, don't automatically assume that the alternator is causing the problem. First check the following items:

a) *Check the drivebelt tension and condition (see Chapter 1). Renew it if it's worn or deteriorated.*
b) *Make sure the alternator mounting and adjustment bolts are tight.*
c) *Inspect the alternator wiring harness and the connectors at the alternator and voltage regulator. They must be in good condition and tight.*
d) *Check the fusible link (if applicable) located between the starter solenoid and the alternator. If it's blown, determine the cause, repair the circuit and renew the link (the car won't start and/or the accessories won't work if the fusible link blows). Sometimes a fusible link may look good, but still be bad. If in doubt, remove it and check for continuity.*
e) *Start the engine and check the alternator for abnormal noises (a shrieking or squealing sound indicates a bad bearing)*
f) *Check the specific gravity of the battery electrolyte. if it's low, charge the battery (doesn't apply to maintenance-free batteries).*
g) *Make sure the battery is fully charged (one bad cell in a battery can cause overcharging by the alternator).*
h) *Disconnect the battery cables (negative first, then positive).*
i) *Inspect the battery posts and the cable clamps for corrosion. Clean them thoroughly if necessary (see Chapter 1). Reconnect the cable to the positive terminal.*
j) *With the key off, connect a test light between the negative battery post and the disconnected negative cable clamp.*
 1) *It the test light does not come on, reattach the clamp and proceed to the next step.*
 2) *If the test light comes on brightly (it will glow dimly because of normal draws from the ECM, radio and clock), there is a short (drain) in the electrical system of the car. The short must be repaired before the charging system can be checked. If*

12.1a Disconnect the 3-pin connector from the back of the alternator

12.1b Probe the black/yellow wire and check for battery voltage

12.1c Earth the white/blue wire and check that the charge warning light is ON

the light stays on bright, pull each fuse until the light dims (this will tell you which circuit is shorted).

k) Disconnect the alternator wiring harness from the backside of the alternator (see illustration). Turn the ignition key to ON (engine not running).

l) If the charging light goes out, fit the connector onto the alternator and proceed to paragraph 3.

m) Check the number 12 (15 amp) fuse (without SRS) or number 24 (15 amp) fuse (with SRS) in the dash fuse box (see Chapter 12). If it is blown, the charge warning light will remain ON even though the system is charging.

n) With the ignition key ON (engine not running), there should be battery voltage between the black/yellow wire and body earth (see illustration). If there is no voltage, check for an open in the circuit .

o) Now check the bulb itself. Turn the ignition key ON (engine not running) - the charge warning light should be ON. If it does not light, unplug the alternator connector and short the pin of the white/blue terminal to earth (see illustration). The light should come ON. If it does not come on, check for a bad bulb, an open circuit in the white/blue wire between the warning light and the dash fuse box an open circuit in the black/yellow wire between the warning light and the dash fuse box or an open circuit between the dash fuse box and the ignition switch. Note: Consult Chapter 6 and test the ELD (Electric Load Detector) for additional information concerning the charging system.

2 Using a voltmeter, check the battery voltage with the engine off. It should be approximately 12 volts.

3 Start the engine and check the battery voltage again. It should now be around 14 to 15 volts.

4 Turn on the headlights. The voltage should drop, and then come back up, if the charging system is working properly.

5 If the voltage reading is more than the specified charging voltage, renew the voltage regulator (see Section 14). If the voltage is

less, the alternator diode(s), stator or rectifier may be bad or the voltage regulator may be malfunctioning.

13 Alternator - removal and refitting

Removal

1 Detach the cable from the negative terminal of the battery. ***Caution: If the radio in your car is equipped with an anti-theft system, make sure you have the correct activation code before disconnecting the battery.***

2 Mark and detach the electrical connector and any earth straps from the alternator.

3 Loosen the alternator adjusting and pivot bolts, then detach the drivebelt **(see illustration)**.

4 Remove the adjusting and pivot bolts and separate the alternator from the engine. **Note:** *To remove the alternator from the engine bay, it will be necessary to remove the alternator bracket from the engine and lower the alternator through the bottom carefully angling the unit around the engine block.*

5 If you are replacing the alternator, take the old one with you when purchasing a renewal unit. Make sure the new/rebuilt unit looks identical to the old alternator. Look at the terminals - they should be the same in number, size and location as the terminals on the old alternator. Finally, look at the identification numbers - they will be stamped into the housing or printed on a tag attached to the

housing. Make sure the numbers are the same on both alternators.

6 Many new/rebuilt alternators DO NOT have a pulley fitted, so you may have to switch the pulley from the old unit to the new/rebuilt one.

Refitting

7 Refitting is the reverse of removal.

8 After the alternator is fitted, adjust the drivebelt tension (see Chapter 1).

9 Check the charging voltage to verify proper operation of the alternator (see Section 11).

14 Voltage regulator and alternator brushes - renewal

Note: *Don't attempt to overhaul the alternator. If renewal of the brushes and regulator does not solve the alternator problem, take the alternator to a dealer service department or other garage and have it overhauled.*

1 Remove the alternator (see Section 13) and place it on a clean workbench.

Nippondenso alternators

Brushes

2 Remove the three rear cover nuts, the nut and terminal insulator and the rear cover **(see Illustration)**.

3 Remove the two brush holder retaining screws **(see illustration)**.

4 Remove the brush holder from the rear end frame.

13.3 Loosen the adjustment bolt located at the bottom of the alternator

14.2 Remove the three nuts (arrowed) and detach the rear cover from the alternator

14.3 Remove the two screws (arrowed) that retain the brush holder

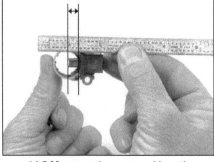

14.5 Measure the exposed length of the brushes

14.12 Remove the voltage regulator screws (arrowed) . . .

14.13 . . . and remove the regulator from the alternator assembly

14.16 Remove the through bolts (arrowed) from the alternator body

14.18 Remove the nut (arrowed) from the back of the alternator body

5 Measure the exposed length of the brush **(see illustration)** and compare it to the specified minimum length. If the length of the brush is less than specified, renew the brush.

6 Make sure that each brush moves smoothly in the brush holder.

7 Fit the brush holder by depressing the brush with a screwdriver to clear the shaft.

8 Fit the brush holder screws into the rear frame.

9 Fit the rear cover and tighten the three nuts.

10 Fit the terminal insulator and tighten it with the nut.

11 Fit the alternator (see Section 13).

Voltage regulator

12 Remove the three retaining screws from the rear end frame **(see illustration)**.

13 Lift the voltage regulator from the alternator assembly **(see illustration)**.

14 Refitting is the reverse of removal.

Mitsubishi alternators

15 Remove the alternator (see Section 13).

16 Remove the through-bolts from the alternator body **(see illustration)**.

17 Mount the front of the alternator face down in a vice. Using rags as a cushion, clamp the front case portion of the alternator in the jaws of the vice.

18 Remove all the nuts from the back of the alternator **(see illustration)**.

19 Insert two standard screwdrivers into the two halves of the alternator (not too deep or you will damage the stator) and prise the rear case off the alternator. *Caution: Prise gently or you will break the aluminium case.*

Note: *If necessary, use a heat gun to warm the case bearings from the outside of the alternator body. This will allow easier separation of the two halves (see illustration).*

20 Separate the rotor from the alternator body **(see illustration)**.

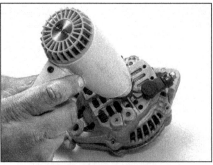

14.19 Use a heat gun to warm the bearing surface of the alternator

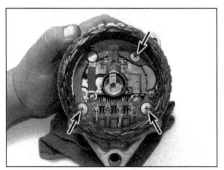

14.21 Regulator/brush assembly and rectifier retaining screws (arrowed)

21 Separate the stator, regulator/brush assembly and rectifier from the alternator body **(see illustration)**.

22 Unsolder the regulator/brush holder assembly **(see illustration)**. **Note:** *While applying heat to electrical components, it's a*

14.20 Separate the rotor assembly from the alternator body

14.22 To separate the brush holder, unsolder the two connectors (arrowed)

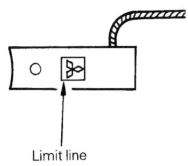

Limit line

14.23a If the brushes are worn past the wear limit line, they should be replaced

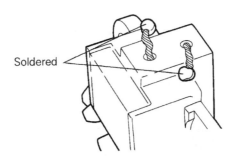

Soldered

14.23b If the brushes are being replaced, unsolder and solder the pigtails as shown

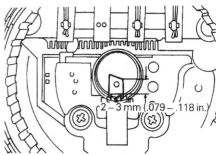

2 – 3 mm (.079 – .118 in.)

14.24 When fitting new brushes, they should extend out of the holder the correct amount

good idea to use a pair of needle nose pliers as a heat sink. Don't apply heat for more than about five seconds.

23 Measure the length of the brushes **(see illustration)** and compare it to the minimum length in this Chapter's Specifications. If the length of the brush is less than specified, renew the brush. Renew them, if necessary, by unsoldering the pigtails **(see illustration)**.

24 When refitting new brushes, solder the pigtails so the brush limit line will be about 0.079 to 0.118 inches above the end of the brush holder **(see illustration)**.

25 To reassemble, compress the brushes into their holder and retain them with a straight piece of wire that can be pulled from the back of the alternator when reassembled **(see illustration)**.

26 The remainder of refitting is the reverse of removal.

15 Starting system - general information and precautions

The sole function of the starting system is to turn over the engine quickly enough to allow it to start.

The starting system consists of the battery, the starter motor, the starter solenoid and the wires connecting them. The solenoid is mounted directly on the starter motor.

The solenoid/starter motor assembly is located on the upper part of the engine, next to the transmission bellhousing.

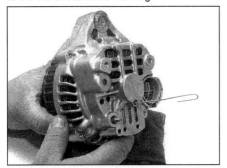

14.25 When reassembling the alternator, use a piece of wire inserted through the rear case and into the brush holder to retain the brushes in the holder

When the ignition key is turned to the Start position, the starter solenoid is actuated through the starter control circuit. The starter solenoid then connects the battery to the starter. The battery supplies the electrical energy to the starter motor, which does the actual work of cranking the engine.

The starter motor on some models equipped with manual transmission can only be operated when the clutch pedal is depressed; the starter on models equipped with automatic transmissions can only be operated when the selector lever is in Park or Neutral.

Always observe the following precautions when working on the starting system:

a) *Excessive cranking of the starter motor can overheat it and cause serious damage. Never operate the starter motor for more than 15 seconds at a time without pausing to allow it to cool for at least two minutes.*

b) *The starter is connected directly to the battery and could arc or cause a fire if mishandled, overloaded or shorted out.*

c) *Always detach the cable from the negative terminal of the battery before working on the starting system.*

16 Starter motor - in-car check

Note: *Before diagnosing starter problems, make sure the battery is fully charged.*

1 If the starter motor does not turn at all when the switch is operated, make sure the gearchange lever is in Neutral or Park (automatic transmission) or the clutch pedal is depressed where applicable (manual transmission).

2 Make sure the battery is charged and all cables, both at the battery and starter solenoid terminals, are clean and secure.

3 If the starter motor spins but the engine is not cranking, the overrunning clutch in the starter motor is slipping and the starter motor must be replaced. Also, the ring gear on the flywheel or driveplate may be worn.

4 If, when the switch is actuated, the starter motor does not operate at all but the solenoid

clicks, the problem lies with either the battery, the main solenoid contacts or the starter motor itself (or the engine is seized).

5 If the solenoid plunger cannot be heard when the switch is actuated, the battery is bad, the fusible link is burned (the circuit is open) or the solenoid itself is defective.

6 To check the solenoid, connect a jumper lead between the battery and the ignition switch wire terminal (the small terminal) on the solenoid. If the starter motor now operates, the solenoid is OK and the problem is in the ignition switch, neutral start switch or the wiring.

7 If the starter motor still does not operate, remove the starter/solenoid assembly for dismantling, testing and repair.

8 If the starter motor cranks the engine at an abnormally slow speed, first make sure that the battery is charged and that all terminal connections are tight. If the engine is partially seized, or has the wrong viscosity oil in it, it will crank slowly.

9 Run the engine until normal operating temperature is reached, then disconnect the coil wire from the distributor cap and earth it on the engine.

10 Connect a voltmeter positive lead to the positive battery post and connect the negative lead to the negative post.

11 Crank the engine and take the voltmeter readings as soon as a steady figure is indicated. Do not allow the starter motor to turn for more than 15 seconds at a time. A reading of nine volts or more, with the starter motor turning at normal cranking speed, is normal. If the reading is nine volts or more but the cranking speed is slow, the motor, solenoid contacts or circuit connections are faulty. If the reading is less than nine volts and the cranking speed is slow, the starter motor is probably bad.

17 Starter motor - removal and refitting

Removal

1 Detach the cable from the negative terminal of the battery. *Caution: If the radio in your*

17.2 Remove the bracket assembly that retains the wiring loom to the transmission

17.3 Leave removing the starter connector until after the unit has been removed

18.4a Remove the solenoid mounting bolts from the starter unit (Hitachi type shown)

car is equipped with an anti-theft system, make sure you have the correct activation code before disconnecting the battery.
2 Clearly label, then disconnect the wires from the terminals on the starter motor solenoid. Disconnect any clips securing the wiring to the starter **(see illustration)**.
3 Remove the mounting bolts **(see illustration)** and detach the starter.

Refitting

4 Refitting is the reverse of removal.

18 Starter solenoid -
 removal and refitting

Removal

1 Disconnect the cable from the negative terminal of the battery. *Caution: If the radio in your car is equipped with an anti-theft system, make sure you have the correct activation code before disconnecting the battery.*
2 Remove the starter motor (see Section 17).
3 Disconnect the large wire from the solenoid to the starter motor terminal.
4 Remove the screws which secure the solenoid to the starter motor gear housing and detach the solenoid from the gear housing. **(see illustrations).**

5 While the solenoid is removed, check the overrunning clutch by sliding it along its shaft. If it doesn't move freely, or if the clutch slips when you rotate the armature while holding the drive gear, renew the clutch assembly. If the gear is worn or damaged, renew the complete overrunning clutch assembly (the

gear isn't available separately). If the starter gear teeth are damaged, you should also inspect the flywheel or driveplate ring gear for damage.

Refitting

6 Refitting is the reverse of removal.

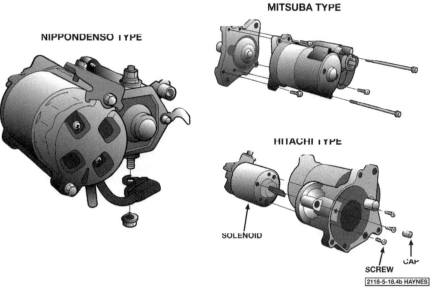

18.4b Various type starter/solenoid assembly details

Chapter 6
Emissions and engine control systems

Contents

Degrees of difficulty

| **Easy,** suitable for novice with little experience | | **Fairly easy,** suitable for beginner with some experience | | **Fairly difficult,** suitable for competent DIY mechanic | | **Difficult,** suitable for experienced DIY mechanic | | **Very difficult,** suitable for expert DIY or professional | |

Specifications

General

Oxygen sensor voltage
  Closed throttle deceleration . . . . Less than 0.4 volts
  Cruising (4,000 rpm) . . . . More than 0.6 volts
CKP circuit resistance . . . . 350 to 700 ohms
CYP circuit resistance . . . . 350 to 700 ohms
TDC circuit resistance . . . . 350 to 700 ohms
Inlet air temperature sensor resistance . . . . 1K to 4 k-ohms at room temperature

1 General information

To prevent pollution of the atmosphere from incompletely burned and evaporating gases, and to maintain good driveability and fuel economy, a number of emission control systems are incorporated. They include the:

Self diagnosis system
Electronic engine controls
(PGM-FI and PGM-CARB)
Electronic Load Detector (ELD)
Exhaust Gas Recirculation (EGR) system
Evaporative Emissions Control
(EVAP) system
Positive Crankcase Ventilation
(PCV) system
Catalytic converter

The Sections in this Chapter include general descriptions, checking procedures within the scope of the home mechanic and component renewal procedures (when possible) for each of the systems listed above.

Before assuming that an emissions control system is malfunctioning, check the fuel and ignition systems carefully. The diagnosis of some emission control devices requires specialised tools, equipment and training. If checking and servicing become too difficult or if a procedure is beyond your ability, consult a dealer service department or other garage. Remember, the most frequent cause of emissions problems is simply a loose or broken wire or vacuum hose, so always check the hose and wiring connections first.

This doesn't mean, however, that emissions control systems are particularly difficult to maintain and repair. You can quickly and easily perform many checks and do most of the regular maintenance at home with common tune-up and hand tools. **Note:** *Because of a warranty which covers the emissions control system components, check with your dealer about warranty coverage before working on any emissions-related systems. Once the warranty has expired, you may wish to perform some of the component checks and/or renewal procedures in this Chapter to save money.*

Pay close attention to any special precautions outlined in this Chapter. It should be noted that the illustrations of the various systems may not exactly match the system installed on your vehicle because of changes made by the manufacturer during production or from year-to-year.

In certain countries a Vehicle Emissions Control Information (VECI) label is attached to the underside of the bonnet **(see illustration)**. This label contains important emissions specifications and adjustment information. Part of this label, the Vacuum Hose Routing Diagram, provides a vacuum hose schematic with emissions components identified. When servicing the engine or emissions systems, the VECI label and the vacuum hose routing diagram in your particular vehicle should always be checked for up-to-date information.

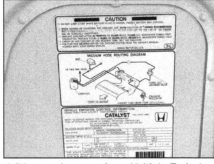

1.5 In certain countries a Vehicle Emission Control Information (VECI) label is located on the underside of the bonnet

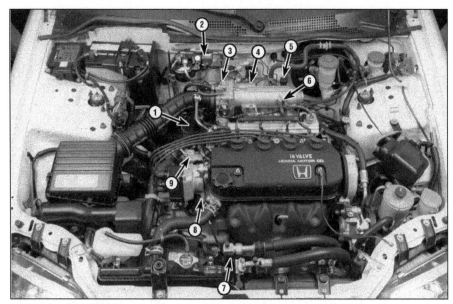

2.1 Typical PGM-FI emission and engine control components (LHD model shown)

1 Charcoal canister
2 MAP sensor
3 Throttle Position Sensor (TPS)
4 Intake Air Temperature (IAT) sensor
5 Purge Control Solenoid

6 Positive Crankcase Ventilation (PCV) valve
7 Oxygen sensor
8 Coolant temperature sensor
9 CYP, TDC, CKP sensor

2 Programmed Fuel Injection (PGM-FI) and carburettor (PGM-CARB) - general

The Programmed PGM-FI and PGM-CARB systems **(see illustration)** consist of three sub-systems: air inlet, electronic control and fuel delivery. The system uses an Engine Control Module (ECM) along with the sensors (coolant temperature sensor, Throttle Position Sensor, Manifold Absolute Pressure (MAP) sensor etc.) to determine the proper fuel/air ratio under all operating conditions.

The fuel injection or carburettor system and the emission control system are closely linked in function and design. For additional information, refer to Chapter 4.

The electronic control system consists of an eight-bit microprocessor (computer), output actuators and various sensors:

The distributor is driven off the end of the camshaft. The crank angle sensor (CRANK on PGM-FI), which is an integral part of the distributor assembly, determines the timing for the fuel injection and ignition and also detects the rpm of the engine (the PGM-CARB system uses an ignition coil signal). On the PGM-FI system the CYL sensor detects the position of the no. 1 cylinder as the base for sequential injection; the TDC sensor determines the injection timing for each cylinder. The TDC sensor also monitors engine speed to help determine the basic discharge duration for different operating conditions. **Note:** On later models the CRANK, CYL and TDC circuits are referred to as CKP, CYP and TDC circuits respectively.

The Manifold Absolute Pressure (MAP) sensor converts manifold pressure readings into electrical voltage signals and sends them to the ECM. This data, along with the data from the TDC and CYL sensors, enables the ECM to determine the correct fuel/air mixture.

The coolant temperature (TW) sensor uses a temperature-dependent resistor (thermistor) to measure differences in the coolant temperature. The resistance of the thermistor decreases with a rise in coolant temperature. The ECM uses this input to control the fuel/air mixture.

The Inlet Air Temperature (IAT or TA) sensor, which is located in the inlet manifold, is also a thermistor. In operation, it's similar to the coolant temperature sensor but has a lower thermal capacity for quicker response time.

A vehicle speed sensor detects pulses from the front wheels which in turn determines the actual speed the car is moving. This data is sent to the ECM for processing the correct air/fuel ratio delivered from the fuel injectors/carburettor and the air inlet system.

On the fuel injection system the Throttle Position Sensor (TPS) is a variable resistor. The sensor is mounted on the side of the throttle body and engages the throttle shaft. As the throttle valve is rotated, the resistance varies, altering the output voltage to the control unit, which in turn alters the fuel discharge duration.

The oxygen sensor monitors the oxygen content in the exhaust gas and sends a variable voltage signal to the ECM, which alters the fuel/air mixture.

When the ignition key is turned to Start, the ignition switch sends a signal to the ECM which increases the amount of fuel in accordance with the engine temperature. The amount of fuel is gradually reduced once the engine is started. Refer to Chapter 4 for additional information on the fuel injection and carburettor systems and diagnosing the components.

3 Self diagnosis system - description and diagnostic trouble codes

Note: The ECM is under the instrument panel, behind the carpet on the passenger side. The codes can be read by jumping the diagnostic connector and reading the CHECK engine light on the instrument panel.

1 To view self-diagnosis information from the ECM memory, fit a jumper wire into the diagnostic terminal **(see illustrations)** located in the left corner under the dash, then turn the ignition switch to the ON position. The codes are stored in the memory of the ECM and when accessed, they blink a sequence on the CHECK light on the instrument panel to relay a number or code that represents a system or component failure.

2 The CHECK light will blink a longer blink to represent the first digit of a two digit number

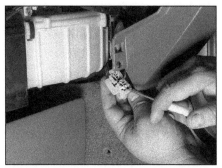

3.1a The diagnostic connector is under the glovebox behind the kick panel. Using a small screwdriver, remove the plastic cover from the electrical connectors

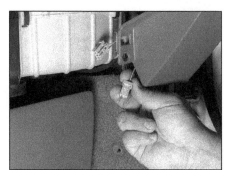

3.1b To activate diagnostic codes, remove the two-terminal electrical connector and bridge the terminals with a jumper wire or paper clip, then turn on the ignition

and then will blink short for the second digit (for example, 1 long blink then 6 short blinks for the code 16 [fuel injector]). **Note:** *If the system has more than one problem, the codes will be displayed in sequence then a pause and the codes will repeat.*

3 When the ECM sets a trouble code, the CHECK engine light will come on and a trouble code will be stored in the memory. The trouble code will stay in the ECM memory until the voltage to the ECM is interrupted. To clear the memory, remove the BACK-UP fuse **(see illustration)** from the relay box located in the left side of the engine compartment. **Note:** *Disconnecting the BACK-UP fuse also cancels the radio preset stations and the clock setting. Be sure to make a note of the various*

radio stations that are programmed into the memory before removing the fuse.

4 The table below is a list of the typical trouble codes which may be encountered while diagnosing the system. Also included are simplified troubleshooting procedures. If the problem persists after these checks have been made, more detailed service procedures will have to be done by a dealer service department or other garage. *Caution: To prevent damage to the ECM, the ignition switch must be off when disconnecting or connecting power to the ECM (this includes disconnecting and connecting the battery). If the stereo in your car is equipped with an anti-theft system, make sure you have the activation code before disconnecting the battery.*

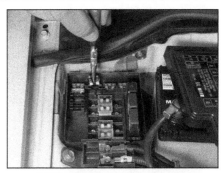

3.3 To clear the codes from the ECM memory, remove BACK-UP fuse (7.5 amp) from the fusebox (LHD shown)

Trouble code	Circuit or system	Corrective action
Code 0	Faulty ECM	Check the ECM electrical connector. If no loose connectors are found, have the ECM diagnosed by a dealer service department.
Code 1	Oxygen content	Check the oxygen sensor, heater and the oxygen sensor circuit (see Section 4).
Code 2	Vehicle speed pulser	Check the Vehicle speed pulser (see Section 4)
Codes 3 and 5	Manifold Absolute Pressure	Check the MAP sensor and circuit (see Section 4).
Code 4 (PGM-FI)	Crank angle sensor (CKP)	Check the crank angle sensor and circuit (see Section 4).
Code 4 (PGM-CARB)	Vacuum switch signal	See vehicle dealer service department or other garage.
Code 6	Coolant temperature	Check the coolant temperature sensor and circuit (Section 4).
Code 7	Throttle angle (TPS)	Check Throttle Position Sensor (TPS) and the circuit (Section 4).
Code 8 (PGM-FI)	TDC Position	Check the TDC sensor and the circuit (see Section 4).
Code 8 (PGM-CARB)	Ignition coil signal	See vehicle dealer service department or other garage.
Code 9 (PGM-FI)	No. 1 cylinder position (CYP)	Check the CYP sensor and the circuit (see Section 4).
Code 9 (PGM-CARB)	Electronic load detector (ELD)	Check the ELD system (see Section 8).
Code 10	Inlet Air Temperature (IAT) sensor	Check the TA sensor and the circuit (see Section 4).
Code 11	A/T lock-up control solenoid valve	Have the car checked at a dealer service garage.
Code 12	Exhaust Gas Recirculation	Check the hoses, the EGR valve lift sensor and the system EGR valve (see Section 6).
Code 13	Barometric Pressure	Have the car checked at a dealer service garage.
Code 14	Idle Air Control (IAC) valve	Check the IAC valve and system (see Chapter 4).
Code 15	Ignition output signal	Check the ignition system (see Chapter 5).
Code 16	Fuel injector	Check the fuel injection system and fuel injectors (Chapter 4).
Code 17	Vehicle speed sensor	Have the car checked at a dealer service department or other garage.
Code 19	Lock-up Control Solenoid	On automatic transmissions, check the solenoid (Chapter 7B).
Code 20	Electronic load detector (ELD)	Check the ELD system (see Section 8).
Code 21	Variable Valve Timing and Valve Lift Solenoid	See Chapter 2A VTEC Solenoid checks.
Code 22	Variable Valve Timing and control pressure switch	See Chapter 2A VTEC Pressure switch checks.
Code 30	A/T FI signal A (automatic transmission vehicles)	Have the car checked at a dealer service department or other garage.
Code 41	Oxygen sensor heater	Check the heater for the proper voltage signal (see Section 4).
Code 43	Fuel supply system	Check the fuel pressure, fuel pressure regulator (see Chapter 4) Also, check for any oxygen sensor vacuum leaks (Section 4).
Code 48	Heated Oxygen sensor	Check the heater for the proper voltage signal (D15Z1 engine, except Ca), (see Section 4).

---

4 Information sensors

Oxygen sensor

General description

1 The oxygen sensor, which is located in the exhaust manifold, monitors the oxygen content of the exhaust gas stream. The oxygen content in the exhaust reacts with the oxygen sensor to produce a voltage output which varies from 0.1-volt (high oxygen, lean mixture) to 0.9-volts (low oxygen, rich mixture). The ECM constantly monitors this variable voltage output to determine the ratio of oxygen to fuel in the mixture. The ECM alters the air/fuel mixture ratio by controlling the pulse width (open time) of the fuel injectors or by controlling the carburettor. A mixture ratio of 14.7 parts air to 1 part fuel is the ideal mixture ratio for minimising exhaust emissions, thus allowing the catalytic

converter to operate at maximum efficiency. It is this ratio of 14.7 to 1 which the ECM and the oxygen sensor attempt to maintain at all times.

2 The oxygen sensor produces no voltage when it is below its normal operating temperature of about 316°C. During this initial period before warm-up, the ECM operates in OPEN LOOP mode.

3 If the engine reaches normal operating temperature and/or has been running for two or more minutes, and if the oxygen sensor is

4.7 Fit a pin into the connector and backprobe the oxygen sensor electrical connector white wire (terminal B)

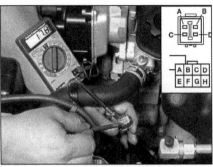

4.10 Measure the resistance of the oxygen sensor heater. Check terminals C and D, it should be 10 to 40 ohms

4.17 Remove the oxygen sensor from the exhaust manifold with a socket specially designed for this purpose

producing a steady signal voltage below 0.45-volts at 1,500 rpm or greater, the ECM will set a Code 1. The ECM will also set a code 41 or 48 if it detects any problem with the heater circuit.

4 When there is a problem with the oxygen sensor or its circuit, the ECM operates in the open loop mode - that is, it controls fuel delivery in accordance with a programmed default value instead of feedback information from the oxygen sensor.

5 The proper operation of the oxygen sensor depends on four conditions:

a) *Electrical - The low voltages generated by the sensor depend upon good, clean connections which should be checked whenever a malfunction of the sensor is suspected or indicated.*

b) *Outside air supply - The sensor is designed to allow air circulation to the internal portion of the sensor. Whenever the sensor is removed and installed or replaced, make sure the air passages are not restricted.*

c) *Proper operating temperature - The ECM will not react to the sensor signal until the sensor reaches approximately 316°C. This factor must be taken into consideration when evaluating the performance of the sensor.*

d) *Unleaded fuel - The use of unleaded fuel is essential for proper operation of the sensor. Make sure the fuel you are using is of this type.*

6 In addition to observing the above conditions, special care must be taken whenever the sensor is serviced.

a) *The oxygen sensor has a permanently attached pigtail and electrical connector which should not be removed from the sensor. Damage or removal of the pigtail or electrical connector can adversely affect operation of the sensor.*

b) *Grease, dirt and other contaminants should be kept away from the electrical connector and the louvered end of the sensor.*

c) *Do not use cleaning solvents of any kind on the oxygen sensor.*

d) *Do not drop or roughly handle the sensor.*

e) *The silicone boot must be installed in the correct position to prevent the boot from being melted and to allow the sensor to operate properly.*

Check

7 Locate the oxygen sensor electrical connector and insert a long pin into the oxygen sensor connector terminal B (signal voltage) (white wire) **(see illustration)**. Fit the positive probe of a voltmeter onto the pin and the negative probe to earth. **Note:** *Consult the wiring diagrams at the end of Chapter 12 for additional information on the oxygen sensor electrical connector wire colour designations.*

8 Monitor the voltage signal (millivolts) as the engine goes from cold to warm.

9 The oxygen sensor will produce a steady voltage signal at first (open loop) of approximately 0.1 to 0.2 volts with the engine cold. After a period of approximately two minutes, the engine will reach operating temperature and the oxygen sensor will start to fluctuate between 0.1 to 0.9 volts (closed loop). If the oxygen sensor fails to reach the closed loop mode or there is a very long period of time until it does switch into closed loop mode (lazy oxygen sensor), renew the oxygen sensor.

10 Also inspect the oxygen sensor heater. Disconnect the oxygen sensor electrical connector and connect an ohmmeter between the A and B terminals **(see illustration)**. It should measure across terminals:

   A to B 2 to 13 ohms
   C to D 10 to 40 ohms

11 Also on models equipped with the D15Z1 engine, check for continuity between terminal A and terminals C through H individually. There should be NO continuity. If there is, renew the oxygen sensor with a new part.

12 Check for proper supply voltage to the heater. Measure the voltage between the yellow/black wire (+) and the black wire (-) on the oxygen sensor electrical connector. There should be battery voltage with the ignition key ON (engine not running). If there is no voltage, check the circuit between the main relay, the ECM and the sensor.

13 If the oxygen sensor fails any of these tests, renew it.

Renewal

Note: *Because it is installed in the exhaust manifold or pipe, which contracts when cool, the oxygen sensor may be very difficult to loosen when the engine is cold. Rather than risk damage to the sensor (assuming you are planning to reuse it in another manifold or pipe), start and run the engine for a minute or two, then shut it off. Be careful not to burn yourself during the following procedure.*

14 Disconnect the cable from the negative terminal of the battery. **Caution: If the stereo in your car is equipped with an anti-theft system, make sure you have the correct activation code before disconnecting the battery.**

15 Raise the car and place it securely on axle stands (see "*Jacking and Vehicle Support*").

16 Carefully disconnect the electrical connector from the sensor.

17 Carefully unscrew the sensor from the exhaust manifold **(see illustration)**.

18 Anti-seize compound must be used on the threads of the sensor to facilitate future removal. The threads of new sensors will already be coated with this compound, but if an old sensor is removed and reinstalled, recoat the threads.

19 Refit the sensor and tighten it securely.

20 Reconnect the electrical connector of the pigtail lead to the main engine wiring harness.

21 Lower the car, take it on a test drive and check to see that no trouble codes set.

Manifold Absolute Pressure (MAP) sensor

General description

22 The Manifold Absolute Pressure (MAP) sensor monitors the inlet manifold pressure changes resulting from changes in engine load and speed and converts the information into a voltage output. The ECM uses the MAP sensor to control fuel delivery and ignition timing. The ECM will receive information as a voltage signal that will vary from 1.0 to 1.5 volts at closed throttle (high vacuum) and 4.0 to 4.5 volts at wide open throttle (low vacuum). The MAP sensor is located inside the control box which is attached to the bulkhead.

4.26 Using a voltmeter, check for reference voltage to MAP sensor (yellow/red (+) wire)

4.27 Fit a vacuum pump to the MAP sensor and check the signal voltage on white wire

4.28 Next, apply 10 in-Hg of vacuum and check for the MAP sensor voltage

23 A failure in the MAP sensor circuit should set a Code 3 or a Code 5.

Check

24 Check the vacuum hose from the throttle body to the MAP sensor for cracking and general deterioration. Renew it if necessary. The vacuum hose for the MAP sensor is attached to the inlet plenum (coded number 21).
25 Check the electrical connector at the sensor for a snug fit. Check the terminals in the connector and the wires leading to it for looseness and breaks. Repair as required.
26 Disconnect the MAP sensor connector, turn the ignition key ON (engine not running) and check for voltage on the reference wire (yellow/red wire (+) and earth) **(see illustration)**. There should be approximately 5 volts.
27 Check for voltage on the signal wire (white wire) and earth with the ignition key ON (engine not running). There should be approximately 5 volts. This checks signal voltage to the MAP sensor **(see illustration)**.
28 Apply vacuum to the MAP sensor vacuum hose and probe the signal wire (white wire) with the positive probe of the voltmeter **(see illustration)**. Voltage should decrease as vacuum increases. If the readings are incorrect, renew the MAP sensor with a new part.

Renewal

29 Disconnect the electrical connector and the vacuum hose from the MAP sensor.
30 Remove the bolts that retain the MAP sensor to the bulkhead and remove the MAP sensor.
31 Installation is the reverse of removal.

CKP/TDC and CYP sensors

General description

32 On these models, the crank angle sensor (CKP) determines the timing for the fuel injection and ignition on each cylinder. It also detects engine RPM. The TDC sensor determines the ignition timing at start-up (engine cranking) and the CYP sensor determines the position of the cylinder for sequential fuel injection to each cylinder on fuel injection models. All three sensors are built into the distributor. Diagnostics for all

three sensors are performed by checking for the diagnostic codes (codes 4, 8 and 9) and then checking for the proper resistance at the electrical connector.

Check

33 To check the CKP sensor, disconnect the electrical connector at the distributor and probe terminals B and F with an ohmmeter **(see illustration)**. Check the resistance listed in this Chapter's Specifications.
34 Check for continuity to earth on each terminal. Continuity should NOT exist. If the test results are incorrect, renew the distributor unit (see Chapter 5).
35 If the test results are all correct, have the system diagnosed by a dealer service department.
36 To check the TDC sensor, disconnect the ignition harness connector at the distributor and probe terminals C and G with an ohmmeter **(see illustration 4.33)**. Check the resistance listed in the Specifications.
37 Check for continuity to earth on each terminal. Continuity should NOT exist. If the test results are incorrect, renew the distributor unit (see Chapter 5).
38 If the test results are all correct, have the system diagnosed by a dealer service department.
39 To check the CYP sensor, disconnect the ignition harness connector at the distributor and probe terminals D and H with an ohmmeter **(see illustration 4.33)**. Check the resistance listed in the Specifications.
40 Check for continuity to earth on each terminal. Continuity should NOT exist. If the

test results are incorrect, renew the distributor unit (see Chapter 5).
41 If the test results are all correct, have the system tested by a dealer service department.

Coolant temperature sensor

General description

42 The coolant temperature sensor is a thermistor (a resistor which varies the value of its voltage output in accordance with temperature changes). The change in the resistance values will directly affect the voltage signal from the water thermosensor. As the sensor temperature DECREASES, the resistance values will INCREASE. As the sensor temperature INCREASES, the resistance values will DECREASE. A failure in this sensor circuit should set a Code 6. This code indicates a failure in the water thermosensor circuit, so in most cases the appropriate solution to the problem will be either repair of a wire or renewal of the sensor.

Check

43 To check the sensor, check the resistance value **(see illustration)** of the coolant temperature sensor while it is completely cold (10° to 27°C = 2,200 to 2,700 ohms). Next, start the engine and warm it up until it reaches operating temperature. The resistance should be lower (82° to 93°C = 280 to 350 ohms). **Note:** *Access to the coolant temperature sensor makes it difficult to position probes of the meter on the terminals. If necessary, remove the sensor and perform the tests in a pan of heated water to simulate the conditions.*

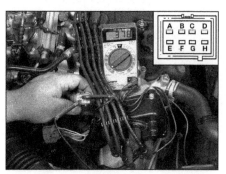

4.33 Check the CRANK sensor resistance by probing terminals B and F

4.43 Check the resistance of the coolant temperature sensor

4.44 Check for supply voltage to the coolant temperature sensor

4.50 Check for reference voltage to the TPS sensor on the yellow/white wire

4.51a Check the voltage from the signal wire (red/blue) and earth wire (green/white)

44 Check the supply voltage (red/white wire) with the ignition key ON (engine not running). It should be approximately 5.0 volts **(see illustration)**. If not, check for an open circuit in the red/white wire from the sensor to the ECM.

Renewal

 Warning: Wait until the engine has cooled completely before beginning this procedure.

45 Before refitting the new sensor, wrap the threads with Teflon sealing tape to prevent leakage and thread corrosion.
46 To remove the sensor, depress the locking tab, unplug the electrical connector, then carefully unscrew the sensor. Coolant will leak out when the sensor is removed, so fit the new sensor as quickly as possible. *Caution: Handle the coolant sensor with care. Damage to this sensor will affect the operation of the entire fuel injection system.*
47 Refitting is the reverse of removal.

Throttle Position (Angle) Sensor (TPS) - fuel injection system

General description

48 The Throttle Position Sensor (TPS) is on the end of the throttle shaft on the throttle body. By monitoring the output voltage from the TPS, the ECM can determine fuel delivery based on throttle valve angle (driver demand). A broken or loose TPS can cause intermittent bursts of fuel and an unstable idle because the ECM thinks the throttle is moving.

Check

49 Follow the wiring harness from the TPS to the back of the inlet manifold and remove it from the bulkhead. This will give you more room to probe the electrical terminals.
50 Using a voltmeter, check the reference voltage from the ECM. Fit the probes on the yellow/white wire **(see illustration)**. It should read approximately 5.0 volts.
51 Next, check the TPS signal voltage. With the engine Off, throttle fully closed and TPS electrical connector connected, fit the probes of the voltmeter onto the red/blue wire (positive probe) and earth (negative probe) **(see illustrations)**. Gradually open the throttle valve and observe the TPS sensor voltage. With the throttle valve fully closed, the voltage should read about 0.5 volts. Slowly move the throttle valve and observe a distinct change in the voltage values as the sensor travels from idle to full throttle. The voltage should increase smoothly to about 4.5 volts. If the readings are incorrect, renew the TPS sensor.
52 A problem in any of the TPS circuits will set a Code 7. Once a trouble code is set, the ECM will use an artificial default value for TPS and some vehicle performance will return.

Inlet Air Temperature (IAT) sensor

Check

53 With the ignition switch ON, disconnect the electrical connector from the IAT sensor, which is located on the inlet manifold. Using an ohmmeter, measure the resistance between the two terminals on the sensor. It should be between 1,000 and 4,000 ohms depending upon the temperature. Refer to the Specifications listed in this Chapter.

54 With the ignition key ON (engine not running), check for voltage at the electrical connector (red/yellow wire) to the sensor **(see illustration)**. It should be about 5.0 volts.
55 If the test results are incorrect, renew the IAT sensor.
56 If the sensor appears okay but there is still a problem, have the car checked at a dealer service department or other qualified garage, as the ECM may be malfunctioning.

Renewal

57 Unplug the electrical connector from the IAT sensor.
58 Remove the screws that retain the sensor to the inlet manifold and remove the IAT sensor.
59 Refitting is the reverse of removal.

Vehicle Speed Sensor

General description

60 The Vehicle Speed Sensor (VSS) is located on the transmission. This sensor is a permanent magnetic variable reluctance sensor that produces a pulsing voltage whenever vehicle speed is over 3 mph. These pulses are translated by the ECM and provided for other systems for fuel and transmission gearchange control.

Check

61 To check the vehicle speed sensor, remove the electrical connector in the wiring harness at the sensor. Using a voltmeter, check for voltage at the electrical connector (yellow/blue wire) to the sensor **(see illustration)**. The circuit should have battery available. If there is no voltage available,

4.51b Rotate the throttle valve until wide open and check the voltage signal

4.54 With the ignition ON (engine not running), check for voltage to IAT sensor

4.61 Checking for supply voltage on the vehicle speed sensor (VSS)

check for an open circuit between the VSS and the fuse box. Using an ohmmeter, check the black wire of the connector for continuity to earth.

62 Raise the front of the car and place it securely on axle stands (see "*Jacking and Vehicle Support*"). Block the rear wheels and place the transmission in Neutral. Connect the electrical connector to the VSS, turn the ignition to On and backprobe the VSS connector yellow/white wire with a voltmeter positive lead. Connect the negative lead of the meter to body earth. While holding one wheel steady, rotate the other wheel by hand. The voltmeter should pulse between zero and 5 volts. If it doesn't, renew the sensor.

Renewal

63 To renew the VSS, disconnect the electrical connector from the VSS.
64 Remove the retaining bolt and lift the VSS from the transmission.
65 Refitting is the reverse of removal.

Barometric (BARO) pressure sensor

General description

66 The barometric pressure sensor is incorporated into the ECM. In the event the self diagnosis system exhibits a code 13, have the system checked by a dealer service department or other qualified repair facility.

Lock-up Control Solenoid (automatic transmission only)

General description

67 The Lock-up Control Solenoid is a computer controlled output actuator that is used to activate the lock-up torque converter on vehicles equipped with the automatic transmission. Refer to Chapter 7B for the check and renewal procedures.

5 Positive Crankcase Ventilation (PCV) system

1 The Positive Crankcase Ventilation (PCV) system (see illustration) reduces hydrocarbon emissions by scavenging crankcase vapours. It does this by circulating fresh air from the air cleaner through the crankcase, where it mixes with blow-by gases and is then re-routed through a PCV valve to the inlet manifold.
2 The main components of the PCV system are the PCV valve, a blow-by filter and the vacuum hoses connecting these two components with the engine.
3 To maintain idle quality, the PCV valve restricts the flow when the inlet manifold vacuum is high. If abnormal operating conditions (such as piston ring problems) arise, the system is designed to allow excessive amounts of blow-by gases to flow back through the crankcase vent tube into the air cleaner to be consumed by normal combustion.

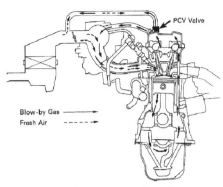

Blow-by Gas
Fresh Air

5.1 Gas flow in a typical PCV system

4 Checking and renewal of the PCV valve is covered in Chapter 1.

6 Exhaust Gas Recirculation (EGR) system

General description

1 The EGR system reduces oxides of nitrogen by recirculating exhaust gas through the EGR valve and inlet manifold into the combustion chambers.
2 The EGR system consists of the EGR valve, the CVC valve, the EGR control solenoid valve, the Electronic Control Module (ECM) and various sensors. The ECM memory is programmed to produce the ideal EGR valve lift for each operating condition. An EGR valve lift sensor detects the amount of EGR valve lift and sends this information to the ECM. The ECM then compares it with the ideal EGR valve lift, which is determined by data received from the other sensors. If there's any difference between the two, the ECM triggers the EGR control solenoid valve to reduce the amount of vacuum applied to the EGR valve.

Check

3 Start the engine and warm it to its normal operating temperature (wait for the electric cooling fan to come on).
4 Detach the number 16 vacuum hose from the EGR valve and attach a vacuum gauge to the hose (see illustration).

6.7 Apply vacuum to the EGR valve and observe that the valve diaphragm moves up and down freely without any binding

5 There should be NO vacuum. If there is no vacuum, proceed to paragraph 7.
6 If vacuum exists, disconnect the electrical connector from the control box (see illustration 6.9) and check for vacuum at the number 16 vacuum hose. If vacuum does not exist, have the ECM diagnosed by a dealer service department. If vacuum is present, check all the vacuum lines to make sure they are routed properly.
7 If there originally was no vacuum, fit a hand held vacuum pump to the EGR valve and apply 8 in-Hg of vacuum to the valve and observe that the engine stalls (see illustration). Also, does the EGR valve hold vacuum? If not, renew the EGR valve.
8 Check for battery voltage to the EGR Control Solenoid valve. Disconnect the two-pin connector from the control box (see illustration) and check for battery voltage at the black/yellow (+) terminal on the main harness. There should be battery voltage.
9 Reconnect the vacuum gauge to the number 16 hose, start the engine and allow it to idle. Connect the battery positive cable with a jumper wire to the A terminal on the two-pin connector (see illustration). While observing the vacuum gauge, earth terminal B with another jumper wire. Vacuum should increase within one second. If there is no vacuum, renew the EGR control solenoid.
10 Next, check the operation of the EGR valve lift sensor. Disconnect the three pin electrical connector from the top of the EGR valve (if applicable) and with the ignition key ON (engine not running), check for reference

6.4 Check for vacuum to the EGR valve on number 16 vacuum hose

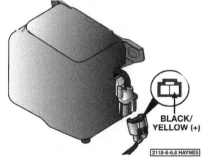

BLACK/
YELLOW (+)

2118-6-6.8 HAYNES

6.8 Check the battery voltage at the black/yellow (+) wire on the harness side of the connector

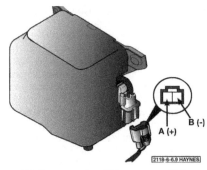

6.9 Vacuum should increase within 1 second after jumping terminal A (+) with battery voltage from the positive cable and terminal B (–) from the negative cable

6.13 Remove the two nuts (arrowed) from the base of the EGR valve

voltage on the yellow/white terminal (see illustration). There should be about 5.0 volts.
11 Further checking of the EGR control system requires special tools and equipment. Take the car to a dealer service department or other qualified garage for checking.

Component renewal

EGR valve

12 Unplug the electrical connector for the EGR valve lift sensor.
13 Remove the two nuts that secure the EGR valve and detach the EGR valve (see illustration).
14 Clean the mating surfaces of the EGR valve and adapter.
15 Fit the EGR valve, using a new gasket. Tighten the nuts securely.
16 Plug in the electrical connector.

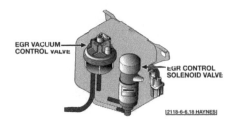

6.18 Details of the EGR control box and components

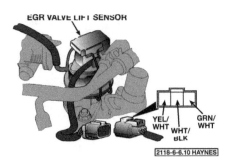

6.10 Check for battery voltage on the yellow/white wire located on the EGR valve position sensor

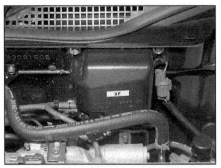

6.17 EGR control box location on the bulkhead

EGR control solenoid

17 Remove the control box located on the bulkhead and separate the cover from the main body (see illustration).
18 Locate the EGR control solenoid (see illustration) and remove the two mounting screws.
19 Lift the solenoid from the control box.
20 Refitting is the reverse of removal.

7 Evaporative emissions control (EVAP) system

General description

1 The fuel evaporative emissions control system absorbs fuel vapours and, during engine operation, releases them into the engine inlet where they mix with the incoming air-fuel mixture.
2 Every evaporative system employs a canister filled with activated charcoal to absorb fuel vapours. The means by which these vapours are controlled, however, varies considerably from one system to another. The following descriptions of a typical system for the models covered by this manual should provide you enough information to understand the system on your car. **Note:** *The following descriptions are not intended as a specific description of the evaporative system on your particular car. Rather, they are intended as a general description of a typical*

system used on fuel-injected vehicles. Although the following components are most likely all used on your particular system, there may also be other devices, not included here, which are unique to your system.
3 The fuel filler cap is fitted with a two-way valve as a safety device. The valve vents fuel vapours to the atmosphere if the evaporative control system fails.
4 Another fuel cut-off valve (two-way valve), mounted on the fuel tank, regulates fuel vapour flow from the fuel tank to the charcoal canister, based on the pressure or vacuum caused by temperature changes.
5 After passing through the two-way valve, fuel vapour is carried by vent hoses to the charcoal canister in the engine compartment. The activated charcoal in the canister absorbs and stores these vapours.
6 When the engine is running and warmed to a pre-set temperature, a purge cut-off solenoid valve near the canister closes, allowing a purge control diaphragm valve in the charcoal canister to be opened by inlet manifold vacuum. Fuel vapours from the canister are then drawn through the purge control diaphragm valve by inlet manifold vacuum.

Check

Note: *Complete checking of the evaporative emissions control system is beyond the scope of the average home mechanic. The EVAP system probably won't fail during the service life of the car; however, if it does, the hoses or charcoal canister are usually to blame.*
7 Always check the hoses first. A disconnected, damaged or missing hose is the most likely cause of a malfunctioning EVAP system. Repair any damaged hoses or renew any missing hoses as necessary.
8 Disconnect the vacuum hose from the purge control diaphragm valve (located on the charcoal canister) and connect a vacuum gauge to the hose (see illustration). Start the engine and allow it to idle. There should be NO vacuum present. **Note:** *The temperature of the engine must be below 75°C.*
9 If there is no vacuum present, proceed to paragraph 13.
10 If there is vacuum present, disconnect the two-pin connector and measure the voltage

7.8 Attach a vacuum gauge to the hose (arrowed) and, with the engine idling (cold engine), there should be no vacuum

7.13 With the engine warmed up, check for vacuum at the number 7 hose

7.16 Connect a vacuum gauge to purge air hose and check for vacuum at 3500 rpm

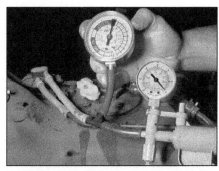

7.18 With the fuel tank removed, check the two-way valve for correct operation

between the yellow/black (+) terminal and the red (-) terminal. There should be battery voltage.

11 If battery voltage is present, renew the purge cut-off solenoid valve.

12 If there is no battery voltage, repair the wiring harness to the ECM and/or the number two fuse.

13 Warm the engine up to normal operating temperature (cooling fan must come on). If there originally was no vacuum on the purge control diaphragm valve, check for vacuum on the number 7 hose **(see illustration)**.

14 If there is vacuum present, proceed to paragraph 16.

15 If there is no vacuum present, disconnect the two-pin connector and check for manifold vacuum now. If there is no vacuum, check to make sure the vacuum hoses are routed correctly. If there is vacuum, check for a short in the wiring harness between the two-pin connector and the ECM.

16 If vacuum was originally present, reconnect the number 7 hose and connect a vacuum gauge to the purge air hose **(see illustration)** and raise the engine rpm to 3,500. Vacuum should be present within one minute. If there is vacuum, check the two-way valve.

Two-way valve

17 Remove the fuel tank (see Chapter 4).

18 Detach the vapour line from the fuel tank and connect a T-fitting into a vacuum pump and vacuum gauge **(see illustration)**.

19 Apply vacuum slowly and steadily and observe the gauge. Vacuum should stabilise momentarily at 0.2 to 0.6 in-Hg. If the valve opens (stabilises) before the correct vacuum, renew it with a new part.

20 Move the hand held vacuum pump over to the pressure fitting (same vacuum line arrangement). Pressurise the line and observe the gauge. Pressure should stabilise at 0.4 to 1.4 in-Hg (valve opens).

21 If the valve opens (stabilises) before or after the correct vacuum, renew it with a new part.

8 Electronic Load Detector (ELD) system

General information

1 The ELD system detects excess amperage draw (load) on the electrical circuits that govern the headlights, fuel injection, charging system etc. The prime symptom of an electrical overload is a driveability problem, usually occurring when the engine is idling. Any trouble with the ELD system will set a code 20.

Check

2 Disconnect the electrical connector from the ELD system and measure voltage **(see illustration)** between the black/yellow (+) wire and the black (-) wire (two outside terminals) with the ignition key ON (engine not running). There should be battery voltage. If no voltage is present, check the wiring harness back to the fuse box (under the dash) and the main fuse box (engine compartment).

3 Measure voltage with the ignition key ON (engine not running) between the green/red (+) terminal and the black (-) terminal **(see illustration)**. There should be 4.5 to 5.0 volts. If no voltage is present, check the ELD circuit between the engine and the alternator).

4 Reconnect the three-pin connector to the ELD system. With the ignition key ON (engine not running) and the headlights ON (low beam), measure the voltage on the green/red terminal (+) (middle wire). There should be approximately 2.5 to 3.5 volts.

8.2 Measure voltage between the black/yellow (+) wire and the black (-) wire

5 Now, turn the switch to high beam and check the voltage. It should be 1.5 to 2.5 volts.

6 If the test results are not correct, renew the ELD unit. This means changing the entire main fusebox. The unit is not available separately.

9 Engine Control Module (ECM) - general information and renewal

> **Warning: Most models covered by this manual are equipped with a Supplemental Restraint System (SRS), more commonly known as an airbag(s). Always disable the airbag system before working in the vicinity of the SRS unit, steering column or instrument panel to avoid the possibility of accidental deployment of the airbag, which could cause personal injury (see Chapter 12).**

1 The Engine Control Module (ECM) is located on the left-hand side of the passenger compartment under the instrument panel. The units for both the PGM-FI and PGM-CARB systems are located in the same position.

2 Disable the airbag system (see Chapter 12). **Caution: If the stereo in your car is equipped with an anti-theft system, make sure you have the correct activation code before disconnecting the battery.**

3 Remove the carpet from the lower panel assembly and the floor area (see Chapter 11) under the dash. Place the carpet sufficiently out of the way.

8.3 Measure voltage between green/red (+) terminal and the black (-) terminal

9.4 Remove the nuts (arrowed) from the kick plate and lift the plate out to gain access to the ECM

4 Remove the kick plate to expose the relay panel and the ECM **(see illustration)**.
5 Unplug the electrical connectors from the ECM. *Caution: The ignition switch must be turned OFF when pulling out or plugging in the electrical connectors to prevent damage to the ECM.*
6 Remove the nut from the ECM bracket.
7 Carefully remove the ECM. **Note**: *Avoid any static electricity damage to the computer by earthing yourself to the body before touching the ECM and using a special anti-static pad to store the ECM on once it is removed.*
8 Refitting is a reversal of removal.

10 Catalytic converter

Note: *Because of the vehicle warranty, be sure to check with a dealer service department before replacing the converter at your own expense.*

General description

1 The catalytic converter is an emission control device added to the exhaust system to reduce pollutants from the exhaust gas stream. There are two types of converters. The conventional oxidation catalyst reduces the levels of hydrocarbon (HC) and carbon monoxide (CO). The three-way catalyst lowers the levels of oxides of nitrogen (NOx) as well as hydrocarbons (HC) and carbon monoxide (CO).

Checking

2 The test equipment for a catalytic converter is expensive and highly sophisticated. If you suspect that the converter on your car is malfunctioning, take it to a dealer or authorised emissions inspection facility for diagnosis and repair.
3 Whenever the car is raised for servicing of underbody components, check the converter for leaks, corrosion, dents and other damage. Check the welds/flange bolts that attach the front and rear ends of the converter to the exhaust system. If damage is discovered, the converter should be replaced.
4 Although catalytic converters don't break too often, they can become blocked. The easiest way to check for a restricted converter is to use a vacuum gauge to diagnose the effect of a blocked exhaust on inlet vacuum.

a) *Open the throttle until the engine speed is about 2000 rpm.*
b) *Release the throttle quickly.*
c) *If there is no restriction, the gauge will quickly drop to not more than 2 in-Hg or more above its normal reading.*
d) *If the gauge does not show 5 in-Hg or more above its normal reading, or seems to momentarily hover around its highest reading for a moment before it returns, the exhaust system, or the converter, is blocked (or an exhaust pipe is bent or dented, or the core inside the silencer has shifted).*

Component renewal

5 Refer to the exhaust system removal and refitting section in Chapter 4.

Chapter 7 Part A:
Manual transmission

Contents

Degrees of difficulty

Easy, suitable for novice with little experience	Fairly easy, suitable for beginner with some experience	Fairly difficult, suitable for competent DIY mechanic	Difficult, suitable for experienced DIY mechanic	Very difficult, suitable for expert DIY or professional

Specifications

Torque wrench settings	Nm	lbf ft
Lower transmission-to-engine bolts		
Front bolt	64	47
Rear bolt	83	61
Lower rear engine-to-transmission bolt	64	47
Upper transmission-to-engine bolts	64	47
Right transmission mount		
Mount bolt and nuts	64	47
Engine bracket-to-mount through-bolt	73	54
Front stopper bracket		
Short bolt	45	33
Long bolts	64	47
Splash shield bolts	10	7
Clutch cover bolts	12	9
Engine stiffeners (D16Z6)		
Short bolts	23	17
Long bolts	45	33

1 General information

The vehicles covered by this manual are equipped with either a five-speed manual transmission or a four-speed automatic transmission. Information on the manual transmission is included in this Part of Chapter 7. Service procedures for the automatic transmission are contained in Chapter 7, Part B.

The manual transmission is a compact, two-piece, lightweight aluminium alloy housing containing both the transmission and differential assemblies.

2 Driveshaft oil seals - renewal

1 Oil leaks frequently occur due to wear of the driveshaft oil seals. Renewal of these seals is relatively easy, since the repair can usually be performed without removing the transmission from the vehicle.
2 The driveshaft oil seals are located at the sides of the transmission, where the driveshafts are attached. If leakage at the seal is suspected, raise the car and support it securely on axle stands (see "Jacking and Vehicle Support"). If the seal is leaking, lubricant will be found on the sides of the transmission, below the seals.
3 Refer to Chapter 8 and remove the driveshafts.

4 Using a screwdriver or lever, carefully prise the oil seal out of the transmission bore (see illustration).

2.4 Insert the tip of a large screwdriver or lever behind the oil seal and very carefully prise it out

2.6 Using a large socket or a pipe, drive the new seal squarely into the bore

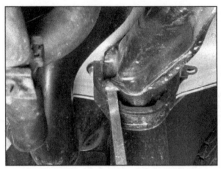

3.2 To check the transmission mount, insert a large screwdriver and try moving it

4.1a Remove this gearchange lever boot and the dust seal underneath

5 If the oil seal cannot be removed with a screwdriver or lever, a special oil seal removal tool (available at motor factors) will be required.

6 Using a large section of pipe or a large deep socket (as large as the outside diameter of the seal) as a drift, fit the new oil seal **(see illustration)**. Drive it into the bore squarely and make sure it's completely seated. Coat the seal lip with transmission lubricant.

7 Refit the driveshaft(s). Be careful not to damage the lip of the new seal.

3 Transmission mount - check and renewal

1 Raise the front of the car and place it on axle stands (see "*Jacking and Vehicle Support*").

2 Insert a large screwdriver or lever between the mount and the transmission and try to lever the transmission up or down **(see illustration)**.

3 The transmission should not move more than about 1/2 to 3/4-inch away from the mount. If it does, renew the mount.

4 To renew the mount, support the transmission with a jack, remove the nuts and bolts and remove the mount. It may be necessary to raise the transmission slightly to provide enough clearance to remove the mount.

> ⚠ **Warning: Do not place any part of your body under the transmission when it's supported only by a jack.**

5 Refitting is the reverse of removal.

4 Gearchange lever and linkage - removal and refitting

Removal

1 Unscrew the gear lever knob. Remove the centre console (see Chapter 11). Remove the

rubber gear lever boot and the dust seal underneath **(see illustrations)**.

2 Raise the car and place it securely on axle stands (see "*Jacking and Vehicle Support*").

3 To disconnect the extension rod from the transmission, simply remove the bolt that attaches it to the extension bracket **(see illustration)**.

4 To disconnect the gearchange rod from the transmission, push the dust boot forward **(see illustration)**, remove the clip and drive out the spring pin with a pin punch. Discard the spring pin - do not re-use it.

5 To disconnect the rear end of the gearchange rod from the gear lever, remove the nut and bolt **(see illustration)**.

6 Remove the two nuts and washers that retain the change ball holder to the underside

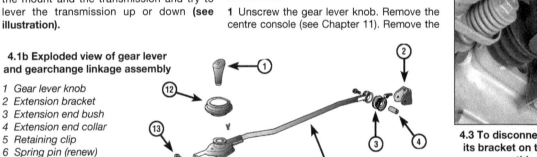

4.3 To disconnect the extension rod from its bracket on the transmission, remove this bolt (arrowed)

4.4 To disconnect the gearchange rod from the transmission, push the dust boot forward, remove the clip (arrowed) and pull out the spring pin

4.1b Exploded view of gear lever and gearchange linkage assembly

1 Gear lever knob
2 Extension bracket
3 Extension end bush
4 Extension end collar
5 Retaining clip
6 Spring pin (renew)
7 Change ball holder
8 Lower gear lever dust seal
9 Gear lever ball seat
10 Gearchange rod
11 Extension rod
12 Upper gear lever dust seal
13 Extension mounting rubber
14 Bushings
15 Extension mounting bracket
16 Gear lever
17 Bush
18 O-rings (renew)
19 Bushings
20 Thrust shim

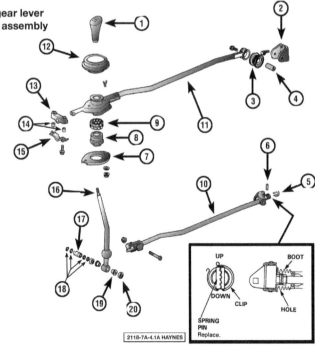

2118-7A-4.1A HAYNES

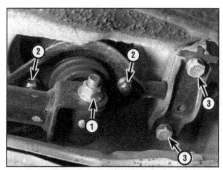

4.5 To disconnect the gearchange rod, remove nut and bolt (1); to disconnect the extension rod, remove two small nuts above (2) and two bolts (3) retaining the extension mounting bracket and cushion

of the extension rod **(see illustration 4.5)** and remove the change ball holder, lower gear lever dust seal, gear lever ball seat, gear lever and extension rod **(see illustration 4.1b)**.

7 Inspect the bush at the front end of the extension rod and renew it if it's cracked, torn or worn.

8 Renew the O-rings in the base of the gear lever.

Refitting

9 Refitting is the reverse of removal. Lubricate the new O-rings and the bushings with silicone grease. Use a new spring pin to attach the gearchange rod to the transmission. Tighten all fasteners to the specified torque values.

10 Check the operation of the gear lever.

5 Reversing light switch - check and renewal

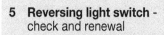

Check

1 Before testing the reversing light switch, check the No. 15 10-amp fuse in the under-dash fuse/relay box.

2 Put the gear lever in Reverse and turn the ignition switch to On. The reversing lights should go on. Turn off the ignition switch.

3 If the reversing lights don't go on, check the reversing light bulbs in the tail light assembly.

4 If the fuse and bulbs are both OK, locate the reversing light switch on top of the transmission **(see illustration)**, trace the leads back to the electrical connector, unplug the connector and hook up an ohmmeter or continuity tester across the two terminals **(see illustration)**.

5 With the gear lever in Reverse, there should be continuity; with the lever in any other gear, there should be no continuity.

6 If the switch fails this test, renew it (see below).

7 If the switch is OK, but the reversing lights aren't coming on, check for a poor earth in the circuit; if the grounds are good, look for opens in the circuits.

5.4a The reversing light switch (arrowed) is located on top of the transmission housing

Renewal

8 Unplug the reversing light switch electrical connector.

9 Unscrew the reversing light switch.

10 Discard the old washer.

11 Using a new washer, fit the new switch.

12 Plug in the connector.

6 Transmission - removal and refitting

Removal

1 Disconnect the negative, *then* the positive, cables from the battery and remove the battery. *Caution: If the radio in your car is equipped with an anti-theft system, make sure you have the correct activation code before disconnecting the battery.*

2 Remove the resonator, inlet air duct and air cleaner (see Chapter 4).

3 Disconnect the starter motor cables and remove the upper starter motor mounting bolt (see Chapter 5).

4 Disconnect the transmission earth cable, unplug the reversing light switch connector (see Section 5) and detach the wiring harness clamp from the transmission. Unplug the vehicle speed sensor electrical connector **(see illustration)**.

5 Loosen the front wheel nuts, raise the car and support it securely on axle stands (see "*Jacking and Vehicle Support*"). Remove the front wheels.

6 Remove the splash shield, if applicable.

6.4 Unplug the electrical connector (arrowed) from the vehicle speed sensor

5.4b The reversing light switch should have continuity only with the lever in Reverse

7 Remove the elbow-shaped exhaust pipe section under the transmission (Chapter 4).

8 Drain the transmission lubricant (see Chapter 1).

9 Disconnect the gearchange and extension rods from the transmission (see Section 4).

10 Remove the clutch fluid hose-to-clutch fluid pressure line junction, the clutch fluid pressure line, the slave cylinder and the slave cylinder pushrod (see Chapter 8). *Caution: Be careful not to bend or kink the clutch fluid pressure line, and don't depress the clutch pedal while the clutch slave cylinder is removed.*

11 Remove the driveshafts (see Chapter 8). Tie plastic bags over the inner CV joints to keep them clean.

12 On D16Z6 (1.6L 16-valve SOHC VTEC) engines, remove the front and rear engine stiffeners (The stiffeners are cast L-shaped pieces bolted to the transmission and the underside of the block by three bolts (one in the transmission and two in the block).

13 Remove the clutch access cover bolts **(see illustration 17.1 in Chapter 4)** and remove the cover.

14 Remove the distributor mounting bolt and attach an engine hoist to the cylinder head to support the engine (see Section 6 in Chapter 2B), then lift the engine slightly to take the load off the engine and transmission mounts.

15 Remove the splash guard (if applicable) and front stopper bracket **(see illustration)**.

16 Place a floor jack under the transmission, place a block of wood between the jack head and the transmission and raise it just enough to take the weight off the mounts.

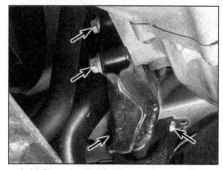

6.15 Remove the front stopper bracket bolts (arrowed) and remove the bracket

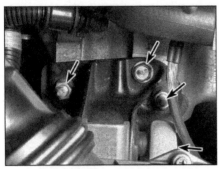

6.17 Remove the transmission mount retaining bolts and nuts (arrowed); bracket-to-mount through bolt (lower arrow) is not visible in this photo

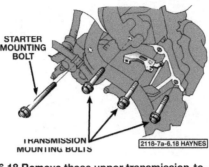

6.18 Remove these upper transmission-to-engine mounting bolts (arrowed)

6.19 Remove the lower transmission-to-engine mounting bolt (arrowed)

6.20 Remove the three rear transmission mounting bracket bolts (arrowed)

17 Remove the right side transmission mounting bracket bolts and nuts (see illustration).

18 Remove the four upper transmission-to-engine mounting bolts (see illustration).

19 Remove the front lower transmission-to-engine bolt (see illustration). Then remove the rear lower transmission-to-engine bolt immediately above the right driveshaft.

20 Remove the three rear transmission mounting bracket bolts (see illustration).

21 Make a final check that all wires and hoses have been disconnected from the transmission, then carefully pull the transmission and jack away from the engine.

22 Once the input shaft is clear, lower the transmission and remove it from under the car.

23 With the transmission removed, the clutch components are now accessible and can be inspected. In most cases, new clutch components should be routinely installed when the transmission is removed (see Chapter 8).

Refitting

24 If removed, refit the clutch components (see Chapter 8).

25 Make sure the two dowel pins are fitted. With the transmission secured to the jack with a chain, raise it into position behind the engine, then carefully slide it forward, engaging the two dowel pins on the transmission with the corresponding holes in the block and the input shaft with the clutch plate hub splines. Do not use excessive force to fit the transmission - if the input shaft does not slide into place, readjust the angle of the transmission so it is level and/or turn the input shaft so the splines engage properly with the clutch plate hub.

26 Refit the transmission housing-to-engine bolts and the transmission rear mounting bracket bolts and tighten them to the torque listed in this Chapter's Specifications.

27 Refit the three upper transmission-to-engine bolts and the lower starter motor mounting bolt and tighten them to the torque listed in this Chapter's Specifications.

28 Raise the transmission slightly, then refit the right transmission mounting bracket and the bracket bolt and nuts. First, tighten the bolt and nuts that attach the mount to the body, then tighten the longer through-bolt that attaches the engine bracket to the mount. Tighten the bolts and nuts to the torque listed in this Chapter's Specifications.

29 Refit the front stopper bracket and tighten the bolts to the torque listed in this Chapter's Specifications.

30 Refit the splash shield and tighten the bolts to the specified torque.

31 Remove the chain hoist and refit the distributor mounting bolt.

32 Refit the clutch cover and, on models with a D16Z6 engine, refit the engine stiffeners. Tighten the clutch cover and engine stiffener bolts to the torque listed in this Chapter's Specifications.

33 The remainder of refitting is the reverse of removal. On 1994 and 1995 models, make sure that the "F" mark on the breather cap points at an angle of 30° to the left of the front of the car. Turn it to this angle if it's off.

34 Refill the transmission with the specified amount of lubricant (see Chapter 1).

35 Bleed the clutch hydraulic system (see Chapter 8).

36 Road test the car for proper operation and check for leaks.

7 Transmission overhaul - general information

Overhauling a manual transmission is a difficult and involved job for the DIY home mechanic. In addition to dismantling and reassembling many small parts, clearances must be precisely measured and, if necessary, changed by selecting shims and spacers. Internal transmission components are also often difficult to obtain, and in many instances, extremely expensive. Because of this, if the transmission develops a fault or becomes noisy, the best course of action is to have the unit overhauled by a specialist repairer, or to obtain an exchange reconditioned unit. Be aware that some transmission repairs can be carried out with the transmission in the car.

Nevertheless, it is not impossible for the more experienced mechanic to overhaul the transmission, provided the special tools are available, and the job is done in a deliberate step-by-step manner, so that nothing is overlooked.

The tools necessary for an overhaul include internal and external circlip pliers, bearing pullers, a slide hammer, a set of pin punches, a dial test indicator, and possibly a hydraulic press. In addition, a large, sturdy workbench and a vice will be required.

During dismantling of the transmission, make careful notes of how each component is fitted, to make reassembly easier and more accurate.

Before dismantling the transmission, it will help if you have some idea what area is malfunctioning. Certain problems can be closely related to specific areas in the transmission, which can make component examination and replacement easier. Refer to the Fault finding Section at the end of this manual for more information.

Chapter 7 Part B:
Automatic transmission

Contents

Degrees of difficulty

Easy, suitable for novice with little experience	Fairly easy, suitable for beginner with some experience	Fairly difficult, suitable for competent DIY mechanic	Difficult, suitable for experienced DIY mechanic	Very difficult, suitable for expert DIY or professional

Specifications

Gearchange lock solenoid clearance . . . . 2.4 mm ± 0.4 mm
Lock-up control solenoid resistance . . . . 14.1 to 15.5 ohms (at 25°C)

Torque wrench settings	Nm	lbf ft
Gearchange lock solenoid self-locking nuts	10	7
Lock-up control solenoid valve assembly bolts	12	9
Transmission-to-engine bolts	58	43
Engine-to-transmission bolt	58	43
Rear transmission mount bolts	83	61
Engine stiffeners		
Short bolts	23	17
Long bolts	45	33
Driveplate/torque converter cover	12	9
Driveplate-to-torque converter bolts	12	9
Stopper mount		
Short bolts	38	28
Long bolts	64	47

1 General information

All vehicles covered in this manual come equipped with either a five-speed manual or a four-speed automatic transmission. All information on the automatic transmission is included in this Part of Chapter 7. Information for the manual transmission can be found in Part A of this Chapter.

Due to the complexity of the automatic transmissions covered in this manual and to the specialised equipment necessary to perform most service operations, this Chapter contains only those procedures related to general diagnosis, routine maintenance, adjustment and removal and refitting.

If the transmission requires major repair work, it should be left to a dealer service department or an automotive or transmission garage. You can, however, remove and refit the transmission yourself and save the expense, even if the repair work is done by a transmission specialist.

2 Diagnosis - general

Note: Automatic transmission malfunctions may be caused by five general conditions: poor engine performance, improper adjustments, hydraulic malfunctions, mechanical malfunctions or malfunctions in the computer or its signal network. Diagnosis of these problems should always begin with a check of the easily repaired items: fluid level and condition (see Chapter 1), gearchange control cable adjustment and throttle control cable adjustment. Next, perform a road test to determine if the problem has been corrected or if more diagnosis is necessary. If the problem persists after the preliminary tests and corrections are completed, additional diagnosis should be done by a dealer service department or transmission garage. Refer to the "Fault finding" section at the front of this manual for information on symptoms of transmission problems.

Preliminary checks

1 Drive the car to warm the transmission to normal operating temperature.
2 Check the fluid level (refer to Chapter 1):
 a) If the fluid level is unusually low, add enough fluid to bring the level within the designated area of the dipstick, then check for external leaks (see below).
 b) If the fluid level is abnormally high, drain off the excess, then check the drained fluid for contamination by coolant. The presence of engine coolant in the automatic transmission fluid indicates that a failure has occurred in the internal radiator walls that separate the coolant from the transmission fluid (Chapter 3).

c) If the fluid is foaming, drain it and refill the transmission, then check for coolant in the fluid, or a high fluid level.

3 Check the engine idle speed. **Note:** If the engine is malfunctioning, do not proceed with the preliminary checks until it has been repaired and runs normally.

4 Check the throttle control cable for freedom of movement. Adjust it if necessary (Section 3). **Note:** The cable may function properly when the engine is shut off and cold, but it may malfunction once the engine is hot. Check it cold and at normal operating temperature.

5 Inspect the gearchange cable linkage (see Section 4). Make sure that it's properly adjusted and that the linkage operates smoothly.

Fluid leak diagnosis

6 Most fluid leaks are easy to locate visually. Repair usually consists of replacing a seal or gasket. If a leak is difficult to find, the following procedure may help.

7 Identify the fluid. Make sure it's transmission fluid and not engine oil or brake fluid (automatic transmission fluid is a deep red colour).

8 Try to pinpoint the source of the leak. Drive the car several miles, then park it over a large sheet of cardboard. After a minute or two, you should be able to locate the leak by determining the source of the fluid dripping onto the cardboard.

9 Make a careful visual inspection of the suspected component and the area immediately around it. Pay particular attention to gasket mating surfaces. A mirror is often helpful for finding leaks in areas that are hard to see.

10 If the leak still cannot be found, clean the suspected area thoroughly with a degreaser or solvent, then dry it.

11 Drive the car for several miles at normal operating temperature and varying speeds. After driving the car, visually inspect the suspected component again.

12 Once the leak has been located, the cause must be determined before it can be properly repaired. If a gasket is replaced but the sealing flange is bent, the new gasket will not stop the leak. The bent flange must be straightened.

13 Before attempting to repair a leak, check to make sure that the following conditions are corrected or they may cause another leak. **Note:** Some of the following conditions cannot be fixed without highly specialised tools and expertise. Such problems must be referred to a transmission specialist or a dealer service department.

Gasket leaks

14 Check the right side cover periodically. Make sure the bolts are tight, no bolts are missing, the gasket is in good condition and the cover is not damaged.

15 If the leak is from the right side cover area, the bolts may be too tight, the sealing surface of the transmission housing may be damaged,

the gasket may be damaged or the transmission casting may be cracked or porous. If sealant instead of gasket material has been used to form a seal between the cover and the transmission housing, it may be the wrong sealant.

Seal leaks

16 If a transmission seal is leaking, the fluid level or pressure may be too high, the vent may be plugged, the seal bore may be damaged, the seal itself may be damaged or improperly installed, the surface of the shaft protruding through the seal may be damaged or a loose bearing may be causing excessive shaft movement.

17 Make sure the dipstick tube seal is in good condition and the tube is properly seated. Periodically check the area around the speedometer gear or sensor for leakage. If transmission fluid is evident, check the O-ring for damage.

Case leaks

18 If the case itself appears to be leaking, the casting is porous and will have to be repaired or replaced.

19 Make sure the oil cooler hose fittings are tight and in good condition.

Fluid comes out vent pipe or fill tube

20 If this condition occurs, the transmission is overfilled, there is coolant in the fluid, the case is porous, the dipstick is incorrect, the vent is plugged or the drain-back holes are plugged.

3 Throttle control (kickdown) cable - check and adjustment

Check

1 Before you check the throttle control cable, make sure the accelerator cable freeplay (see Chapter 4) and the idle speed (see Chapter 1) are correct.

2 Warm up the engine to its proper operating temperature.

3 Verify that the throttle control lever is synchronised with the throttle linkage while depressing and releasing the accelerator pedal.

4 If the throttle control lever isn't synchronised with the throttle linkage, adjust the throttle control cable (see below).

5 Verify that there's play in the throttle control lever while depressing the accelerator pedal to the full-throttle position.

6 Disconnect the end of the throttle control cable from the throttle control lever.

7 Verify that the throttle control lever moves smoothly.

8 Reconnect the throttle control cable to the throttle control lever.

Adjustment

9 Follow Steps 1 and 2 above.

10 Verify that the throttle linkage is in the fully-closed position.

11 Loosen the throttle control cable locknut at the upper end, near the throttle body.

12 While pushing the throttle control lever to the fully-closed position, remove all freeplay from the throttle control cable by tightening the upper locknut.

13 Tighten the locknut.

14 After the locknut is tightened, check the synchronisation and throttle control lever movement.

15 After tightening the locknuts, check the operation of the throttle control cable.

4 Gearchange cable - renewal and adjustment

Renewal

⚠ **Warning:** Most models covered by this manual are equipped with a Supplemental Restraint System (SRS), more commonly known as an airbag(s). Always disable the airbag system before working in the vicinity of the SRS unit, steering column or instrument panel to avoid the possibility of accidental deployment of the airbag, which could cause personal injury (see Chapter 12).

1 Remove the centre console (Chapter 11).

2 Put the selector lever in the Neutral position, then remove the retaining clip from the cable adjuster **(see illustration)**.

3 Unbolt the gearchange cable bracket **(see illustration)**.

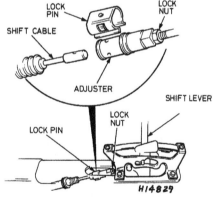

4.2 An exploded view of the gearchange cable, adjuster and retaining clip assembly

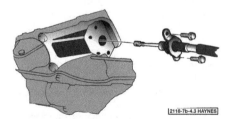

4.3 Gearchange cable bracket details

4.10 Make sure the hole in the adjuster is perfectly aligned with the hole in the gearchange cable

4 Unbolt the gearchange cable holder from the floorpan.
5 Remove the gearchange cable cover.
6 Remove the control lever from the control shaft, then remove the gearchange cable. Be careful not to bend the cable when removing or refitting it.
7 Refitting is the reverse of removal. Be sure to adjust the gearchange cable when you have finished.

Adjustment

8 Remove the centre console, if not already done (see Chapter 11).
9 Gearchange to the Neutral position, then remove the retaining clip from the cable adjuster **(see illustration 4.2)**.
10 There are two holes in the end of the gearchange cable. They're positioned 90° apart to allow cable adjustments in 1/4-turn increments. Verify that the hole in the adjuster is perfectly aligned with the hole in the gearchange cable **(see illustration)**.
11 If the two holes aren't perfectly aligned, loosen the locknut on the gearchange cable and adjust it as required, then retighten the locknut.
12 Fit the retaining clip on the adjuster. If the clip feels as if it's binding as you fit it, the cable is still out of adjustment and must be readjusted.
13 Start the engine and check the selector lever in all gears. If any gear doesn't work properly, refer to Section 2.

5 Gearchange indicator panel - adjustment

1 Verify that the index mark on the selector lever is aligned with the Neutral mark on the gearchange indicator panel when the transmission is in Neutral. If they're not aligned, adjust the gearchange indicator panel.
2 Remove the centre console (see Chapter 11).
3 Remove the gearchange indicator panel mounting screws and align the marks by moving the panel.
4 Fit the panel screws and tighten them securely.
5 Refit the console (see Chapter 11).

6 Gear position switch - check, adjustment and renewal

Check

 Warning: Most models covered by this manual are equipped with a Supplemental Restraint System (SRS), more commonly known as an airbag(s). Always disable the airbag system before working in the vicinity of the SRS unit, steering column or instrument panel to avoid the possibility of accidental deployment of the airbag, which could cause personal injury (see Chapter 12).

1 Remove the console (see Chapter 11).
2 Unplug the 14-pin electrical connector from the gearchange position console switch **(see illustration)**.
3 Check for continuity between the indicated terminals in each switch position in accordance with the accompanying tables **(see illustrations)**. Move the selector lever back and forth at each switch position without touching the push-button and check for continuity within the range of selector lever freeplay (about 2.0 mm).
4 If there's no continuity within the range of selector lever freeplay at each selector lever position, adjust the position of the console switch.

6.2 Terminal guide for the 14-pin connector

Adjustment

5 Move the selector lever to the Park position and loosen the switch mounting nuts **(see illustration 6.11)**.
6 Slide the switch toward the Drive positions until there's continuity between terminals 7 and 10, within the range of selector lever freeplay (about 2.0 mm).
7 Recheck continuity as described above in paragraph 3. Make sure the engine starts when the selector lever is in the Neutral position.
8 If there's still no continuity at each selector lever position, inspect the selector lever detent and bracket for damage. If they're undamaged, renew the gearchange position console switch.

Renewal

9 Remove the console (see Chapter 11).

SHIFT POSITION SWITCH (Without cruise control)

TERMINAL ▶ POSITION ▼	7	6	3	2	1	8	9	10	BACK-UP LIGHT SWITCH 4	5	NEUTRAL SAFETY SWITCH 11	12
1	O	O										
2	O		O									
D3	O			O								
D4	O				O							
N	O						O				O	O
R	O					O			O	O		
P	O							O			O	O

6.3a Continuity table for the gear position switch (without cruise control)

Shift Position Switch (With cruise control)

TERMINAL POSITION	13	7	6	3	2	1	8	9	10	Back-up Light Switch 4	5	Neutral Safety Switch 11	12
1		O	O										
2	O	O		O									
D3	O	O			O								
D4	O	O				O							
N		O						O				O	O
R		O					O			O	O		
P		O							O			O	O

6.3b Continuity table for the gear position switch (with cruise control)

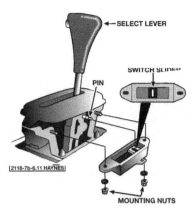

6.11 Refitting details for the gear position switch (note the slider position for refitting the switch)

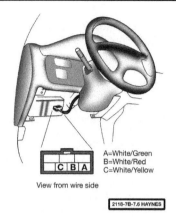

A=White/Green
B=White/Red
C=White/Yellow

View from wire side

7.6 Terminal guide for the key interlock solenoid connector (as seen from the back side of the connector)

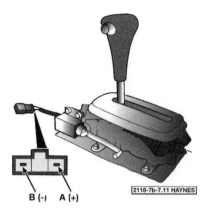

B (-) A (+)

7.11 Terminal guide for the gearchange lock solenoid connector (as seen from the back side of the connector)

10 Unplug the 12-pin connector (see illustration 6.2).
11 Remove the two console switch mounting nuts and washers (see illustration).
12 Position the switch slider at the Neutral position (see illustration 6.11).
13 Move the selector lever to the Neutral position, then fit the new switch.
14 Attach the new switch with the two nuts and washers.
15 Test the new switch as described above in paragraph 3. Make sure the engine starts when the selector lever is in the Neutral position.
16 Reconnect the connector. Clamp the harness.
17 Refit the console (see Chapter 11).

---

7 Interlock system - description, check, solenoid renewal and adjustment

Description

1 Vehicles with automatic transmission have an interlock system to prevent unintentional shifting. The interlock system consists of two subsystems: a gearchange lock system and a key interlock system.

Key interlock system

2 The key interlock system prevents the ignition key from being removed from the ignition switch unless the selector lever is in the Park position. If you insert the key when the selector lever is in any position other than Park, a solenoid is activated, making it impossible for you to remove the key until the selector lever is moved to the Park position.

Gearchange lock system

3 The gearchange lock system prevents the selector lever from moving from the Park position into the Reverse or Drive positions unless the brake pedal is depressed. Nor can the selector lever be shifted when the brake pedal and the accelerator pedal are depressed at the same time. In the event of a system

malfunction, you can release the selector lever by inserting a key into the release slot near the selector lever.

Check

4 The following checks are simple tests of the key interlock solenoid and the gearchange lock solenoid you can do at home. Further testing of the interlock system should be left to a dealer service department.

Key interlock solenoid

5 Remove the lower instrument panel and knee bolster (see Chapter 11).
6 Unplug the 7-pin connector (see illustration) from the main wire harness.
7 Check for continuity between the terminals in each switch position. With the key pushed in, there should be continuity between terminals A, B and C; with the key released, there should be continuity only between terminals B and C.
8 Verify that the key can't be removed when the battery is connected to terminals A and B.
9 If the key can't be removed, the key interlock solenoid is okay; if the key can be removed, the steering lock assembly needs to be replaced (the key interlock solenoid isn't available separately).

Gearchange lock solenoid

10 Remove the console (see Chapter 11).
11 Unplug the three-pin connector for the gearchange lock solenoid (see illustration) from the dashboard wiring harness.
12 Using a pair of jumper wires, momentarily touch a positive battery lead to the A terminal of the three-pin connector and a negative lead to the B terminal and note whether the solenoid clicks on or not. *Caution: Make sure you don't connect the battery voltage leads to the wrong connector terminals. Reversing the polarity can damage or destroy the diode inside the solenoid.*
  a) If the solenoid doesn't operate, renew it.
  b) If the solenoid does operate, but you have been having problems with the gearchange lock system, it may be necessary to adjust the solenoid at its Off and On positions (see below).

13 While the solenoid is on, it's a good idea to check the clearance between the gearchange lock lever and the lock pin groove (see below).
14 With the solenoid turned off, note whether or not the lock pin is blocked by the gearchange lock lever. If it isn't, adjust the position of the gearchange lock solenoid until it is (see below).

Solenoid renewal and adjustment

Note: *The following procedure pertains only to the gearchange lock solenoid. For information on how to renew the key interlock solenoid, refer to the "Ignition switch/key lock cylinder renewal" Section in Chapter 12. The key interlock solenoid isn't available separately.*

15 Remove the gearchange lock collar and the solenoid pin (see illustration).
16 Remove the self-locking nuts and the gearchange lock solenoid. Discard the old nuts.
17 Refitting is the reverse of removal. Don't tighten the new nuts until you have adjusted the solenoid as follows.

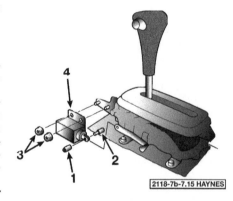

7.15 An exploded view of the gearchange lock solenoid assembly

1 Gearchange lock collar
2 Solenoid pin
3 Self-locking nuts (renew)
4 Gearchange lock solenoid

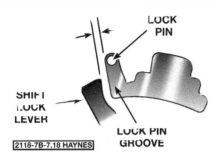

7.18 Energise the solenoid, check the clearance between the gearchange lock lever and the lock pin groove (arrowed)

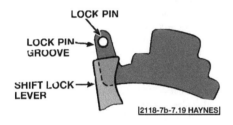

7.19 When the gearchange lock solenoid is Off, make sure the lock pin is blocked by the gearchange lock lever

18 To adjust the gearchange lock solenoid, energise the solenoid and check the clearance between the gearchange lock lever and the lock pin groove **(see illustration)** and compare your measurement to the clearance listed in this Chapter's Specifications. Position the solenoid so that the clearance is correct, then tighten the new self-locking nuts to the torque listed in this Chapter's specifications. **Note:** *Be sure to use new self-locking nuts.*

19 With the solenoid turned off, note whether or not the lock pin is blocked by the gearchange lock lever **(see illustration)**. If it isn't, readjust the position of the gearchange lock solenoid until it is.

8 Lock-up control solenoid valve - check and renewal

Check

1 Unplug the connector from the lock-up control solenoid valve **(see illustration)**.
2 Measure the resistance between each of the connector terminals (solenoid side) and earth **(see illustration)** and compare your measurements to the resistance listed in this Chapter's Specifications. If the resistance is out of specification for either terminal, renew the entire solenoid assembly.
3 Connect each of the connector terminals to the battery positive terminal with a jump lead. You should hear a clicking sound as each solenoid valve is energised. If you don't, take

8.1 The lock-up control solenoid valve is located on top of the transmission

the car to a dealer and have the ECM and lock-up control solenoid valve circuits checked out.

Renewal

Note: *You cannot renew only one solenoid valve; the lock-up control solenoid valve assembly must be replaced as a single unit.*
4 Remove the mounting bolts **(see illustration)** and remove the lock-up control solenoid valve assembly.
5 Clean the mounting surface and oil passages; make sure all dirt and dust is removed.
6 Fit a new base gasket and refit the new lock-up control solenoid valve assembly. Tighten the solenoid valve bolts to the torque listed in this Chapter's Specifications.
7 Check the electrical connector for dirt, corrosion and oil; clean it thoroughly if necessary. Reconnect it.
8 Check the solenoid valves as described above and make sure the new unit is functioning properly.

9 Automatic transmission - removal and refitting

Removal

1 Disconnect the negative cable from the battery. *Caution: If the radio in your car is equipped with an anti-theft system, make sure you have the correct activation code before disconnecting the battery.*
2 Remove the resonator, inlet air duct and air cleaner housing (see Chapter 4)
3 Remove the starter motor cables and cable bracket from the starter (see Chapter 5).
4 Disconnect the transmission earth cable from the transmission.
5 Unplug the electrical connector from the lock-up control solenoid (see Section 8).
6 Unplug the speed sensor electrical connector (see Chapter 7A).
7 Remove the three upper transmission-to-engine mounting bolts and the rear engine mounting bolt **(see illustration)**.
8 Raise the car and support it on axle stands (see *"Jacking and Vehicle Support"*).

8.2 Measure the resistance between each of the terminals (solenoid side) and earth

8.4 To renew the lock-up control solenoid valve, remove these bolts (arrowed)

9 Drain the transmission fluid (see Chapter 1). Be sure to use a new sealing washer when you refit the drain plug.
10 Disconnect the lower arms from the steering knuckles (see Chapter 10).
11 Separate the driveshafts from the differential (see Chapter 8). Cover the inner CV joints with plastic bags to keep them clean.
12 Remove the right suspension strut (see Chapter 10).
13 Remove the driveshafts (see Chapter 8).
14 Remove the splash shield.
15 Remove the elbow-shaped exhaust pipe section from underneath the engine (see Chapter 4).

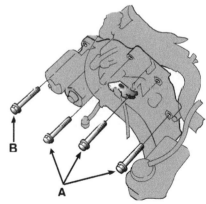

9.7 Remove the three upper transmission-to-engine mounting bolts (A) and the rear engine mounting bolt (B)

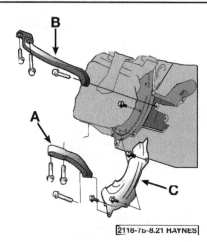

9.20 An exploded view of the front engine stiffener (A), the rear engine stiffener (B) and the torque converter access plate (C)

16 Remove the gearchange cable cover, then remove the control lever and gearchange cable. It's not necessary to disconnect the gearchange cable from the control lever.

17 Remove the stopper mount (refer to Chapter 7A).

18 Disconnect the throttle control cable from the throttle control lever (see Section 3).

19 Disconnect the transmission fluid cooler hoses from the cooler lines. Turn the hoses up to prevent fluid from flowing out, then plug the lines to prevent contamination.

20 Remove the engine stiffener(s) **(see illustration)**. Note: *Only the D16Z6 uses a rear engine stiffener.*

21 Remove the torque converter access plate.

22 Mark the relationship of the torque converter to the driveplate so that they can be reinstalled in the same relationship to one another **(see illustration)**.

23 Remove the eight torque converter-to-driveplate bolts one at a time by rotating the crankshaft pulley for access to each bolt.

24 Remove the distributor mounting bolt, then attach an engine hoist to the engine.

25 Place a transmission jack or a floor jack under the transmission. Raise the transmission assembly just enough to take the load off the transmission mount.

26 Remove the transmission side mount **(see illustration)**.

27 Remove the lower transmission-to-engine bolt, the lower engine-to-transmission bolt and the rear engine mount bolts **(see illustration)**.

28 Move the transmission back to disengage it from the engine block dowel pins and make sure the torque converter is detached from the driveplate. Secure the torque converter to the transmission so it will not fall out during removal. Lower the transmission from the car. **Note:** *It may be necessary to slowly lower the jack supporting the engine while the jack supporting the transmission is being lowered. This will provide more clearance between the transmission and the body.*

Refitting

29 Honda recommends flushing the transmission cooler and the cooler hoses and lines with solvent whenever the transmission is removed from the car. Use an approved solvent, such as Honda J-35944-20 or equivalent. Flush the lines and fluid cooler thoroughly and make sure no solvent remains in the lines or cooler after flushing.

30 Refit the starter motor (see Chapter 5).

31 Prior to refitting, make sure that the torque converter hub is securely engaged in the pump. With the transmission secured to the jack, raise it into position. Be sure to keep it level so the torque converter does not slide out.

32 Turn the torque converter to line it up with the driveplate. The marks you made on the torque converter and the driveplate must line up.

33 Make sure the two dowel pins are still installed, then move the transmission forward carefully until the dowel pins and the torque converter are engaged.

34 Refit the lower transmission-to-engine bolt and the lower engine-to-transmission bolt. Tighten them to the torque listed in this Chapter's Specifications. *Caution: Don't use the bolts to force the transmission and engine together. If the transmission doesn't slide easily up against the engine, find out why before you tighten the bolts.*

35 The remainder of refitting is the reverse of removal.

36 Refill the transmission with fluid to the specified level (see Chapter 1). Note that the transmission may require more fluid than in a normal fluid and filter change, since the torque converter may be empty (the converter is not drained during a fluid change).

37 Start the engine, apply the handbrake and gearchange the transmission through all gears three times. Make sure the gearchange cable is working properly (see Section 4).

38 Check and, if necessary, adjust the ignition timing (see Chapter 1).

39 Allow the engine to reach its proper operating temperature with the transmission in Park or Neutral, then turn it off and check the fluid level.

40 Road test the car and check for fluid leaks.

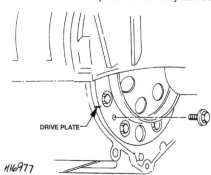

9.22 Before removing the driveplate-to-torque converter bolts, make alignment marks on the edge of the driveplate and torque converter

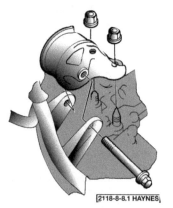

9.26 Transmission side mount details

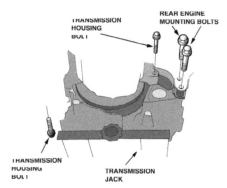

9.27 Remove lower transmission-to-engine bolt, lower engine-to-transmission bolt and rear engine mount bolts

Chapter 8
Clutch and driveshafts

Contents

Degrees of difficulty

| Easy, suitable for novice with little experience | | Fairly easy, suitable for beginner with some experience | | Fairly difficult, suitable for competent DIY mechanic | | Difficult, suitable for experienced DIY mechanic | | Very difficult, suitable for expert DIY or professional | |

Specifications

General
Clutch pedal disengagement height . . . . 83.0 mm
Clutch pedal freeplay . . . . 12 to 21 mm
Clutch pedal standard height . . . . 164 mm
Clutch pedal stroke . . . . 135 mm

Driveshafts
Dynamic damper (distance from inner CV gaiter)
    Left . . . . 76 mm +/- 2.8 mm
    Right . . . . 56 mm +/- 2.8 mm

Torque wrench settings

	Nm	lbf ft
Clutch pressure plate bolts	26	19
Driveshaft/hub nut	182	134
Intermediate shaft bearing support bolts	39	29

1 General information

The information in this Chapter deals with the components from the rear of the engine to the front wheels, except for the transmission, which is dealt with in the previous Chapter. For the purposes of this Chapter, these components are grouped into two categories - clutch and driveshafts. Separate Sections within this Chapter offer general descriptions and checking procedures for components in each of the two groups.

Since nearly all the procedures covered in this Chapter involve working under the car, make sure it's securely supported on sturdy axle stands (see "Jacking and Vehicle Support") or on a hoist where the car can be easily raised and lowered.

2 Clutch - description and check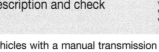

1 All vehicles with a manual transmission use a single dry-plate, diaphragm-spring type clutch. The clutch disc has a splined hub which allows it to slide along the splines of the transmission input shaft. The clutch and pressure plate are held in contact by spring pressure exerted by the diaphragm in the pressure plate.
2 The clutch release system is operated by hydraulic pressure. The hydraulic release system consists of the clutch pedal, a master cylinder and fluid reservoir, the hydraulic line, a release (or slave) cylinder which actuates the clutch release lever and the clutch release bearing.
3 When pressure is applied to the clutch pedal to release the clutch, hydraulic pressure is exerted against the outer end of the clutch release lever. As the lever pivots the shaft fingers push against the release bearing. The bearing pushes against the fingers of the diaphragm spring of the pressure plate assembly, which in turn releases the clutch plate.
4 Terminology can be a problem when discussing the clutch components because common names are in some cases different from those used by the manufacturer. For example, the driven plate is also called the clutch plate or disc, the clutch release bearing is sometimes called a throwout bearing, the slave cylinder is sometimes called the operating or slave cylinder.
5 Other than to renew components with obvious damage, some preliminary checks should be performed to diagnose clutch problems. These checks assume that the transmission is in good working condition.

a) The first check should be of the fluid level in the clutch master cylinder (Chapter 1). If the fluid level is low, add fluid as necessary and inspect the hydraulic system for leaks. If the master cylinder reservoir has run dry, bleed the system as described in Section 5 and retest the clutch operation.

b) To check "clutch spin-down time," run the engine at normal idle speed with the transmission in Neutral (clutch pedal up - engaged). Disengage the clutch (pedal down), wait several seconds and gearchange the transmission into Reverse. No grinding noise should be heard. A grinding noise would most likely indicate a problem in the pressure plate or the clutch disc.

c) To check for complete clutch release, run the engine (with the handbrake applied to prevent movement) and hold the clutch pedal approximately 1/2-inch from the floor. Shift the transmission between 1st gear and Reverse several times. If the gearchange is rough, component failure is indicated. Check the slave cylinder pushrod travel. With the clutch pedal depressed completely, the slave cylinder pushrod should extend substantially. If it doesn't, check the fluid level in the clutch master cylinder.

d) Visually inspect the pivot bush at the top of the clutch pedal to make sure there is no binding or excessive play.

e) Crawl under the car and make sure the clutch release lever is solidly mounted on the ball stud.

3 Clutch master cylinder - removal and refitting
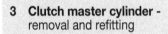

Removal

1 Disconnect the cable from the negative battery terminal. *Caution: If the radio in your car is equipped with an anti-theft system, make sure you have the correct activation code before disconnecting the battery.*

2 Working under the dashboard, remove the split pin from the master cylinder pushrod clevis. Pull out the clevis pin to disconnect the pushrod from the pedal.

3 Detach the clutch master cylinder reservoir **(see illustration)**. Clamp a pair of locking pliers onto the clutch fluid feed hose, a couple of inches downstream of the reservoir **(see illustration)**. The pliers should be just tight enough to prevent fluid flow when the hose is disconnected.

4 Disconnect the hydraulic lines at the cylinder **(see illustration)**. Loosen the fluid feed hose clamp and detach the hose from the cylinder. Have rags handy as some fluid will be lost as the line is removed. Cap or plug the ends of the lines (and/or hose) to prevent fluid leakage and the entry of contaminants. *Caution: Don't allow brake fluid to come into contact with the paint as it will damage the finish.*

5 Working under the dash, unscrew the two clutch master cylinder retaining nuts **(see illustration)** and remove the cylinder.

3.3a To get at the clutch master cylinder, remove these two bolts (arrowed) and lift the fluid reservoir out of the way

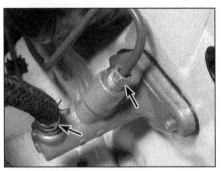

3.4 To remove the clutch master cylinder, loosen the hose clamp (left arrow) and the pressure line fitting (right arrow

Refitting

6 Place the master cylinder in position and refit the mounting bolts finger tight.

7 Connect the hydraulic lines to the master cylinder. Move the cylinder slightly as necessary to thread the fitting into the cylinder (don't tighten the fitting yet). Attach the fluid feed hose to the cylinder and tighten the hose clamp.

8 Tighten the mounting bolts securely, then tighten the hydraulic line fitting securely.

9 Connect the pushrod to the clutch pedal. Use a new split pin to secure the clevis pin.

10 Remove the locking pliers from the feed hose. Fill the clutch master cylinder reservoir with brake fluid conforming to DOT 3 specifications and bleed the clutch system as outlined in Section 5.

4.3 Loosen the clutch fluid line fitting (arrowed) at the slave cylinder

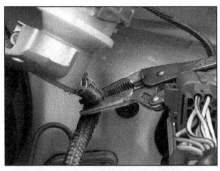

3.3b Pinch off the fluid hose between the reservoir and clutch master cylinder to prevent fluid loss

3.5 To detach the clutch master cylinder from the bulkhead, remove the two mounting nuts (arrowed)

4 Clutch slave cylinder - removal and refitting

Removal

1 Disconnect the negative cable from the battery. *Caution: If the radio in your car is equipped with an anti-theft system, make sure you have the correct activation code before disconnecting the battery.*

2 Raise the car and support it on axle stands (see "Jacking and Vehicle Support").

3 Disconnect the fluid hose at the cylinder. Use a flare nut spanner so you don't strip the corners off the fitting **(see illustration)**. Be prepared for fluid spillage as the line is removed.

4 Remove the two slave cylinder mounting bolts **(see illustration)**.

4.4 Remove the two mounting bolts (arrowed) from the clutch slave cylinder

5 Remove the slave cylinder.

Refitting

6 Refit the slave cylinder on the clutch housing, but don't completely tighten the bolts yet. Make sure the pushrod is seated in the release fork pocket.

7 Connect the hydraulic line to the slave cylinder, then tighten the slave cylinder mounting bolts securely. Using a flare-nut spanner, tighten the hydraulic fitting securely.

8 Fill the clutch master cylinder with brake fluid conforming to DOT 3 specifications.

9 Bleed the system as described in Section 5.

10 Lower the car and connect the negative battery cable.

5 Clutch hydraulic system - bleeding

1 Bleed the hydraulic system whenever any part of the system has been removed or the fluid level has fallen so low that air has been drawn into the master cylinder. The bleeding procedure is very similar to bleeding a brake system.

2 Fill the master cylinder with new brake fluid conforming to DOT 3 specifications. *Caution: Do not re-use any of the fluid coming from the system during the bleeding operation or use fluid which has been inside an open container for an extended period of time.*

3 Raise the car and place it securely on axle stands (see "*Jacking and Vehicle Support*") to gain access to the slave cylinder, which is located on the front of the transmission.

4 Remove the dust cap which fits over the bleeder valve and push a length of plastic hose over the valve. Place the other end of the hose into a clear container with about two inches of brake fluid. The hose end must be in the fluid at the bottom of the container.

5 Have an assistant depress the clutch pedal and hold it. Open the bleeder valve on the slave cylinder, allowing fluid to flow through the hose. Close the bleeder valve when the flow of fluid (and bubbles) ceases. Once closed, have your assistant release the pedal.

6 Continue this process until all air is evacuated from the system, indicated by a solid stream of fluid being ejected from the bleeder valve each time with no air bubbles in the hose or container. Keep a close watch on the fluid level inside the clutch master cylinder reservoir - if the level drops too far, air will get into the system and you'll have to start again.

7 Refit the dust cap and lower the car. Check carefully for proper operation before placing the car into normal service.

6 Clutch components - removal, inspection and refitting

Warning: Dust produced by clutch wear and deposited on clutch components may contain asbestos, which is hazardous to your health. DO NOT blow it out with compressed air and DO NOT inhale it. DO NOT use fuel or petroleum-based solvents to remove the dust. Brake system cleaner should be used to flush the dust into a drain pan. After the clutch components are wiped clean with a rag, dispose of the contaminated rags and cleaner in a covered, marked container.

Removal

1 Access to the clutch components is normally accomplished by removing the transmission, leaving the engine in the car. If the engine is being removed for major overhaul, check the clutch for wear and renew worn components as necessary. However, the relatively low cost of the clutch components compared to the time and trouble spent gaining access to them warrants their renewal anytime the engine or transmission is removed, unless they are new or in near-perfect condition. The following procedures are based on the assumption the engine will stay in place.

2 Remove the transmission from the car (see Chapter 7, Part A). Support the engine while the transmission is out. Preferably, an engine hoist should be used to support it from above. However, if a jack is used underneath the engine, make sure a piece of wood is positioned between the jack and sump to spread the load. *Caution: The pick-up for*

the oil pump is very close to the bottom of the sump. If the pan is bent or distorted in any way, engine oil starvation could occur.

3 The clutch fork and release bearing can remain attached to the transmission housing for the time being.

4 To support the clutch disc during removal, fit a clutch alignment tool through the clutch disc hub.

5 Inspect the flywheel and pressure plate for indexing marks. The marks are usually an X, an O or a white letter. If they cannot be found, scribe or paint marks yourself so the pressure plate and the flywheel will be in the same alignment during refitting **(see illustration)**.

6 Turning each bolt a little at a time, loosen the pressure plate-to-flywheel bolts **(see illustration)**. Work in a criss-cross pattern until all spring pressure is relieved. Then hold the pressure plate securely and completely remove the bolts, followed by the pressure plate and clutch disc.

Inspection

7 Ordinarily, when a problem occurs in the clutch, it can be attributed to wear of the clutch driven plate assembly (clutch disc). However, all components should be inspected at this time.

8 Inspect the flywheel for cracks, heat checking, grooves and other obvious defects. If the imperfections are slight, a machine shop can machine the surface flat and smooth, which is highly recommended regardless of the surface appearance. Refer to Chapter 2 for the flywheel removal and refitting procedure.

9 Inspect the lining on the clutch disc. There should be at least 1.5 mm of lining above the rivet heads. Check for loose rivets, distortion, cracks, broken springs and other obvious damage **(see illustration)**. As mentioned above, ordinarily the clutch disc is routinely replaced, so if in doubt about the condition, renew it.

10 The release bearing should also be replaced along with the clutch disc (Section 7).

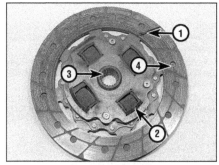

6.9 The clutch disc
1 **Lining** - this will wear down in use
2 **Springs or dampers** - check for cracking and deformation
3 **Splined hub** - the splines must not be worn, and should slide smoothly on the transmission input shaft splines
4 **Rivets** - these secure the lining, and will damage the flywheel if allowed to contact it

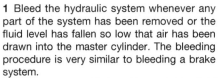
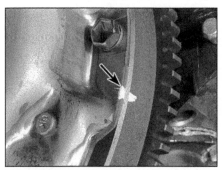

6.5 Mark the relationship of the pressure plate to the flywheel (just in case you're going to re-use the old pressure plate)

6.6 Remove the pressure plate bolts (arrowed) gradually and evenly in a criss-cross pattern

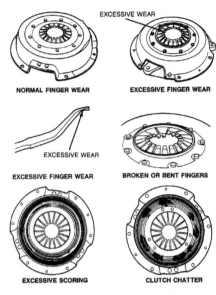

6.11 Renew the pressure plate if any of these conditions are noted

11 Check the machined surfaces and the diaphragm spring fingers of the pressure plate (see illustration). If the surface is grooved or otherwise damaged, renew the pressure plate. Also check for obvious damage, distortion, cracking, etc. Light glazing can be removed with emery cloth or sandpaper. If a new pressure plate is required, new and factory-rebuilt units are available.

Refitting

12 Before refitting, clean the flywheel and pressure plate machined surfaces with brake cleaner, lacquer thinner or acetone. It's important that no oil or grease is on these surfaces or the lining of the clutch disc. Handle the parts only with clean hands.
13 Position the clutch disc and pressure plate against the flywheel with the clutch held in place with an alignment tool (see illustration). Make sure the disc is installed properly (most renewal clutch discs will be marked "flywheel side" or something similar - if not marked, fit the clutch disc with the damper springs toward the transmission).
14 Tighten the pressure plate-to-flywheel bolts only finger tight, working around the pressure plate.
15 Centre the clutch disc by ensuring that the alignment tool extends through the splined hub and into the pocket in the crankshaft. Wiggle the tool up, down or side-to-side as needed to centre the disc. Tighten the pressure plate-to-flywheel bolts a little at a time, working in a criss-cross pattern to prevent distorting the cover. After all of the bolts are snug, tighten them to the specified torque. Remove the alignment tool.
16 Using high-temperature grease, lubricate the inner groove of the release bearing (see Section 7). Also place grease on the release lever contact areas and the transmission input shaft bearing retainer.

6.13 Centre the clutch disc in the pressure plate with a clutch alignment tool

17 Refit the clutch release bearing (see Section 7).
18 Refit the transmission and all components removed previously.

7 Clutch release bearing and fork - removal, inspection and refitting

Removal

⚠ **Warning: Dust produced by clutch wear and deposited on clutch components may contain asbestos, which is hazardous to your health. DO NOT blow it out with compressed air and DO NOT inhale it. DO NOT use fuel or petroleum-based solvents to remove the dust. Brake system cleaner should be used to flush the dust into a drain pan. After the clutch components are wiped clean with a rag, dispose of the contaminated rags and cleaner in a labelled, covered container.**

1 Unbolt the clutch slave cylinder (see Section 4), but don't disconnect the fluid line between the master cylinder and the slave cylinder. Suspend the slave cylinder out of the way with a piece of wire.
2 Remove the transmission (see Chapter 7A).
3 Slide the release bearing off the input shaft, disengage the clutch release fork retention spring from the ball stud and remove the fork (see illustrations).

7.3b . . . then disengage the fork from the ball stud by popping the fork retention spring off the ball stud with your finger

Inspection

4 Hold the bearing by the outer race and rotate the inner race while applying pressure. If the bearing doesn't turn smoothly or if it's noisy, renew the bearing/hub assembly with a new one. Wipe the bearing with a clean rag and inspect it for damage, wear and cracks. It's common practice to renew the bearing with a new one whenever a clutch job is performed, to decrease the possibility of a bearing failure in the future. Don't immerse the bearing in solvent - it's sealed for life and to do so would ruin it. Also check the release lever for cracks and bends.
5 If the new bearing is not equipped with a bearing holder (hub), drive the holder from the old bearing and fit it to the new one. A seal/bush driver or an appropriately sized socket can be used to accomplish this.

Refitting

6 Fill the inner groove of the release bearing with high temperature grease. Also apply a light coat of the same grease to the transmission input shaft splines and the front bearing retainer (see illustration).
7 Lubricate the release fork ball socket, fork ends and slave cylinder pushrod socket with high temperature grease (see illustration).
8 Fit the release bearing to the release fork.
9 Slide the release bearing onto the transmission input shaft front bearing retainer while passing the end of the release fork through the opening in the clutch housing. Push the clutch release fork onto the ball stud until it's firmly seated.

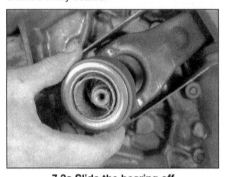

7.3a Slide the bearing off the input shaft . . .

7.6 Fill the release bearing inner groove with grease and apply a little to the input shaft splines and the front bearing retainer

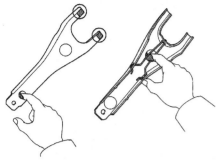

7.7 Lubricate the release fork ball socket, fork ends and slave cylinder pushrod socket with high temperature grease

10 Apply a light coat of high temperature grease to the face of the release bearing where it contacts the pressure plate diaphragm fingers.
11 The remainder of refitting is the reverse of the removal procedure.

8 Clutch pedal - adjustment

1 Loosen locknut A **(see illustration)**, then back off clutch pedal switch A.
2 Loosen locknut C, then turn the pushrod in or out until the stroke and height of the pedal are within the range listed in the Specifications at the beginning of this Chapter.
3 Tighten locknut C.
4 Screw in clutch pedal switch A until it contacts the clutch pedal.
5 Turn clutch pedal switch A another 3/4 to 1 full turn further.
6 Tighten locknut A.
7 Loosen locknut B and clutch pedal switch B.
8 Push the clutch pedal to the floor, then raise it about 3/4-inch.
9 Screw in clutch pedal switch B until it contacts the clutch pedal.
10 Turn the switch another 3/4 to 1 full turn.
11 Tighten locknut B.

9 Starter/clutch interlock switch - check, renewal and adjustment

Check

1 The starter/clutch interlock switch is located near the upper end of the clutch pedal (pedal switch B in illustration 8.1). It has two wires - one coming from the starter relay and one going to earth. When the ignition switch key is turned to the Start position and the clutch pedal is depressed, the starter relay's path to earth is closed by the starter/clutch interlock switch and the starter motor is activated.
2 If the engine will not crank when the clutch pedal is depressed, adjust the switch (see

8.1 Clutch pedal adjustment details

1 *Locknut A*
2 *Clutch pedal switch A*
3 *Locknut B*
4 *Clutch pedal switch B*
5 *Assist spring*
6 *Clutch master cylinder*
7 *Locknut C*
8 *Stroke at clutch pedal*
9 *Clutch pedal play*
10 *Clutch pedal height*
11 *Clutch pedal disengagement height*

`2118-8-8.1 HAYNES`

paragraph 6) and try again. If it still will not turn over, check the switch (see paragraph 3) and, if necessary, renew it (see paragraph 5). If the engine rotates when the clutch pedal isn't depressed, adjust the switch and try again.
3 If the engine will not start when the clutch pedal is depressed, either there's no voltage from the starter relay to the switch, or there's no continuity between the two terminals on the switch.
4 Check the voltage to the switch with a voltmeter or test light. When you turn the ignition key to the Start position and depress the clutch pedal, there should be voltage in the wire from the starter relay. If there isn't, look for an open or short circuit condition somewhere between the starter relay and the switch. If there is voltage in this wire, check the other side of the switch for voltage (with the pedal depressed). If there's voltage on both sides of the switch, the switch should be operating correctly. Try adjusting it (see paragraph 6). If voltage isn't present on both sides, the switch is bad.

Renewal

5 Unplug the electrical connector, loosen the adjustment nut and unscrew the switch from its mounting bracket. Refitting is the reverse of removal.

Adjustment

6 Loosen the locknut and turn the switch in or out, as necessary, to provide continuity through the switch when the clutch pedal is depressed.

10 Driveshafts - removal and refitting

Removal

1 Loosen the front wheel nuts. Raise the front of the car and place it securely on axle stands (see "*Jacking and Vehicle Support*"). Remove the wheel nuts and the front wheel. If the driveshaft/hub nut is staked, Unstake it with a punch or chisel **(see illustration)**; if it's secured by locking tabs, bend the tabs out.
2 Loosen the hub nut with a socket and large extension bar. To prevent the hub from turning, place a lever between two of the wheel studs, then loosen the nut **(see illustration and Tool Tip)**.
3 Drain the transmission lubricant (see Chapter 1).
4 Disconnect the damper fork from the shock

10.1 If the driveshaft nut is "staked," use a centre punch to unstake it

10.2 To prevent the hub from turning while you're loosening it, place a lever between two of the wheel studs

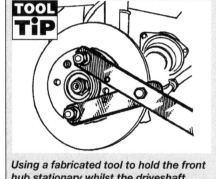

Using a fabricated tool to hold the front hub stationary whilst the driveshaft retaining nut is slackened

10.6 Swing the hub/knuckle out (away from the car) and pull the driveshaft from the hub

absorber assembly and the lower control arm (see Chapter 10).

5 Separate the lower control arm from the steering knuckle (see Chapter 10).

6 Swing the knuckle/hub assembly out (away from the car) until the end of the driveshaft is free of the hub **(see illustration)**. Support the outer end of the driveshaft with a piece of wire to avoid unnecessary strain on the inner CV joint.

7 Carefully prise the inner end of the driveshaft from the transmission - or, on convertible models, the intermediate shaft - using a large screwdriver or lever positioned between the transmission or bearing support and the CV joint housing **(see illustrations)**. Support the CV joints and carefully remove the driveshaft from the car. To prevent damage to the intermediate shaft seal or the differential seal, hold the inner CV joint horizontal until the driveshaft is clear of the intermediate shaft or transmission.

Refitting

8 Prise the old spring clip from the inner end of the driveshaft and fit a new one **(see illustrations)**. Lubricate the differential or intermediate shaft seal with multi-purpose grease and raise the driveshaft into position while supporting the CV joints.

9 Insert the splined end of the inner CV joint into the differential side gear (or, on convertible models, the intermediate shaft)

and make sure the spring clip locks in its groove **(see illustration)**.

10 Apply a light coat of multi-purpose grease to the outer CV joint splines, pull out on the strut/steering knuckle assembly and refit the stub axle into the hub.

11 Insert the stud of the lower control arm balljoint into the steering knuckle and tighten the nut (see the torque specifications in Chapter 10). Be sure to use a new split pin. Refit the damper fork (see Chapter 10).

12 Fit the hub nut (and, if applicable, a new locking tab washer). Lock the disc as described in paragraph 2 so it can't turn, then tighten the hub nut securely. Don't try to tighten it to the actual torque specification until you've lowered the car to the earth.

13 Grasp the inner CV joint housing (not the driveshaft) and pull out to make sure the driveshaft has seated securely in the transmission.

14 Refit the wheel and wheel nuts, then lower the car.

15 Tighten the wheel nuts to the torque listed in the Chapter 1 Specifications. Tighten the hub nut to the torque listed in this Chapter's Specifications. Using a hammer and punch, stake the nut to the groove in the driveshaft. If the hub nut uses a locking tab, be sure to bend the tabs up against the nut. Refit the wheel cover (if applicable).

16 Refill the transmission with the recommended type and amount of lubricant (see Chapter 1).

10.7a Use a large screwdriver or a lever to remove the inner end of the driveshaft from the transmission, or . . .

10.7b . . . if removing the left driveshaft from a convertible model, lever between intermediate shaft bearing and driveshaft

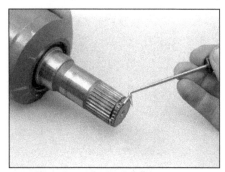

10.8a Prise the old spring clip from the inner end of the driveshaft with a small screwdriver or awl

10.8b To refit the new spring clip, start one end in the groove and work the clip over the shaft end, into the groove

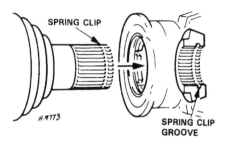

10.9 When refitting the driveshaft, make sure the spring clip pops into place in its groove - if it's seated properly, you shouldn't be able to pull it out by hand

11 Intermediate shaft (where applicable) - removal and refitting

Removal

1 Loosen the left front wheel nuts, raise the front of the car and support it on axle stands (see "*Jacking and Vehicle Support*"). Remove the wheel.

2 Drain the transmission oil (see Chapter 1).

3 Separate the left lower control arm from the steering knuckle (see Chapter 10).

4 Prise the inner CV joint housing from the intermediate shaft. Position the driveshaft out of the way and hang it with a piece of wire. Do not allow it to hang unsupported, as the outer CV joint may be damaged.

5 Remove the three bearing support-to-engine block bolts (see illustration) and slide the intermediate shaft out of the transmission. Be careful not to damage the differential seal when pulling the shaft out.

6 Check the support bearing for smooth operation by turning the shaft while holding the bearing. If you feel any roughness, take the bearing support to a dealer service department or other garage to have a new bearing installed. To do the job at home, you would need specialised tools.

Refitting

7 Lubricate the lips of the differential seal with multi-purpose grease. Carefully guide the intermediate shaft into the differential side gear then fit the mounting bolts through the bearing support. Tighten the bolts to the torque listed in this Chapter's Specifications.

8 Fit a new spring clip on the inner CV joint **(see illustrations 10.8a and 10.8b)** and seat the driveshaft into the intermediate shaft splines.

9 Connect the lower control arm to the steering knuckle and tighten the balljoint stud nut to the torque listed in the Chapter 10 Specifications.

10 Refit the wheel and wheel nuts, lower the car and tighten the wheel nuts to the torque listed in the Chapter 1 Specifications.

11 Refill the transmission with the proper type and amount of lubricant (see Chapter 1).

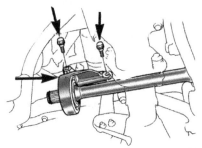

11.5 Location of the intermediate shaft bearing support bolts (arrowed) - third bolt not visible here

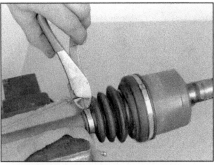

12.3a Cut off the gaiter clamps and discard them - don't try to re-use old clamps

12.3b Slide the gaiter down the driveshaft, out of the way

12 Driveshaft gaiter renewal and constant velocity (CV) joint overhaul

Note 1: *If the CV joints are worn, indicating the need for an overhaul (usually due to torn gaiters), explore all options before beginning the job. Complete rebuilt driveshafts are available on an exchange basis, which eliminates much time and work. If you decide to rebuild a CV joint, check the cost and availability of parts before dismantling the driveshaft.*

Note 2: *Some motor factors carry "split" type renewal gaiters, which can be fitted without removing the driveshaft from the car. This is a convenient alternative; however, the driveshaft should be removed and the CV joint disassembled and cleaned to ensure that the joint is free from contaminants such as moisture and dirt which will accelerate CV joint wear.*

1 Remove the driveshaft from the car (see Section 10) then measure the overall length of it so that it can be adjusted before tightening the new gaiters.

2 Mount the driveshaft in a vice. The jaws of the vice should be lined with wood or rags to prevent damage to the driveshaft.

Inner CV joint and gaiter

Dismantling

3 Cut off both gaiter clamps and slide the gaiter towards the centre of the driveshaft **(see illustrations)**.

4 Scribe or paint alignment marks on the outer race and the tripod bearing assembly **(see illustration)** so they can be returned to their original position, then slide the outer race off the tripod bearing assembly.

5 Remove the circlip from the end of the driveshaft, then mark the relationship of the tripod bearing assembly to the driveshaft **(see illustration)**.

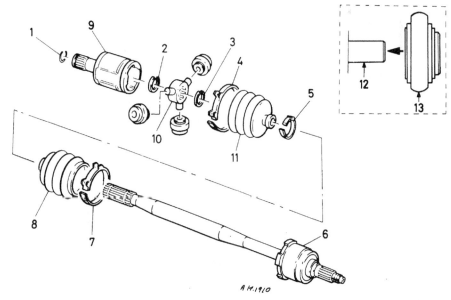

12.3c An exploded view of a typical driveshaft assembly

1 Spring clip	6 Outer CV joint	9 Inner CV joint	12 Tripod post
2 Circlip	assembly	housing/outer race	13 Roller bearing
3 Stop-ring	7 Gaiter clamp	10 Tripod assembly	
5 Gaiter clamp	8 Gaiter	11 Gaiter	

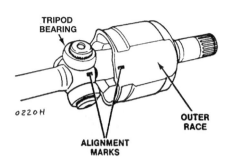

12.4 Scribe or paint alignment marks on the tripod assembly and the outer race, then slide the outer race off

12.5 Remove the circlip from the end of the driveshaft, then mark the tripod bearing assembly in relation to the driveshaft

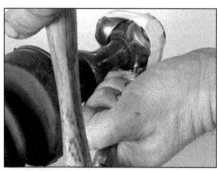

12.6 Secure the bearing rollers with tape, drive the tripod off with a hammer and brass drift, then remove the stop-ring

12.10a Wrap the splined area of the driveshaft with tape to prevent damage to the gaiter when refitting it

12.10b Refit the stop-ring on the driveshaft, making sure it seats in its groove

12.12 Refit the tripod assembly on the driveshaft, making sure the punch marks are lined up, then refit the circlip

12.13 Use plenty of CV joint grease to hold the needle bearings in place when you refit the roller assemblies on the tripod

12.14 Pack the outer race with grease and slide it over the tripod - enure the match marks on outer race and tripod align

14 Pack the outer race with half of the grease furnished with the new gaiter and place the remainder in the gaiter. Fit the outer race **(see illustration)**. Make sure the marks you made on the tripod assembly and the outer race are aligned.
15 Seat the gaiter in the grooves in the outer race and the driveshaft, then adjust the driveshaft to the proper length **(see illustration)**.
16 With the driveshaft set to the proper length, equalise the pressure in the gaiter by inserting a blunt screwdriver between the gaiter and the outer race **(see illustration)**. Don't damage the gaiter with the tool.
17 Fit and tighten the new gaiter clamps **(see illustrations)**.
18 Refit the driveshaft assembly (Section 10).

6 Secure the bearing rollers with tape, then remove the tripod bearing assembly from the driveshaft with a brass drift and a hammer **(see illustration)**. Remove the tape, but don't let the rollers fall off and get mixed up.
7 Remove the stop-ring, slide the old gaiter off the driveshaft and discard it.

Inspection

8 Clean the old grease from the outer race and the tripod bearing assembly. Carefully dismantle each section of the tripod assembly, one at a time so as not to mix up the parts, and clean the needle bearings with solvent.
9 Inspect the rollers, tripod, bearings and outer race for scoring, pitting or other signs of abnormal wear, which will warrant the renewal of the inner CV joint.

Reassembly

10 Wrap the splines of the driveshaft with tape to avoid damaging the new gaiter, then slide the gaiter onto the driveshaft **(see illustration)**. Remove the tape and slide the inner circlip into place **(see illustration)**.
11 Align the match marks you made before dismantling and tap the tripod assembly onto the driveshaft with a hammer and brass drift.
12 Fit the outer circlip **(see illustration)**.
13 Apply a coat of CV joint grease to the inner bearing surfaces to hold the needle bearings in place when reassembling the tripod assembly **(see illustration)**. Make sure each roller is installed on the same post as before. **Note:** *If the rollers have a flat, rectangular shaped surface, make sure the flat sides are positioned closest to the driveshaft.*

Outer CV joint and gaiter

Dismantling

19 Following Steps 3 to 7, remove the inner CV joint from the driveshaft and dismantle it.
20 If the driveshaft has a dynamic damper,

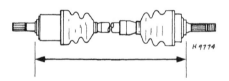

12.15 Before tightening the gaiter clamps, adjust the driveshaft length to the dimension noted on removal

12.16 Equalise the pressure inside the gaiter using a small, dull screwdriver

12.17b . . . and flatten the tabs to hold it in place

scribe or paint a location mark on the driveshaft along the outer edge of the damper (the side facing the outer CV joint), cut the retaining clamp and slide the damper off. **Note:** *If you're planning to renew the driveshaft and outer CV joint assembly, the specified distance between the inner CV joint gaiter and the dynamic damper is listed in this Chapter's Specifications.*

12.17a To refit the new clamps, bend the tang down . . .

12.23 Inspect the bearing surfaces for wear and damage

21 Cut the gaiter clamps from the outer CV joint. Slide the gaiter off the shaft. **Note:** *The outer CV joint can't be disassembled or removed from the shaft.*

Inspection

22 Thoroughly wash the inner and outer CV joints in clean solvent and blow them dry with compressed air, if available.

 Warning: Wear eye protection when using compressed air.

Note: *Because the outer joint can't be disassembled, it is difficult to wash away all the old grease and to rid the bearing of solvent once it's clean. But it is imperative that the job be done thoroughly, so take your time and do it right.*
23 Bend the outer CV joint housing at an angle to the driveshaft to expose the bearings, inner race and cage **(see illustration)**. Inspect the bearing surfaces for signs of wear. If the bearings are damaged or worn, renew the driveshaft.

Reassembly

24 Slide the new outer gaiter onto the driveshaft. It's a good idea to wrap tape around the splines of the shaft to prevent damage to the gaiter **(see illustration 12.10a)**. When the gaiter is in position, add the specified amount of grease (included in the gaiter renewal kit) to the outer joint and the gaiter (pack the joint with as much grease as it will hold and put the rest into the gaiter). Slide the gaiter on the rest of the way and fit the new clamps **(see illustrations 12.17a and 12.17b)**.
25 Slide the dynamic damper, if applicable, onto the shaft. Make sure its outer edge is aligned with the previously applied mark. **Note:** *If you're using a new driveshaft and outer CV joint assembly, the specified distance between the inner CV joint gaiter and the dynamic damper is listed in this Chapter's Specifications.* Fit a new retaining clamp.
26 Clean and reassemble the inner CV joint by following Steps 8 through 17, then refit the driveshaft as outlined in Section 10.

Chapter 9
Braking system

Contents

Degrees of difficulty

Easy, suitable for novice with little experience		Fairly easy, suitable for beginner with some experience		Fairly difficult, suitable for competent DIY mechanic		Difficult, suitable for experienced DIY mechanic		Very difficult, suitable for expert DIY or professional	

Specifications

General

Brake pedal freeplay	1 to 5 mm
Brake pedal height	
Manual transmission	165 mm
Automatic transmission	160 mm
Handbrake lever travel	See Chapter 1
Brake servo pushrod-to-master cylinder piston	
clearance (with a vacuum of 30 in-Hg applied to servo)	0.0 to 0.4 mm

Disc brakes

Brake pad minimum thickness	See Chapter 1
Disc minimum thickness	Refer to minimum thickness cast into disc
Thickness variation (parallelism)	No more than 0.015 mm
Runout limit	0.10 mm

Drum brakes

Brake lining minimum thickness	See Chapter 1
Drum diameter	Refer to maximum diameter cast into drum

Torque wrench settings

	Nm	lbf ft
Brake hose-to-caliper banjo bolt (front or rear)	34	25
Front caliper bolts		
Models with two (upper and lower) mounting bolts	33	24
Models with lower mounting bolt only	27	20
Front caliper mounting bracket bolts	109	80
Rear caliper bolts	23	17
Rear caliper bracket bolts	38	28
Wheel cylinder nuts	10	7
Brake servo mounting nuts	12	9

1 General information

General

All vehicles covered by this manual have hydraulically operated power assisted brake systems. All front brake systems are disc type. Some models use drum type brakes at the rear, others have with disc brakes.

All brakes are self-adjusting. The front and rear disc brakes automatically compensate for pad wear, while the rear drum brakes incorporate an adjustment mechanism which is activated as the brakes are applied, either through the pedal or the handbrake lever.

The hydraulic system is a diagonally-split design, meaning there are separate circuits for the left front/right rear and the right front/left rear brakes. If one circuit fails, the other circuit will remain functional and a warning indicator will light up on the dashboard when a substantial amount of brake fluid is lost, showing that a failure has occurred.

Master cylinder

The master cylinder is bolted to the brake servo, which is mounted on the driver's side of the bulkhead. To locate the master cylinder, look for the large fluid reservoir on top. The fluid reservoir is a removable plastic cup, secured to the master cylinder by a clamp.

The master cylinder is designed for the "split system" mentioned earlier and has separate piston assemblies for each circuit.

Proportioning valve

The proportioning valve assembly is located on the bulkhead. On cars equipped with the Anti-lock Brake System (ABS), it is an integral part of the modulator/solenoid unit, which is located on the right (passenger's) side of the bulkhead, behind the transmission.

The proportioning valve regulates the hydraulic pressure to the rear brakes during heavy braking to eliminate rear wheel lock-up. Under normal braking conditions, it allows full pressure to the rear brake system until a predetermined pedal pressure is reached. Above that point, the pressure to the rear brakes is limited.

The proportioning valve is not serviceable - if a problem develops with the valve, it must be replaced as an assembly.

Brake servo

The brake servo, which uses engine manifold vacuum and atmospheric pressure to provide assistance to the hydraulically operated brakes, is mounted on the bulkhead in the engine compartment.

Handbrake

A handbrake lever inside the car operates a single front cable attached to a pair of rear cables, each of which is connected to its respective rear brake. When the handbrake lever is pulled on drum brake models, each rear cable pulls on a lever attached to the brake shoe assembly, causing the shoes to expand against the drum. When the lever is pulled on models with rear disc brakes, the rear cables pull on levers that are attached to screw-type actuators in the caliper housings, which apply force to the caliper pistons, clamping the brake pads against the brake disc.

Precautions

There are some general cautions and warnings involving the brake system on these vehicles:

a) Use only brake fluid conforming to DOT 3 specifications.
b) The brake pads and linings may contain asbestos fibres which are hazardous to your health if inhaled. Whenever you work on brake system components, clean all parts with brake system cleaner. Do not allow the fine dust to become airborne.
c) Safety should be paramount whenever any servicing of the brake components is performed. Do not use parts or fasteners which are not in perfect condition, and be sure that all clearances and torque specifications are adhered to. If you are at all unsure about a certain procedure, seek professional advice. Upon completion of any brake system work, test the brakes carefully in a controlled area before putting the car into normal service.
d) No part of the brake hydraulic system on a car equipped with an Anti-lock Brake System (ABS) should be disconnected, as special tools are required to properly bleed the system. Take the car to a dealer service department or other qualified garage for repairs which require opening of the system.
e) If a problem is suspected in the brake system, don't drive the car until it's fixed.

2 Anti-lock Brake System (ABS) - general information and trouble codes

⚠️ **Warning: No part of the hydraulic brake system on a vehicle equipped with an Anti-lock Brake System (ABS) should be disconnected, as special tools are needed to properly bleed the system. Take the vehicle to a dealer service department or other garage for repairs which require opening of the system.**

General information

In a conventional braking system, if you press the brake pedal too hard, the wheels can "lock up" (stop turning) and the car can go into a skid. If the wheels lock up, you can lose control of the car. The Anti-lock Brake System (ABS) prevents the wheels from locking up by modulating (pulsing on and off) the pressure of the brake fluid at each caliper.

The Anti-lock Brake System has two basic subsystems: One is an electrical system and the other is hydraulic. The electrical half has four "gear pulsers," four wheel sensors, a computer and an electrical circuit connecting all the components. The hydraulic part of the system consists of a solenoid/modulator, the disc brake calipers and the hydraulic fluid lines between the solenoid/modulator and the calipers.

In principle, the system is pretty simple: Each wheel has a wheel sensor monitoring a gear pulser (a ring with evenly-spaced raised ridges cast into its circumference). The wheel sensor "counts" the ridges of the gear pulser as they pass by, converts this information into an electrical output and transmits it back to the computer. The computer constantly "samples" the voltage inputs from all four wheel sensors and compares them to each other. As long as the gear pulsers at all four wheels are rotating at the same speed, the Anti-lock Brake System is inactive. But when a wheel locks up, the voltage signal from that wheel sensor deviates from the signals coming from the other wheels.

So the computer "knows" the wheel is locking up. It sends an electrical signal to the solenoid/modulator assembly, which releases the brake fluid pressure to the brake caliper at that wheel. As soon as the wheel unlocks and resumes turning at the same rate of speed as the other wheels, its wheel sensor voltage output once again matches the output of the other wheels and the computer deactivates the signal to the solenoid/modulator.

In reality, the Anti-lock Brake System is far more complex than it sounds, so we do not recommend that you attempt to diagnose or service it. If the Anti-lock Brake System on your car develops problems, take it to a dealer service department or other qualified garage.

ABS trouble codes (where applicable)

1 Normally, the ABS indicator light should come on when the engine is started, then go off immediately. Under certain conditions, however, the indicator light may remain on. If this occurs, the ABS computer has stored a diagnostic trouble code because it has detected a problem in the ABS system. You can have the ABS indicator display the diagnostic trouble code as follows:
2 Unplug the service check connector from the connector cover located underneath the glove box (see Chapter 6).
3 Bridge the two terminals of the service check connector with a jumper wire.
4 Turn the ignition switch to On, but don't start the engine. One second after you turn on the ignition, the ABS computer will begin displaying any stored diagnostic trouble code(s) by blinking the ABS indicator light on and off. The sequence begins with a two-second pause, followed by a series of blinks representing the main code, followed by a one-second pause, followed by another series of blinks representing the sub-code (if any), followed by a five-second pause, then the next main code/sub-code blinks, another five second pause, the next main code/sub-code combination, etc. The ABS computer can indicate up to three codes.
5 Count the number of main code and sub-code blinks and jot them down, then refer to the accompanying table (see illustration). If you miscount, turn the ignition switch to Off, then back to On, to recycle the ABS computer.

3 Disc brake pads - renewal

Note: *This procedure applies to front and rear disc brakes.*

⚠️ *Warning: Disc brake pads must be replaced on both front wheels at the same time - never renew the pads on only one wheel. Also, the dust created by the brake system may contain asbestos,*

TROUBLE CODE		MALFUNCTIONING COMPONENT/ SYSTEM	WHEELS-AFFECTED				OTHER COMPONENTS POSSIBLY INVOLVED
MAIN CODE	SUB-CODE		FRONT RIGHT	FRONT LEFT	REAR RIGHT	REAR LEFT	
1	—	Pump motor over-run	—	—	—	—	Pressure switch
	2	Pump motor circuit problem	—	—	—	—	Motor relay, Unit fuse, Motor fuse
	3	High pressure leakage	—	—	—	—	Solenoid
	4	Pressure switch	—	—	—	—	
	8	Accumulator gas leakage	—	—	—	—	
2	1	Parking brake switch-related problem	—	—	—	—	Brake fluid level switch [BRAKE] light
3	1	Pulser(s)	○				
	2			○			
	4				○	○	
4	1	Speed sensor	○				
	2			○			
	4				○		
	8					○	
5	—	Speed sensor(s)			○	○	Modulator
	4				○		
	8					○	
6	—	Fail-safe relay (Open, short)	—	—	—	—	Front or rear fail-safe relay
	1		—	—	—	—	Front fail-safe relay
	4		—	—	—	—	Rear fail-safe relay
7	1	Solenoid related problem (Open)	○				ABS B1 fuse
	2			○			Front fail-safe relay
	4				○	○	Rear fail-safe relay

2118-9-2.5 HAYNES

2.5 ABS trouble codes (not applicable in all countries)

3.5 Using a large C-clamp, push the piston back into the caliper

3.6a Before removing anything, spray with brake system cleaner to remove dust - DO NOT blow it off with compressed air, nor inhale any of it

3.6b Remove caliper bolt (lower arrow) (upper arrow shows banjo fitting for brake hose, which should not be disconnected unless you're removing the caliper

3.6c Swing the caliper up and off its upper locating pin (on this caliper, there's no upper bolt; the locating pin is a stud that's an integral part of the caliper bracket)

which is harmful to your health. Never blow it out with compressed air and don't inhale any of it. An approved filtering mask should be worn when working on the brakes. Do not, under any circumstances, use petroleum-based solvents to clean brake parts. Use brake system cleaner only!

1 Remove the cap from the fluid reservoir.
2 Loosen the wheel nuts, raise the front, or rear, of the car and support it on axle stands (see "Jacking and Vehicle Support").
3 Remove the front, or rear, wheels. Work on one brake assembly at a time, using the assembled brake for reference if necessary.
4 Inspect the brake disc carefully as outlined in Section 5. If machining is necessary, follow the information in that Section to remove the disc, at which time the calipers and pads can be removed as well.

Front pads

5 Push the piston back into the bore to provide room for the new brake pads. A C-clamp can be used to accomplish this (see illustration). As the piston is depressed to the bottom of the caliper bore, the fluid in the master cylinder will rise. Make sure it doesn't overflow. If necessary, siphon off some of the fluid.
6 Follow the accompanying illustrations, beginning with 3.6a, for the actual pad renewal procedure. Be sure to stay in order and read the caption under each illustration. **Note:** *The sequence shown here depicts the procedure for changing the pads on one of several typical front calipers used on the cars covered by this manual. If your car is equipped with either of the other two calipers* (see illustrations), *refer to the accompanying exploded views. These calipers have two pins*

3.6d Hang the caliper out of the way with a piece of coat hanger wire

3.6e Remove the outer brake pad and shim

3.6f Remove the inner brake pad (some models don't have a shim on the inner pad)

3.6g Remove and inspect the upper and lower brake pad retainer clips (upper clip shown); the inner pad also has a pair of clips just like the two outer clips

3.6h The pad retainer clips should fit snugly into their respective grooves in the caliper mounting bracket; if they don't, renew them (lower outer clip shown)

3.6i Apply anti-squeal compound to the back of the inner pads

3.6j Fit the new inner pad; ensure the "ears" on the upper and lower ends of the pad are fully engaged with their respective grooves and the pad retainer clips

3.6k Refit the new outer pad and shim (if the new pad has no shim, take the old shim off the old pad and fit it on the new outer pad)

3.6l Before refitting the caliper, remove the caliper pin dust boots and inspect them for tears and cracks; if they're damaged, renew them

3.6m Clean off the upper caliper pin and coat it with high-temperature grease; do the same thing with the lower caliper retaining bolt

3.6n Slide the caliper onto the upper locating pin like this (or on models that use bolts, refit the upper bolt), then swing the caliper down over the disc and new pads

3.6o Refit the lower bolt and tighten it to the torque listed in this Chapter's Specifications

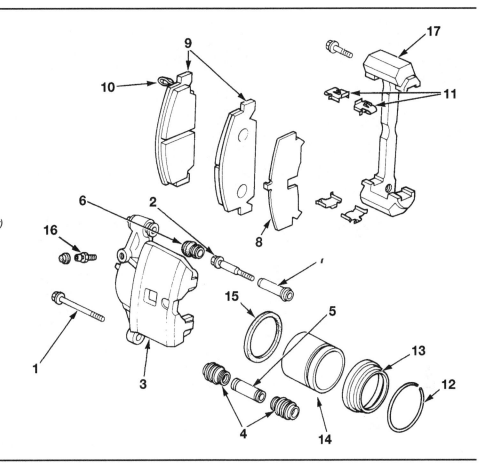

**3.6p An exploded view
of an Akebono caliper**

1 Lower caliper pin (bolt)
2 Upper caliper pin (bolt)
3 Caliper body
4 Dust boot
5 Sleeve
6 Dust boot
7 Sleeve
8 Pad shim
9 Outer pad
10 Inner pad (with wear indicator)
11 Pad retainers
12 Boot clip
13 Piston boot
14 Piston
15 Piston seal
16 Bleeder screw
17 Caliper mounting bracket

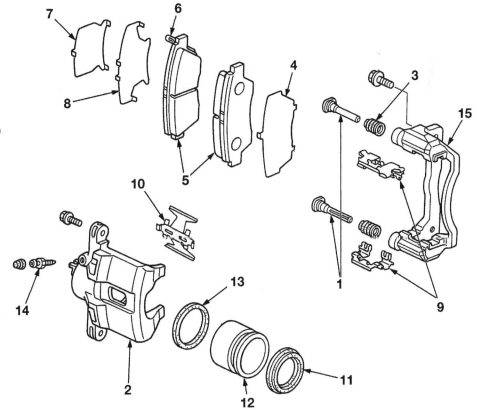

**3.6q An exploded view
of a Nissin caliper**

1 Caliper pins (bolts)
2 Caliper body
3 Dust boot
4 Outer pad shim
5 Outer pad
6 Inner pad (with wear indicator)
7 Inner shim
8 Inner shim
9 Retainers
10 Pad spring
11 Piston boot
12 Piston
13 Piston seal
14 Bleeder screw
15 Caliper mounting bracket

3.7a Remove the caliper shield bolts (arrowed) and the shield

3.7b Remove the two caliper mounting bolts (arrowed) . . .

3.7c . . . lift the caliper from its mounting bracket; hang it out of the way on a wire

3.7d Remove the outer shim and pad

3.7e Remove the inner shim and pad

3.7f Remove the brake pad retainers from the caliper (lower shown, upper identical)

3.8 Before refitting the brake pads, apply a coat of disc brake anti-squeal compound or copper-based brake grease to the backing plates of the pads

3.12 To provide clearance for the new brake pads, back the piston into the caliper bore by rotating it with a pair of needle-nose pliers

(caliper bolts) instead of one, and one of them uses a pair of inner pad shims and different pad retainers. Other than these details differences, however, the procedure for replacing the pads or overhauling either caliper is similar to the sequence shown here for pad renewal, and the overhaul procedure shown in the next section.

Rear pads

7 Follow the accompanying illustrations, beginning with 3.7a, for the actual pad renewal procedure. Be sure to stay in order and read the caption under each illustration. When you have completed the steps described in the accompanying photos, proceed to paragraph 8.
8 Apply a thin coat of disc brake anti-squeal compound, in accordance with the

manufacturer's recommendations, on the backing plates of the new pads **(see illustration)**.
9 Fit the shims onto their respective pads.
10 Fit the pad retainers in the caliper mounting bracket. Lubricate the retainers with a thin film of silicone grease.
11 Fit the new pads and shims to the caliper mounting bracket.
12 Retract the piston by engaging the tips of a pair of needle-nose pliers with two of the grooves in the top of the piston and turning it clockwise until it bottoms out **(see illustration)**. Now, rotate the piston out until one of its grooves is aligned with the tab on the inner brake pad when you fit the caliper. You may have to adjust the piston position by turning it back and forth until the tab fits. If the piston dust boot becomes distorted when the

piston is turned, turn the piston in the opposite direction to restore the shape of the boot, but make sure the cut-out still lines up.
13 Fit the caliper protector.

Front or rear pads

14 Refit the wheel and wheel nuts, lower the car and tighten the wheel nuts to the torque specified in Chapter 1.
15 Check the brake fluid level and add fluid, if necessary (see Chapter 1).
16 Apply and release the brake pedal and (if you replaced rear pads) the hand brake lever several times to bring the pads into contact with the brake discs. Check the operation of the brakes in an isolated area before driving the car in traffic.

---

4   Disc brake caliper - removal, overhaul and refitting

⚠️ *Warning: Dust created by the brake system may contain asbestos, which is harmful to your health. Never blow or clean with compressed air and don't inhale any of it. An approved filtering mask should be worn when working on the brakes. Do not, under any circumstances, use petroleum-based solvents to clean brake parts. Use brake system cleaner only!*

Note: If an overhaul is indicated (usually because of fluid leakage), explore all options before beginning the job. New and factory

4.2 The handbrake cable is secured to the caliper by a clevis pin held by a split pin

4.3 Using a short piece of rubber hose, plug the brake line banjo fitting like this

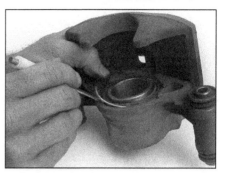

4.5 Use a screwdriver to remove the dust boot retaining ring (not on all calipers)

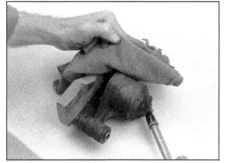

4.6 With the caliper padded to catch the piston, use compressed air to force the piston out of its bore

4.8 The piston seal should be removed with a plastic or wooden tool to avoid damage to the bore and seal groove

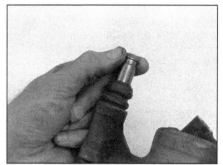

4.9 On each side of the caliper, push the mounting bolt sleeves through the boot and pull them free; remove the dust boots

rebuilt calipers are available on an exchange basis, which makes this job quite easy. If you decide to rebuild the calipers, make sure a rebuild kit is available before proceeding. Always rebuild the calipers in pairs - never rebuild just one of them.

Removal

1 Loosen - but don't remove - the wheel nuts on the front, or rear wheels. Raise the front, or rear, of the car and place it securely on axle stands (see "Jacking and Vehicle Support"). Remove the front, or rear, wheels.

2 If you're removing a rear caliper, remove the split pin from the clevis pin that connects the handbrake cable to the handbrake lever **(see illustration)**. Pull out the pin and detach the cable.

3 Disconnect the brake line from the caliper **(see illustration 3.6b)** and plug it to keep contaminants out of the brake system and to prevent losing any more brake fluid than is necessary **(see illustration)**.

4 Refer to Section 3 and remove the caliper (it's part of the brake pad renewal procedure).

Overhaul

Front caliper

Note: In addition to the illustrations accompanying this Section, refer to the exploded views accompanying Section 2 in this Chapter. The models covered by this book include a number of different caliper assemblies. They're all similar in design, but when you buy a caliper rebuild kit, be sure to

tell the parts counter person the year and model of your car so you do not get the wrong kit.

5 Place the caliper on a clean workbench. If there are any pad retainers in the caliper, note how they're installed, then remove them. If the dust boot is held in place by a ring, remove it **(see illustration)**. Prise out the dust boot.

6 Before you remove the piston, place a wood block between the piston and caliper to prevent damage as it is removed. To remove the piston from the caliper, apply compressed air to the brake fluid hose connection on the caliper body **(see illustration)**. Use only enough pressure to ease the piston out of its bore.

> ⚠ **Warning: Be careful not to place your fingers between the piston and the caliper, as the piston may come out with some force.**

7 Inspect the mating surfaces of the piston and caliper bore wall. If there is any scoring, rust, pitting or bright areas, renew the complete caliper unit with a new one.

8 If these components are in good condition, remove the piston seal from the caliper bore using a wooden or plastic tool **(see illustration)**. Metal tools may damage the cylinder bore.

9 Push the mounting bolt sleeves out of the caliper ears **(see illustration)** and remove the rubber boots from both ends (this doesn't apply to all models). Slide the bush sleeves out of the caliper ears.

10 Wash all the components with brake system cleaner.

11 To reassemble the caliper, you should already have the correct rebuild kit for the car.

12 Submerge the new piston seal in brake fluid and fit it in the lower groove in the caliper bore, making sure it isn't twisted.

13 If the caliper doesn't use a retaining ring on the piston dust boot (calipers marked NISSIN), fit the boot in the upper groove in the caliper bore. Make sure the flange on the boot seats in the groove completely.

14 Lubricate the piston with clean brake fluid, carefully slide it through the new boot, position it squarely in the caliper bore and apply firm (but not excessive) pressure to fit it. Make sure the piston boot seats in the groove in the piston **(see illustration)**.

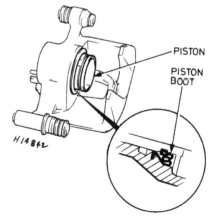

4.14 Stretch the boot over the base of the piston, and push the piston into the bore

5.3 The brake pads on this car were obviously neglected - note the deep grooves cut into the disc

5.4a Make sure the disc retaining screws or wheel nuts are tight, then rotate the disc and check the runout with a dial indicator

5.4b Using a swirling motion, remove the glaze from the disc with emery cloth or sandpaper

15 If the caliper uses a retaining ring for the piston dust boot (Akebono type - no markings), fit the new boot and retaining. Make sure the boot seats in the groove in the piston.

16 Lubricate the sliding bushings and sleeves with silicone-based grease (usually supplied in the kit) and push them into the caliper ears. Fit the dust covers. Also lubricate the caliper upper mounting pin or guide pin bolt with silicone grease **(see illustration 3.6m)**.

Rear caliper

17 Dismantling of the rear caliper requires special tools not generally available to the home mechanic. If the rear calipers need to be overhauled, take them to a dealer service department or other garage or exchange them for new or rebuilt ones.

Refitting

18 Refit the caliper by reversing the removal procedure. Remember to renew the sealing washer on either side of the brake line fitting (they should be included with the rebuild kit).

19 Bleed the brake system (see Section 11).

20 Refit the wheels, hand tighten the wheel nuts, remove the safety stands and lower the car. Tighten the wheel nuts to the torque listed in the Chapter 1 Specifications.

5 **Brake disc** - inspection, removal and refitting

Note: *This procedure applies to both the front and (on cars so equipped) rear brake discs.*

Inspection

1 Loosen the wheel nuts, raise the car and support it securely on axle stands (see *"Jacking and Vehicle Support"*). Remove the wheel and fit two wheel nuts with 3 mm thick washers under them to hold the disc in place (if the two disc retaining screws are still in place, this will be unnecessary). If you're checking the rear disc, release the handbrake.

2 Remove the brake caliper (see Section 4). It's not necessary to disconnect the brake hose. After removing the caliper bolts,

suspend the caliper out of the way with a piece of wire.

3 Visually inspect the disc surface for scoring or damage **(see illustration)**. Light scratches and shallow grooves are normal after use and may not always be detrimental to brake operation, but deep scoring requires refinishing by an specialist machine shop. Be sure to check both sides of the disc.

4 If you've noted pulsation during braking, suspect disc runout. To check disc runout, place a dial indicator at a point about 1/2-inch from the outer edge of the disc **(see illustration)**. Set the indicator to zero and turn the disc. The indicator reading should not exceed the specified allowable runout limit. If it does, have the disc refinished by a machine shop. **Note:** *Professionals recommend that the discs be resurfaced regardless of the dial indicator reading, as this will impart a smooth*

5.5a The minimum allowable thickness is stamped into the disc (typical)

5.6a Remove the front caliper mounting bracket-to-steering knuckle bolts (arrowed) and the bracket

finish and ensure a perfectly flat surface, eliminating any brake pedal pulsation or other undesirable symptoms related to questionable discs. At the very least, if you elect not to have the discs resurfaced, remove the glazing from the surface with emery cloth or sandpaper using a swirling motion **(see illustration)**.

5 It is critical that the disc not be machined to a thickness less than the minimum allowable thickness. The minimum wear (or discard) thickness is stamped on the disc **(see illustration)**. The disc thickness can be checked with a micrometer **(see illustration)**.

Removal

6 Remove the two caliper mounting bracket-to-steering knuckle bolts **(see illustration)** or, on rear calipers, the bracket-to-trailing arm bolts **(see illustration)**, and remove the mounting bracket.

5.5b A micrometer is used to measure disc thickness

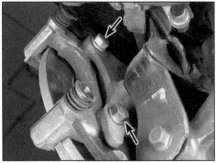

5.6b Remove the rear caliper-to-trailing arm bolts (arrowed), then remove the caliper mounting bracket

5.7a If the disc retaining screws are stuck, use an impact driver to loosen them

5.7b If the disc is stuck, thread two bolts into the disc and tighten them to force the disc off the hub

5.7c As you remove the disc, make sure you don't damage the threads on the studs for the wheel nuts

7 Remove the two wheel nuts which were put on to hold the disc in place, or the two disc retaining screws, if present **(see illustration)** and remove the disc from the hub. If the disc is stuck to the hub and won't come off, thread two bolts into the holes provided **(see illustration)** and tighten them. Alternate between the bolts, turning them a couple of turns at a time, until the disc is free **(see illustration)**.

Refitting

8 Place the disc in position over the threaded studs. Refit the disc retaining screws
9 Refit the caliper mounting bracket, brake pads and caliper over the disc. Tighten the mounting bracket and caliper bolts to the torque listed in this Chapter's Specifications.
10 Refit the wheel, then lower the car to the earth. Depress the brake pedal a few times to bring the brake pads into contact with the disc. Bleeding of the system will not be necessary unless the fluid hose was disconnected from the caliper. Check the operation of the brakes carefully before placing the car into normal service.

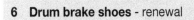

6 Drum brake shoes - renewal

Warning: Drum brake shoes must be replaced on both wheels at the same time - never renew the shoes on only one

6.2 If the drum is hard to pull off, thread a pair of 8 mm bolts into the holes provided and press the drum off

wheel. Also, the dust created by the brake system may contain asbestos, which is harmful to your health. Never blow it out with compressed air and don't inhale any of it. An approved filtering mask should be worn when working on the brakes. Do not, under any circumstances, use petroleum-based solvents to clean brake parts. Use brake system cleaner only!

Caution: Whenever the brake shoes are replaced, the return and hold-down springs should also be replaced. Due to the continuous heating/cooling cycle that the springs are subjected to, they lose their tension over a period of time and may allow the shoes to drag on the drum and wear at a much faster rate than normal.
1 Loosen the wheel nuts, raise the rear of the car and support it securely on axle stands (see *"Jacking and Vehicle Support"*). Block the front wheels to keep the car from rolling. Remove the rear wheels. Release the handbrake.

2 Remove the brake drum. It should simply pull straight off the hub. If the drum won't come off, tap it carefully with a soft-faced mallet, or screw a couple of 8.0 mm bolts into the tapped holes **(see illustration)**. If it still won't budge, the shoes have probably carved wear grooves into the drum. To get the drum off, you'll have to retract them. Remove the rubber plug in the backing plate. Use one screwdriver inserted through the hole in the backing plate to hold the self-adjuster lever away from the adjuster bolt, then use another screwdriver to rotate the adjuster bolt until the drum can be removed.
3 Replacing the shoes is easier if you remove the rear wheel bearing cap, spindle nut and washer, and slide off the hub (Chapter 10).
4 Follow **illustrations 6.4a to 6.4r** for the inspection and renewal of the brake shoes. Be sure to stay in order and read the caption under each illustration. All four rear brake shoes must be replaced at the same time, but to avoid mixing up parts, work on only one brake assembly at a time.

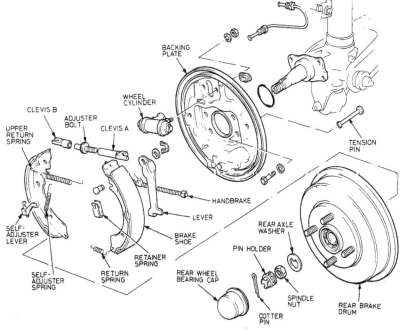

6.4a An exploded view of a typical rear drum brake assembly

6.4b Before removing anything, clean the brake assembly with brake cleaner and allow it to dry

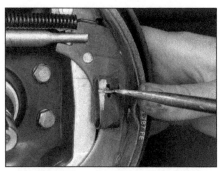

6.4c Push down on the retainer spring, then turn the pin to align its blade with the slot in the retainer spring - the spring should pop off (repeat on the other spring)

6.4d Pull the shoe assembly away from the backing plate (hub removed for clarity) . . .

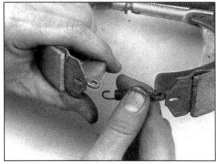

6.4e . . . and unhook the return spring

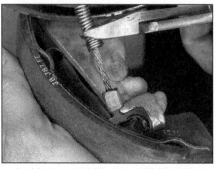

6.4f Pull back on the handbrake cable spring and grip the cable, holding the spring in the compressed position; unhook the cable end from the handbrake lever

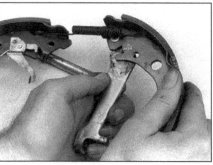

6.4g Swing the handbrake lever away from the trailing shoe, which will force the adjuster bolt clevis out of its groove in the shoe; the two shoes can now be separated

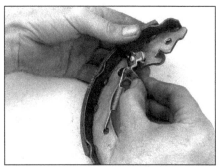

6.4h Remove the self-adjuster lever and spring from the leading shoe

6.4i Prise open the handbrake lever retaining clip and separate the lever from the shoe; be careful not to lose the wave washer that is under the clip

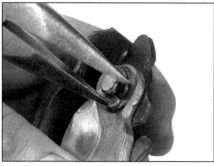

6.4j Put the new trailing shoe on the lever, place the wave washer over the pin, then refit the clip; crimp the ends of the clip together with a pair of needle-nose pliers

6.4k Clean the adjuster bolt and clevis, then lubricate the threads and ends with high-temperature grease

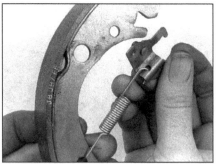

6.4l Connect the self-adjuster lever spring to the leading brake shoe, then insert the pin on the lever into its hole in the shoe

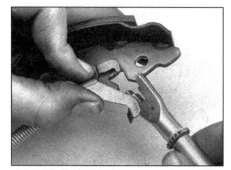

6.4m Insert the short clevis of the adjuster bolt into its slot in the leading shoe; make sure it catches the self-adjuster lever

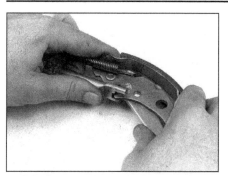

6.4n Connect the upper return spring between the two shoes, prise the lower ends of the shoes apart and insert the clevis at the other end of the adjuster bolt into the slot in the shoe; note position of the stepped portion of the clevis opening

6.4o Lubricate the brake shoe contact areas on the backing plate with high-temperature grease

6.4p Compress the handbrake cable spring, hold it in position and connect the cable end to the handbrake lever (again, if you use diagonal cutting pliers, be careful not to cut or nick the cable)

6.4q Place the brake shoe assembly against the backing plate, engaging the upper ends of the shoes in the slots in the wheel cylinder pistons. Connect the lower return spring between the shoes

6.4r With the brake shoes in position, pass the tension pins through the back plate and brake shoes, then refit the retainer springs (see illustration 6.4c) - ensure the handbrake cable spring and lower return spring are seated behind the anchor plate, as shown

7 Wheel cylinder - removal and refitting

Note: *If the wheel cylinders leak, they must be replaced with new ones - the manufacturer does not recommend overhauling them.*

Removal

1 Raise the rear of the car and support it securely on axle stands (see "*Jacking and Vehicle Support*"). Block the front wheels to keep the car from rolling.
2 Remove the brake shoe assembly (see Section 6).
3 Remove all dirt and foreign material from around the wheel cylinder.
4 Unscrew the brake line fitting **(see illustration)**. Don't pull the brake line away from the wheel cylinder.
5 Remove the wheel cylinder mounting bolts.
6 Detach the wheel cylinder from the brake backing plate and place it on a clean workbench. Immediately plug the brake line to prevent fluid loss and contamination. **Note:** *If the brake shoe linings are contaminated with brake fluid, fit new brake shoes and clean the drums with brake system cleaner.*

5 Before reinstalling the drum it should be checked for cracks, score marks, deep scratches and hard spots, which will appear as small discoloured areas. If the hard spots cannot be removed with fine emery cloth or if any of the other conditions listed above exist, the drum must be taken to an automotive machine shop to have it machined. **Note:** *Professionals recommend resurfacing the drums whenever a brake job is done. Resurfacing will eliminate the possibility of out-of-round drums.* If the drums are worn so

much that they can't be resurfaced without exceeding the maximum allowable diameter (stamped into the drum*)* **(see illustration)**, then new ones will be required. At the very least, if you elect not to have the drums resurfaced, remove the glazing from the surface with sandpaper or emery cloth using a swirling motion.
6 Fit the hub and bearing unit, the washer and a new spindle nut (if removed previously). Tighten the nut to the torque in the Chapter 10 Specifications. Refit the brake drum.
7 Mount the wheel, refit the wheel nuts, then lower the car. Tighten the wheel nuts to the torque listed in the Chapter 1 Specifications.
8 Make a number of forward and reverse stops to adjust the brakes until satisfactory pedal action is obtained.
9 Check brake operation before driving the car in traffic.

 Warning: Do not operate the car if you are in doubt about the effectiveness of the brake system.

6.5 The maximum allowable diameter is cast into the drum (typical)

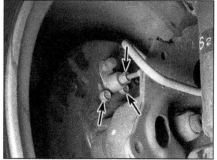

7.4 To remove the wheel cylinder, unscrew the brake line fitting (upper arrow), then remove the two wheel cylinder retaining bolts (lower arrows)

Refitting

7 Apply RTV sealant to the mating surface of the wheel cylinder and brake back plate, place the cylinder in position and connect the brake line. Don't tighten the fitting completely yet.

8 Refit the mounting bolts, tightening them securely. Tighten the brake line fitting. Fit the brake shoe assembly.

9 Bleed the brakes (see Section 11).

10 Check brake operation before driving the car in traffic.

 Warning: Do not operate the car if you are in doubt about the effectiveness of the brake system.

8 Master cylinder - removal and refitting

 Warning: This procedure should not be undertaken on a car equipped with an Anti-lock Brake System (ABS), since special tools are needed to properly bleed the brakes. Take the car to a dealer service department or other garage that has the proper tools.

Note: *If the master cylinder is defective, it must be renewed - the manufacturer does not recommend rebuilding it.*

Removal

1 The master cylinder is located in the engine compartment, mounted to the brake servo.

2 Remove as much fluid as you can from the reservoir with a syringe.

3 Place rags under the fluid fittings and prepare caps or plastic bags to cover the ends of the lines once they are disconnected. *Caution: Brake fluid will damage paint. Cover all body parts and be careful not to spill fluid during this procedure.*

4 Loosen the tube nuts at the ends of the brake lines where they enter the master cylinder **(see illustration)**. To prevent rounding off the corners on these nuts, the use of a flare-nut spanner, which wraps around the nut, is preferred.

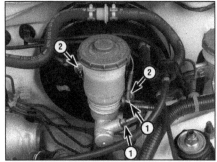

8.4 Use a flare-nut spanner to unscrew the threaded fittings (1) at the master cylinder then remove the two nuts (2)

5 Pull the brake lines slightly away from the master cylinder and plug the ends to prevent contamination.

6 Disconnect the electrical connector at the master cylinder, then remove the nuts attaching the master cylinder to the power servo. Pull the master cylinder off the studs and out of the engine compartment. Again, be careful not to spill the fluid as this is done.

Refitting

7 Bench bleed the new master cylinder before refitting it. Because it will be necessary to apply pressure to the master cylinder piston and, at the same time, control flow from the brake line outlets, it is recommended that the master cylinder be mounted in a vice, with the jaws of the vice clamping on the mounting flange.

8 Insert threaded plugs into the brake line outlet holes and snug them down so there will be no air leakage past them, but not so tight that they cannot be easily loosened (if you don't have any plugs, see paragraph 13).

9 Fill the reservoir with brake fluid of the recommended type (see Chapter 1).

10 Remove one plug and push the piston assembly into the master cylinder bore to expel the air from the master cylinder. A large crosshead screwdriver can be used to push on the piston assembly.

11 To prevent air from being drawn back into the master cylinder, the plug must be replaced and seated before releasing the pressure on the piston assembly.

12 Repeat the procedure until only brake fluid is expelled from the brake line outlet hole. When only brake fluid is expelled, repeat the procedure with the other outlet hole and plug. Be sure to keep the master cylinder reservoir filled with brake fluid to prevent the introduction of air into the system.

13 Since high pressure is not involved in the bench bleeding procedure, an alternative to the removal and renewal of the plugs with each stroke of the piston assembly is available. Before pushing in on the piston assembly, remove the plug as described in paragraph 10. Before releasing the piston, however, instead of replacing the plug, simply put your finger tightly over the hole to keep air from being drawn back into the master cylinder. Wait several seconds for brake fluid to be drawn from the reservoir into the piston bore, then depress the piston again, removing your finger as brake fluid is expelled. Be sure to put your finger back over the hole each time before releasing the piston, and when the bleeding procedure is complete for that outlet, renew the plug and snug it before going on to the other port.

14 Refit the master cylinder over the studs on the brake servo and tighten the attaching nuts only finger tight at this time.

15 Thread the brake line fittings into the master cylinder. Since the master cylinder is still a bit loose, it can be moved slightly in order for the fittings to thread in easily. Do not strip the threads as the fittings are tightened.

9.1 To renew the proportioning valve, unscrew all the threaded fittings with a flare nut spanner, and unbolt the valve

16 Fully tighten the mounting nuts, then the brake line fittings.

17 Fill the master cylinder reservoir with fluid, then bleed the master cylinder and the brake system as described in Section 11. To bleed the cylinder on the car, have an assistant pump the brake pedal several times and then hold the pedal to the floor. Loosen the fitting nut to allow air and fluid to escape. Repeat this procedure on both fittings until the fluid is clear of air bubbles. Test the operation of the brake system carefully before placing the car into normal service.

 Warning: Do not operate the car if you are in doubt about the effectiveness of the brake system.

9 Proportioning valve - renewal

1 The proportioning valve **(see illustration)** is mounted on the bulkhead. Its purpose is to limit hydraulic pressure to the rear brakes under heavy braking conditions to prevent rear wheel lockup.

2 The valve is not serviceable; if you suspect it's malfunctioning, have it checked by a dealer service department or garage equipped with the necessary pressure gauges.

3 If the valve is defective, renew it by unscrewing the brake lines (using a flare-nut spanner, if available) and unbolting the valve from its mounting bracket. After the new valve is installed, bleed the complete brake system as described in Section 11.

10 Brake hoses and lines - inspection and renewal

 Warning: The brake hoses on cars with an Anti-lock Brake System (ABS) should not be disconnected or replaced by the DIY mechanic, since special tools are required to properly bleed the brakes. Take the car to a dealer service department or qualified garage.

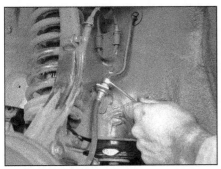

10.4a Use a flare-nut spanner to break loose the brake line-to-hose fitting . . .

1 About every six months the flexible hoses which connect the steel brake lines with the rear brakes and front calipers should be inspected for cracks, chafing of the outer cover, leaks, blisters, and other damage.
2 Renewal steel and flexible brake lines are commonly available from dealer parts departments and motor factors.

 Warning: Do not, under any circumstances, use anything other than genuine steel brake lines or approved flexible brake hoses as renewal items.

3 When refitting the brake line, leave at least 20 mm clearance between the line and any moving or vibrating parts.
4 To disconnect a hose and line, use a flare-nut spanner **(see illustration)**. Then remove the clip and slide the hose out of the bracket **(see illustration)**.
5 When disconnecting two hoses, use normal spanners on the hose fittings. When connecting two hoses, make sure they are not twisted or strained.
6 Steel brake lines are usually retained along their span with clips. Always remove these clips completely before removing a fixed brake line. Always fit these clips, or new ones if the old ones are damaged, when replacing a brake line, as they provide support and keep the lines from vibrating, which can eventually break them.
7 When replacing brake lines be sure to use the correct parts. NEVER use copper tubing! Purchase steel brake lines from a dealer or auto parts store.
8 When refitting a steel line, make sure it's securely supported in the brackets and has plenty of clearance between moving or hot components.
9 After refitting, check the fluid level in the master cylinder and add fluid as necessary. Bleed the brake system as described in Section 11 and test the brakes carefully before driving the car in traffic.

 Warning: Do not operate the car if you are in doubt about the effectiveness of the brake system.

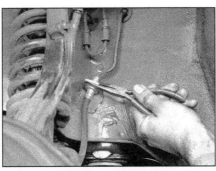

10.4b . . . then remove the clip and slide the hose out of the bracket

11 Brake hydraulic system - bleeding

 Warning: This procedure should not be undertaken on a car equipped with an Anti-lock Brake System (ABS), since special tools are needed to properly bleed the brakes. Take the car to a dealer service department or other garage that has the proper tools. Wear eye protection when bleeding the brake system. If the fluid comes in contact with your eyes, immediately rinse them with water and seek medical attention.

1 Bleeding the hydraulic system is necessary to remove any air that finds its way into the system when it's been opened during removal and refitting of a hose, line, caliper or master cylinder. It will probably be necessary to bleed the system at all four brakes if air has entered the system due to low fluid level, or if the brake lines have been disconnected at the master cylinder.
2 If a brake line was disconnected only at a wheel, then only that caliper or wheel cylinder must be bled.
3 If a brake line is disconnected at a fitting located between the master cylinder and any of the brakes, that part of the system served by the disconnected line must be bled.
4 Remove any residual vacuum from the brake servo by applying the brake several times with the engine off.
5 Remove the master cylinder reservoir cover and fill the reservoir with brake fluid. Fit the cover. **Note:** *Check the fluid level often during the bleeding operation and add fluid as necessary to prevent the fluid level from falling low enough to allow air bubbles into the master cylinder.*
6 Have an assistant on hand, and a supply of new brake fluid, a glass jar partially filled with clean brake fluid, a length of plastic, rubber or vinyl tubing to fit over the bleed screw and a spanner to open and close the bleed screw.
7 Beginning at the right rear wheel, loosen the bleed screw slightly, then tighten it to a point where it is snug but can still be loosened quickly and easily.

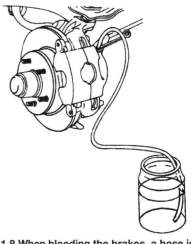

11.8 When bleeding the brakes, a hose is connected to the bleed screw at the caliper or wheel cylinder and then submerged in brake fluid

8 Place one end of the tubing over the bleed screw and submerge the other end in brake fluid in the container **(see illustration)**.
9 Have the assistant pump the brakes slowly a few times to get pressure in the system, then hold the pedal firmly depressed.
10 While the pedal is held depressed, open the bleed screw just enough to allow a flow of fluid to leave the screw. Watch for air bubbles to exit the submerged end of the tube. When the fluid flow slows after a couple of seconds, close the screw and have your assistant release the pedal.
11 Repeat Steps 9 and 10 until no more air is seen leaving the tube, then tighten the bleed screw and proceed to the left front wheel, the left rear wheel and the right front wheel, in that order, and perform the same procedure. Be sure to check the fluid in the master cylinder reservoir frequently.
12 Never use old brake fluid. It contains moisture which boils during (or after) heavy braking, rendering the brakes inoperative.
13 Refill the master cylinder with fluid at the end of the operation.
14 Check the operation of the brakes. The pedal should feel solid when depressed, with no sponginess. If necessary, repeat the process.

 Warning: Do not operate the car if you are in doubt about the operation of the brake system.

12 Brake servo - check, removal and refitting

Operating check

1 Depress the brake pedal several times with the engine off and make sure there is no change in the pedal reserve distance.
2 Depress the pedal and start the engine. If the pedal goes down slightly, operation is normal.

12.10 Remove the four brake servo mounting nuts (two left nuts shown; the right nuts aren't visible in this photo)

Airtightness check

3 Start the engine and turn it off after one or two minutes. Depress the brake pedal several times slowly. If the pedal goes down further the first time but gradually rises after the second or third depression, the servo is airtight.

4 Depress the brake pedal while the engine is running, then stop the engine with the pedal depressed. If there is no change in the pedal reserve travel after holding the pedal for 30 seconds, the servo is airtight.

Removal

5 Brake servo units should not be disassembled. They require special tools not normally found in most automotive repair stations or shops. They are fairly complex and because of their critical relationship to brake performance it is best to renew a defective servo unit with a new or rebuilt one.

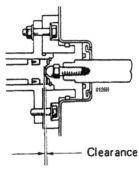

12.13a The servo pushrod-to-master cylinder clearance must be as specified

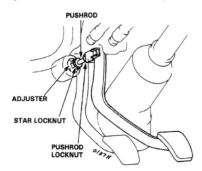

12.13b Servo pushrod adjustment details

6 To remove the servo, first remove the brake master cylinder as described in Section 8.

7 Disconnect the hose leading from the engine to the servo. Be careful not to damage the hose when removing it from the servo fitting.

8 Locate the pushrod clevis pin connecting the servo to the brake pedal. This is accessible from under the dash panel in front of the driver's seat.

9 Remove the split pin with pliers and pull out the clevis pin.

10 Remove the four nuts and washers **(see illustration)** holding the brake servo to the bulkhead. You may need a light to see them, because they are up under the dash area.

11 Slide the servo straight out from the bulkhead until the studs clear the holes and pull the servo, brackets and gaskets from the engine compartment area.

Refitting

12 Refitting procedures are basically the reverse of those for removal. Tighten the servo mounting nuts to the torque listed in this Chapter's Specifications. Also, be sure to use a new split pin on the clevis pin.

13 If the power servo unit is being replaced, the clearance between the master cylinder piston and the pushrod in the vacuum servo must be measured. Using a depth micrometer or vernier calipers, measure the distance from the seat (recessed area) in the master cylinder piston to the master cylinder mounting flange. Next, apply a vacuum of 20 in-Hg to the servo (using a hand vacuum pump) and measure the distance from the end of the vacuum servo pushrod to the mounting face of the servo (including gasket, if used) where the master cylinder mounting flange seats. Subtract the two measurements to get the clearance **(see illustration)**. If the clearance is more or less than specified, loosen the star locknut and turn the adjuster on the power servo pushrod until the clearance is within the specified limit **(see illustration)**. After adjustment, tighten the locknut.

14 After the final refitting of the master cylinder and brake hoses and lines, bleed the brakes as described in Section 11.

13 Handbrake - adjustment

1 Remove the gear lever knob (Chapter 7).

2 Remove the centre console (Chapter 11).

3 Block the front wheels, raise the rear of the car and support it securely on axle stands (see "Jacking and Vehicle Support"). Apply the handbrake lever until you hear one click.

4 Turn the adjusting nut on the equaliser **(see illustration)** clockwise while rotating the rear wheels. Stop turning the nut when the brakes just start to drag on the rear wheels.

5 Release the handbrake lever and check to see that the brakes don't drag when the rear

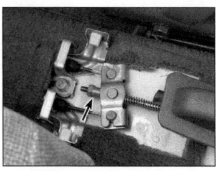

13.4 The handbrake adjusting nut (arrowed) is on the equaliser assembly

wheels are turned. The travel on the handbrake lever should be as listed in the Chapter 1 Specifications when properly adjusted.

6 Lower the car and refit the console (see Chapter 11).

14 Handbrake cable(s) - renewal

1 Block the front wheels and loosen the rear wheel nuts. Raise the rear of the car and support it securely on axle stands (see "Jacking and Vehicle Support").

2 On cars with rear drum brakes, remove the brake drum(s) (see Section 6).

3 Following the procedure in the previous Section, loosen the cable adjusting nut. Remove the cable clamp from the cable housing **(see illustration 13.4)**. Unhook the cable from the equaliser.

4 On models with rear drum brakes, remove the brake shoes (see Section 6) and disconnect the cable end from the lever on the trailing brake shoe **(see illustration 6.4f)**. Depress the tangs on the cable housing retainer and pass the cable through the backing plate. You can do this by passing an offset 12 mm box end spanner over the end of the cable and onto the retainer **(see illustration)**. This compresses all the tangs simultaneously.

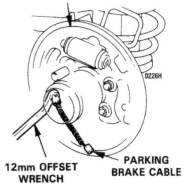

14.4 Compress the tangs on the retainer by sliding a 12 mm offset ring spanner over the end of the cable onto the retainer, and pull the cable out of the backing plate

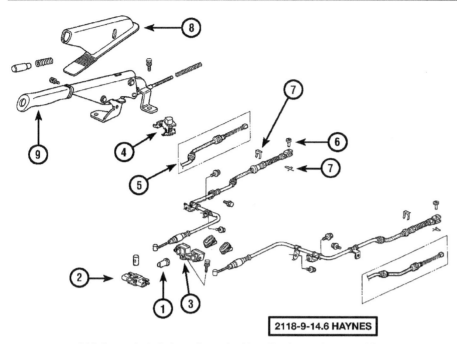

2118-9-14.6 HAYNES

14.6 An exploded view of a typical handbrake cable assembly

1 Adjusting nut	3 Bracket	5 Drum brake	7 Clip	9 Handbrake
2 Equaliser	4 Switch	6 Clevis pin	8 Cover	lever

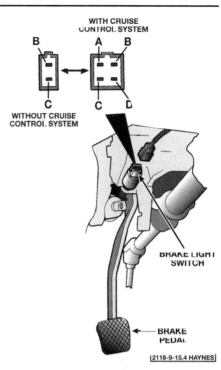

[2118-9-15.4 HAYNES]

15.4 Terminal guide for the brake light switch assembly

5 On models with rear disc brakes, remove the clip and clevis to disconnect the cable end from the actuator lever on the caliper **(see illustration 4.2)**, then remove the spring clip to free the cable housing from the support bracket.

6 Unbolt the cable housing clamps from the underbody, noting how the cable is routed, then remove the cable from the car. It may be necessary to remove the exhaust pipe heat shield bolts at the rear to allow cable removal **(see illustration)**.

7 If both cables are to be removed, repeat the above steps to remove the remaining cable.

8 Refitting is the reverse of the removal procedure. After the cable(s) are installed, be sure to adjust them according to the procedure described in Section 13.

---

15 Brake light switch - check, renewal and adjustment

Check

1 To check the brake light switch, push on the brake pedal and verify that the brake lights come on.

2 If they don't, check the brake light fuse (see Chapter 12 or check your owner's manual for fuse locations). Also check the brake light bulbs in both tail light assemblies (while you're at it, don't forget to check the high-mount brake light).

3 If the fuse and the bulbs are okay, locate the brake light switch at the top of the brake pedal.

4 Unplug the switch electrical connector **(see illustration)**.

5 Check for continuity across switch terminals B and C with an ohmmeter. When the brake pedal is depressed, there should be continuity; when it's released, there should be no continuity. If the switch doesn't operate as described, renew it.

Renewal

6 Disconnect the electrical connector from the switch, if you have not already done so.

7 Remove the locknut on the pedal side of the switch and unscrew the switch from the bracket.

8 Refitting of the brake light switch is the reverse of the removal procedure.

Adjustment

9 Loosen the brake light switch locknut and back off the brake light switch until it's not touching the brake pedal.

10 Loosen the pushrod locknut and screw the pushrod in or out with pliers until the pedal height from the floor is correct (as listed in this Chapter's Specifications).

11 Tighten the locknut securely.

12 Screw in the brake light switch until its plunger is fully depressed (threaded end touching the pad on the pedal arm), then back off the switch 1/2-turn and tighten the locknut.

13 Depress the pedal with your hand and measure the pedal freeplay. It should be within the dimensions listed in this Chapter's Specifications. Make sure the brake lights operate when the pedal is depressed and go off when the pedal is released.

Notes

Chapter 10
Suspension and steering

Contents

Degrees of difficulty

Easy, suitable for novice with little experience	Fairly easy, suitable for beginner with some experience	Fairly difficult, suitable for competent DIY mechanic	Difficult, suitable for experienced DIY mechanic	Very difficult, suitable for expert DIY or professional
				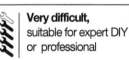

Specifications

General

Power steering fluid type .... See Chapter 1

Torque wrench settings	Nm	lbf ft
Front suspension		
Shock absorber		
Shock absorber-to-body mounting nuts	64	47
Shock absorber strut rod upper nut	30	22
Strut fork		
Pinch bolt	43	32
Fork-to-lower arm through-bolt nut	64	47
Lower control arm		
Front pivot bolt	64	47
Rear pivot stud nut	83	61
Bush clamp bolts	90	66
Anti-roll bar		
Link nuts (upper and lower)	22	16
Bush clamp nuts	22	16
Steering knuckle (lower) balljoint nut	49 to 58	36 to 43
Upper control arm		
Anchor bolt nuts	64	47
Pivot bolt nuts	30	22
Balljoint nut	39 to 48	29 to 35

Torque wrench settings (continued)

	Nm	lbf ft
Rear suspension		
Compensator arm		
Compensator arm-to-body pivot bolt	64	47
Compensator arm-to-trailing arm bolt	64	47
Hub-to-spindle nut	182	134
Lower arm		
Lower arm-to-body pivot bolt	54	40
Lower arm-to-trailing arm bolt	54	40
Shock absorber		
Strut rod nut	30	22
Shock-to-lower arm bolt	54	40
Shock upper mounting nuts	49	36
Trailing arm bush bracket-to-body bolts	64	47
Upper arm		
Bush bracket-to-body bolts	39	29
Upper arm-to-trailing arm bolt	54	40
Upper control arm inner mounting bolts	38	28
Steering system		
Steering wheel nut	49	36
Airbag module Torx bolts	10	7
Steering gear mounting bolts		
Left (driver's side)	58	43
Right (passenger's side)	38	28
Track rod end-to-steering knuckle nut	43	32
Intermediate shaft pinch-bolt	22	16

1 General information

The front suspension **(see illustration)** is a fully independent design with upper and lower control arms, shock absorber/coil spring assemblies and an anti-roll bar.

The rear suspension uses trailing arms, upper and lower control arms, "compensator" arms and shock absorber/coil spring units **(see illustration)**.

All models use rack-and-pinion steering. Some models are power-assisted. The power steering system employs an engine-driven pump connected by hoses to the steering gear.

Frequently, when working on the suspension or steering system components, you may come across nut and bolts which seem impossible to loosen. These nuts/bolts on the underside of the vehicle are continually subjected to water, road grime, mud, etc., and can become rusted or "seized," making them extremely difficult to remove. In order to unscrew these without damaging them (or other components), be sure to use lots of penetrating oil and allow it to soak in for a while. Using a wire brush to clean exposed threads will also ease removal of the nut or bolt and prevent damage to the threads. Sometimes a sharp blow with a hammer and punch is effective in breaking the bond between a nut and bolt threads, but care must be taken to prevent the punch from slipping off and ruining the threads. Heating the stuck nut/bolt and surrounding area with a torch sometimes helps too, but isn't recommended because of the obvious dangers associated with fire. Long socket bars and extension, or "cheater" pipes will increase leverage, but never use an extension pipe on a ratchet - the ratcheting mechanism could be damaged. Sometimes, turning the nut or bolt in the tightening (clockwise) direction first will help to break it loose. Nuts and bolts that require drastic measures to loosen should always be replaced with new ones.

Since most of the procedures that are dealt with in this chapter involve jacking up the vehicle and working underneath it, a good pair of axle stands will be needed. A hydraulic floor jack is the preferred type of jack to lift the vehicle, and it can also be used to support certain components during various operations.

1.1 Front suspension and steering components

1 Steering gear
2 Lower control arm bush clamp
3 Lower control arm
4 Strut fork
5 Steering knuckle
6 Shock absorber/coil spring assembly

1.2 Rear suspension components

1 Shock absorber/coil   2 Upper arm   4 Compensator arm
   spring assembly   3 Lower arm   5 Trailing arm

⚠ *Warning: Never, under any circumstances, rely on a jack to support the vehicle while working on it. Whenever any of the suspension or steering fasteners are loosened or removed they must be inspected and, if necessary, be replaced with new ones of the same part number or of original equipment quality and design. Torque specifications must be followed for proper reassembly and component retention. Never attempt to heat or straighten any suspension or steering component. Instead, replace any bent or damaged part with a new one.*

2 Anti-roll bar (front) - removal and refitting

Removal

1 Apply the handbrake. Loosen the front wheel nuts, raise the front of the car and support it on axle stands (see *"Jacking and Vehicle Support"*). Remove the wheels.

2 Remove the bolts which attach the anti-roll bar brackets to the underside of the car **(see illustration)**.

3 Detach the anti-roll bar link bolts from the lower control arms **(see illustration)**. Note the

order in which the spacers, washers and bushings are arranged on the link bolt.

4 Remove the bar from under the car.

5 Pull the brackets off the anti-roll bar and inspect the bushings for cracks, hardness and other signs of deterioration. If the bushings are damaged, renew them.

Refitting

6 Refitting is the reverse of removal.

3 Shock absorber/coil spring (front) - removal and refitting

Removal

1 Loosen the wheel nuts, raise the car and support it on axle stands (see *"Jacking and Vehicle Support"*). Remove the wheel.

2 Unbolt the brake hose from the shock absorber assembly.

3 Disconnect the anti-roll bar from the lower control arm (see Section 2).

4 Place a floor jack under the lower control arm to support it when the shock absorber assembly is removed. Remove the strut fork pinch bolt **(see illustration)**.

5 Remove the strut fork-to-lower control arm bolt and remove the fork **(see illustrations)**. It may be necessary to tap the fork from the shock absorber.

6 Support the shock absorber and coil spring assembly and remove the two upper mounting nuts **(see illustration)**. Remove the unit from the wheel arch.

2.2 Remove the bolts (arrowed) attaching the anti roll bar bracket to the chassis

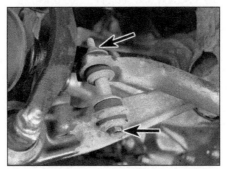

2.3 Remove the nut and bolt (arrowed) and remove the anti roll bar link assembly

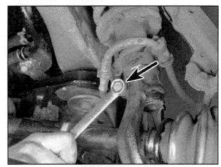

3.4 Remove the strut fork pinch bolt (arrowed)

3.5a Remove the through-bolt that connects strut fork to lower control arm

3.5b Detach the strut fork from the shock absorber

3.6 Remove the nuts (arrowed) from the shock absorber mounting studs

Refitting

7 Guide the shock absorber assembly up into the front wheel arch and insert the upper mounting studs through the holes in the body. Once the studs protrude from the holes, fit the nuts so the assembly won't fall back through, but don't tighten the nuts completely yet. The shock absorber is heavy and awkward, so get an assistant to help you, if possible.

8 Insert the lower end of the shock absorber into the strut fork. Make sure the aligning tab on the back of the shock body enters the slot in the strut fork.

9 Connect the strut fork to the lower control arm, tightening the self-locking nut to the torque listed in this Chapter's Specifications. Now tighten the strut fork pinch bolt to the torque listed in this Chapter's Specifications.

10 Attach the brake hose to its bracket and tighten the bolt securely.

11 Refit the wheel and wheel nuts, lower the car and tighten the wheel nuts to the torque listed in the Chapter 1 Specifications.

12 Tighten the upper mounting nuts to the torque listed in this Chapter's Specifications.

4 Shock absorber/coil spring - renewal

1 Remove the shock absorber/coil spring assembly (see Section 3 or 9).

2 Check the shock absorber for leaking fluid, dents, cracks or other obvious damage. Check the coil spring for chips or cracks which could cause premature failure and inspect the spring seats for hardness or general deterioration. The shock absorber assemblies, complete with the coil springs, are available on an exchange basis which eliminates much time and work. So, before disassembling your shock to renew individual components, check on the availability of parts and the price of a complete rebuilt unit.

⚠️ *Warning: Disassembling a shock absorber/coil spring assembly is a potentially dangerous undertaking and utmost attention must be directed to the job, or serious injury may result. Use only a high quality spring compressor and carefully follow the manufacturer's instructions furnished with the tool. After removing the coil spring from the shock absorber, set it aside in a safe, isolated area.*

3 Mount the shock absorber assembly in a vice. Line the vice jaws with wood or rags to prevent damage to the unit and don't tighten the vice excessively.

4 Mark the relationship of the strut mounting base to the spring (or if the spring is being replaced, put the mark on the strut unit). This will ensure correct positioning of the mounting base when the unit is reassembled.

5 Following the tool maker's instructions, fit

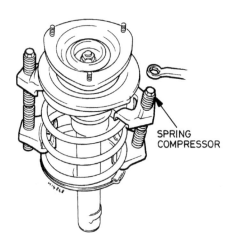

4.5 Refit the spring compressor according to the tool manufacturer's instructions and compress the spring until all pressure is relieved from the mounting base

the spring compressor (which can be obtained at most motor factors or equipment hire shops on a daily rental basis) on the spring and compress it sufficiently to relieve all pressure from the strut mounting base **(see illustration)**.

6 Remove the strut cap **(see illustration)**. Unscrew the self-locking nut while holding the strut shaft with an Allen spanner to prevent it from turning. Remove the parts from the upper part of the shock and lay them out in the exact order in which they're removed.

7 Carefully lift the compressed spring from the assembly and set it in a safe place, such as inside a steel cabinet.

⚠️ *Warning: Keep the ends of the spring facing away from your body!*

8 Slide the rest of the parts off the strut shaft and lay them out in the exact order in which they're removed.

9 Fit the bump stop, bump stop plate (if applicable), dust cover and dust cover plate onto the new strut unit. Extend the strut shaft as far as it will go and slide the components down to the strut body.

10 Carefully place the coil spring onto the shock absorber body, with the end of the spring resting in the lowest part of the seat.

11 Fit the spring mounting rubber, lower mounting rubber, strut mounting collar, strut mounting base, seal, upper mounting rubber, strut mounting washer and a new self-locking nut. Before tightening the nut, align the previously applied marks on the mounting base and the spring (or strut body).

12 Tighten the self-locking nut to the torque listed in this Chapter's Specifications, again using the Allen spanner to prevent the shaft from turning. Remove the spring compressor. Fit the strut cap.

13 Fit the shock absorber/coil spring assembly (see Section 3 or 9).

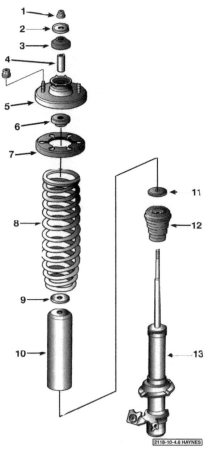

4.6 Exploded view of a typical front shock absorber/coil spring assembly

1 Self-locking nut	8 Spring
2 Mounting washer	9 Dust cover plate
3 Mounting rubber	10 Dust cover
4 Mounting collar	11 Bump stop plate
5 Mounting base	12 Bump stop
6 Mounting rubber	13 Strut unit
7 Spring mounting rubber	

5 Lower control arm (front) - removal and refitting

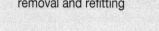

Removal

1 Loosen the front wheel nuts, raise the car, place it securely on axle stands (see *"Jacking and Vehicle Support"*) and remove the wheel.

2 Detach the anti-roll bar from the lower control arm (see Section 2).

3 Detach the strut fork from the shock absorber (see Section 3).

4 Remove the split pin from the castle nut on the lower balljoint stud. Loosen the nut, but do not remove it yet. Using a puller, separate the lower control arm from the balljoint in the steering knuckle **(see illustration)**. Remove the nut.

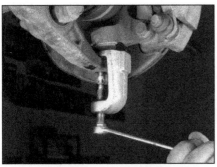

5.4 Separate the lower control arm from the steering knuckle balljoint with a puller

5.5 Remove the pivot bolt (arrowed) from the inner end of the arm

5 Remove the pivot bolt from the inner end of the lower control arm **(see illustration)** and separate the arm from the chassis.
6 Remove the nut from the rear pivot stud **(see illustration)**, pull the stud out of the bush and remove the arm. **Note:** *It is not necessary to remove the three bush clamp retaining bolts unless the bush is to be replaced.*

Refitting
7 Refitting is the reverse of removal.

6 Upper control arm (front) - removal and refitting

Removal
1 Loosen the front wheel nuts, raise the car,

6.2 Loosen - but do not remove - the upper balljoint castle nut (arrowed)

5.6 To detach the lower arm's rear pivot stud from its bush, remove middle nut (arrowed); it is not necessary to remove the three bush clamp bolts (arrowed), unless you're fitting a new bush

place it securely on axle stands (see "*Jacking and Vehicle Support*") and remove the wheel. Support the lower control arm with a floor jack.
2 Remove the split pin and loosen, but do not remove, the castle nut **(see illustration)** from the upper balljoint stud. The nut will prevent the upper control arm and the steering knuckle from separating violently in the next step.
3 Separate the upper control arm from the steering knuckle with a puller **(see illustration)**. Don't let the top of the steering knuckle fall out. If necessary, secure it to the shock absorber with a piece of wire.
4 Remove the upper control arm pivot nuts and bolts **(see illustration)** and the balljoint nut, then remove the upper control arm. Note that the heads of the pivot bolts face *away* from each other - be sure to fit them the same way.
5 If the inner pivot bushings are worn, remove the anchor bolts from the inner wheel arch, mount the anchor bolts in a vice and drive the bushings out with an appropriately-sized drift. Press the new ones in with the jaws of the vice.

Refitting
6 Refitting is the reverse of removal. Be sure to tighten all of the fasteners to the torque values listed in this Chapter's Specifications.

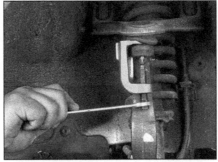

6.3 Refit a two-jaw puller and separate the upper control arm balljoint stud from the steering knuckle

7 Steering knuckle and hub assembly - removal and refitting

Removal
1 Remove the wheel cover, if applicable. Loosen the driveshaft/hub nut (Chapter 8). Loosen the wheel nuts, raise the front of the car and support it securely on axle stands (see "*Jacking and Vehicle Support*"). Remove the wheel and the driveshaft/hub nut.
2 Unbolt the brake hose bracket from the steering knuckle. Unbolt the brake caliper, hang it out of the way with a piece of wire, remove the caliper mounting bracket and remove the brake disc (see Chapter 9).
3 Disconnect the track rod end from the steering knuckle (see Section 13).
4 Separate the lower control arm from the balljoint in the bottom of the steering knuckle (see Section 5).
5 Separate the upper end of the knuckle from the upper control arm balljoint (see Section 6).
6 Carefully pull the knuckle and hub assembly off the driveshaft. Tap the end of the driveshaft with a soft-faced hammer to break the driveshaft loose from the hub. Support the driveshaft with a piece of wire to prevent damage to the inner CV joint.
7 Due to the special tools and expertise required to press the hub and bearing from the steering knuckle, the assembly should be taken to a dealer service department or other garage to have the bearings replaced, if they are worn.

Refitting
8 Apply a light coat of wheel bearing grease to the driveshaft splines. Insert the driveshaft through the splined bore of the hub while guiding the steering knuckle into position.
9 Connect the upper end of the knuckle to the upper control arm balljoint (see Section 6). Tighten the balljoint stud nut to the torque listed in this Chapter's Specifications.
10 Connect the balljoint on the bottom of the knuckle to the lower control arm (Section 5).
11 Refit the brake disc, caliper mount and caliper (Chapter 9). Fit the brake hose bracket.

6.4 Separate the knuckle from the upper control arm and remove the two pivot bolts and nuts (arrowed)

9.4 Shock absorber mounting bolt (right arrow); also note lower arm-to-trailing arm bolt (left arrow)

10.3 Using a hammer and chisel, remove the dust cover

10.4 Unstake the hub nut

12 Fit the driveshaft nut and tighten securely.
13 Refit the wheel and wheel nuts, lower the car and tighten the wheel nuts to the torque listed in the Chapter 1 Specifications.
14 Tighten the driveshaft nut to the torque specified in Chapter 8.
15 Drive the car to a wheel alignment specialist and have the front end alignment checked and, if necessary, adjusted.

8 Balljoints - renewal

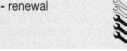

The front suspension uses two balljoints. The upper balljoint, located in the upper control arm, cannot be removed. If it is worn or damaged, renew the upper control arm (see Section 6).

The lower balljoint, located in the steering knuckle, can be removed, but special tools are needed. If it's worn or damaged, remove the knuckle (see Section 7) and take it to a dealer service department or other garage to have it replaced.

9 Shock absorber/coil spring (rear) - removal and refitting

Removal

1 Loosen the rear wheel nuts, raise the car, place it securely on axle stands (see "Jacking and Vehicle Support") and remove the rear wheels.
2 Remove the strut upper cover from the rear seat lining.
3 Remove the shock absorber upper mounting nuts.
4 Remove the shock absorber lower mounting bolt **(see illustration)**.
5 Pull down on the lower arm and remove the shock absorber/coil spring assembly.
6 To inspect or renew the shock absorber or coil spring, see Section 4.

Refitting

7 Refitting is the reverse of removal. Be sure

to tighten all fasteners to the torque values listed in this Chapter's Specifications.

10 Hub and bearing assembly (rear) - removal and refitting

Note: *The rear hub and bearing are combined into a single assembly. The bearing is sealed for life and requires no lubrication or attention. If the bearing is worn or damaged, renew the entire hub and bearing assembly.*

Removal

1 Loosen the rear wheel nuts, raise the car, place it securely on axle stands (see "Jacking and Vehicle Support") and remove the rear wheel.
2 Remove the brake drum or caliper and disc (see Chapter 9).
3 Remove the dust cover **(see illustration)**.
4 Unstake the hub retaining nut **(see illustration)**, unscrew the nut, then remove the thrustwasher and the hub assembly.

Refitting

5 Refit the new hub assembly and thrustwasher, tighten the new nut to the torque listed in this Chapter's Specifications, then stake its edge into the groove in the spindle **(see illustration)**.
6 Fit the dust cover by tapping lightly around the edge until it is seated.
7 The remainder of refitting is the reverse of removal.

11 Rear suspension arms - removal and refitting

1 Loosen the rear wheel nuts, raise the car, place it securely on axle stands (see "Jacking and Vehicle Support") and remove the wheel.

Upper arm

Removal

2 Remove the upper arm-to-trailing arm bolt and nut **(see illustration)**.

10.5 Stake the hub nut back into place

3 Remove the mounting bolts from the upper arm inner bush and remove the upper arm.
4 Inspect the bush for cracking or deterioration. If it's worn, have it pressed out, and a new one installed, by a dealer service department or other garage.

Refitting

5 Refitting is the reverse of removal. Be sure to tighten all fasteners to the torque listed in this Chapter's Specifications.

Lower arm

Removal

6 Remove the lower arm-to-trailing arm bolt **(see illustration 9.4)**.
7 Remove the shock absorber-to-lower arm bolt (see Section 9).

11.2 Remove the upper arm-to-trailing arm bolt and nut (right arrows), then remove the two bolts (left arrows) that attach the inner bush to the body

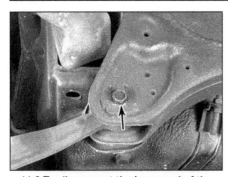

11.8 To disconnect the inner end of the lower arm from the chassis, remove the pivot bolt (arrowed)

8 Remove the inner pivot bolt and nut from the lower arm **(see illustration)** and remove the lower arm.
9 Inspect the lower arm bushings for cracks and deterioration. If any of them are worn, have them pressed out, and new ones installed, by a dealer service department or other garage.

Refitting

10 Refitting is the reverse of removal. Be sure to tighten all fasteners to the torque listed in this Chapter's Specifications.

Compensator arm

Removal

11 Remove the compensator arm-to-trailing arm bolt **(see illustration)**.
12 Remove the compensator arm-to-body nut and bolt and remove the compensator arm.
13 Inspect the compensator arm bushings for wear and deterioration. If either of them need to be replaced, have them pressed out, and new ones installed, by a dealer service department or an automotive machine shop.

Refitting

14 Refitting is the reverse of removal. Be sure to tighten both fasteners to the torque listed in this Chapter's Specifications.

Trailing arm

Removal

15 Disconnect the brake hose from the wheel cylinder or rear caliper and plug the hose to

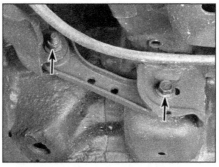

11.11 Remove the compensator arm-to-trailing arm bolt (left arrow), then remove the arm-to-body bolt (right arrow)

prevent leakage or contamination. Remove the brake drum and brake shoes, or the rear caliper and disc. Disconnect the handbrake cable (see Chapter 9).
16 Remove the rear hub and bearing assembly (see Section 10).
17 Remove the brake backing plate.
18 Detach the upper, lower and compensator arms from the trailing arm (see above).
19 Disconnect the handbrake cable bracket from the trailing arm, then remove the bolts from the trailing arm bush **(see illustrations)** and remove the trailing arm.
20 Inspect the trailing arm bush for cracks and deterioration. If it needs to be replaced, have it pressed out, and a new one installed, by a dealer service department or other garage.

Refitting

21 Refitting is the reverse of removal. Be sure to tighten all fasteners to the torque listed in this Chapter's Specifications and bleed the brake hydraulic system (see Chapter 9).

12 Steering wheel -
removal and refitting

Removal

> ⚠ **Warning: Most models covered by this manual are equipped with a Supplemental Restraint System (SRS), more commonly known as an airbag(s). Always disable the**

11.19a To disconnect the trailing arm from the body, remove the left bush retaining bolt (arrowed) . . .

11.19b . . . and the right bolt (right arrow); detach the bracket for the handbrake cable by removing this bolt (left arrow)

airbag system before working in the vicinity of the SRS unit, steering column or instrument panel to avoid the possibility of accidental deployment of the airbag, which could cause personal injury (Chapter 12).

1 Disconnect the cable from the negative battery terminal, then disconnect the positive battery cable. *Caution: If the stereo in your car is equipped with an anti-theft system, make sure you have the correct activation code before disconnecting the battery.*
2 Rotate the wheel 180° so the access panel is facing up. Remove the access plate and remove the short connector from the access plate **(see illustrations)**. Unplug the airbag module-to-cable reel connector; plug the short connector into the airbag module side of this connector to disable the airbag module **(see illustrations)**.

12.2a Remove this screw and remove the short connector access plate

12.2b The short connector is stowed on the inside of the access plate

12.2c Unplug the yellow connector for the airbag module . . .

12.2d . . . plug the short connector into the airbag module connector to disable the airbag module

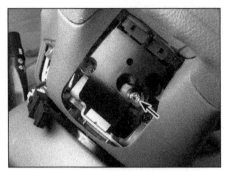

12.3a Remove the left Torx screw (arrowed) that attaches the airbag module to the steering wheel

12.3b Rotate the steering wheel and remove the right Torx screw (arrowed)

12.4 Remove the airbag module from the steering wheel and set it aside (store the airbag module with trim side facing UP)

12.6 After removing the steering wheel nut, mark the relationship of the wheel to the shaft

12.9 Make sure the wheels are pointed straight ahead and "Top" mark points up; also note yellow gear tooth at 7 o'clock

3 Remove both airbag module Torx screws from the side of the steering wheel facing the instrument panel **(see illustrations)**.

4 Pull off the module **(see illustration)** and carefully set the module aside with the trim side facing up.

5 Unplug the electrical connectors for the horn and, if applicable, the cruise control system.

6 Remove the steering wheel nut. Make a mark indicating the relationship of the steering wheel hub to the steering shaft **(see illustration)**.

7 Remove the steering wheel by pulling it straight off the shaft.

 Warning: While the steering wheel is removed, DO NOT turn the steering shaft. If you do, the airbag reel could be damaged.

Refitting

8 Make sure that the wheels are pointed straight ahead.

9 Make absolutely sure that the cable reel is centred with the arrow on the cable reel pointing up as shown **(see illustration)**. This shouldn't be a problem as long as you have not turned the steering shaft while the wheel was removed. If for some reason the shaft was turned, centre the cable reel as follows:

a) *Turn the cable reel clockwise until it stops.*

b) *Rotate the cable reel anti-clockwise about two turns until the yellow gear tooth lines up with the mark on the cover and the arrow on the cable reel points straight up.*

10 Be sure to align the index mark on the steering wheel hub with the mark on the shaft when you slip the wheel onto the shaft. And make sure the locating pins on the steering column engage the holes in the backside of the steering wheel. Fit the mounting nut and tighten it to the specified torque.

11 Plug in the horn connector and, if applicable, the cruise control connector.

12 Reattach the airbag module with NEW Torx bolts and tighten the bolts to the torque listed in this Chapter's Specifications. Fit the Torx bolt access panels.

13 Unplug the short connector from the airbag connector.

14 Plug the airbag and cable reel connector halves together.

15 Secure the short connector to the access plate and refit the access plate.

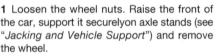

13 Track rod ends - removal and refitting

Removal

1 Loosen the wheel nuts. Raise the front of the car, support it securely on axle stands (see "*Jacking and Vehicle Support*") and remove the wheel.

2 Retain the track rod end with a second spanner and carefully loosen the lock nut just enough to mark the position of the track rod end in relation to the threads **(see illustrations)**.

3 Remove the split pin and loosen the nut on the track rod end stud. Don't completely remove the nut.

13.2a Using a spanner to prevent the track rod end from turning, loosen the lock nut

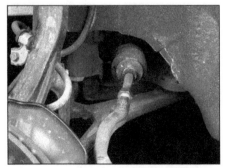

13.2b Make a mark on the exposed threads, along the edge of the track rod

13.4 Use a puller to separate the track rod end from the steering knuckle arm

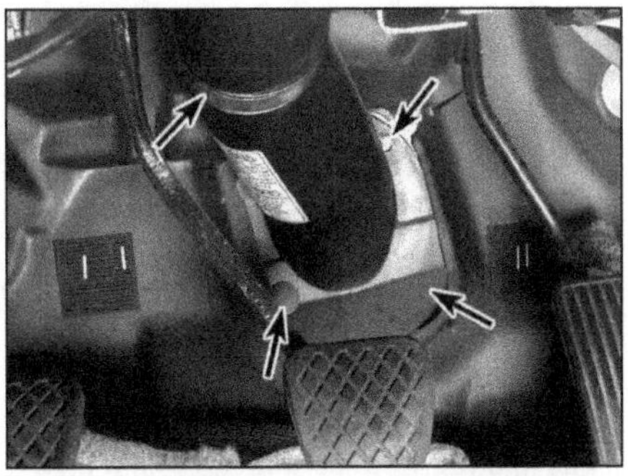
15.1 Steering joint cover lower clamp (upper left arrow) - upper clamp hidden, and plastic clip (lower left arrow); on refitting, note the two locating pin holes (right arrows)

15.2 Mark the relationship of the intermediate shaft to the steering gear input shaft and remove the pinch bolt (arrowed)

4 Separate the track rod from the steering knuckle arm with a puller **(see illustration)**. Remove the nut and detach the track rod.
5 Unscrew the track rod end from the track rod.

Refitting

6 Thread the track rod end on to the marked position and insert the track rod stud into the steering knuckle arm. Don't tighten the lock nut yet.
7 Fit the nut on the stud and tighten it to the torque listed in this Chapter's Specifications. Fit a new split pin.
8 Tighten the lock nut securely.
9 Refit the wheel and wheel nuts. Lower the car and tighten the wheel nuts to the torque listed in the Chapter 1 Specifications.
10 Have the alignment checked by a dealer service department or an alignment shop.

14 Steering gear gaiters - renewal

1 Loosen the wheel nuts, raise the front of the car and support it securely on axle stands (see "*Jacking and Vehicle Support*"). Remove the wheel.
2 Remove the track rod end and lock nut (see Section 13).
3 Remove the steering gear gaiter clamps and slide off the gaiter.
4 Before fitting the new gaiter, wrap the threads and serration's on the end of the track rod with a layer of tape so the small end of the new gaiter isn't damaged.
5 Slide the new gaiter into position on the steering gear until it seats in the groove in the steering rod and fit new clamps.
6 Remove the tape and fit the track rod end (see Section 13).
7 Refit the wheel and wheel nuts. Lower the car and tighten the wheel nuts to the torque listed in the Chapter 1 Specifications.

15 Steering gear - removal and refitting

Removal

1 Working under the instrument panel, remove the steering joint cover **(see illustration)**. Pop off the upper and lower clamps, pop out the single plastic clip and slide off the cover.
2 Mark the relationship of the intermediate shaft universal joint to the steering gear input shaft **(see illustration)** and remove the pinch bolt.
3 Raise the front of the car and support it securely on axle stands. Apply the handbrake. Lock the steering wheel with the ignition key.
Caution: DO NOT allow the steering wheel to rotate with the steering gear removed or damage to the SRS coil may result.
4 Remove the gearchange rods (manual transmission) or gearchange control cable (automatic transmission) from the transmission (Chapter 7).
5 Remove the catalytic converter (Chapter 4).
6 Place a drain pan under the steering gear. Disconnect the power steering fluid lines **(see illustration)** and cap them to prevent contamination and loss of fluid.
7 Separate the track rod ends from the steering knuckle arms (see Section 13). Remove the left track rod end.
8 Support the steering gear and remove the mounting bolts **(see illustrations)**. Lower the unit, separating the intermediate shaft from the steering gear input shaft. Move the steering gear as far as possible to the right. Rotate the steering gear so that the input shaft is facing forward. Lower the left end past the frame and remove the steering gear from the car as you move it to the left side.

Refitting

9 Raise the steering gear into position and connect the intermediate shaft, aligning the marks.
10 Fit the steering gear mounting bolts and washers and tighten them to the torque listed in this Chapter's Specifications.
11 Fit the left track rod end and connect the track rod ends to the steering knuckle arms (see Section 13).
12 Connect the power steering hoses/lines to the steering gear.

15.6 Loosen the power steering fluid line fittings (arrowed); detach the lines and plug them to prevent leakage and dirt ingress

15.8a Remove these bolts (arrowed) from the left end (driver's side) of the steering gear

15.8b Remove these bolts (arrowed) from the right (passenger side) steering gear mounting clamp and remove the clamp

13 Refit the transmission control rods or cable and the catalytic converter.

14 Lower the car, refit the intermediate shaft pinch bolt and tighten it to the torque listed in this Chapter's Specifications. Refit the steering joint cover and clamps. Make sure the two holes in the flange at the lower end of the shield are aligned with the locating pins in the floor.

15 Fill the power steering pump reservoir with the recommended fluid (see Chapter 1) and bleed the steering system (Section 17).

16 Power steering pump - removal and refitting

Removal

1 Disconnect the cable from the negative battery terminal, then disconnect the positive battery cable. *Caution: If the stereo in your car is equipped with an anti-theft system, make sure you have the correct activation code before disconnecting the battery.*

2 Disconnect the fluid hoses at the pump **(see illustration)**. Note the difference between the pressure and the return hoses; the return hose is held to the pump with a spring type clamp, and the pressure line has two bolts holding it to the pump body. Cap or plug both hoses to prevent leakage or contamination. Fit a new O-ring on the end of the pressure line.

3 Remove the pump adjusting bolt.

4 Remove the pump mounting bolts and remove the pump from the engine.

Refitting

5 Refitting is the reverse of removal. Be sure to bleed the power steering system (see Section 17) and adjust the drivebelt tension (see Chapter 1).

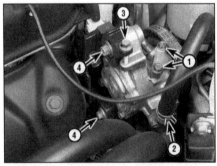

16.2 To remove the power steering pump, disconnect the pressure line bolts (1) and the return line clamp (2), then remove the adjuster bolt (3) and the mounting bolts (4)

17 Power steering system - bleeding

1 Following any operation in which the power steering fluid lines have been disconnected, the power steering system must be bled to remove all air and obtain proper steering performance.

2 With the front wheels in the straight ahead position, check the power steering fluid level (see Chapter 1). If it's low, add fluid until it reaches the lower mark on the reservoir.

3 Start the engine and allow it to run at fast idle. Recheck the fluid level and add more if necessary to reach the Cold mark on the dipstick.

4 Bleed the system by turning the wheels from side-to-side, without hitting the stops. This will work the air out of the system. Keep the reservoir full of fluid as this is done.

5 When the air is worked out of the system, return the wheels to the straight ahead position and leave the car running for several more minutes before shutting it off.

6 Road test the car to be sure the steering system is functioning normally and noise free.

7 Recheck the fluid level to be sure it is up to the Hot mark on the reservoir while the engine is at normal operating temperature. Add fluid if necessary (see Chapter 1).

18 Wheels and tyres - general information

All cars covered by this manual are equipped with metric-sized steel belted radial tyres. Use of other size or type of tyres may affect the ride and handling of the car. Don't mix different types of tyres, such as radials and bias belted, on the same car as handling may be seriously affected. It's recommended that tyres be replaced in pairs on the same axle, but if only one tyre is being replaced, be sure it's the same size, structure and tread design as the other.

Because tyre pressure has a substantial effect on handling and wear, the pressure on all tyres should be checked at least once a month or before any extended trips (see *"Weekly checks"*).

Wheels must be replaced if they are bent, dented, leak air, have elongated bolt holes, are heavily rusted, out of vertical symmetry or if the wheel nuts won't stay tight.

Tyre and wheel balance is important to the overall handling, braking and performance of the car. Unbalanced wheels can adversely affect handling and ride characteristics as well as tyre life. Whenever a tyre is installed on a wheel, the tyre and wheel should be balanced by a shop with the proper equipment.

19 Wheel alignment - general information

A wheel alignment refers to the adjustments made to the wheels so they are in proper angular relationship to the suspension and the earth. Wheels that are out of proper alignment not only affect steering control, but also increase tyre wear. Toe-in can be adjusted on the front and rear wheels. The front and rear camber and castor angles should be checked to determine if any of the suspension components are worn out or bent .

Getting the proper wheel alignment is a very exacting process, one in which complicated and expensive machines are necessary to perform the job properly. Because of this, you should have a technician with the proper equipment perform these tasks. We will, however, use this space to give you a basic idea of what is involved with wheel alignment so you can better understand the process and deal intelligently with the shop that does the work.

Toe-in is the turning in of the wheels. The purpose of a toe specification is to ensure parallel rolling of the wheels. In a car with zero toe-in, the distance between the front edges of the wheels will be the same as the distance between the rear edges of the wheels. The actual amount of toe-in is normally only a fraction of an inch. At the front end, toe-in is controlled by the track rod end position on the track rod. At the rear it is adjusted by moving the rear lower arm, in or out, within its bracket on the body. Incorrect toe-in will cause the tyres to wear improperly by making them scrub against the road surface.

Camber is the tilting of the wheels from the vertical when viewed from the front or rear of the car. When the wheels tilt out at the top, the camber is said to be positive (+). When the wheels tilt in at the top the camber is negative (-). The amount of tilt is measured in degrees from the vertical and this measurement is called the camber angle. This angle affects the amount of tyre tread which contacts the road and compensates for changes in the suspension geometry when the car is cornering or travelling over an undulating surface. Camber isn't adjustable on these models.

Castor is the tilting of the top of the steering axis from the vertical. A tilt toward the rear is positive castor and a tilt toward the front is negative castor. Castor isn't adjustable on these models.

Chapter 11
Bodywork, trim and fittings

Contents

Degrees of difficulty

Easy, suitable for novice with little experience	**Fairly easy,** suitable for beginner with some experience	**Fairly difficult,** suitable for competent DIY mechanic	**Difficult,** suitable for experienced DIY mechanic	**Very difficult,** suitable for expert DIY or professional

Specifications

Torque wrench settings	Nm	lbf ft
Passenger's airbag retaining nuts	11	8
Bumper mounting bolts		
Front	22	16
Rear	64	47

1 General information

These models feature a "unibody" layout, using a floor pan with front and rear frame side rails which support the body components, front and rear suspension systems and other mechanical components.

Certain components are particularly vulnerable to accident damage and can be unbolted and repaired or replaced. Among these are the body mouldings, bumpers, the bonnet and boot lid (or tailgate) and all glass.

Only general body maintenance practices and body panel repair procedures within the scope of the do-it-yourselfer are included in this Chapter.

2 Body - maintenance

1 The condition of your car's body is very important, because the resale value depends a great deal on it. It's much more difficult to repair a neglected or damaged body than it is to repair mechanical components. The hidden areas of the body, such as the wheel wells, the frame and the engine compartment, are equally important, although they do not require as frequent attention as the rest of the body.
2 Once a year it is a good idea to have the underside of the body steam cleaned. All traces of dirt and oil will be removed and the area can then be inspected carefully for rust, damaged brake lines, frayed electrical wires, damaged cables and other problems.
3 At the same time, clean the engine and the engine compartment with a steam cleaner or water soluble degreaser.
4 The wheel wells should be given close attention, since undercoating can peel away and stones and dirt thrown up by the tyres can cause the paint to chip and flake, allowing rust to set in. If rust is found, clean down to the bare metal and apply an anti-rust paint.
5 The body should be washed about once a week. Wet the car thoroughly to soften the dirt, then wash it down with a soft sponge and plenty of clean soapy water. If the surplus dirt is not washed off very carefully, it can wear down the paint.
6 Spots of tar or asphalt thrown up from the road should be removed with a cloth soaked in solvent.
7 Once every six months, wax the body and chrome trim. If a chrome cleaner is used to remove rust from any of the car's plated parts, remember that the cleaner also removes part of the chrome, so use it sparingly.

3 Vinyl trim - maintenance

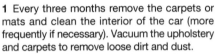

Don't clean vinyl trim with detergents, caustic soap or petroleum based cleaners. Plain soap and water works fine, with a soft brush to clean dirt that may be ingrained. Wash the vinyl as frequently as the rest of the car.

After cleaning, application of a high quality rubber and vinyl protectant will help prevent oxidation and cracks. The protectant can also be applied to weather-stripping, vacuum lines and rubber hoses, which often fail as a result of chemical degradation, and to the tyres.

4 Upholstery and carpets - maintenance

1 Every three months remove the carpets or mats and clean the interior of the car (more frequently if necessary). Vacuum the upholstery and carpets to remove loose dirt and dust.
2 Leather upholstery requires special care. Stains should be removed with warm water and a very mild soap solution. Use a clean, damp cloth to remove the soap, then wipe again with a dry cloth. Never use alcohol, fuel, nail polish remover or thinner to clean leather upholstery.
3 After cleaning, regularly treat leather upholstery with a leather wax. Never use car wax on leather upholstery.
4 In areas where the interior of the car is subject to bright sunlight, cover leather seats with a sheet if the car is to be left out for any length of time.

5 Body repair - minor damage

Repair of minor scratches

1 If the scratch is superficial and does not penetrate to the metal of the body, repair is very simple. Lightly rub the scratched area with a fine rubbing compound to remove loose paint and built up wax. Rinse the area with clean water.
2 Apply touch-up paint to the scratch, using a small brush. Continue to apply thin layers of paint until the surface of the paint in the scratch is level with the surrounding paint. Allow the new paint at least two weeks to harden, then blend it into the surrounding paint by rubbing with a very fine rubbing compound. Finally, apply a coat of wax to the scratch area.
3 If the scratch has penetrated the paint and exposed the metal of the body, causing the metal to rust, a different repair technique is required. Remove all loose rust from the

bottom of the scratch with a pocket knife, then apply rust inhibiting paint to prevent the formation of rust in the future. Using a rubber or nylon applicator, coat the scratched area with glaze-type filler. If required, the filler can be mixed with thinner to provide a very thin paste, which is ideal for filling narrow scratches. Before the glaze filler in the scratch hardens, wrap a piece of smooth cotton cloth around the tip of a finger. Dip the cloth in thinner and then quickly wipe it along the surface of the scratch. This will ensure that the surface of the filler is slightly hollow. The scratch can now be painted over as described earlier in this section.

Repair of dents

4 When repairing dents, the first job is to pull the dent out until the affected area is as close as possible to its original shape. There is no point in trying to restore the original shape completely as the metal in the damaged area will have stretched on impact and cannot be restored to its original contours. It is better to bring the level of the dent up to a point which is about 1/8-inch below the level of the surrounding metal. In cases where the dent is very shallow, it is not worth trying to pull it out at all.
5 If the back side of the dent is accessible, it can be hammered out gently from behind using a soft-face hammer. While doing this, hold a block of wood firmly against the opposite side of the metal to absorb the hammer blows and prevent the metal from being stretched.
6 If the dent is in a section of the body which has double layers, or some other factor makes it inaccessible from behind, a different technique is required. Drill several small holes through the metal inside the damaged area, particularly in the deeper sections. Screw long, self tapping screws into the holes just enough for them to get a good grip in the metal. Now the dent can be pulled out by pulling on the protruding heads of the screws with locking pliers.
7 The next stage of repair is the removal of paint from the damaged area and from an inch or so of the surrounding metal. This is easily done with a wire brush or sanding disc in a drill motor, although it can be done just as effectively by hand with sandpaper. To complete the preparation for filling, score the surface of the bare metal with a screwdriver or the tang of a file or drill small holes in the affected area. This will provide a good grip for the filler material. To complete the repair, see the Section on filling and painting.

Repair of rust holes or gashes

8 Remove all paint from the affected area and from an inch or so of the surrounding metal using a sanding disc or wire brush mounted in a drill motor. If these are not available, a few sheets of sandpaper will do the job just as effectively.
9 With the paint removed, you will be able to

determine the severity of the corrosion and decide whether to renew the whole panel, if possible, or repair the affected area. New body panels are not as expensive as most people think and it is often quicker to fit a new panel than to repair large areas of rust.
10 Remove all trim pieces from the affected area except those which will act as a guide to the original shape of the damaged body, such as headlight shells, etc. Using metal snips or a hacksaw blade, remove all loose metal and any other metal that is badly affected by rust. Hammer the edges of the hole in to create a slight depression for the filler material.
11 Wire brush the affected area to remove the powdery rust from the surface of the metal. If the back of the rusted area is accessible, treat it with rust inhibiting paint.
12 Before filling is done, block the hole in some way. This can be done with sheet metal riveted or screwed into place, or by stuffing the hole with wire mesh.
13 Once the hole is blocked off, the affected area can be filled and painted. See the following subsection on filling and painting.

Filling and painting

14 Many types of body fillers are available, but generally speaking, body repair kits which contain filler paste and a tube of resin hardener are best for this type of repair work. A wide, flexible plastic or nylon applicator will be necessary for imparting a smooth and contoured finish to the surface of the filler material. Mix up a small amount of filler on a clean piece of wood or cardboard (use the hardener sparingly). Follow the manufacturer's instructions on the package, otherwise the filler will set incorrectly.
15 Using the applicator, apply the filler paste to the prepared area. Draw the applicator across the surface of the filler to achieve the desired contour and to level the filler surface. As soon as a contour that approximates the original one is achieved, stop working the paste. If you continue, the paste will begin to stick to the applicator. Continue to add thin layers of paste at 20-minute intervals until the level of the filler is just above the surrounding metal.
16 Once the filler has hardened, the excess can be removed with a body file. From then on, progressively finer grades of sandpaper should be used, starting with a 180-grade paper and finishing with 600-grade wet-or-dry paper. Always wrap the sandpaper around a flat rubber or wooden block, otherwise the surface of the filler will not be completely flat. During the sanding of the filler surface, the wet-or-dry paper should be periodically rinsed in water. This will ensure that a very smooth finish is produced in the final stage.
17 At this point, the repair area should be surrounded by a ring of bare metal, which in turn should be encircled by the finely feathered edge of good paint. Rinse the repair area with clean water until all of the dust produced by the sanding operation is gone.

18 Spray the entire area with a light coat of primer. This will reveal any imperfections in the surface of the filler. Repair the imperfections with fresh filler paste or glaze filler and once more smooth the surface with sandpaper. Repeat this spray-and-repair procedure until you are satisfied that the surface of the filler and the feathered edge of the paint are perfect. Rinse the area with clean water and allow it to dry completely.

19 The repair area is now ready for painting. Spray painting must be carried out in a warm, dry, windless and dust free atmosphere. These conditions can be created if you have access to a large indoor work area, but if you are forced to work in the open, you will have to pick the day very carefully. If you are working indoors, dousing the floor in the work area with water will help settle the dust which would otherwise be in the air. If the repair area is confined to one body panel, mask off the surrounding panels. This will help minimise the effects of a slight mismatch in paint colour. Trim pieces such as chrome strips, door handles, etc., will also need to be masked off or removed. Use masking tape and several thicknesses of newspaper for the masking operations.

20 Before spraying, shake the paint can thoroughly, then spray a test area until the spray painting technique is mastered. Cover the repair area with a thick coat of primer. The thickness should be built up using several thin layers of primer rather than one thick one. Using 600-grade wet-or-dry sandpaper, rub down the surface of the primer until it is very smooth. While doing this, the work area should be thoroughly rinsed with water and the wet-or-dry sandpaper periodically rinsed as well. Allow the primer to dry before spraying additional coats.

21 Spray on the top coat, again building up the thickness by using several thin layers of paint. Begin spraying in the centre of the repair area and then, using a circular motion, work out until the whole repair area and about two inches of the surrounding original paint is covered. Remove all masking material 10 to 15 minutes after spraying on the final coat of paint. Allow the new paint at least two weeks to harden, then use a very fine rubbing compound to blend the edges of the new paint into the existing paint. Finally, apply a coat of wax.

6 Body repair - major damage

1 Major damage must be repaired by an auto body shop specifically equipped to perform unibody repairs. These shops have the specialised equipment required to do the job properly.

2 If the damage is extensive, the body must be checked for proper alignment or the car's handling characteristics may be adversely affected and other components may wear at an accelerated rate.

3 Due to the fact that all of the major body components (bonnet, wings, etc.) are separate and replaceable units, any seriously damaged components should be replaced rather than repaired. Sometimes the components can be found in a breakers yard that specialises in used car components, often at considerable savings over the cost of new parts.

7 Hinges and locks - maintenance

Once every three months, the hinges and latch assemblies on the doors, bonnet and boot (or tailgate) should be given a few drops of light oil or lock lubricant. The door latch strikers should also be lubricated with a thin coat of grease to reduce wear and ensure free movement. Lubricate the door and boot (or tailgate) locks with spray-on graphite lubricant.

8 Windscreen and fixed glass - renewal

Renewal of the windscreen and fixed glass requires the use of special fast-setting adhesive/caulk materials and some specialised tools and techniques. These operations should be left to a dealer service department or a shop specialising in glass work.

9 Bonnet - removal, refitting and adjustment

Removal

Note: *The bonnet is heavy and somewhat awkward to remove and refit - at least two people should perform this procedure.*

1 Use blankets or pads to cover the wings and cowl areas. This will protect the body and paint as the bonnet is lifted off.

2 Scribe or draw alignment marks around the bolt heads to ensure proper alignment during refitting **(see illustration)**.

3 Disconnect any cables or wire harnesses which will interfere with removal.

4 Have an assistant support the weight of the bonnet. Remove the hinge-to-bonnet bolts and any shims, if already installed. If there are any shims, make sure you keep the shims for each side with their respective bolts. Don't mix them up.

5 Lift off the bonnet.

Refitting

6 Refitting is the reverse of removal. If you fit the bonnet so that the hinges fit within the scribe marks you made before loosening the bolts and if you refit the shims, if any, in the same number and location they were in prior to removal, then the bonnet should still be aligned. Of course, if you're refitting a new bonnet, or forgot to scribe the hinge positions, or mixed up the shims, etc. then you'll need to readjust the bonnet position.

Adjustment

7 You can adjust the bonnet fore-and-aft and right-and-left by means of the elongated holes in the hinges.

8 Scribe a line around the entire hinge plate so you can judge the amount of movement.

9 Loosen the bolts and move the bonnet into correct alignment. Move it only a little at a time. Tighten the hinge bolts or nuts and carefully lower the bonnet to check the alignment.

10 If necessary after refitting, the entire bonnet latch assembly can be adjusted up-and-down as well as from side-to-side on the upper radiator support so the bonnet closes securely and is flush with the wings **(see illustration)**. To do this, scribe a line around the bonnet latch mounting bolts to provide a reference point. Then loosen the bolts and reposition the latch assembly as necessary. Following adjustment, retighten the mounting bolts.

11 Adjust the vertical height of the leading

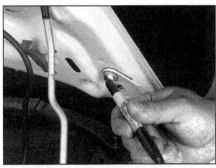

9.2 Scribe or draw alignment marks around the bolt heads (arrowed) and the bonnet hinges to ensure proper alignment of the bonnet when it's reinstalled

9.10 Scribe a line around the bonnet latch so you can judge the movement, then loosen the bolts and adjust the latch position

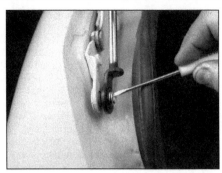

9.11 To adjust the vertical height of the bonnet edge so it's flush with the wings, adjust each edge cushion - clockwise lowers the bonnet, and vice-versa

10.2 Detach the lower strut cover

10.3 Use a small screwdriver to prise off the retaining clip

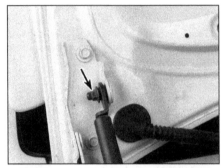
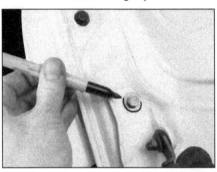

10.4 Remove the screws (arrowed) and detach the upper end of the strut

10.6 Draw alignment marks around the bolt head with a marking pen, for refitting

edge of the bonnet by screwing the edge cushions in or out so that the bonnet, when closed, is flush with the wings **(see illustration)**. Finally, adjust the rear edge of the bonnet until it is flush with the wings by using shims (available at a Honda dealer parts department) between the bonnet and the hinge plates.

12 The bonnet latch assembly, as well as the hinges, should be periodically lubricated with white lithium-base grease to prevent sticking and wear.

10 Boot lid and support struts - removal, refitting and adjustment

Support struts

1 Support the boot lid in the open position.
2 Remove the plastic cover from the lower end of the strut **(see illustration)**.
3 Use a small screwdriver to prise off the clip and detach the strut **(see illustration)**.
4 Remove the nut and detach the strut **(see illustration)**.
5 Refitting is the reverse of removal.

Boot lid

6 Scribe or draw alignment marks around the hinge-to-boot lid bolts **(see illustration)**.
7 While an assistant supports the boot lid, detach the support struts, then remove the hinge-to-boot lid bolts from both sides and lift off the boot lid.
8 Refitting is the reverse of removal. Be sure to align the hinge bolt flanges with the marks made during removal.
9 After refitting, close the lid and see if it's in proper alignment with the adjacent body surfaces. Fore-and-aft and side-to-side adjustments of the lid are controlled by the position of the hinge bolts in the slots. To adjust it, loosen the hinge bolts, reposition the lid and retighten the bolts.
10 The height of the rear of the lid in relation to the surrounding body panels when closed can be adjusted by loosening the lock striker bolts and adding or removing adjusting shims

(available from a Honda dealer parts department) between the striker and the body and retightening the bolts.
11 Finally, you can fine-tune the height of the trailing edge of the boot lid by turning the boot lid edge cushions in or out to lower or raise the boot as necessary.

11 Tailgate and support struts - removal, refitting and adjustment

Note: *The following procedure applies only to Hatchback models.*

Support struts

1 Open the tailgate and support it.
2 Loosen the single locknut at the upper end of each strut, remove the two mounting bolts at the lower end of each strut, then unscrew the stud at the upper end of the strut from the tailgate.
3 Refitting is the reverse of removal. Tighten all fasteners securely.

Tailgate

4 Open the tailgate and cover the upper body area around the opening with pads or cloths to protect the painted surfaces when the tailgate is removed.
5 Unplug all electrical connectors and pull the wire harness out of the tailgate (tie string or wire to the cables so they can be pulled back into the body when the tailgate is refitted).
6 Paint or scribe alignment marks around the tailgate hinge flanges.

7 While an assistant supports the tailgate, detach the support struts (see above).
8 Remove the hinge bolts and detach the tailgate from the car.
9 Refitting is the reverse of removal. Be extremely careful with the wire harness when threading it back into the tailgate or you could cut it on a metal edge.
10 After refitting, close the tailgate and check it's aligned with the surrounding body panels.
11 If the tailgate needs to be adjusted, loosen the hinge bolts slightly, gently close the tailgate and verify that it's centred between the two wings (the striker should centre it). Then carefully open the tailgate and retighten the hinge bolts.

12 Tailgate - removal and refitting

Note: *The following procedure applies only to Hatchback models.*

Removal

1 Open the tailgate.
2 Remove the trim panel and unplug all electrical connectors and pull the wire harness out of the tailgate (tie string or wire to the cables so they can be pulled back into the body when the tailgate is reinstalled).
3 Detach the cable from the tailgate latch.
4 Remove the bolt and detach the tailgate support cable.
5 Paint or scribe alignment marks around the tailgate hinge flanges.

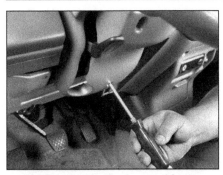

13.3 Use a crosshead screwdriver to remove the steering column cover screws

14.2 Rotate the cover panel down, detach the clip and pull it out

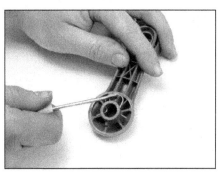

16.1 Remove the window crank by pulling this clip off with a wire hook

6 While an assistant supports the tailgate, remove the hinge bolts and detach the tailgate from the car.

Refitting

7 Refitting is the reverse of removal. Be extremely careful with the wire harness when threading it back into the tailgate or you could cut it on a metal edge.
8 After refitting, close the tailgate and make sure it's in proper alignment with the surrounding body panels.
9 If the tailgate needs to be adjusted, loosen the hinge bolts slightly, gently close the tailgate and verify that it's centred between the two wings (the striker should centre it). Then carefully lower the tailgate and retighten the hinge bolts.

13 Steering column cover - removal and refitting

⚠ **Warning: Most models covered by this manual are equipped with a Supplemental Restraint System (SRS), more commonly known as an airbag(s). Always disable the airbag system before working in the vicinity of the SRS unit, steering column or instrument panel to avoid the possibility of accidental deployment of the airbag, which could cause personal injury (see Chapter 12).**

Caution: The stereo in your car may be equipped with an anti-theft system, refer to the information at the rear of this manual before detaching the battery cable.

Removal

1 Remove the instrument cover lower panel (see Section 14).
2 On tilt steering columns, move the column to the lowest position.
3 Remove the remaining screws, then separate the halves and remove the covers **(see illustration).**

Refitting

4 Refitting is the reverse of the removal procedure.

14 Instrument panel lower cover and knee bolster - removal and refitting

Note: *Refer to the warning at the start of Section 13 before proceeding.* **Caution: If the stereo in your car has an anti-theft code, refer to the information at the rear of this manual before disconnecting the battery.**

Cover

1 Remove the bolts at the panel rear edge.
2 Rotate the panel down to detach the clip, then pull it straight back and remove it from the car **(see illustration).**
3 Refitting is the reverse of removal.

Knee bolster

4 Remove the two bolts and lower the metal knee bolster from under the dash.
5 Refitting is the reverse of removal.

15 Bumpers - removal and refitting

Front bumper

Removal

1 Detach the bumper cover.
2 Disconnect any wiring or other components that would interfere with bumper removal.
3 Support the bumper on a jack or axle stand.
4 Remove the plastic bumper beam absorber and gussets for access, then remove the four bolts and detach the bumper beam.

Refitting

5 Refitting is the reverse of removal.
6 Tighten the retaining bolts securely.
7 Refit the bumper cover and any other components that were removed.

Rear bumper

Removal

8 Detach the bumper cover.
9 Disconnect any wiring or other components that would interfere with bumper removal.
10 Support the bumper on a jack or axle stand.
11 Open the boot lid or tailgate and detach the carpet for access to the retaining bolts.

12 Remove the four bolts in the rear compartment, then remove the detach the bumper beam from the car.

Refitting

13 Refitting is the reverse of removal.
14 Tighten the retaining bolts securely.
15 Refit the bumper cover and any other components that were removed.

16 Door trim panel - removal and refitting

Removal

1 On manual (non-electric) window models, remove the window crank **(see illustration).**
2 Remove the inside handle (see Section 17).
3 Remove the door trim panel retaining screws **(see illustrations),** then carefully prise loose the retaining clips with a trim pad remover or a putty knife between the trim panel and the

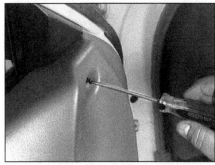

16.3a Remove door trim panel screws . . .

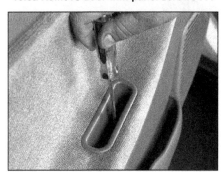

16.3b . . . and the screw in the door pull

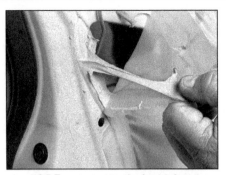

16.4 Lift the door trim panel up and out of the door

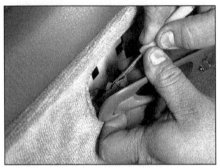

16.5 For access to the inner door mechanisms, carefully peel back the plastic shield - be careful not to tear it

17.1 Remove the inside door handle retaining screw (s)

door. Work slowly and carefully around the outer edge of the trim panel until it is free.

4 Once all of the clips are disengaged, pull the trim panel up, unplug any wiring connectors and remove the panel **(see illustration)**.

5 For access to the door inner panel, carefully peel back the plastic shield **(see illustration)**.

Refitting

6 Prior to refitting of the door trim panel, be sure to refit any clips in the panel which may have come out when you removed the panel.

7 Plug in the wire harness connectors for the power door lock switch and the power window switch, if applicable, and place the panel in position in the door. Press the door panel into place until the clips are seated. Refit the two trim panel retaining screws and the armrest retaining screw. Refit the power door lock switch assembly, if applicable. Refit the manual regulator crank handle.

17 Door inside handle - removal and refitting

Removal

1 Remove the inside door handle retaining screw(s) **(see illustration)**.

2 Carefully pull the door handle assembly out of the door trim panel and disconnect the release rod from the handle lever and remove the handle **(see illustration)**.

3 Unplug the wiring connector (if applicable) and remove the handle **(see illustration)**.

Refitting

4 Refitting is the reverse of removal.

18 Door outside handle, lock cylinder and latch - removal and refitting

Outside door handle

Removal

1 Remove the inside door handle and the door trim panel and plastic shield (see Sections 16 and 17).

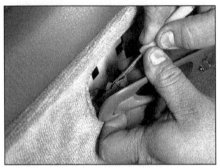

17.2 Disconnect the lock rod with a screwdriver and remove the inside door handle

2 Apply tape around the handle opening to protect the paint.

3 On rear doors it will be necessary to move the rear glass channel out of the way for access. This is done by loosening the upper channel nut and removing the lower bolt and moving the channel forward **(see illustration)**.

4 Remove the door handle retaining bolts. On some rear doors it will be necessary to remove the door latch for access to the bolts (see below).

5 Prise the lock rod loose with a small flat-bladed screwdriver, pull the handle out from

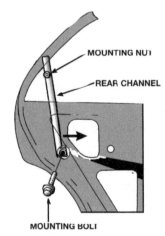

MOUNTING NUT

REAR CHANNEL

MOUNTING BOLT

2118-11-18.3 HAYNES

18.3 On rear doors, you'll have to move the rear glass channel for access to the outer door handle bolts

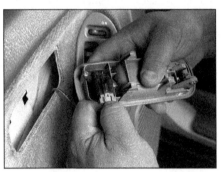

17.3 Unplug the electrical connector

the door and rotate the handle to unscrew it from the release rod.

Refitting

6 Refitting is the reverse of removal.

Lock cylinder

Removal

7 Remove the outer door handle (see above).

8 Pull out the retainer clip and detach the lock cylinder from the handle.

Refitting

9 Refitting is the reverse of removal.

Latch

Removal

10 Disconnect the lock and inner handle rod from the latch.

11 Remove the door latch retaining screws **(see illustration)** and take the door latch off

18.11 Remove the latch bolts in the end of the door (arrowed)

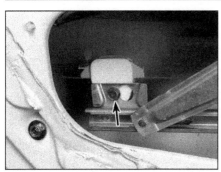

19.4a Lower the glass in the door; working through the access hole remove the rear . . .

and manoeuvre it out of the door. *Caution: Make sure you don't bend the rods.*
12 Disconnect the lock and release rods from the latch assembly and switch them over to the new latch unit.

Refitting
13 Refitting is the reverse of removal.

19 Door window glass - removal and refitting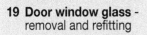

Removal
1 Remove the inside door handle (see Section 17).
2 Remove the door trim panel and plastic shield (see Section 16).
3 On convertible models, remove the nuts and detach the stopper plates at the top of the door.
4 Lower the window so the mounting bolts can be reached through the access holes in the door, then remove the bolts **(see illustrations)**.
5 Lift the door glass up and out of the door window slot, then tilt it and remove it from the door.

Refitting
6 Refitting is the reverse of removal.

20 Window regulator - removal, refitting and adjustment

Removal
1 Remove the inner door handle (Section 17).
2 Remove the door trim panel and plastic shield (see Section 16).
3 Remove the door window glass (see Section 19).
4 Scribe or mark a line around the roller guide adjusting bolt to ensure proper reassembly **(see illustration)**. Remove the window regulator retaining bolts and the two roller guide bolts, then loosen the motor bolts **(see illustration)** and remove the regulator assembly through the hole in the centre of the door. On electric windows, unplug the electrical connector.

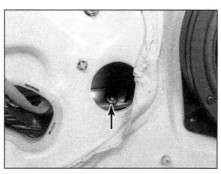

19.4b . . . and front window mounting bolts through the access hole in the door

Refitting
5 Prior to refitting, lubricate all contact surfaces with grease. Refitting is the reverse of removal.
6 To adjust the glass position evenly in the opening, loosen the roller guide or motor mounting bolts. Raise the window as far as possible, making sure it's centred in its channel, then tighten the roller guide or motor mounting bolts securely.

21 Exterior mirrors - removal and refitting

Removal
1 On manual mirrors, remove the cap and screw and pull off the knob.

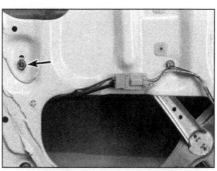

20.4a Before removing the mounting bolts, mark a line around the roller guide bolt (arrowed) (in the slotted hole)

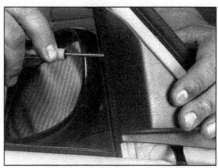

21.2 Use a small screwdriver to prise off the mirror cover

2 Prise off the cover panel **(see illustration)**.
3 Remove the three retaining nuts and lift the mirror off **(see illustration)**. On models equipped with power mirrors, unplug the electrical connector.

Refitting
4 Refitting is the reverse of removal.

22 Door - removal, refitting and adjustment

Removal
1 Remove the door trim panel (Section 16). Disconnect any electrical connectors and push them through the door opening so they won't interfere with door removal.
2 Place a floor jack under the door or have an assistant on hand to support it when the hinge bolts are removed. **Note**: *If a jack is used, be sure to place a rag between the jack head and the door to protect the door's painted surfaces.*
3 Remove the check strap pin **(see illustration)**.
4 Scribe or mark around the door hinges **(see illustration)**.
5 Remove the hinge-to-door bolts, then carefully lift off the door.

Refitting and adjustment
6 Refitting is the reverse of removal.

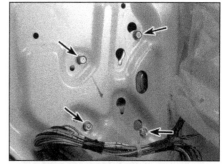

20.4b Regulator bolts (arrowed)

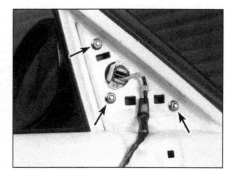

21.3 To remove the mirror, remove these three nuts (arrowed) - on electric mirrors, unplug the electrical connector too

22.3 Use a small hammer to tap out the retaining pin (arrowed)

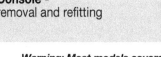

22.4 Scribe around the door hinge bolts with a marking pen

7 Following refitting of the door, check the alignment and adjust it if necessary as follows:

a) *Up-and-down and forward-and-backward adjustments are made by loosening the hinge-to-body bolts and moving the door as necessary.*

b) *The door lock striker can also be adjusted both up-and-down and sideways to provide positive engagement with the lock mechanism. This is done by loosening the mounting bolts and moving the striker as necessary.*

23 Console - removal and refitting

⚠ *Warning: Most models covered by this manual are equipped with a Supplemental Restraint System (SRS), more commonly known as an airbag(s). Always disable the airbag system before working in the vicinity of the SRS unit, steering column or instrument panel to avoid the possibility of accidental deployment of the airbag, which could cause personal injury (see Chapter 12).*

Caution: If the stereo in your car is equipped with an anti-theft system, refer to the information at the rear of this manual before disconnecting the battery.

Removal

1 On models with an automatic transmission, remove the two retaining screws on each side of the gearchange lever knob and pull off the knob.

2 On models with a manual transmission, simply unscrew and remove the shifter knob.

3 Remove the console retaining screws.

4 Detach the console and lift it out of the car **(see illustrations)**.

Refitting

5 Refitting is the reverse of removal.

24 Instrument cluster surround - removal and refitting

Note: *Refer to the warning at the start of Section 23 before proceeding.* **Caution:** *If the stereo in your car is equipped with an anti-theft system, refer to the information at the rear of this manual before detaching the battery cable.*

Removal

1 Prise out any switches from the surround that would interfere with removal, and unplug the electrical connectors **(see illustrations)**.

2 On some models it may be necessary to remove the centre and side air vents.

3 Remove the retaining screws **(see illustration)**.

4 Grasp the surround securely and detach it

23.4a On some models it's possible to remove the console with the forward console in place

23.4b The forward console also has sufficient clearance to be removed separately

24.1a Prise out the instrument panel switches . . .

24.1b . . . and unplug the electrical connector

24.3 Remove the cluster retaining screws with a crosshead screwdriver

24.4a Grasp one end of the trim panel and pull it out of the instrument panel

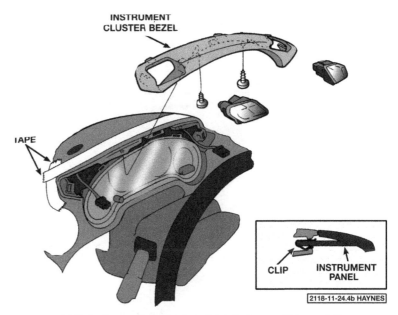

from the instrument panel **(see illustrations)**. Unplug any electrical connectors and remove the surround.

Refitting

5 Refitting is the reverse of removal.

25 Glove box - removal and refitting

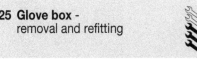

Note: *Refer to the warning at the start of Section 23 before proceeding.* **Caution: If the stereo in your car is equipped with an anti-theft system, refer to the information at the rear of this manual before detaching the battery cable.**

Removal

1 Remove the two screws from the underside of the glove box and remove the glove box **(see illustration)**.
2 Open the glove box and remove it from the car.

Refitting

3 Refitting is the reverse of removal.

26 Instrument panel - removal and refitting

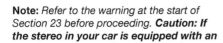

Note: *Refer to the warning at the start of Section 23 before proceeding.* **Caution: If the stereo in your car is equipped with an**

25.1 Remove the two glove box screws (arrow points to other screw location)

24.4b Instrument cluster bezel details (convertible model)

anti-theft system, refer to the information at the rear of this manual before detaching the battery cable.

Removal

1 Remove the front seats (see Section 27).
2 Remove the console (see Section 23).
3 Remove the stereo (see Chapter 12).
4 Remove the heater control panel (see Chapter 3).

5 Remove the instrument panel lower cover and knee bolster (see Section 14).
6 Remove the instrument cluster trim panel (see Section 24).
7 Remove any switches that will interfere with instrument panel removal.
8 Remove the glove box (see Section 25).
9 Remove the caps from the ends of the dashboard **(see illustration)** and remove the screws from each end of the dash.

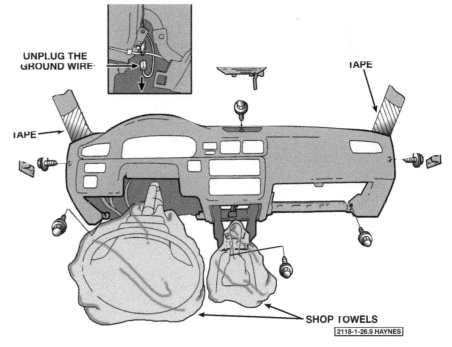

26.9 Civic instrument panel details (left-hand-drive shown)

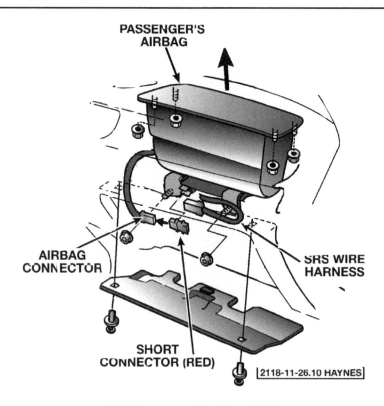

PASSENGER'S
AIRBAG

AIRBAG
CONNECTOR

SRS WIRE
HARNESS

SHORT
CONNECTOR (RED)

2118-11-26.10 HAYNES

26.12 Passenger side airbag details

27.1a Front seat track retaining bolt
(arrowed) (left bolt shown,
right bolt identical)

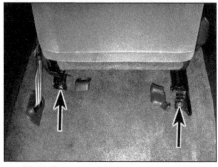

27.1b Seat track rear retaining bolts
(arrowed)

10 Remove the carpet clips from the carpet and peel back the carpet from the forward end of the console tunnel, then remove the lower dash retaining bolts.
11 Remove the steering column covers (see Section 13).
12 On models so equipped, remove the

 Warning: Always connect the short (red) connector on the airbag harness to the airbag when the airbag harness is disconnected to avoid the possibility of accidental deployment of the airbag, which could cause personal injury (Chapter 12).

passenger side airbag **(see illustration)**.
13 Remove the nuts and the wiring harness clip bolts and lower the steering column.
14 Pull out the dash assembly far enough to unplug all instrument panel wiring connectors.
15 Remove the instrument panel assembly.

Refitting

16 Refitting is the reverse of removal.

27 Seats - removal and refitting

Removal

Remove the front and rear seat track retaining bolts **(see illustrations)** and remove the seat. Unplug any electrical connectors.

Refitting

Refitting is the reverse of removal.

28 Seat belt check

1 Check the seat belts, buckles, latch plates and guide loops for obvious damage and signs of wear.
2 Check that the seat belt reminder light comes on when the key is turned to the Run and Start positions. A chime should also sound.
3 The seat belts are designed to lock up during a sudden stop or impact, yet allow free movement during normal driving. Check that the retractors return the belt against your chest while driving and rewind the belt completely when the buckle is unlatched.
4 If any of the above checks reveal problems with the seat belts, renew parts as necessary.

Chapter 12
Body electrical system

Contents

Degrees of difficulty

| Easy, suitable for novice with little experience | | Fairly easy, suitable for beginner with some experience | | Fairly difficult, suitable for competent DIY mechanic | | Difficult, suitable for experienced DIY mechanic | | Very difficult, suitable for expert DIY or professional | |

---

1 General information

The electrical system is a 12-volt, negative earth type. Power for the lights and all electrical accessories is supplied by a lead/acid-type battery which is charged by the alternator.

This Chapter covers repair and service procedures for the various electrical components not associated with the engine. Information on the battery, alternator, distributor and starter motor can be found in Chapter 5. It should be noted that when portions of the electrical system are serviced, the negative battery cable should be disconnected from the battery to prevent electrical shorts and/or fires. **Caution: The stereo in your car may be equipped with an anti-theft system. Refer to the information at the rear of this manual before detaching the battery cables.**

2 Electrical troubleshooting - general information

 Warning: Most models covered by this manual are equipped with a Supplemental Restraint System (SRS), more commonly known as an airbag(s). Always disable the airbag system before working in the *vicinity of the SRS unit, steering column or instrument panel to avoid the possibility of accidental deployment of the airbag, which could cause personal injury (see Section 24).*

A typical electrical circuit consists of an electrical component, any switches, relays, motors, fuses, fusible links or circuit breakers related to that component and the wiring and connectors that link the component to both the battery and the chassis. To help you pinpoint an electrical circuit problem, wiring diagrams are included at the end of this book.

Before tackling any troublesome electrical circuit, first study the appropriate wiring diagrams to get a complete understanding of what makes up that individual circuit. Trouble spots, for instance, can often be narrowed down by noting if other components related to the circuit are operating properly. If several components or circuits fail at once, the problem is likely in a fuse or earth connection, because several circuits are often routed through the same fuse and earth connections.

Electrical problems usually stem from simple causes, such as loose or corroded connections, a blown fuse, a melted fusible link or a bad relay. Visually inspect the condition of all fuses, wires and connections in a problem circuit before troubleshooting it.

If testing instruments are going to be utilised, use the diagrams to plan ahead of time where you will make the necessary connections in order to accurately pinpoint the trouble spot.

The basic tools needed for electrical troubleshooting include a circuit tester or voltmeter (a 12-volt bulb with a set of test leads can also be used), a continuity tester, which includes a bulb, battery and set of test leads, and a jumper wire, preferably with a circuit breaker incorporated, which can be used to bypass electrical components. Before attempting to locate a problem with test instruments, use the wiring diagram(s) to decide where to make the connections.

Voltage checks

Voltage checks should be performed if a circuit is not functioning properly. Connect one lead of a circuit tester to either the negative battery terminal or a known good earth. Connect the other lead to a connector in the circuit being tested, preferably nearest to the battery or fuse. If the bulb of the tester lights, voltage is present, which means that the part of the circuit between the connector and the battery is problem free. Continue checking the rest of the circuit in the same fashion. When you reach a point at which no voltage is present, the problem lies between that point and the last test point with voltage. Most of the time the problem can be traced to a loose connection. **Note:** *Keep in mind that some circuits receive voltage only when the ignition key is in the Accessory or Run position.*

Finding a short

One method of finding shorts in a circuit is to remove the fuse and connect a test light or voltmeter in its place to the fuse terminals. There should be no voltage present in the circuit. Move the wiring harness from side-to-side while watching the test light. If the bulb goes on, there is a short to earth somewhere in that area, probably where the insulation has rubbed through. The same test can be performed on each component in the circuit, even a switch.

Earth check

Perform an earth test to check whether a component is properly earthed. Disconnect the battery and connect one lead of a self-powered test light, known as a continuity tester, to a known good earth. Connect the other lead to the wire or earth connection being tested. If the bulb goes on, the earth is good. If the bulb does not go on, the earth is not good. *Caution: If the radio in your car is equipped with an anti-theft system. Make sure you have the activation code before disconnecting the battery.*

Continuity check

A continuity check is done to determine if there are any breaks in a circuit - if it is passing electricity properly. With the circuit off (no power in the circuit), a self-powered continuity tester can be used to check the circuit. Connect the test leads to both ends of the circuit (or to the "power" end and a good earth), and if the test light comes on the circuit is passing current properly. If the light doesn't come on, there is a break somewhere in the circuit. The same procedure can be used to test a switch, by connecting the continuity tester to the switch terminals. With the switch turned On, the test light should come on.

Finding an open circuit

When diagnosing for possible open circuits, it is often difficult to locate them by sight because oxidation or terminal misalignment are hidden by the connectors. Merely wiggling a connector on a sensor or in the wiring harness may correct the open circuit condition. Remember this when an open circuit is indicated when troubleshooting a circuit. Intermittent problems may also be caused by oxidised or loose connections.

Electrical troubleshooting is simple if you keep in mind that all electrical circuits are basically electricity running from the battery, through the wires, switches, relays, fuses and fusible links to each electrical component (light bulb, motor, etc.) and to earth, from which it is passed back to the battery. Any electrical problem is an interruption in the flow of electricity to and from the battery.

3 Fuses - general information

1 The electrical circuits of the car are protected by a combination of fuses and circuit breakers. The two fuse blocks are

3.1a The interior fuse box is located under the driver's side of the instrument panel, under a cover

located under the instrument panel and on the left side of the engine compartment **(see illustrations)**. Models with ABS have an additional fuse block (including relays) on the left-hand side of the engine compartment in front of the suspension strut.

2 Each of the fuses is designed to protect a specific circuit (or circuits), and the various circuits are identified on the fuse panel itself.

3 Miniaturised fuses are employed in the fuse block. These compact fuses, with blade terminal design, allow fingertip removal and renewal. If an electrical component fails, always check the fuse first. To check the fuses, turn the ignition key to the On position and, using a test light, probe each exposed terminal of each fuse. If the test light glows on both terminals of a fuse, the fuse is good. If power is available on one side of the fuse but not the other, the fuse is blown. When removed, a blown fuse is easily identified through the clear plastic body. Visually inspect the element for evidence of damage **(see illustration)**.

4 Be sure to renew blown fuses with the correct type. Fuses of different ratings are physically interchangeable, but only fuses of the proper rating should be used. Replacing a fuse with one of a higher or lower value than specified is not recommended. Each electrical circuit needs a specific amount of protection. The amperage value of each fuse is moulded into the fuse body.

5 If the renewal fuse immediately fails, don't renew it again until the cause of the problem

3.3 To test for a blown fuse you can pull it out and inspect it for a broken element (1) or, with the circuit activated, use a test light between earth and the terminals (2)

3.1b The engine compartment fuse box is located in the rear corner of the engine compartment (LHD model shown)

is isolated and corrected. In most cases, the cause will be a short circuit in the wiring caused by a broken or deteriorated wire.

6 All models are equipped with a main fuse (either an 80A or 100A) which protects all the circuits coming from the battery. If these circuits are overloaded, the main fuse blows, preventing damage to the main wiring harness. The main fuse consists of a metal strip which will be visibly melted when overloaded. Always disconnect the battery before replacing a main fuse (available from your dealer). *Caution: If the stereo in your car is equipped with an anti-theft system, refer to the information at the rear of this manual before disconnecting the battery.*

6 The main fuse is located in the engine compartment fuse block. It's very similar in appearance to standard fuses and is replaced in the same way. If you have to renew a main fuse, make sure you fit a replacement unit that's equivalent to the old fuse. In other words, if the old main fuse is an 80A unit, renew it with an 80A fuse. Don't switch amperage ratings on the main fuse!

4 Circuit breakers - general information

Circuit breakers protect components such as sunroof motors, power window motors and airbag inflator resistors.

On some models the circuit breaker resets itself automatically, so an electrical overload in a circuit breaker protected system will cause the circuit to fail momentarily, then come back on. If the circuit does not come back on, check it immediately. Once the condition is corrected, the circuit breaker will resume its normal function. Some circuit breakers must be reset manually.

5 Relays - general information

Several electrical accessories such as the heated rear window, the blower motor, the cooling fan and the anti-lock brake system use relays, which are remote switches that allow a small amount of current in one circuit to open or close a switch in a circuit with more current. If the relay is defective, the circuit it controls won't operate properly.

Relays are located in both main fuse boxes and under the right-hand side of the instrument panel (see Section 3):

Interior fuse box (under right side of instrument panel) and right footwell:
Sunroof open and close relays
Horn relay
Power window relay
Direction indicator/hazard relay

Engine compartment fuse box (left rear corner of engine compartment):
Heated rear window relay
Blower motor relay
Cooling fan relay

They are also located in various other locations throughout the car:

Anti-lock brake motor relay - anti-lock brake fuse box on left side of engine compartment

Condenser fan relay - front left corner of the engine compartment

Air conditioner compressor clutch relay - front left corner of the engine compartment next to condenser fan relay

PGM-FI main relay - in right end of instrument panel

If you suspect a faulty relay, remove it and have it tested by a dealer service department or a garage. Defective relays must be replaced - they can't be serviced.

---

6 Hazard/direction indicator flashers - check and renewal

⚠ **Warning: Most models covered by this manual are equipped with a Supplemental Restraint System (SRS), more commonly** known as an airbag(s). **Always disable the airbag system before working in the vicinity of the SRS unit, steering column or instrument panel to avoid the possibility of accidental deployment of the airbag, which could cause personal injury (see Section 24).**

Caution: The stereo in your car may be equipped with an anti-theft system. Refer to the information at the rear of this manual before disconnecting the battery.

1 The hazard/direction indicator flasher is a small square relay on the interior fuse block under the right side of the instrument panel.

2 If the flasher unit is functioning properly, you can hear an audible clicking sound when it's operating. If the direction indicators fail on one side or the other and the flasher unit doesn't make its characteristic clicking sound, look for a faulty direction indicator bulb.

3 If both direction indicators fail to blink, the problem may be due to a blown fuse (in the engine compartment fuse box), a faulty flasher unit, a broken switch or a loose or open connection. If a quick check of the fuse box indicates that the direction indicator fuse has blown, check the wiring for a short before refitting a new fuse.

4 To renew the flasher, simply pull it out of the fuse block.

5 Make sure that the new unit is identical to the original. Compare the old one to the new one before fitting it.

6 Fit the new unit using a reversal of the removal procedure.

---

7 Combination switch - check and renewal

Note: *Refer to the warning at the start of Section 6 before proceeding.*

Caution: The stereo in your car may be equipped with an anti-theft system. Refer to the information at the rear of this manual before disconnecting the battery.

Check

1 Remove the steering column covers (see Chapter 11).

2 Remove the instrument panel lower cover (see Chapter 11).

3 Remove the affected switch (see below) and unplug the electrical connector.

4 Check the connector terminals for continuity with the switch in each position **(see illustrations)**. If the continuity is not as specified, renew the switch.

Renewal

Direction indicator/ headlight/dimmer switch

5 Remove the two retaining screws, detach the switch, unplug the electrical connector and remove the switch from the housing **(see illustrations)**.

6 Refitting is the reverse of removal.

Windscreen wiper/washer switch

7 Remove the two retaining screws, then use a small screwdriver to carefully detach the

---

1	2	3	4			5	6	7	8	9
10	11	12	13	14	15	16	17	18	19	20

2118-12-7.4A HAYNES

7.4a Terminal guide for the lighting/dimmer/passing switch and direction indicator switch (wire harness side of connector shown)

LIGHTIMG/DIMMER PASSING SWITCH

POSITION	TERMINAL		D	E	F	G (CANADA)	I	J
HEADLIGHT SWITCH	OFF							
	•		O——	——O				
	LOW		O——	——O	O——	——O——	——O	
	HIGH		O——	——O		O——		——O
PASSING SWITCH	OFF							
	ON						O——	——O

TURN SIGNAL SWITCH

POSITION	TERMINAL	A	B	C
RIGHT		O———		———O
NEUTRAL				
LEFT		O———	———O	

2118-12-7.4b HAYNES

7.4b Continuity table for the lighting/dimmer/passing switch and direction indicator switch

---

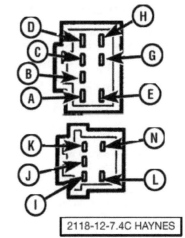

2118-12-7.4C HAYNES

7.4c Terminal guide for the front and rear wiper/washer switch (wire harness side of connector shown)

TERMINAL POSITION	A	B	C	D	H	G	E
OFF	O					O	
INT	O		O—O			O	
LO	O						O
HI		O					O
Mist switch "ON"		O					O
Washer switch "ON"				O—O			

7.4d Continuity table for the windscreen wiper/washer switch

Rear Window Wiper/Washer Switch

TERMINAL POSITION	L	K	H	I	J
OFF			O—O		
Washer switch "ON"	O—O		O—O		
ON			O——O		
Washer switch "ON"	O—O		O——O		

7.4e Continuity table for the rear wiper/washer switch

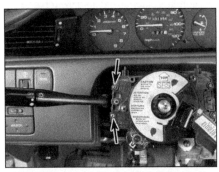

7.5a To remove the headlight/dimmer/direction indicator switch, remove the two screws (arrowed) (steering wheel removed)

7.5b Pull the headlight/dimmer/direction indicator switch out for access, then unplug connector (steering wheel removed)

7.7a Remove the two wiper/washer switch retaining screws (arrowed) (steering wheel removed for clarity). . .

1 Remove the steering column covers, instrument panel lower cover and bolster (see Chapter 11).

Switch

2 Remove the dash lower cover (Chapter 11). Disconnect the negative battery cable, then the positive battery cable.

3 Trace the wire harness for the ignition switch/key lock cylinder assembly to the fuse box under the left side of the dash, then unplug the connectors from the fuse box.

4 Check the connector for continuity between the connector terminals as shown with the key in each position (see illustration).

5 If the continuity is not as specified, renew the switch.

6 Remove the steering column covers (see Chapter 11).

7 Unplug the seven-pin connector from the fuse box.

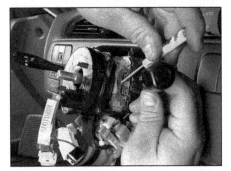

7.7b . . . use a small screwdriver to prise the switch free as you guide it out of the housing (steering wheel removed) . . .

7.7c . . . then pull the switch out of the way and unplug the electrical connector (steering wheel removed for clarity)

Caution: The stereo in your car may be equipped with an anti-theft system. Refer to the information at the rear of this manual before disconnecting the battery.

switch from the housing and unplug the electrical connector (see illustrations)

8 Refitting is the reverse of removal.

8 Ignition switch/key lock cylinder - check and renewal

Warning: Most models covered by this manual are equipped with a Supplemental Restraint System (SRS), more commonly known as an airbag(s). Always disable the airbag system before working in the vicinity of the SRS unit, steering column or instrument panel to avoid the possibility of accidental deployment of the airbag, which could cause personal injury (see Section 24).

TERMINAL POSITION	WHT/BLK (ACC)	WHT (BAT)	BLK/YEL (IG1)	YEL (IG2)	BLK/WHT (ST)	BLU/WHT (KEY)	BLU/WHT (GND)
O							
I	O—O						
II	O—O—O—O						
III		O—O			O		
Key OUT						O—O	

8.4 Continuity table for the ignition switch terminals

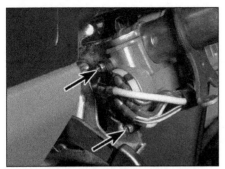

8.9 Remove the two ignition switch screws (arrowed) and remove the switch

9.1 Carefully prise the defogger switch out of the dash with a small screwdriver

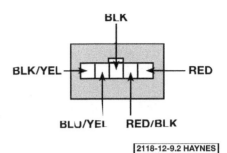

2118-12-9.2 HAYNES

9.2 Terminal guide for the heated rear window switch

8 Insert the key and turn it to the "O" position.
9 Remove the two retaining screws and detach the switch (see illustration).
10 Refitting is the reverse of removal.

Lock cylinder and steering column lock assembly

11 Check the lock cylinder in each position to make sure it isn't worn or loose and that the key position corresponds to the markings on the housing. If the lock cylinder is faulty, the entire steering column lock assembly will have to be replaced.
12 Disconnect the negative battery cable, then the positive battery cable (see Caution and Warning above).
13 Remove the steering column cover and lower instrument panel (see Chapter 11).
14 Remove the retaining nuts and lower the steering column.
15 The lock assembly is clamped to the steering column by two shear-head bolts. Use a centre punch to make a dimple in the head of each bolt, then drill them out. Alternatively, make slots with a hammer and chisel in the bolt heads and unscrew them with a screwdriver. Separate the clamp and remove the assembly from the steering column.
16 Place the new switch in position without the key inserted and tighten the bolts.
17 Insert the key and check the lock cylinder for proper operation.
18 Tighten the bolts until their heads break off.
19 The remainder of refitting is the reverse of removal.
20 Connect the positive battery cable, followed by the negative cable.

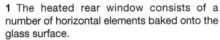

9 Heated rear window switch - check and renewal

1 Using a small screwdriver, carefully prise the switch from the dash, then unplug it from the connector (see illustration).
2 Check for battery voltage between the indicated terminals of the connector (see illustration) as follows: With the ignition On, there should be battery voltage between the BLK/YEL+ and BLK- terminals. If there is no voltage, connect a jumper wire between the BLK/YEL and BLU/YEL terminals.
3 Turn the ignition switch On and check the heated rear window. If it works, the switch is faulty and must be replaced.

10 Heated rear window - check and repair

1 The heated rear window consists of a number of horizontal elements baked onto the glass surface.
2 Small breaks in the element can be repaired without removing the rear window.

Check

3 Turn the ignition switch and heated rear window system switches On.
4 Earth the negative lead of a voltmeter to terminal B and the positive lead to terminal A (see illustration).
5 The voltmeter should read between 10 and 15 volts. If the reading is lower there is a poor earth connection.
6 Connect the negative lead to a good body earth. The reading should stay the same.
7 Connect the negative lead to the earth bus bar (point "B"), then touch each grid line at the mid-point with the positive lead.
8 The reading should be approximately six volts. If the reading is 0, there is a break between the mid-point "C" and the battery voltage bus bar point "A").
9 A 10 to 14 volt reading is an indication of a break between mid-point "C" and earth.

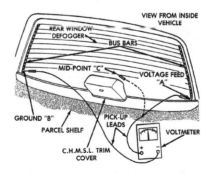

10.4 Heated rear window test points

10 Move the lead toward the break; the voltage will change when the break is crossed.

Repair

11 Repair the break in the line using a repair kit specifically recommended for this purpose. Included in this kit is plastic conductive epoxy.
12 Prior to repairing a break, turn off the system and allow it to de-energise for a few minutes.
13 Lightly buff the element area with fine steel wool, then clean it thoroughly with rubbing alcohol.
14 Use masking tape to mask off the area being repaired (see illustration).
15 Mix the epoxy thoroughly, following the instructions provided with the repair kit.
16 Apply the epoxy material to the slit in the masking tape, overlapping the undamaged area about 20 mm on either end.
17 Allow the repair to cure for 24 hours before removing the tape and using the system.

11 Stereo and speakers - removal and refitting

⚠️ *Warning: Most models covered by this manual are equipped with a Supplemental Restraint System (SRS), more commonly known as an airbag(s). Always disable the airbag system before working in the*

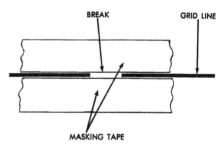

10.14 To repair a broken grid, first apply a strip of masking tape to either side of the grid to mask off the area

11.3 Reach under the stereo and remove the screws, pull it out far enough to unplug the connectors and remove the unit

11.6 Remove the screws, pull the speaker out and unplug it

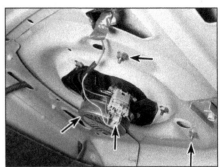

11.10 Remove the speaker grill nuts (arrowed) from underneath

vicinity of the SRS unit, steering column or instrument panel to avoid the possibility of accidental deployment of the airbag, which could cause personal injury (Section 24).

Caution: The stereo in your car may be equipped with an anti-theft system. Refer to the information at the rear of this manual before disconnecting the battery.

Stereo

1 Detach the cable from the negative terminal of the battery, then detach the positive cable (see the Caution and Warning above).
2 Remove the centre console (Chapter 11).
3 Reach under the radio and remove the two retaining screws. Pull out the stereo, unplug the electrical connector and aerial lead, then remove the stereo **(see illustration)**.
4 Refitting is the reverse of removal.

Speakers

Front speakers

5 Remove the door trim panel.
6 Remove the speaker mounting screws, pull out the speaker and unplug the electrical connector **(see illustration)**.
7 Refitting is the reverse of removal.

Rear speakers

Coupe

8 Open the boot, remove the nuts and clips and detach the trim panel between the seat back and the rear window.
9 Inside the car, remove the screws and lift the speaker and adapter out as an assembly.

Saloon

10 Working in the boot, remove the speaker grill nuts and unplug the wires from the speaker **(see illustration)**.
11 Working inside the car, remove the screws, detach the speaker and lift it out.
12 Refitting is the reverse of removal.

12 Aerial - removal and refitting

Saloon

Removal

1 Disconnect the aerial lead at the radio (see Section 11).
2 Connect a piece of string or wire to the aerial lead at the radio end.
3 Remove the mounting screws and pull the aerial out of the body pillar.

Refitting

4 Fasten the string to the lead of the new aerial. Lower the aerial into place, pulling the new lead into the pillar with the wire or string
5 Disconnect the string or wire and connect the aerial lead to the radio. Refit the aerial mounting screws and tighten them securely.

Convertible

Removal

6 Remove the locknut, then unscrew the mast, nut and spacer.

7 Remove the right side interior panel.
8 Remove the mounting nut, unplug the aerial lead and withdraw the assembly through the opening in the wing.

Refitting

9 Refitting is the reverse of removal.

13 Headlight bulb - removal and refitting

⚠️ *Warning: Halogen gas-filled bulbs are under pressure and may shatter if the surface is scratched or the bulb is dropped. Wear eye protection and handle the bulbs carefully, grasping only the base whenever possible. Do not touch the surface of the bulb with your fingers because the oil from your skin could cause it to overheat and fail prematurely.*

Removal

1 Open the bonnet.
2 If you're removing a right-side bulb, pull straight up on the air cleaner tube to remove it.
3 Reach behind the headlight assembly, unplug the electrical connector, then remove the rubber boot **(see illustration)**.
4 Release the bulb holder retaining clip, then pull out the bulb/holder assembly **(see illustrations)**.

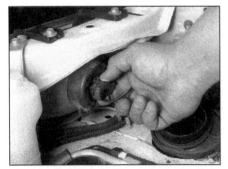

13.3 Unplug the electrical connector and remove the rubber boot

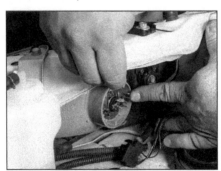

13.4a Detach the wire clip . . .

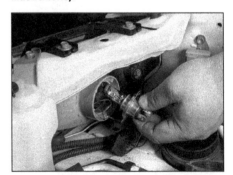

13.4b . . . then pull out the bulb assembly straight out of the housing

14.1a Headlight adjuster closest to the outer wing controls the horizontal movement, the one closest to the radiator controls vertical movement

Refitting

5 Insert the new bulb assembly and lock it in place with the clip. Refit the rubber boot and plug in the connector.

14 Headlights - adjustment

Note: The headlights must be aimed correctly. If adjusted incorrectly they could blind the driver of an oncoming car and cause a serious accident or seriously reduce your ability to see the road. The headlights should be checked for proper aim regularly and any time a new headlight is fitted or front end body work is performed. It should be emphasised that the following procedure is only an interim step which will provide temporary adjustment until the headlights can be adjusted by a properly equipped garage.

1 Headlights have spring-loaded adjusting screws for controlling up-and-down (inner) and left-and-right movement (outer - nearest the sidelight) **(see illustrations)**.
2 There are several methods of adjusting the headlights. The simplest method requires a blank wall 25 feet in front of the car and a level floor.
3 Position masking tape vertically on the wall in reference to the car centreline and the centrelines of both headlights.
4 Position a horizontal tape line in reference to the centreline of all the headlights. **Note:** It may be easier to position the tape on the wall with the car parked only a few inches away.
5 Adjustment should be made with the car sitting level, the fuel tank half-full and no unusually heavy load in the car.
6 Starting with the low beam adjustment, position the high intensity zone so it is 50 mm below the horizontal line and 50 mm to the left of the headlight vertical line. Adjustment is made by turning the vertical adjusting screw. The horizontal adjusting screw should be used to move the beam left or right.
7 With the main beams on, the main intensity zone should be vertically centred with the exact centre just below the horizontal line.

14.1b The screwdriver fits into a geared housing adjuster like this (horizontal adjuster shown)

Note: It may not be possible to position the headlight aim exactly for both main and dip beams. If a compromise must be made, keep in mind that the dip beams are the most used and have the greatest effect on driver safety.
8 Have the headlights adjusted by a dealer service department or service station at the earliest opportunity.

15 Headlight housing - renewal

Warning: Most models covered by this manual are equipped with a Supplemental Restraint System (SRS), more commonly

15.4a There are three headlight retaining fasteners, two of them (arrowed) are on the radiator support panel . . .

15.4c . . . and a nut (arrowed) at the inner corner

known as an airbag(s). Always disable the airbag system before working in the vicinity of the SRS unit, steering column or instrument panel to avoid the possibility of accidental deployment of the airbag, which could cause personal injury (see Section 24).

Caution: The stereo in your car may be equipped with an anti-theft system. Refer to the information at the rear of this manual before disconnecting the battery.
1 Unplug the electrical connectors, and remove the halogen bulbs (see Section 13).
2 Remove the side marker light retaining screw, pull off the light and unplug the electrical connector (see Section 16).
3 On convertible models, remove the front bumper (see Chapter 11).
4 Remove the headlight housing mounting bolts/nuts and remove the housing **(see illustrations)**.
5 Refitting is the reverse of removal. After have finished, adjust the headlights (see Section 14).

16 Bulb renewal

Front direction indicator/ marker light

1 Open the bonnet and remove the screw that secures the direction indicator/marker

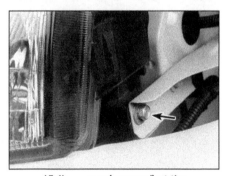

15.4b . . . one (arrowed) at the lower corner . . .

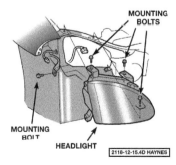

15.4d Convertible headlight housing details

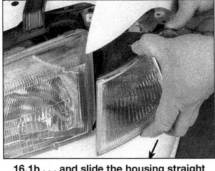

16.1a Remove the direction indicator housing screw (arrowed) . . .

16.1b . . . and slide the housing straight forward to detach it

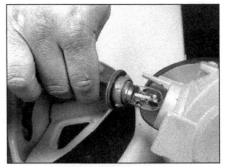

16.2 Rotate the bulb housing anti-clockwise and remove it

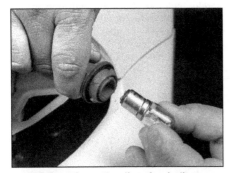

16.3 Push in on the direction indicator bulb, turn it anti-clockwise and remove it

16.5 Press the tab with your thumb and detach to tail light bulb housing cover

16.6 The tail light bulbs are removed by turning the housing anti-clockwise

16.9 Reach up into the high-mounted brake light housing, turn the bulb holder 1/8-turn and remove it

16.17 To remove an instrument cluster light bulb, depress it and turn it anti-clockwise to release it

Instrument panel lights

16 To gain access to the instrument panel lights, the instrument cluster will have to be removed first (see Section 18).
17 Rotate the bulb holder anti-clockwise and remove it from the instrument cluster (see illustration).
18 Pull the bulb straight out of the holder.
19 Refitting is the reverse of removal.

Number plate lights

20 Remove the two screws and pull out the lens.
21 On hatchback models, rotate the bulb holder 1/8-turn anti-clockwise and detach it from the lens housing.
22 Pull the bulb straight out of the holder.
23 Refitting is the reverse of removal.

Interior lights

24 Prise the lens off to access the bulb.
25 Remove the bulb from the terminals. It may be necessary to prise the bulb out - if this is the case, prise only on the ends of the bulb (otherwise the glass may shatter).
26 Refitting is the reverse of removal.

light housing, then pull the housing straight forward (see illustrations).
2 Turn the bulb holder 1/8-turn anti-clockwise and pull it out of the housing (see illustration).
3 Push in on the bulb and turn it anti-clockwise, then pull it out of the bulb holder (see illustration).
4 Refitting is the reverse of removal.

Tail light bulb

5 Remove the cover for the tail light bulb housing (see illustration).
6 Turn the bulb holder 1/8-turn anti-clockwise and pull it out of the housing (see illustration).
7 Push in on the bulb and turn it anti-clockwise, then pull it out of the bulb holder (see illustration 16.3).
8 Refitting is the reverse of removal.

High-mounted brake light

Coupe/Saloon models

9 Open the boot, then reach up through the hole in the rear shelf and twist the bulb holder anti-clockwise to remove it (see illustration).
10 Push in on the bulb and turn it anti-clockwise, then pull it out of the bulb holder (see illustration 16.3).
11 Refitting is the reverse of removal.

Hatchback models

12 Open the tailgate and carefully prise off the cover below the high-mounted brake light housing.
13 Twist the bulb holder 1/8-turn anti-clockwise and pull it out of the housing.
14 Pull the bulb straight out of the housing.
15 Refitting is the reverse of removal.

17 Wiper motor -
check and renewal

Windscreen wiper motor

Check

1 Disconnect the electrical connector from the wiper motor assembly.

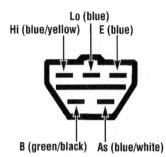

17.2 Terminal guide for the electrical connector for the windscreen wiper motor

Lo (blue)
Hi (blue/yellow)   E (blue)
B (green/black)   As (blue/white)

17.4 To remove a wiper arm, remove this nut and pull the arm off its splined shaft

Renewal

15 Detach the wiper arm and remove the rubber seal, shaft nut and washer.
16 Open the tailgate, remove the wiper motor cover and unplug the electrical connector.
17 Support the motor with one hand while removing the three retaining nuts, then lower the wiper motor from the car.
18 Refitting is the reverse of removal.

18 Instrument cluster - removal and refitting

Warning: Most models covered by this manual are equipped with a Supplemental Restraint System (SRS), more commonly known as an airbag(s). Always disable the airbag system before working in the vicinity of the SRS unit, steering column or instrument panel to avoid the possibility of accidental deployment of the airbag, which could cause personal injury (see Section 24).

Caution: The stereo in your car may be equipped with an anti-theft system. Refer to the information at the rear of this manual before disconnecting the battery.

Removal

1 Disconnect the negative cable from the battery, then the positive cable. **Caution: If the radio in your car has an anti-theft system. Make sure you have the activation code before disconnecting the battery.**
2 Remove the instrument cluster surround (see Chapter 11).
3 Remove the instrument cluster screws, pull out the cluster and unplug the electrical connectors **(see illustrations)**.

Refitting

4 Refitting is the reverse of removal. Be sure to connect the positive cable to the battery first, then the negative cable.

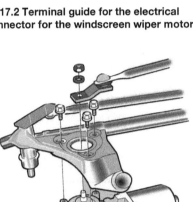

17.9 Windscreen wiper-to-frame attachment details

2118-12-17.9 HAYNES

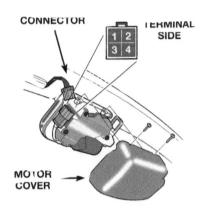

CONNECTOR

TERMINAL SIDE

1 | 2
3 | 4

MOTOR COVER

2118-12-17.13 HAYNES

17.13 Rear window wiper terminal details

2 Using a pair of jumper wires, apply battery voltage to the B terminal (green/black wire) and earth the Lo terminal (blue wire) **(see illustration)**. The wiper should operate at low speed. Then connect the battery positive terminal to the B terminal again and the negative terminal to the Hi terminal (blue/yellow wire). The wiper motor should operate at high speed.
3 If the motor fails to run at low or high speed, renew it.

Renewal

4 Detach the wiper arms **(see illustration)**.
5 Remove the bonnet seal and cowl panel by levering off the trim clips and removing the screws.
6 Unplug the electrical connector.
7 Remove the four wiper motor and linkage frame mounting bolts.
8 Turn the frame assembly over for access to the motor and linkage.
9 Remove the retaining nut, detach the linkage from the motor, then remove the three motor-to-frame mounting bolts and separate the motor from the wiper linkage **(see illustration)**.
10 Refitting is otherwise the reverse of removal. Before refitting the new motor assembly, lubricate the contact points of the wiper linkage with multi-purpose grease.

Rear wiper motor

Check

11 Open the tailgate and remove the wiper motor cover.
12 Disconnect the electrical connector from the wiper motor assembly.
13 Using a pair of jumper wires, apply battery voltage to the number 2 terminal (green/black wire) and earth the number 4 terminal (green wire) **(see illustration)**. The wiper should run smoothly.
14 If the motor fails to run, renew it.

18.3a Remove the instrument cluster screws (arrowed)

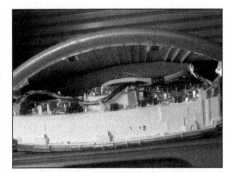

18.3b Pull the cluster out of the dash, turn it over and unplug the electrical connectors from the backside

19 Horn - check and renewal

 Warning: Most models covered by this manual are equipped with a Supplemental Restraint System (SRS), more commonly known as an airbag(s). Always disable the airbag system before working in the vicinity of the SRS unit, steering column or instrument panel to avoid the possibility of accidental deployment of the airbag, which could cause personal injury (see Section 24).

Caution: The stereo in your car may be equipped with an anti-theft system. Refer to the information at the rear of this manual before detaching the battery cables.

Note: *Check the fuses before beginning electrical diagnosis.*

1 Remove the front bumper (see Chapter 11).
2 Unplug the electrical connector from the horn.
3 To test the horn, connect battery voltage to the two terminals with a pair of jumper wires. If the horn doesn't sound, renew it. If it does sound, the problem lies in the switch, relay or the wiring between the components.
4 To renew the horn, unplug the electrical connector and remove the bracket bolt.
5 Refitting is the reverse of removal.
6 Refit the front bumper (see Chapter 11).

20 Cruise control system - description and check

1 The cruise control system maintains car speed with a vacuum actuated servo motor located in the engine compartment, which is connected to the throttle linkage by a cable. The system consists of the servo motor, brake switch, control switches, a relay, the car speed sensor and associated vacuum hoses. Cruise controls all work by the same basic principles; however, the hardware used varies considerably depending on model and year of manufacture. Listed below are some general procedures that may be used to locate common problems.
2 Locate and check the fuse (see Section 3).
3 Have an assistant operate the brake lights while you check their operation (voltage from the brake light switch deactivates the cruise control).
4 If the brake lights don't come on or don't switch off, correct the problem and retest the cruise control.
5 Inspect the cable linkage between the cruise control actuator and the throttle linkage. The cruise control servo is located under a cover and is next to the brake fluid reservoir **(see illustration)**.

20.5 The cruise control servo (arrowed) is located in the left front corner of the engine compartment

6 Visually inspect the vacuum hose(s) and wires connected to the cruise control actuator and renew as necessary.
7 The car speed sensor is located on top of the transmission **(see illustration)**. Raise the front of the car and support it on axle stands (see "*Jacking and Vehicle Support*"). Unplug the electrical connector and touch one probe of a digital voltmeter to the yellow/white wire of the connector and the other to a good earth. With the car in Neutral and key On, measure the voltage while rotating one wheel with the other one blocked. If the voltage doesn't vary as the wheel rotates, the sensor is defective.
8 Test drive the car to determine if the cruise control is now working. If it isn't, take it to a dealer service department or an automotive electrical specialist for diagnosis and repair.

21 Electric window system - description and check

1 The electric window system consists of the control switches, the motors, glass mechanisms (regulators), and associated wiring.
2 Electric windows are wired so they can be lowered and raised from the master control switch by the driver or by remote switches located at the individual windows. Each window has a separate motor which is reversible. The position of the control switch determines the polarity and therefore the direction of operation. The system is equipped with a relay that controls current flow to the motors.
3 The electric window system operates when the ignition switch is ON. In addition, these models have a window lockout switch at the master control switch which, when activated, disables the switches at the rear windows and, sometimes, the switch at the passenger's window also. Always check these items before troubleshooting a window problem.
4 These procedures are general in nature, so if you cannot find the problem using them, take the car to a dealer service department or other qualified garage.
5 If the electric windows don't work at all, check the fuse or circuit breaker.

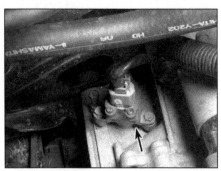

20.7 The vehicle speed sensor (arrowed) is located on the transmission

6 If only the rear windows are inoperative, or if the windows only operate from the master control switch, check the rear window lockout switch for continuity in the unlocked position. Renew it if it doesn't have continuity.
7 Check the wiring between the switches and fuse panel for continuity. Repair the wiring, if necessary.
8 If only one window is inoperative from the master control switch, try the other control switch at the window. **Note:** *This does not apply to the drivers door window.*
9 If the same window works from one switch, but not the other, check the switch for continuity.
10 If the switch tests OK, check for a short or open in the wiring between the affected switch and the window motor.
11 If one window is inoperative from both switches, remove the trim panel from the affected door and check for voltage at the motor while the switch is operated.
12 If voltage is reaching the motor, disconnect the glass from the regulator (see Chapter 11). Move the window up and down by hand while checking for binding and damage. Also check for binding and damage to the regulator. If the regulator is not damaged and the window moves up and down smoothly, renew the motor (see Chapter 11). If there's binding or damage, lubricate, repair or renew parts, as necessary.
13 If voltage isn't reaching the motor, check the wiring in the circuit for continuity between the switches and motors. Check that the relay is earthed properly and receiving voltage from the switches. Also check that the relay sends voltage to the motor when the switch is turned on. If it doesn't, renew the relay.
14 Test the windows after you have finished to confirm correct repairs.

22 Central locking system - description and check

 Warning: Most models covered by this manual are equipped with a Supplemental Restraint System (SRS), more commonly known as an airbag(s). Always disable the

airbag system before working in the vicinity of the SRS unit, steering column or instrument panel to avoid the possibility of accidental deployment of the airbag, which could cause personal injury (see Section 24).

Caution: The stereo in your car may be equipped with an anti-theft system. Refer to the information at the rear of this manual before disconnecting the battery.

1 Central locking systems are operated by bi-directional solenoids located in the doors. The lock switches have two operating positions: Lock and Unlock. These switches activate a relay which in turn connects voltage to the door lock solenoids. Depending on which way the relay is activated, it reverses polarity, allowing the two sides of the circuit to be used alternately as the feed (positive) and earth side.

2 Always check the circuit protection first. Some cars use a combination of circuit breakers and fuses.

3 Operate the door lock switches in both directions (Lock and Unlock) with the engine off. Listen for the faint click of the relay operating.

4 If there's no click, check for voltage at the switches. If no voltage is present, check the wiring between the fuse panel and the switches for shorts and opens.

5 If voltage is present but no click is heard, test the switch for continuity. Renew it if there's not continuity in both switch positions.

6 If the switch has continuity but the relay doesn't click, check the wiring between the switch and relay for continuity. Repair the wiring if there's no continuity.

7 If the relay is receiving voltage from the switch but is not sending voltage to the solenoids, check for a bad earth at the relay case. If the relay case is earthing properly, renew the relay.

8 If all but one lock solenoid operates, remove the trim panel from the affected door (see Chapter 11). and check for voltage at the solenoid while the lock switch is operated. One of the wires should have voltage in the Lock position; the other should have voltage in the unlock position.

9 If the inoperative solenoid is receiving voltage, renew the solenoid.

10 If the inoperative solenoid is not receiving voltage, check for an open or short in the wire between the lock solenoid and the relay.

Note: *It's common for wires to break in the portion of the harness between the body and door (opening and closing the door fatigues and eventually breaks the wires).*

23 Electric rear view mirrors - description and check

1 Most electric rear view mirrors use two motors to move the glass; one for up-and-

23.6 Use a small screwdriver to carefully prise the mirror switch out of the instrument panel

down adjustments and one for left-to-right adjustments. In addition, some mirrors have electrically heated glass defroster circuits, which are usually powered through the rear window defogger relay.

2 The control switch usually has a selector portion which sends voltage to the left or right side mirror. With the ignition ON but the engine OFF, roll down the windows and operate the mirror control switch through all functions (left-right and up-down) for both the left and right side mirrors.

3 Listen carefully for the sound of the electric motors running in the mirrors.

4 If the motors can be heard but the mirror glass doesn't move, there's probably a problem with the drive mechanism inside the mirror. Remove and dismantle the mirror to locate the problem.

5 If the mirrors don't operate and no sound comes from the mirrors, check the fuse (see Chapter 1).

6 If the fuse is OK, remove the mirror control switch from its mounting without disconnecting the wires attached to it **(see illustration).** Turn the ignition ON and check for voltage at the switch. There should be voltage at one terminal. If there's no voltage at the switch, check for an open or short in the wiring between the fuse panel and the switch.

7 If there's voltage at the switch, disconnect it. Check the switch for continuity in all its operating positions. If the switch does not have continuity, renew it.

8 Re-connect the switch. Locate the wire going from the switch to earth. Leaving the switch connected, connect a jumper wire between this wire and earth. If the mirror works normally with this wire in place, repair the faulty earth connection.

9 If the mirror still doesn't work, remove the cover and check the wires at the mirror for voltage with a test light **(see illustration).** Check with ignition ON and the mirror selector switch on the appropriate side. Operate the mirror switch in all its positions. There should be voltage at one of the switch-to-mirror wires in each switch position (except the neutral "off" position).

10 If there's not voltage in each switch position, check the wiring between the mirror and control switch for opens and shorts.

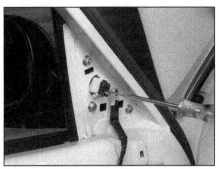

23.9 Use a test light to make sure there is power going to the mirror motor

11 If there's voltage, remove the mirror and test it off the car with jumper wires. Renew the mirror if it fails this test (see Chapter 11).

24 Airbag - general information

Description

1 Most models are equipped with a Supplemental Restraint System (SRS), more commonly known as an airbag. Later models may have two airbags, one for the driver and one for the front seat passenger. The SRS system is designed to protect the driver (and on later models, the passenger as well) from serious injury in the event of a head-on or frontal collision.

2 The SRS system on 1992 and 1993 models consists of an SRS unit, two dash-mounted impact sensors and an airbag assembly in the centre of the steering wheel. The SRS system on 1994 and later models consists of an SRS unit - which contains an impact sensor, safing sensor, self-diagnosis circuit and a back-up power circuit - located under the dash, right in front of the floor console, an airbag assembly in the centre of the steering wheel and, on some later models, a second airbag assembly for the front seat passenger, located in the top of the dash right above the glove box.

Operation

3 For the airbag(s) to deploy, the impact and safing sensors must be activated. When this condition occurs, the circuit to the airbag inflator is closed and the airbag inflates. If the battery is destroyed by the impact, or is too low to power the inflator, a back-up power unit inside the SRS unit provides power.

Self-diagnosis system

4 A self-diagnosis circuit in the SRS unit displays a light when the ignition switch is turned to the On position. If the system is operating normally, the light should go out after about six seconds. If the light doesn't come on, or does not go out after six seconds, or if it comes on while you're driving the car, there is a malfunction in the SRS

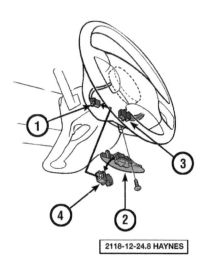

2118-12-24.8 HAYNES

24.8 To prevent the possibility of accidental deployment of the driver's side airbag, remove the two screws from the maintenance lid under the steering wheel, pull off the lid, remove the short connector, unplug the three-pin connector between the airbag and the cable reel and plug the short connector into the airbag side of the three-pin connector

1 *Airbag connector*
2 *Access cover*
3 *Cable reel connector*
4 *Short connector (red)*

system. Have it inspected and repaired as soon as possible. Do not attempt to troubleshoot or service the SRS system yourself. Even a small mistake could cause the SRS system to malfunction when you need it.

Servicing components near the SRS system

5 Nevertheless, there are times when you need to remove the steering wheel, radio or service other components on or near the dash. At these times, you'll be working around components and wire harnesses for the SRS

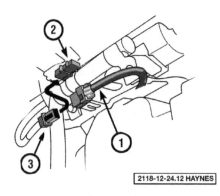

2118-12-24.12 HAYNES

24.12 When disabling the passenger's side airbag, unplug the airbag electrical connector from the SRS main harness and refit the red short connector to the airbag electrical connector

1 *SRS main harness*
2 *Short connector (red)*
3 *Front passenger's airbag three-pin connector*

system. SRS wires are easy to identify: They're all bright yellow. Do not unplug the connectors for these wires. And do not use electrical test equipment on yellow wires. *ALWAYS DISABLE THE SRS SYSTEM BEFORE WORKING NEAR THE SRS SYSTEM COMPONENTS OR RELATED WIRING.*

Disabling the SRS system

6 Disconnect the battery negative cable, then disconnect the positive cable and wait three minutes. *Caution: The radio in your car may be equipped with an anti-theft system. Make sure you have the correct activation code before disconnecting the battery cables.*
7 Connect the short (red) connectors to the airbag side of the connectors as described in the following steps.

Driver's side airbag

8 Remove the access panel below the airbag

and remove the short (red) connector **(see illustration)**.
9 Unplug the three-pin connector between the airbag and the cable reel.
10 Plug the short (red) connector into the airbag side of the three-pin connector.

Passenger's side airbag

11 Remove the glove box (see Chapter 11).
12 Unplug the electrical connector between the passenger side airbag and the SRS main wiring harness. Fit the red short connector on the airbag side of the connector **(see illustration)**.

Either airbag

13 After you've disabled the airbag and performed the necessary service, unplug the short connector from the airbag connector and plug in the three-pin airbag connector into the three-pin cable reel connector (driver's side) or the SRS main harness (passenger's side) attach the short connector to its holder and refit the lid to the underside of the steering wheel or refit the glove box.
14 Reattach the positive (first) and negative (last) battery cables (see Chapter 5).

25 Wiring diagrams - general information

Since it is not possible to include all wiring diagrams for every year and model covered by this manual, the following diagrams are those that are typical and most commonly needed. The selection of wiring diagrams are for left-hand drive models however right-hand drive models are similar.

Prior to troubleshooting any circuits, check the fuse and circuit breakers (if applicable) to make sure they're in good condition. Make sure the battery is properly charged and check the cable connections (see Chapter 1).

When checking a circuit, make sure that all connectors are clean, with no broken or loose terminals. When unplugging a connector, do not pull on the wires. Pull only on the connector housings themselves.

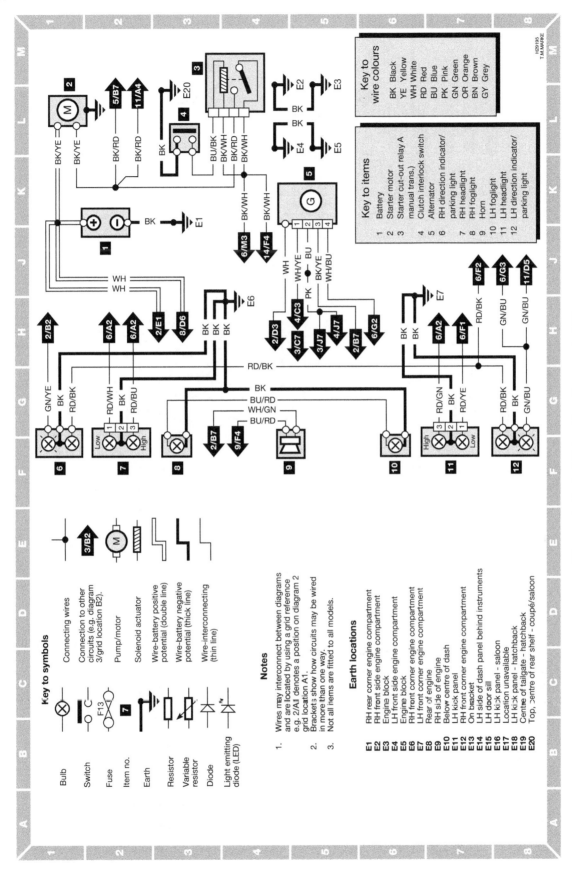

Diagram 1 : Typical Civic wiring diagram - 1 of 15

Key to wire colours

BK Black
YE Yellow
WH White
RD Red
BU Blue
PK Pink
GN Green
OR Orange
BN Brown
GY Grey

Key to items

1 Battery
2 Starter motor
3 Starter cut-out relay A (manual trans.)
4 Clutch interlock switch
5 Alternator
6 RH direction indicator/ parking light
7 RH headlight
8 RH foglight
9 Horn
10 LH foglight
11 LH headlight
12 LH direction indicator/ parking light

Key to symbols

Bulb — Connecting wires

Switch — Connection to other circuits (e.g. diagram 3/grid location B2).

Fuse — Pump/motor

Item no. — Solenoid actuator

Earth — Wire-battery positive potential (double line)

Resistor — Wire-battery negative potential (thick line)

Variable resistor — Wire-interconnecting (thin line)

Diode

Light emitting diode (LED)

Notes

1. Wires may interconnect between diagrams and are located by using a grid reference e.g. 2/A1 denotes a position on diagram 2 grid location A1.
2. Brackets show how circuits may be wired in more than one way.
3. Not all items are fitted to all models.

Earth locations

E1 RH rear corner engine compartment
E2 RH front side engine compartment
E3 Engine block
E4 LH front side engine compartment
E5 Engine block
E6 RH front corner engine compartment
E7 LH front corner engine compartment
E8 Rear of engine
E9 RH side of engine
E10 Below centre of dash
E11 LH kick panel
E12 RH front corner engine compartment
E13 On bracket
E14 LH side of dash panel behind instruments
E15 LH door sill
E16 LH kick panel - saloon
E17 Location unavailable
E18 LH kick panel - hatchback
E19 Centre of tailgate - hatchback
E20 Top, centre of rear shelf - coupé/saloon

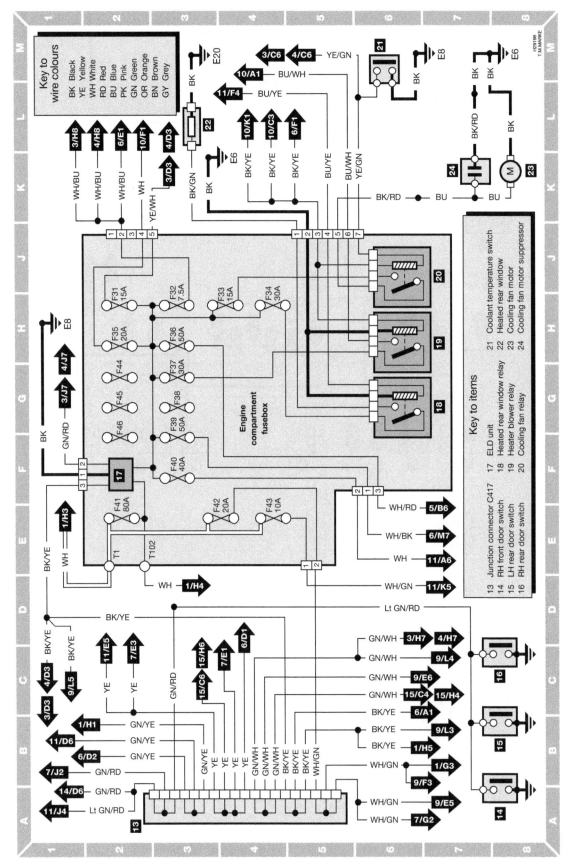

Diagram 2 : Typical Civic wiring diagram - 2 of 15

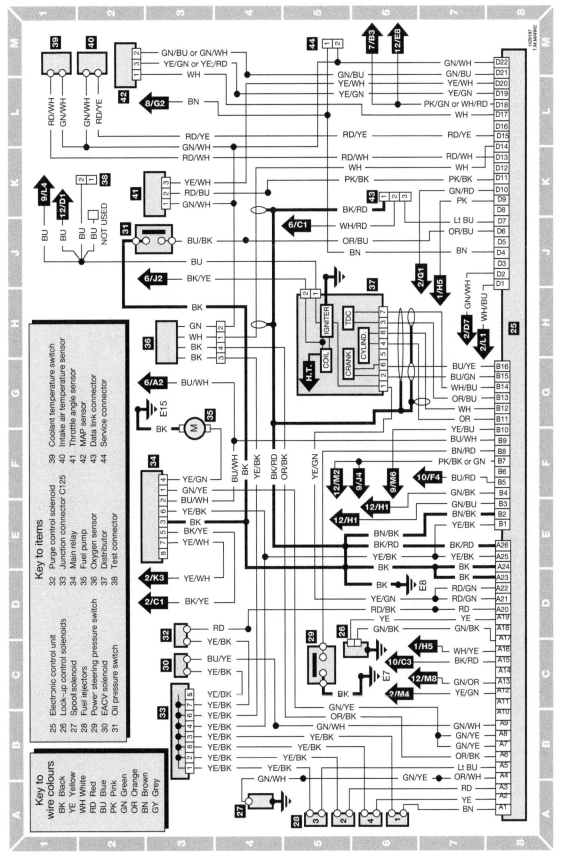

Diagram 3 : Typical Civic wiring diagram - 3 of 15

Key to items

25	Electronic control unit
26	Lock-up control solenoids
27	Spool solenoid
28	Fuel injectors
29	Power steering pressure switch
30	EACV solenoid
31	Oil pressure switch
32	Purge control solenoid
33	Junction connector C125
34	Main relay
35	Fuel pump
36	Oxygen sensor
37	Distributor
38	Test connector
39	Coolant temperature switch
40	Intake air temperature sensor
41	Throttle angle sensor
42	MAP sensor
43	Data link connector
44	Service connector

Key to wire colours

BK	Black
YE	Yellow
WH	White
RD	Red
BU	Blue
PK	Pink
GN	Green
OR	Orange
BN	Brown
GY	Grey

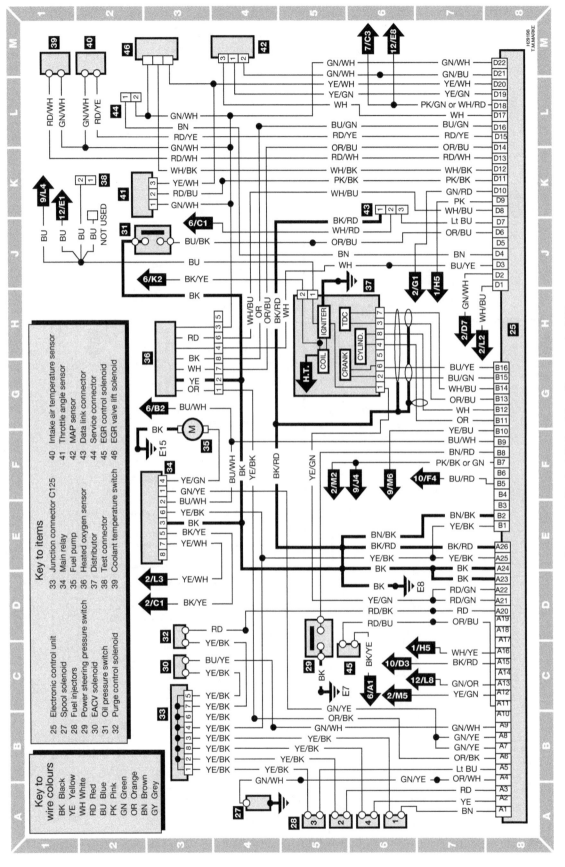

Diagram 4 : Typical Civic wiring diagram - 4 of 15

Key to items

33 Junction connector C125
34 Main relay
35 Fuel pump
36 Heated oxygen sensor
37 Distributor
38 Test connector
39 Coolant temperature switch

25 Electronic control unit
27 Spool solenoid
28 Fuel injectors
29 Power steering pressure switch
30 EACV solenoid
31 Oil pressure switch
32 Purge control solenoid

40 Intake air temperature sensor
41 Throttle angle sensor
42 MAP sensor
43 Data link connector
44 Service connector
45 EGR control solenoid
46 EGR valve lift solenoid

Key to wire colours

BK Black
YE Yellow
WH White
RD Red
BU Blue
PK Pink
GN Green
OR Orange
BN Brown
GY Grey

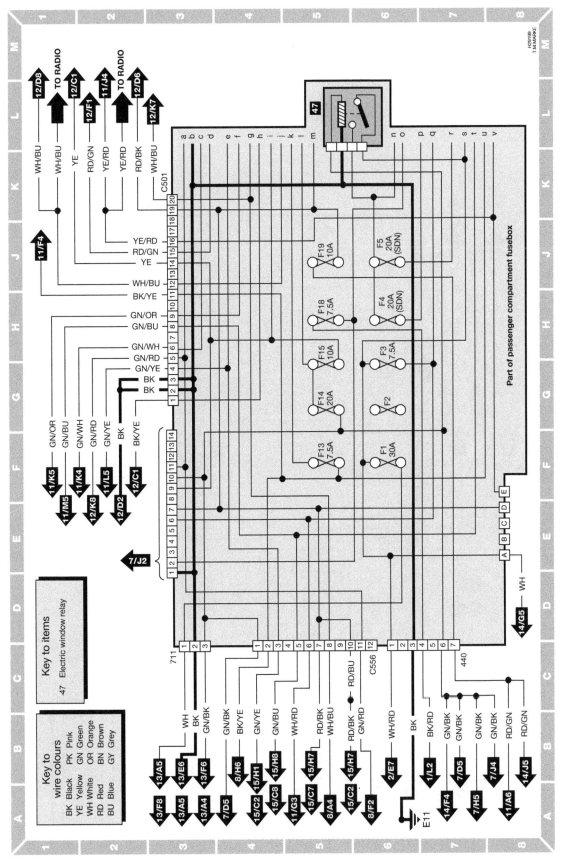

Diagram 5 : Typical Civic wiring diagram - 5 of 15

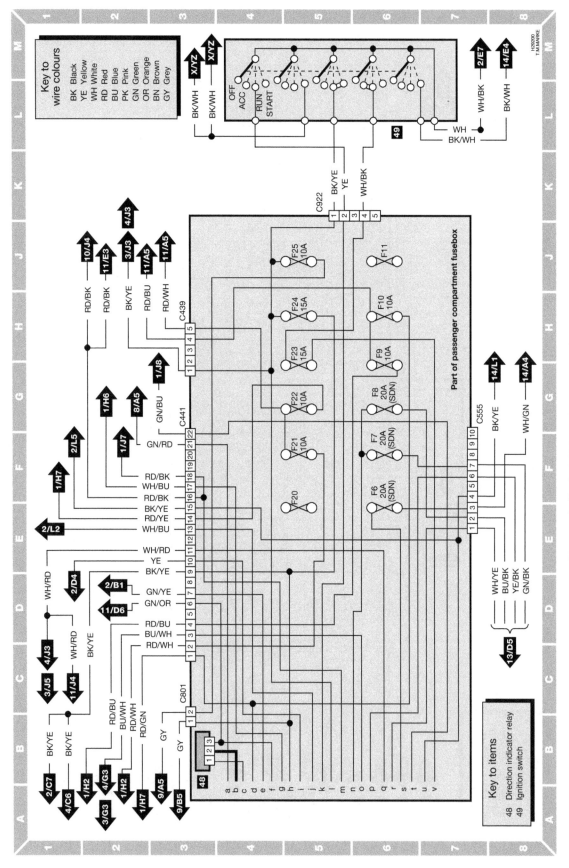

Diagram 6 : Typical Civic wiring diagram - 6 of 15

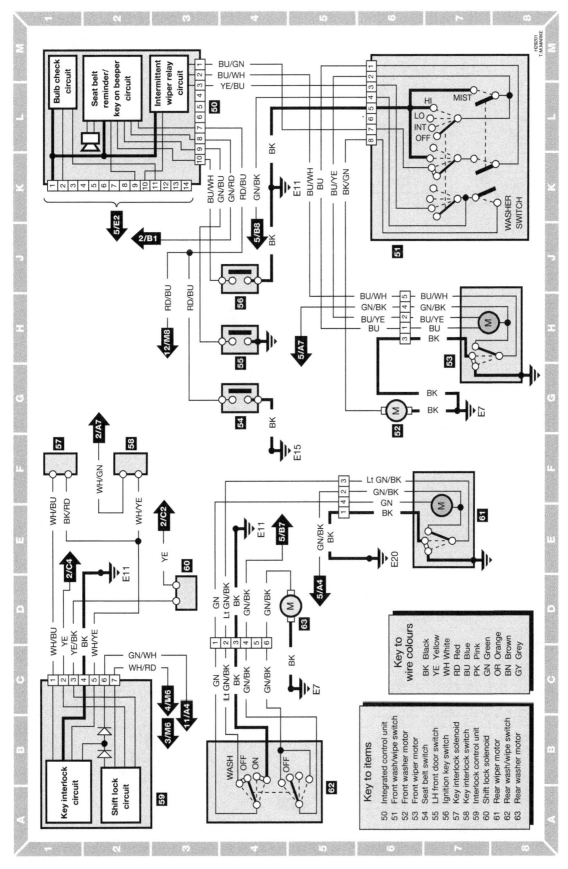

Diagram 7 : Typical Civic wiring diagram - 7 of 15

Key to wire colours

BK Black
YE Yellow
WH White
RD Red
BU Blue
PK Pink
GN Green
OR Orange
BN Brown
GY Grey

Key to items

50 Integrated control unit
51 Front wash/wipe switch
52 Front washer motor
53 Front wiper motor
54 Seat belt switch
55 LH front door switch
56 Ignition key switch
57 Key interlock solenoid
58 Key interlock switch
59 Interlock control unit
60 Shift lock solenoid
61 Rear wiper motor
62 Rear wash/wipe switch
63 Rear washer motor

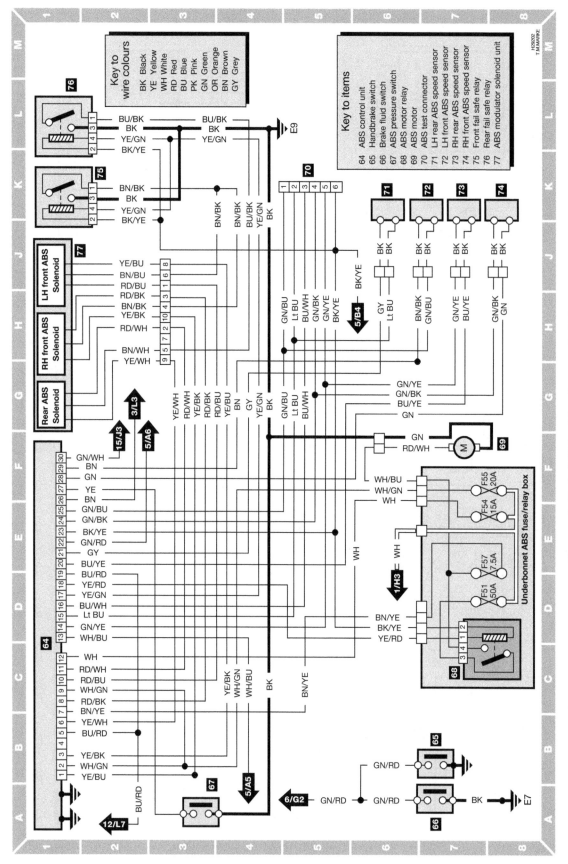

Key to wire colours
BK Black
YE Yellow
WH White
RD Red
BU Blue
PK Pink
GN Green
OR Orange
BN Brown
GY Grey

Key to items
64 ABS control unit
65 Handbrake switch
66 Brake fluid switch
67 ABS pressure switch
68 ABS motor relay
69 ABS motor
70 ABS test connector
71 LH rear ABS speed sensor
72 LH front ABS speed sensor
73 RH rear ABS speed sensor
74 RH front ABS speed sensor
75 Front fail safe relay
76 Rear fail safe relay
77 ABS modulator solenoid unit

Diagram 8 : Typical Civic wiring diagram - 8 of 15

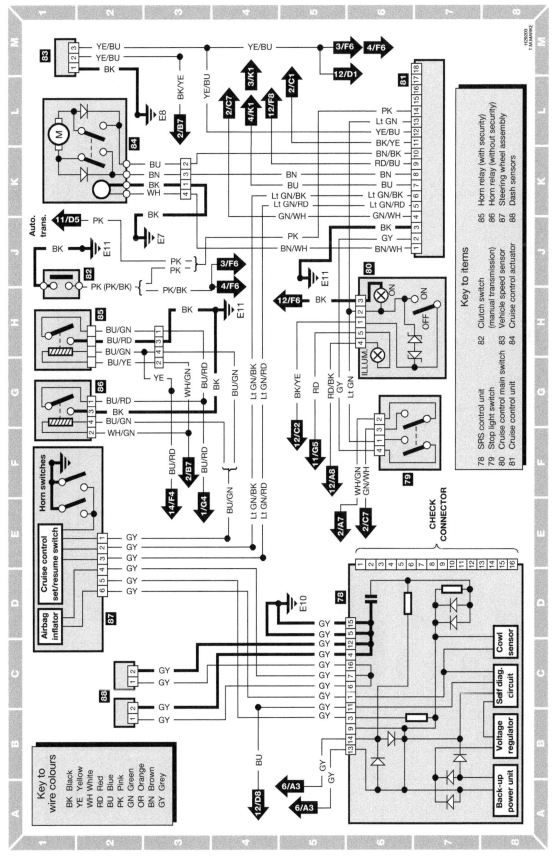

Diagram 9 : Typical Civic wiring diagram - 9 of 15

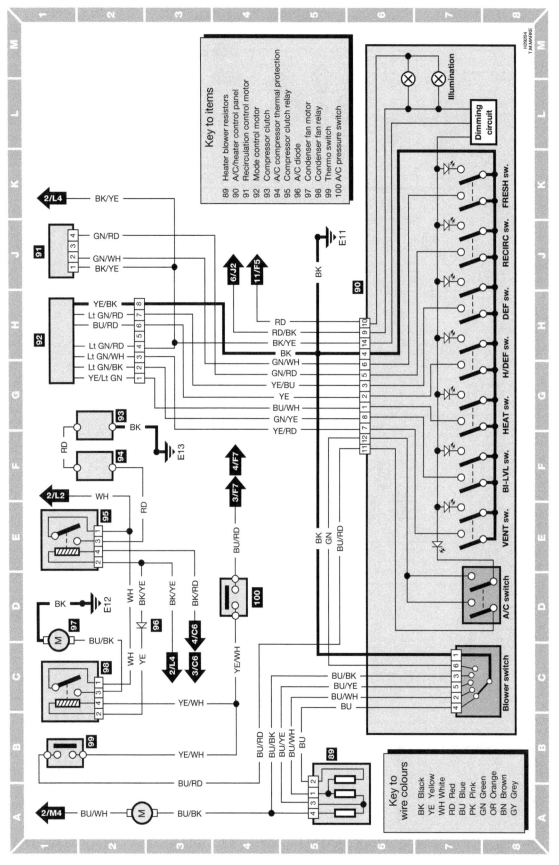

Key to items

89 Heater blower resistors
90 A/C/heater control panel
91 Recirculation control motor
92 Mode control motor
93 Compressor clutch
94 A/C compressor thermal protection
95 Compressor clutch relay
96 A/C diode
97 Condenser fan motor
98 Condenser fan relay
99 Thermo switch
100 A/C pressure switch

Key to wire colours

BK Black
YE Yellow
WH White
RD Red
BU Blue
PK Pink
GN Green
OR Orange
BN Brown
GY Grey

Diagram 10 : Typical Civic wiring diagram - 10 of 15

H29204
T.M.MARKE

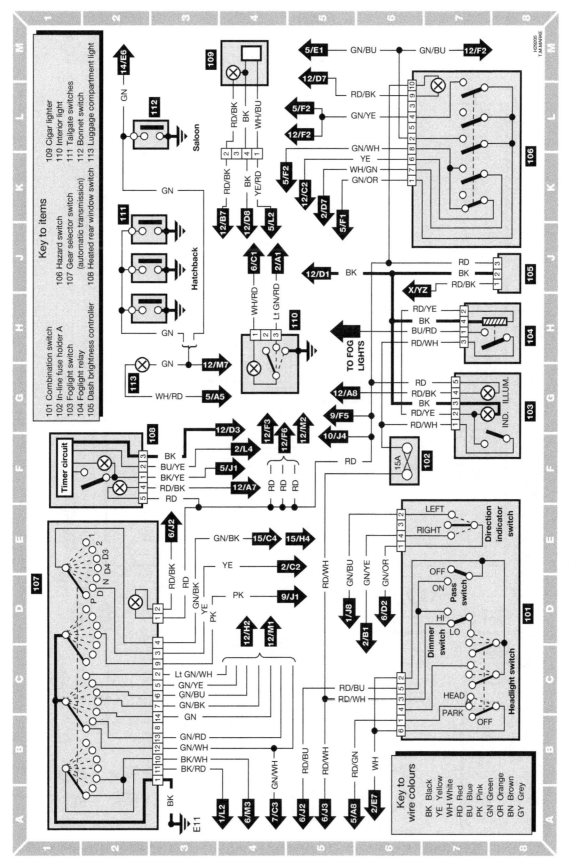

Diagram 11 : Typical Civic wiring diagram - 11 of 15

Key to items

101 Combination switch
102 In-line fuse holder A
103 Foglight switch
104 Foglight relay
105 Dash brightness controller
106 Hazard switch
107 Gear selector switch (automatic transmission)
108 Heated rear window switch
109 Cigar lighter
110 Interior light
111 Tailgate switches
112 Bonnet switch
113 Luggage compartment light

Key to wire colours

BK Black
YE Yellow
WH White
RD Red
BU Blue
PK Pink
GN Green
OR Orange
BN Brown
GY Grey

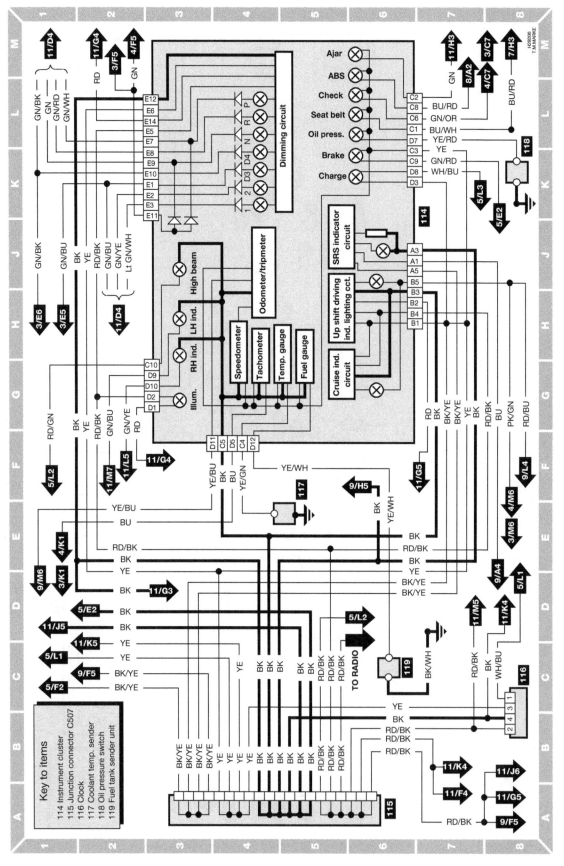

Diagram 12 : Typical Civic wiring diagram - 12 of 15

Key to items

114 Instrument cluster
115 Junction connector C507
116 Clock
117 Coolant temp. sender
118 Oil pressure switch
119 Fuel tank sender unit

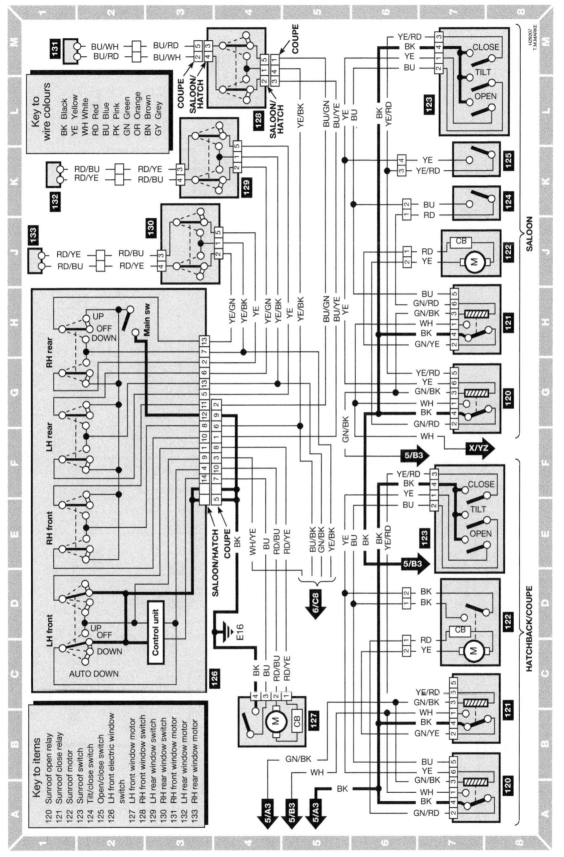

Diagram 13 : Typical Civic wiring diagram - 13 of 15

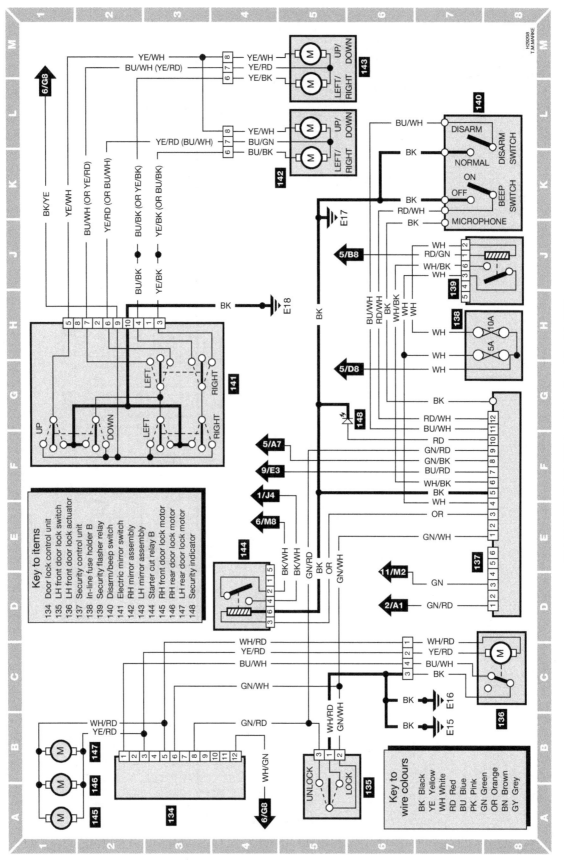

Diagram 14 : Typical Civic wiring diagram - 14 of 15

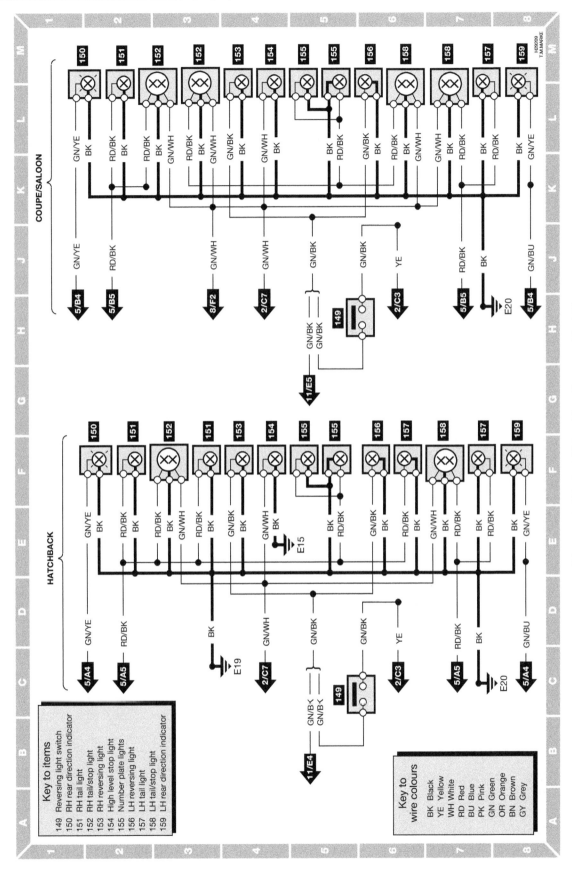

Diagram 15 : Typical Civic wiring diagram - 15 of 15

COUPE/SALOON

HATCHBACK

Key to items
149 Reversing light switch
150 RH rear direction indicator
151 RH tail light
152 RH tail/stop light
153 RH reversing light
154 High level stop light
155 Number plate lights
156 LH reversing light
157 LH tail light
158 LH tail/stop light
159 LH rear direction indicator

Key to wire colours
BK Black
YE Yellow
WH White
RD Red
BU Blue
PK Pink
GN Green
OR Orange
BN Brown
GY Grey

Notes

Reference REF•1

General dimensions and weights

Note: *All figures are approximate, and may vary according to model. Refer to manufacturer's data for exact figures.*

Dimensions
Overall length	4405 mm
Overall width	1695 mm
Overall height (unladen)	1375 mm
Wheelbase	2620 mm
Track	
Front	1475 mm
Rear	1465 mm

Weights
Kerb weight	970 to 1155 kg*
Maximum gross vehicle weight	1500 to 1545 kg*
Maximum towing weight (trailer with brakes)	700 to 1000 kg*
Maximum trailer nose weight	50 kg

Depending on model and specification.

Conversion Factors

Length (distance)

Inches (in)	25.4	= Millimetres (mm)	x 0.0394	=	Inches (in)
Feet (ft)	0.305	= Metres (m)	x 3.281	=	Feet (ft)
Miles	1.609	= Kilometres (km)	x 0.621	=	Miles

Volume (capacity)

Cubic inches (cu in; in³)	x 16.387	= Cubic centimetres (cc; cm³)	x 0.061	=	Cubic inches (cu in; in³)
Imperial pints (Imp pt)	x 0.568	= Litres (l)	x 1.76	=	Imperial pints (Imp pt)
Imperial quarts (Imp qt)	x 1.137	= Litres (l)	x 0.88	=	Imperial quarts (Imp qt)
Imperial quarts (Imp qt)	x 1.201	= US quarts (US qt)	x 0.833	=	Imperial quarts (Imp qt)
US quarts (US qt)	x 0.946	= Litres (l)	x 1.057	=	US quarts (US qt)
Imperial gallons (Imp gal)	x 4.546	= Litres (l)	x 0.22	=	Imperial gallons (Imp gal)
Imperial gallons (Imp gal)	x 1.201	= US gallons (US gal)	x 0.833	=	Imperial gallons (Imp gal)
US gallons (US gal)	x 3.785	= Litres (l)	x 0.264	=	US gallons (US gal)

Mass (weight)

Ounces (oz)	x 28.35	= Grams (g)	x 0.035	=	Ounces (oz)
Pounds (lb)	x 0.454	= Kilograms (kg)	x 2.205	=	Pounds (lb)

Force

Ounces-force (ozf; oz)	x 0.278	= Newtons (N)	x 3.6	=	Ounces-force (ozf; oz)
Pounds-force (lbf; lb)	x 4.448	= Newtons (N)	x 0.225	=	Pounds-force (lbf; lb)
Newtons (N)	x 0.1	= Kilograms-force (kgf; kg)	x 9.81	=	Newtons (N)

Pressure

Pounds-force per square inch (psi; lbf/in²; lb/in²)	x 0.070	= Kilograms-force per square centimetre (kgf/cm²; kg/cm²)	x 14.223	=	Pounds-force per square inch (psi; lbf/in²; lb/in²)
Pounds-force per square inch (psi; lbf/in²; lb/in²)	x 0.068	= Atmospheres (atm)	x 14.696	=	Pounds-force per square inch (psi; lbf/in²; lb/in²)
Pounds-force per square inch (psi; lbf/in²; lb/in²)	x 0.069	= Bars	x 14.5	=	Pounds-force per square inch (psi; lbf/in²; lb/in²)
Pounds-force per square inch (psi; lbf/in²; lb/in²)	x 6.895	= Kilopascals (kPa)	x 0.145	=	Pounds-force per square inch (psi; lbf/in²; lb/in²)
Kilopascals (kPa)	x 0.01	= Kilograms-force per square centimetre (kgf/cm²; kg/cm²)	x 98.1	=	Kilopascals (kPa)
Millibar (mbar)	x 100	= Pascals (Pa)	x 0.01	=	Millibar (mbar)
Millibar (mbar)	x 0.0145	= Pounds-force per square inch (psi; lbf/in²; lb/in²)	x 68.947	=	Millibar (mbar)
Millibar (mbar)	x 0.75	= Millimetres of mercury (mmHg)	x 1.333	=	Millibar (mbar)
Millibar (mbar)	x 0.401	= Inches of water (inH₂O)	x 2.491	=	Millibar (mbar)
Millimetres of mercury (mmHg)	x 0.535	= Inches of water (inH₂O)	x 1.868	=	Millimetres of mercury (mmHg)
Inches of water (inH₂O)	x 0.036	= Pounds-force per square inch (psi; lbf/in²; lb/in²)	x 27.68	=	Inches of water (inH₂O)

Torque (moment of force)

Pounds-force inches (lbf in; lb in)	x 1.152	= Kilograms-force centimetre (kgf cm; kg cm)	x 0.868	=	Pounds-force inches (lbf in; lb in)
Pounds-force inches (lbf in; lb in)	x 0.113	= Newton metres (Nm)	x 8.85	=	Pounds-force inches (lbf in; lb in)
Pounds-force inches (lbf in; lb in)	x 0.083	= Pounds-force feet (lbf ft; lb ft)	x 12	=	Pounds-force inches (lbf in; lb in)
Pounds-force feet (lbf ft; lb ft)	x 0.138	= Kilograms-force metres (kgf m; kg m)	x 7.233	=	Pounds-force feet (lbf ft; lb ft)
Pounds-force feet (lbf ft; lb ft)	x 1.356	= Newton metres (Nm)	x 0.738	=	Pounds-force feet (lbf ft; lb ft)
Newton metres (Nm)	x 0.102	= Kilograms-force metres (kgf m; kg m)	x 9.804	=	Newton metres (Nm)

Power

Horsepower (hp)	x 745.7	= Watts (W)	x 0.0013	=	Horsepower (hp)

Velocity (speed)

Miles per hour (miles/hr; mph)	x 1.609	= Kilometres per hour (km/hr; kph)	x 0.621	=	Miles per hour (miles/hr; mph)

Fuel consumption*

Miles per gallon (mpg)	x 0.354	= Kilometres per litre (km/l)	x 2.825	=	Miles per gallon (mpg)

It is common practice to convert from miles per gallon (mpg) to litres/100 kilometres (l/100km), where mpg x l/100 km = 282

Temperature

Degrees Fahrenheit = (°C x 1.8) + 32

Degrees Celsius (Degrees Centigrade; °C) = (°F - 32) x 0.56

Spare parts are available from many sources, including maker's appointed garages, accessory shops, and motor factors. To be sure of obtaining the correct parts, it may sometimes be necessary to quote the vehicle identification number. If possible, it can also be useful to take the old parts along for positive identification. Items such as starter motors and alternators may be available under a service exchange scheme - any parts returned should always be clean.

Our advice regarding spare part sources is as follows.

Officially-appointed garages

This is the best source of parts which are peculiar to your car, and are not otherwise generally available (eg badges, interior trim, certain body panels, etc). It is also the only place at which you should buy parts if the vehicle is still under warranty.

Accessory shops

These are very good places to buy materials and parts needed for the maintenance of your car (oil, air and fuel filters, spark plugs, light bulbs, drivebelts, oils and greases, brake pads, touch-up paint, etc). Parts like this sold by a reputable shop are of the same standard as those used by the car manufacturer.

Motor factors

Good factors will stock all the more important components which wear out comparatively quickly and can sometimes supply individual components needed for the overhaul of a larger assembly. They may also handle work such as cylinder block reboring, crankshaft regrinding and balancing, etc.

Tyre and exhaust specialists

These outlets may be independent or members of a local or national chain. They frequently offer competitive prices when compared with a main dealer or local garage, but it will pay to obtain several quotes before making a decision. Also ask what 'extras' may be added to the quote - for instance, fitting a new valve and balancing the wheel are both often charged on top of the price of a new tyre.

Other sources

Beware of parts or materials obtained from market stalls, car boot sales or similar outlets. Such items are not invariably sub-standard, but there is little chance of compensation if they do prove unsatisfactory. In the case of safety-critical components such as brake pads there is the risk not only of financial loss but also of an accident causing injury or death.

Vehicle identification numbers

Modifications are always a continuing and unpublicised process in vehicle manufacture, quite apart from major model changes. Spare parts lists are compiled upon a numerical basis, the individual vehicle identification numbers being essential to correct identification of the component concerned.

When ordering spare parts, always give as much information as possible. Quote the car model, year of manufacture, body and engine numbers, as appropriate.

The Vehicle Identification Number (VIN) and engine number plate is riveted to the left-hand side of the bulkhead in the engine compartment behind the battery. The chassis number is also stamped on the crossmember at the front of the engine compartment.

The Engine number is situated on the front right-hand end of the cylinder block, near the exhaust manifold.

The *Transmission number* is located on the bellhousing near the starter motor on manual transmission models, and on the right front of the transmission case above the dipstick on automatic transmission models.

The Vehicle Identification Number and engine number plate is riveted to the bulkhead

Whenever servicing, repair or overhaul work is carried out on the car or its components, it is necessary to observe the following procedures and instructions. This will assist in carrying out the operation efficiently and to a professional standard of workmanship.

Joint mating faces and gaskets

When separating components at their mating faces, never insert screwdrivers or similar implements into the joint between the faces in order to prise them apart. This can cause severe damage which results in oil leaks, coolant leaks, etc upon reassembly. Separation is usually achieved by tapping along the joint with a soft-faced hammer in order to break the seal. However, note that this method may not be suitable where dowels are used for component location.

Where a gasket is used between the mating faces of two components, ensure that it is renewed on reassembly, and fit it dry unless otherwise stated in the repair procedure. Make sure that the mating faces are clean and dry, with all traces of old gasket removed. When cleaning a joint face, use a tool which is not likely to score or damage the face, and remove any burrs or nicks with an oilstone or fine file.

Make sure that tapped holes are cleaned with a pipe cleaner, and keep them free of jointing compound, if this is being used, unless specifically instructed otherwise.

Ensure that all orifices, channels or pipes are clear, and blow through them, preferably using compressed air.

Oil seals

Oil seals can be removed by levering them out with a wide flat-bladed screwdriver or similar tool. Alternatively, a number of self-tapping screws may be screwed into the seal, and these used as a purchase for pliers or similar in order to pull the seal free.

Whenever an oil seal is removed from its working location, either individually or as part of an assembly, it should be renewed.

The very fine sealing lip of the seal is easily damaged, and will not seal if the surface it contacts is not completely clean and free from scratches, nicks or grooves. If the original sealing surface of the component cannot be restored, and the manufacturer has not made provision for slight relocation of the seal relative to the sealing surface, the component should be renewed.

Protect the lips of the seal from any surface which may damage them in the course of fitting. Use tape or a conical sleeve where possible. Lubricate the seal lips with oil before fitting and, on dual-lipped seals, fill the space between the lips with grease.

Unless otherwise stated, oil seals must be fitted with their sealing lips toward the lubricant to be sealed.

Use a tubular drift or block of wood of the appropriate size to install the seal and, if the seal housing is shouldered, drive the seal down to the shoulder. If the seal housing is unshouldered, the seal should be fitted with its face flush with the housing top face (unless otherwise instructed).

Screw threads and fastenings

Seized nuts, bolts and screws are quite a common occurrence where corrosion has set in, and the use of penetrating oil or releasing fluid will often overcome this problem if the offending item is soaked for a while before attempting to release it. The use of an impact driver may also provide a means of releasing such stubborn fastening devices, when used in conjunction with the appropriate screwdriver bit or socket. If none of these methods works, it may be necessary to resort to the careful application of heat, or the use of a hacksaw or nut splitter device.

Studs are usually removed by locking two nuts together on the threaded part, and then using a spanner on the lower nut to unscrew the stud. Studs or bolts which have broken off below the surface of the component in which they are mounted can sometimes be removed using a stud extractor. Always ensure that a blind tapped hole is completely free from oil, grease, water or other fluid before installing the bolt or stud. Failure to do this could cause the housing to crack due to the hydraulic action of the bolt or stud as it is screwed in.

When tightening a castellated nut to accept a split pin, tighten the nut to the specified torque, where applicable, and then tighten further to the next split pin hole. Never slacken the nut to align the split pin hole, unless stated in the repair procedure.

When checking or retightening a nut or bolt to a specified torque setting, slacken the nut or bolt by a quarter of a turn, and then retighten to the specified setting. However, this should not be attempted where angular tightening has been used.

For some screw fastenings, notably cylinder head bolts or nuts, torque wrench settings are no longer specified for the latter stages of tightening, "angle-tightening" being called up instead. Typically, a fairly low torque wrench setting will be applied to the bolts/nuts in the correct sequence, followed by one or more stages of tightening through specified angles.

Locknuts, locktabs and washers

Any fastening which will rotate against a component or housing during tightening should always have a washer between it and the relevant component or housing.

Spring or split washers should always be renewed when they are used to lock a critical component such as a big-end bearing retaining bolt or nut. Locktabs which are folded over to retain a nut or bolt should always be renewed.

Self-locking nuts can be re-used in non-critical areas, providing resistance can be felt when the locking portion passes over the bolt or stud thread. However, it should be noted that self-locking stiffnuts tend to lose their effectiveness after long periods of use, and should be renewed as a matter of course.

Split pins must always be replaced with new ones of the correct size for the hole.

When thread-locking compound is found on the threads of a fastener which is to be re-used, it should be cleaned off with a wire brush and solvent, and fresh compound applied on reassembly.

Special tools

Some repair procedures in this manual entail the use of special tools such as a press, two or three-legged pullers, spring compressors, etc. Wherever possible, suitable readily-available alternatives to the manufacturer's special tools are described, and are shown in use. In some instances, where no alternative is possible, it has been necessary to resort to the use of a manufacturer's tool, and this has been done for reasons of safety as well as the efficient completion of the repair operation. Unless you are highly-skilled and have a thorough understanding of the procedures described, never attempt to bypass the use of any special tool when the procedure described specifies its use. Not only is there a very great risk of personal injury, but expensive damage could be caused to the components involved.

Environmental considerations

When disposing of used engine oil, brake fluid, antifreeze, etc, give due consideration to any detrimental environmental effects. Do not, for instance, pour any of the above liquids down drains into the general sewage system, or onto the ground to soak away. Many local council refuse tips provide a facility for waste oil disposal, as do some garages. If none of these facilities are available, consult your local Environmental Health Department, or the National Rivers Authority, for further advice.

With the universal tightening-up of legislation regarding the emission of environmentally-harmful substances from motor vehicles, most current vehicles have tamperproof devices fitted to the main adjustment points of the fuel system. These devices are primarily designed to prevent unqualified persons from adjusting the fuel/air mixture, with the chance of a consequent increase in toxic emissions. If such devices are encountered during servicing or overhaul, they should, wherever possible, be renewed or refitted in accordance with the vehicle manufacturer's requirements or current legislation.

OIL CARE

OIL BANK LINE
0800 66 33 66

Note: It is antisocial and illegal to dump oil down the drain. To find the location of your local oil recycling bank, call this number free.

Jacking and Vehicle Support

The jack supplied with the vehicle tool kit should only be used for changing the roadwheels - see *"Wheel changing"* at the front of this manual. When carrying out any other kind of work, raise the vehicle using a hydraulic (or "trolley") jack, and always supplement the jack with axle stands positioned under the vehicle jacking points.

When using a hydraulic jack or axle stands, always position the jack head or axle stand head under, or adjacent to one of the relevant wheel changing jacking points **(see illustration)**.

To raise the front of the vehicle, position the jack with an interposed block of wood underneath the centre of the front valance on the jack lift platform. Similarly to raise the rear of the vehicle, position the jack with an interposed block of wood underneath the centre of the rear valance on the jack lift platform **(see illustration)**. **Do not** jack the vehicle under the sump, or under any of the steering or suspension components.

The jack supplied with the vehicle locates in the jacking points in the ridges on the underside of the sills. Ensure that the jack head is correctly engaged before attempting to raise the vehicle.

Never work under, around, or near a raised vehicle, unless it is adequately supported in at least two places.

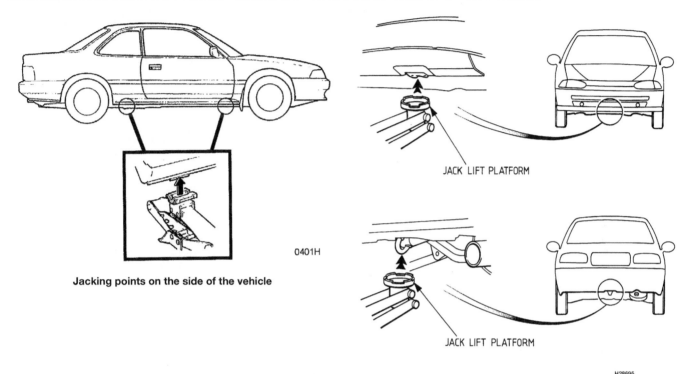

Jacking points on the side of the vehicle

Front (top) and rear (bottom) trolley jack position points

Radio/cassette unit Anti-theft System - Precaution

The radio/cassette unit fitted to later models as standard equipment by Honda is equipped with a built-in security code, to deter thieves. If the power source to the unit is cut, the anti-theft system will activate. Even if the power source is immediately reconnected, the radio/cassette unit will not function until the correct security code has been entered. Therefore if you do not know the correct security code for the unit, **do not** disconnect the battery negative lead, or remove the radio/cassette unit from the vehicle.

To enter the security code, press the "on/off" button; the unit display will show "CODE". The security code can then be entered using the buttons 1 to 6 on the unit. The unit will be activated automatically if the correct code is entered.

If the incorrect code is entered, the unit will lock, and the word "SECURITY" will be displayed for 2 minutes. After 2 minutes, it will be possible to enter a code again. Note that if 3 wrong codes are entered, the unit will lock for 2 hours. To clear the locking function, leave the unit and the ignition switched on during this period.

If the security code is lost or forgotten, see your Honda dealer. On presentation of proof of ownership, a Honda dealer will be able to provide you with a new security code.

Introduction

A selection of good tools is a fundamental requirement for anyone contemplating the maintenance and repair of a motor vehicle. For the owner who does not possess any, their purchase will prove a considerable expense, offsetting some of the savings made by doing-it-yourself. However, provided that the tools purchased meet the relevant national safety standards and are of good quality, they will last for many years and prove an extremely worthwhile investment.

To help the average owner to decide which tools are needed to carry out the various tasks detailed in this manual, we have compiled three lists of tools under the following headings: *Maintenance and minor repair, Repair and overhaul,* and *Special.* Newcomers to practical mechanics should start off with the *Maintenance and minor repair* tool kit, and confine themselves to the simpler jobs around the vehicle. Then, as confidence and experience grow, more difficult tasks can be undertaken, with extra tools being purchased as, and when, they are needed. In this way, a *Maintenance and minor repair* tool kit can be built up into a *Repair and overhaul* tool kit over a considerable period of time, without any major cash outlays. The experienced do-it-yourselfer will have a tool kit good enough for most repair and overhaul procedures, and will add tools from the *Special* category when it is felt that the expense is justified by the amount of use to which these tools will be put.

Maintenance and minor repair tool kit

The tools given in this list should be considered as a minimum requirement if routine maintenance, servicing and minor repair operations are to be undertaken. We recommend the purchase of combination spanners (ring one end, open-ended the other); although more expensive than open-ended ones, they do give the advantages of both types of spanner.

☐ *Combination spanners:*
  Metric - 8 to 19 mm inclusive
☐ *Adjustable spanner - 35 mm jaw (approx.)*
☐ *Spark plug spanner (with rubber insert) - petrol models*
☐ *Spark plug gap adjustment tool - petrol models*
☐ *Set of feeler gauges*
☐ *Brake bleed nipple spanner*
☐ *Screwdrivers:*
  Flat blade - 100 mm long x 6 mm dia
  Cross blade - 100 mm long x 6 mm dia
☐ *Combination pliers*
☐ *Hacksaw (junior)*
☐ *Tyre pump*
☐ *Tyre pressure gauge*
☐ *Oil can*
☐ *Oil filter removal tool*
☐ *Fine emery cloth*
☐ *Wire brush (small)*
☐ *Funnel (medium size)*

Repair and overhaul tool kit

These tools are virtually essential for anyone undertaking any major repairs to a motor vehicle, and are additional to those given in the *Maintenance and minor repair* list. Included in this list is a comprehensive set of sockets. Although these are expensive, they will be found invaluable as they are so versatile - particularly if various drives are included in the set. We recommend the half-inch square-drive type, as this can be used with most proprietary torque wrenches.

The tools in this list will sometimes need to be supplemented by tools from the *Special* list:

☐ *Sockets (or box spanners) to cover range in previous list (including Torx sockets)*
☐ *Reversible ratchet drive (for use with sockets)*
☐ *Extension piece, 250 mm (for use with sockets)*
☐ *Universal joint (for use with sockets)*
☐ *Torque wrench (for use with sockets)*
☐ *Self-locking grips*
☐ *Ball pein hammer*
☐ *Soft-faced mallet (plastic/aluminium or rubber)*
☐ *Screwdrivers:*
  Flat blade - long & sturdy, short (chubby), and narrow (electrician's) types
  Cross blade – Long & sturdy, and short (chubby) types
☐ *Pliers:*
  Long-nosed
  Side cutters (electrician's)
  Circlip (internal and external)
☐ *Cold chisel - 25 mm*
☐ *Scriber*
☐ *Scraper*
☐ *Centre-punch*
☐ *Pin punch*
☐ *Hacksaw*
☐ *Brake hose clamp*
☐ *Brake/clutch bleeding kit*
☐ *Selection of twist drills*
☐ *Steel rule/straight-edge*
☐ *Allen keys (inc. splined/Torx type)*
☐ *Selection of files*
☐ *Wire brush*
☐ *Axle stands*
☐ *Jack (strong trolley or hydraulic type)*
☐ *Light with extension lead*

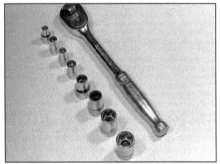
Sockets and reversible ratchet drive

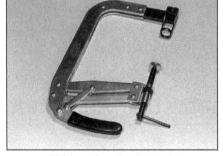
Valve spring compressor

Spline bit set

Piston ring compressor

Clutch plate alignment set

Special tools

The tools in this list are those which are not used regularly, are expensive to buy, or which need to be used in accordance with their manufacturers' instructions. Unless relatively difficult mechanical jobs are undertaken frequently, it will not be economic to buy many of these tools. Where this is the case, you could consider clubbing together with friends (or joining a motorists' club) to make a joint purchase, or borrowing the tools against a deposit from a local garage or tool hire specialist. It is worth noting that many of the larger DIY superstores now carry a large range of special tools for hire at modest rates.

The following list contains only those tools and instruments freely available to the public, and not those special tools produced by the vehicle manufacturer specifically for its dealer network. You will find occasional references to these manufacturers' special tools in the text of this manual. Generally, an alternative method of doing the job without the vehicle manufacturers' special tool is given. However, sometimes there is no alternative to using them. Where this is the case and the relevant tool cannot be bought or borrowed, you will have to entrust the work to a dealer.

☐ Valve spring compressor
☐ Valve grinding tool
☐ Piston ring compressor
☐ Piston ring removal/installation tool
☐ Cylinder bore hone
☐ Balljoint separator
☐ Coil spring compressors (where applicable)
☐ Two/three-legged hub and bearing puller
☐ Impact screwdriver
☐ Micrometer and/or vernier calipers
☐ Dial gauge
☐ Stroboscopic timing light
☐ Dwell angle meter/tachometer
☐ Universal electrical multi-meter
☐ Cylinder compression gauge
☐ Hand-operated vacuum pump and gauge
☐ Clutch plate alignment set
☐ Brake shoe steady spring cup removal tool
☐ Bush and bearing removal/installation set
☐ Stud extractors
☐ Tap and die set
☐ Lifting tackle
☐ Trolley jack

Buying tools

Reputable motor accessory shops and superstores often offer excellent quality tools at discount prices, so it pays to shop around.

Remember, you don't have to buy the most expensive items on the shelf, but it is always advisable to steer clear of the very cheap tools. Beware of 'bargains' offered on market stalls or at car boot sales. There are plenty of good tools around at reasonable prices, but always aim to purchase items which meet the relevant national safety standards. If in doubt, ask the proprietor or manager of the shop for advice before making a purchase.

Care and maintenance of tools

Having purchased a reasonable tool kit, it is necessary to keep the tools in a clean and serviceable condition. After use, always wipe off any dirt, grease and metal particles using a clean, dry cloth, before putting the tools away. Never leave them lying around after they have been used. A simple tool rack on the garage or workshop wall for items such as screwdrivers and pliers is a good idea. Store all normal spanners and sockets in a metal box. Any measuring instruments, gauges, meters, etc, must be carefully stored where they cannot be damaged or become rusty.

Take a little care when tools are used. Hammer heads inevitably become marked, and screwdrivers lose the keen edge on their blades from time to time. A little timely attention with emery cloth or a file will soon restore items like this to a good finish.

Working facilities

Not to be forgotten when discussing tools is the workshop itself. If anything more than routine maintenance is to be carried out, a suitable working area becomes essential.

It is appreciated that many an owner-mechanic is forced by circumstances to remove an engine or similar item without the benefit of a garage or workshop. Having done this, any repairs should always be done under the cover of a roof.

Wherever possible, any dismantling should be done on a clean, flat workbench or table at a suitable working height.

Any workbench needs a vice; one with a jaw opening of 100 mm is suitable for most jobs. As mentioned previously, some clean dry storage space is also required for tools, as well as for any lubricants, cleaning fluids, touch-up paints etc, which become necessary.

Another item which may be required, and which has a much more general usage, is an electric drill with a chuck capacity of at least 8 mm. This, together with a good range of twist drills, is virtually essential for fitting accessories.

Last, but not least, always keep a supply of old newspapers and clean, lint-free rags available, and try to keep any working area as clean as possible.

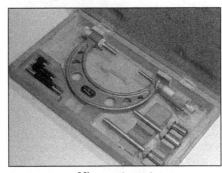

Micrometer set

Dial test indicator ("dial gauge")

Stroboscopic timing light

Compression tester

Stud extractor set

This is a guide to getting your vehicle through the MOT test. Obviously it will not be possible to examine the vehicle to the same standard as the professional MOT tester. However, working through the following checks will enable you to identify any problem areas before submitting the vehicle for the test.

Where a testable component is in borderline condition, the tester has discretion in deciding whether to pass or fail it. The basis of such discretion is whether the tester would be happy for a close relative or friend to use the vehicle with the component in that condition. If the vehicle presented is clean and evidently well cared for, the tester may be more inclined to pass a borderline component than if the vehicle is scruffy and apparently neglected.

It has only been possible to summarise the test requirements here, based on the regulations in force at the time of printing. Test standards are becoming increasingly stringent, although there are some exemptions for older vehicles. For full details obtain a copy of the Haynes publication Pass the MOT! (available from stockists of Haynes manuals).

An assistant will be needed to help carry out some of these checks.

The checks have been sub-divided into four categories, as follows:

1 Checks carried out **FROM THE DRIVER'S SEAT**

2 Checks carried out **WITH THE VEHICLE ON THE GROUND**

3 Checks carried out **WITH THE VEHICLE RAISED AND THE WHEELS FREE TO TURN**

4 Checks carried out on **YOUR VEHICLE'S EXHAUST EMISSION SYSTEM**

---

1 Checks carried out **FROM THE DRIVER'S SEAT**

Handbrake

☐ Test the operation of the handbrake. Excessive travel (too many clicks) indicates incorrect brake or cable adjustment.

☐ Check that the handbrake cannot be released by tapping the lever sideways. Check the security of the lever mountings.

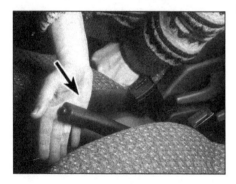

Footbrake

☐ Depress the brake pedal and check that it does not creep down to the floor, indicating a master cylinder fault. Release the pedal, wait a few seconds, then depress it again. If the pedal travels nearly to the floor before firm resistance is felt, brake adjustment or repair is necessary. If the pedal feels spongy, there is air in the hydraulic system which must be removed by bleeding.

☐ Check that the brake pedal is secure and in good condition. Check also for signs of fluid leaks on the pedal, floor or carpets, which would indicate failed seals in the brake master cylinder.

☐ Check the servo unit (when applicable) by operating the brake pedal several times, then keeping the pedal depressed and starting the engine. As the engine starts, the pedal will move down slightly. If not, the vacuum hose or the servo itself may be faulty.

Steering wheel and column

☐ Examine the steering wheel for fractures or looseness of the hub, spokes or rim.

☐ Move the steering wheel from side to side and then up and down. Check that the steering wheel is not loose on the column, indicating wear or a loose retaining nut. Continue moving the steering wheel as before, but also turn it slightly from left to right.

☐ Check that the steering wheel is not loose on the column, and that there is no abnormal

movement of the steering wheel, indicating wear in the column support bearings or couplings.

Windscreen and mirrors

☐ The windscreen must be free of cracks or other significant damage within the driver's field of view. (Small stone chips are acceptable.) Rear view mirrors must be secure, intact, and capable of being adjusted.

290mm

Seat belts and seats

Note: *The following checks are applicable to all seat belts, front and rear.*

☐ Examine the webbing of all the belts (including rear belts if fitted) for cuts, serious fraying or deterioration. Fasten and unfasten each belt to check the buckles. If applicable, check the retracting mechanism. Check the security of all seat belt mountings accessible from inside the vehicle.

☐ The front seats themselves must be securely attached and the backrests must lock in the upright position.

Doors

☐ Both front doors must be able to be opened and closed from outside and inside, and must latch securely when closed.

2 Checks carried out WITH THE VEHICLE ON THE GROUND

Vehicle identification

☐ Number plates must be in good condition, secure and legible, with letters and numbers correctly spaced – spacing at (A) should be twice that at (B).

☐ The VIN plate and/or homologation plate must be legible.

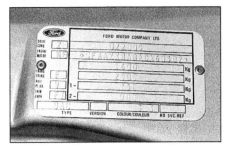

Electrical equipment

☐ Switch on the ignition and check the operation of the horn.

☐ Check the windscreen washers and wipers, examining the wiper blades; renew damaged or perished blades. Also check the operation of the stop-lights.

☐ Check the operation of the sidelights and number plate lights. The lenses and reflectors must be secure, clean and undamaged.

☐ Check the operation and alignment of the headlights. The headlight reflectors must not be tarnished and the lenses must be undamaged.

☐ Switch on the ignition and check the operation of the direction indicators (including the instrument panel tell-tale) and the hazard warning lights. Operation of the sidelights and stop-lights must not affect the indicators - if it does, the cause is usually a bad earth at the rear light cluster.

☐ Check the operation of the rear foglight(s), including the warning light on the instrument panel or in the switch.

Footbrake

☐ Examine the master cylinder, brake pipes and servo unit for leaks, loose mountings, corrosion or other damage.

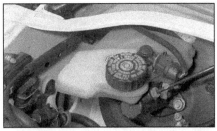

☐ The fluid reservoir must be secure and the fluid level must be between the upper (A) and lower (B) markings.

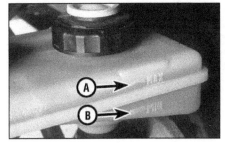

☐ Inspect both front brake flexible hoses for cracks or deterioration of the rubber. Turn the steering from lock to lock, and ensure that the hoses do not contact the wheel, tyre, or any part of the steering or suspension mechanism. With the brake pedal firmly depressed, check the hoses for bulges or leaks under pressure.

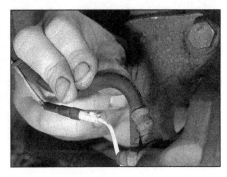

Steering and suspension

☐ Have your assistant turn the steering wheel from side to side slightly, up to the point where the steering gear just begins to transmit this movement to the roadwheels. Check for excessive free play between the steering wheel and the steering gear, indicating wear or insecurity of the steering column joints, the column-to-steering gear coupling, or the steering gear itself.

☐ Have your assistant turn the steering wheel more vigorously in each direction, so that the roadwheels just begin to turn. As this is done, examine all the steering joints, linkages, fittings and attachments. Renew any component that shows signs of wear or damage. On vehicles with power steering, check the security and condition of the steering pump, drivebelt and hoses.

☐ Check that the vehicle is standing level, and at approximately the correct ride height.

Shock absorbers

☐ Depress each corner of the vehicle in turn, then release it. The vehicle should rise and then settle in its normal position. If the vehicle continues to rise and fall, the shock absorber is defective. A shock absorber which has seized will also cause the vehicle to fail.

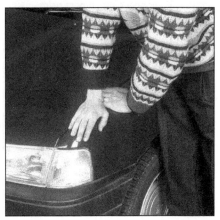

Exhaust system

☐ Start the engine. With your assistant holding a rag over the tailpipe, check the entire system for leaks. Repair or renew leaking sections.

3 Checks carried out
WITH THE VEHICLE RAISED AND THE WHEELS FREE TO TURN

Jack up the front and rear of the vehicle, and securely support it on axle stands. Position the stands clear of the suspension assemblies. Ensure that the wheels are clear of the ground and that the steering can be turned from lock to lock.

Steering mechanism

☐ Have your assistant turn the steering from lock to lock. Check that the steering turns smoothly, and that no part of the steering mechanism, including a wheel or tyre, fouls any brake hose or pipe or any part of the body structure.

☐ Examine the steering rack rubber gaiters for damage or insecurity of the retaining clips. If power steering is fitted, check for signs of damage or leakage of the fluid hoses, pipes or connections. Also check for excessive stiffness or binding of the steering, a missing split pin or locking device, or severe corrosion of the body structure within 30 cm of any steering component attachment point.

Front and rear suspension and wheel bearings

☐ Starting at the front right-hand side, grasp the roadwheel at the 3 o'clock and 9 o'clock positions and shake it vigorously. Check for free play or insecurity at the wheel bearings, suspension balljoints, or suspension mountings, pivots and attachments.

☐ Now grasp the wheel at the 12 o'clock and 6 o'clock positions and repeat the previous inspection. Spin the wheel, and check for roughness or tightness of the front wheel bearing.

☐ If excess free play is suspected at a component pivot point, this can be confirmed by using a large screwdriver or similar tool and levering between the mounting and the component attachment. This will confirm whether the wear is in the pivot bush, its retaining bolt, or in the mounting itself (the bolt holes can often become elongated).

☐ Carry out all the above checks at the other front wheel, and then at both rear wheels.

Springs and shock absorbers

☐ Examine the suspension struts (when applicable) for serious fluid leakage, corrosion, or damage to the casing. Also check the security of the mounting points.

☐ If coil springs are fitted, check that the spring ends locate in their seats, and that the spring is not corroded, cracked or broken.

☐ If leaf springs are fitted, check that all leaves are intact, that the axle is securely attached to each spring, and that there is no deterioration of the spring eye mountings, bushes, and shackles.

☐ The same general checks apply to vehicles fitted with other suspension types, such as torsion bars, hydraulic displacer units, etc. Ensure that all mountings and attachments are secure, that there are no signs of excessive wear, corrosion or damage, and (on hydraulic types) that there are no fluid leaks or damaged pipes.

☐ Inspect the shock absorbers for signs of serious fluid leakage. Check for wear of the mounting bushes or attachments, or damage to the body of the unit.

Driveshafts (fwd vehicles only)

☐ Rotate each front wheel in turn and inspect the constant velocity joint gaiters for splits or damage. Also check that each driveshaft is straight and undamaged.

Braking system

☐ If possible without dismantling, check brake pad wear and disc condition. Ensure that the friction lining material has not worn excessively, (A) and that the discs are not fractured, pitted, scored or badly worn (B).

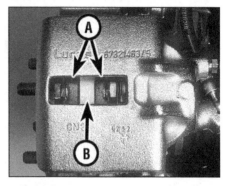

☐ Examine all the rigid brake pipes underneath the vehicle, and the flexible hose(s) at the rear. Look for corrosion, chafing or insecurity of the pipes, and for signs of bulging under pressure, chafing, splits or deterioration of the flexible hoses.

☐ Look for signs of fluid leaks at the brake calipers or on the brake backplates. Repair or renew leaking components.

☐ Slowly spin each wheel, while your assistant depresses and releases the footbrake. Ensure that each brake is operating and does not bind when the pedal is released.

☐ Examine the handbrake mechanism, checking for frayed or broken cables, excessive corrosion, or wear or insecurity of the linkage. Check that the mechanism works on each relevant wheel, and releases fully, without binding.

☐ It is not possible to test brake efficiency without special equipment, but a road test can be carried out later to check that the vehicle pulls up in a straight line.

Fuel and exhaust systems

☐ Inspect the fuel tank (including the filler cap), fuel pipes, hoses and unions. All components must be secure and free from leaks.

☐ Examine the exhaust system over its entire length, checking for any damaged, broken or missing mountings, security of the retaining clamps and rust or corrosion.

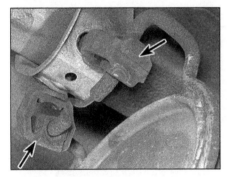

Wheels and tyres

☐ Examine the sidewalls and tread area of each tyre in turn. Check for cuts, tears, lumps, bulges, separation of the tread, and exposure of the ply or cord due to wear or damage. Check that the tyre bead is correctly seated on the wheel rim, that the valve is sound and

properly seated, and that the wheel is not distorted or damaged.

☐ Check that the tyres are of the correct size for the vehicle, that they are of the same size and type on each axle, and that the pressures are correct.

☐ Check the tyre tread depth. The legal minimum at the time of writing is 1.6 mm over at least three-quarters of the tread width. Abnormal tread wear may indicate incorrect front wheel alignment.

Body corrosion

☐ Check the condition of the entire vehicle structure for signs of corrosion in load-bearing areas. (These include chassis box sections, side sills, cross-members, pillars, and all suspension, steering, braking system and seat belt mountings and anchorages.) Any corrosion which has seriously reduced the thickness of a load-bearing area is likely to cause the vehicle to fail. In this case professional repairs are likely to be needed.

☐ Damage or corrosion which causes sharp or otherwise dangerous edges to be exposed will also cause the vehicle to fail.

4 Checks carried out on YOUR VEHICLE'S EXHAUST EMISSION SYSTEM

Petrol models

☐ Have the engine at normal operating temperature, and make sure that it is in good tune (ignition system in good order, air filter element clean, etc).

☐ Before any measurements are carried out, raise the engine speed to around 2500 rpm, and hold it at this speed for 20 seconds. Allow

the engine speed to return to idle, and watch for smoke emissions from the exhaust tailpipe. If the idle speed is obviously much too high, or if dense blue or clearly-visible black smoke comes from the tailpipe for more than 5 seconds, the vehicle will fail. As a rule of thumb, blue smoke signifies oil being burnt (engine wear) while black smoke signifies unburnt fuel (dirty air cleaner element, or other carburettor or fuel system fault).

☐ An exhaust gas analyser capable of measuring carbon monoxide (CO) and hydrocarbons (HC) is now needed. If such an instrument cannot be hired or borrowed, a local garage may agree to perform the check for a small fee.

CO emissions (mixture)

☐ At the time of writing, the maximum CO level at idle is 3.5% for vehicles first used after August 1986 and 4.5% for older vehicles. From January 1996 a much tighter limit (around 0.5%) applies to catalyst-equipped vehicles first used from August 1992. If the CO level cannot be reduced far enough to pass the test (and the fuel and ignition systems are otherwise in good condition) then the carburettor is badly worn, or there is some problem in the fuel injection system or catalytic converter (as applicable).

HC emissions

☐ With the CO emissions within limits, HC emissions must be no more than 1200 ppm (parts per million). If the vehicle fails this test at idle, it can be re-tested at around 2000 rpm; if the HC level is then 1200 ppm or less, this counts as a pass.

☐ Excessive HC emissions can be caused by oil being burnt, but they are more likely to be due to unburnt fuel.

Diesel models

☐ The only emission test applicable to Diesel engines is the measuring of exhaust smoke density. The test involves accelerating the engine several times to its maximum unloaded speed.

Note: *It is of the utmost importance that the engine timing belt is in good condition before the test is carried out.*

☐ Excessive smoke can be caused by a dirty air cleaner element. Otherwise, professional advice may be needed to find the cause.

Engine 1
- [ ] Engine fails to rotate when attempting to start
- [ ] Engine rotates, but will not start
- [ ] Engine difficult to start when cold
- [ ] Engine difficult to start when hot
- [ ] Starter motor noisy or rough in engagement
- [ ] Engine starts, but stops immediately
- [ ] Engine idles erratically
- [ ] Engine misfires at idle speed
- [ ] Engine misfires throughout the speed range
- [ ] Engine hesitates on acceleration
- [ ] Engine stalls
- [ ] Engine lacks power
- [ ] Oil pressure warning light illuminated with engine running
- [ ] Engine runs-on after switching off
- [ ] Engine backfires
- [ ] Engine noises

Cooling system 2
- [ ] Overheating
- [ ] Overcooling
- [ ] External coolant leakage
- [ ] Internal coolant leakage
- [ ] Corrosion

Fuel and exhaust systems 3
- [ ] Excessive fuel consumption
- [ ] Fuel leakage and/or fuel odour
- [ ] Excessive noise or fumes from exhaust system

Clutch 4
- [ ] Pedal travels to floor - no pressure or very little resistance
- [ ] Clutch fails to disengage (unable to select gears)
- [ ] Clutch slips (engine speed increases, with no increase in vehicle speed)
- [ ] Judder as clutch is engaged
- [ ] Noise when depressing or releasing clutch pedal

Manual transmission 5
- [ ] Noisy in neutral with engine running
- [ ] Noisy in one particular gear
- [ ] Difficulty engaging gears
- [ ] Jumps out of gear
- [ ] Vibration
- [ ] Lubricant leaks

Automatic transmission 6
- [ ] Fluid leakage
- [ ] Transmission fluid brown, or has burned smell
- [ ] General gear selection problems
- [ ] Transmission will not downshift (kickdown) with accelerator fully depressed
- [ ] Engine will not start in any gear, or starts in gears other than Park or Neutral
- [ ] Transmission slips, shifts roughly, is noisy, or has no drive in forward or reverse gears

Driveshafts 7
- [ ] Clicking or knocking noise on turns (at slow speed on full-lock)
- [ ] Vibration when accelerating or decelerating

Braking system 8
- [ ] Vehicle pulls to one side under braking
- [ ] Noise (grinding or high-pitched squeal) when brakes applied
- [ ] Excessive brake pedal travel
- [ ] Brake pedal feels spongy when depressed
- [ ] Excessive brake pedal effort required to stop vehicle
- [ ] Judder felt through brake pedal or steering wheel when braking
- [ ] Brakes binding
- [ ] Rear wheels locking under normal braking

Suspension and steering systems 9
- [ ] Vehicle pulls to one side
- [ ] Wheel wobble and vibration
- [ ] Excessive pitching and/or rolling around corners, or during braking
- [ ] Wandering or general instability
- [ ] Excessively-stiff steering
- [ ] Excessive play in steering
- [ ] Lack of power assistance
- [ ] Tyre wear excessive

Electrical system 10
- [ ] Battery will not hold a charge for more than a few days
- [ ] Ignition/no-charge warning light remains illuminated with engine running
- [ ] Ignition/no-charge warning light fails to come on
- [ ] Lights inoperative
- [ ] Instrument readings inaccurate or erratic
- [ ] Horn inoperative, or unsatisfactory in operation
- [ ] Windscreen/tailgate wipers inoperative, or unsatisfactory in operation
- [ ] Windscreen/tailgate washers inoperative, or unsatisfactory in operation
- [ ] Electric windows inoperative, or unsatisfactory in operation
- [ ] Central locking system inoperative, or unsatisfactory in operation

Introduction

The vehicle owner who does his or her own maintenance according to the recommended service schedules should not have to use this section of the manual very often. Modern component reliability is such that, provided those items subject to wear or deterioration are inspected or renewed at the specified intervals, sudden failure is comparatively rare. Faults do not usually just happen as a result of sudden failure, but develop over a period of time. Major mechanical failures in particular are usually preceded by characteristic symptoms over hundreds or even thousands of miles. Those components which do occasionally fail without warning are often small and easily carried in the vehicle.

With any fault-finding, the first step is to decide where to begin investigations. Sometimes this is obvious, but on other occasions, a little detective work will be necessary. The owner who makes half a dozen haphazard adjustments or replacements may be successful in curing a fault (or its symptoms), but will be none the wiser if the fault recurs, and ultimately may have spent more time and money than was necessary. A calm and logical approach will be found to be more satisfactory in the long run. Always take into account any warning signs or abnormalities that may have been noticed in the period preceding the fault - power loss, high or low gauge readings, unusual smells, etc - and remember that failure of components such as fuses or spark plugs may only be pointers to some underlying fault.

The pages which follow provide an easy-reference guide to the more common problems which may occur during the operation of the vehicle. These problems and their possible causes are grouped under headings denoting various components or systems, such as Engine, Cooling system, etc. The Chapter and/or Section which deals with the problem is also shown in brackets. Whatever the fault, certain basic principles apply. These are as follows:

Verify the fault. This is simply a matter of being sure that you know what the symptoms are before starting work. This is particularly important if you are investigating a fault for someone else, who may not have described it very accurately.

Don't overlook the obvious. For example, if the car won't start, is there fuel in the tank? (Don't take anyone else's word on this particular point, and don't trust the fuel gauge either!) If an electrical fault is indicated, look for loose or broken wires before digging out the test gear.

Cure the disease, not the symptom. Substituting a flat battery with a fully-charged one will get you off the hard shoulder, but if the underlying cause is not attended to, the new battery will go the same way. Similarly, changing oil-fouled spark plugs for a new set will get you moving again, but remember that the reason for the fouling (if it wasn't simply an incorrect grade of plug) will have to be established and corrected.

Don't take anything for granted. Particularly, don't forget that a "new" component may itself be defective (especially if it's been rattling around in the boot for months), and don't leave components out of a fault diagnosis sequence just because they are new or recently-fitted. When you do finally diagnose a difficult fault, you'll probably realise that all the evidence was there from the start.

1 Engine

Engine fails to rotate when attempting to start

- ☐ Battery terminal connections loose or corroded (Chapter 1).
- ☐ Battery discharged or faulty (Chapter 5).
- ☐ Broken, loose or disconnected wiring in the starting circuit (Chapter 5).
- ☐ Defective starter solenoid or switch (Chapter 5).
- ☐ Defective starter motor (Chapter 5).
- ☐ Starter pinion or flywheel/driveplate ring gear teeth loose or broken (Chapter 2A or 5).
- ☐ Engine earth strap broken or disconnected (Chapter 2A).

Starter motor turns engine slowly

- ☐ Partially-discharged battery (recharge, use jump leads, or push start) (Chapter 5).
- ☐ Battery terminals loose or corroded (Chapter 1).
- ☐ Battery earth to body defective (Chapter 5).
- ☐ Engine earth strap loose (Chapter 2A).
- ☐ Starter motor (or solenoid) wiring loose (Chapter 5).
- ☐ Starter motor internal fault (Chapter 5).

Engine rotates, but will not start

- ☐ Fuel tank empty.
- ☐ Battery discharged (engine rotates slowly) (Chapter 5).
- ☐ Battery terminal connections loose or corroded (Chapter 1).
- ☐ Ignition components damp or damaged (Chapter 1 and 5).
- ☐ Broken, loose or disconnected wiring in the ignition circuit (Chapters 1 and 5).
- ☐ Worn, faulty or incorrectly-gapped spark plugs (Chapter 1).
- ☐ Faulty choke or carburettor (Chapter 4).
- ☐ Fuel injection system fault (Chapter 4).
- ☐ Major mechanical failure (eg broken timing belt) (Chapter 2B).

Engine difficult to start when cold

- ☐ Battery discharged (Chapter 5).
- ☐ Battery terminal connections loose or corroded (Chapter 1).
- ☐ Worn, faulty or incorrectly-gapped spark plugs (Chapter 1).
- ☐ Faulty choke or carburettor (Chapter 4).
- ☐ Fuel injection system fault (Chapter 4).
- ☐ Other ignition system fault (Chapters 1 and 5).
- ☐ Low cylinder compressions (Chapter 2A).

Engine difficult to start when hot

- ☐ Air filter element dirty or clogged (Chapter 1).
- ☐ Faulty choke or carburettor (Chapter 4).
- ☐ Fuel injection system fault (Chapter 4).
- ☐ Low cylinder compressions (Chapter 2A).

Starter motor noisy or rough in engagement

- ☐ Starter pinion or flywheel/driveplate ring gear teeth loose or broken (Chapter 2A or 5).
- ☐ Starter motor mounting bolts loose or missing (Chapter 5).
- ☐ Starter motor internal components worn or damaged (Chapter 5).

Engine starts, but stops immediately

- ☐ Loose or faulty electrical connections in the ignition circuit (Chapters 1 and 5).
- ☐ Vacuum leak at carburettor, throttle body or inlet manifold (Chapter 4).
- ☐ Faulty carburettor (Chapter 4).
- ☐ Fuel injection system fault (Chapter 4).

Engine idles erratically

- ☐ Incorrectly-adjusted idle speed (Chapter 1).
- ☐ Air filter element clogged (Chapter 1).
- ☐ Vacuum leak at the carburettor, throttle body, inlet manifold or associated hoses (Chapter 4).
- ☐ Worn, faulty or incorrectly-gapped spark plugs (Chapter 1).
- ☐ Uneven or low cylinder compressions (Chapter 2A).
- ☐ Camshaft lobes worn (Chapter 2A).
- ☐ Faulty carburettor (Chapter 4).
- ☐ Fuel injection system fault (Chapter 4).

Engine misfires at idle speed

- ☐ Worn, faulty or incorrectly-gapped spark plugs (Chapter 1).
- ☐ Faulty spark plug HT leads (Chapter 1).
- ☐ Vacuum leak at the carburettor, throttle body, inlet manifold or associated hoses (Chapter 4).
- ☐ Faulty carburettor (Chapter 4).
- ☐ Fuel injection system fault (Chapter 4).
- ☐ Distributor cap cracked or tracking internally (Chapter 1).
- ☐ Uneven or low cylinder compressions (Chapter 2A).
- ☐ Disconnected or leaking crankcase ventilation hoses (Chapter 4).

Engine misfires throughout the speed range

- ☐ Fuel filter choked (Chapter 1).
- ☐ Fuel pump faulty, or delivery pressure low (Chapter 4).
- ☐ Fuel tank vent blocked, or fuel pipes restricted (Chapter 4).
- ☐ Vacuum leak at the carburettor, throttle body, inlet manifold or associated hoses (Chapter 4).
- ☐ Worn, faulty or incorrectly-gapped spark plugs (Chapter 1).
- ☐ Faulty spark plug HT leads (Chapter 1).
- ☐ Distributor cap cracked or tracking internally (Chapter 1).
- ☐ Faulty ignition coil (Chapter 5).
- ☐ Uneven or low cylinder compressions (Chapter 2A).
- ☐ Faulty carburettor (Chapter 4).
- ☐ Fuel injection system fault (Chapter 4).

1 Engine (continued)

Engine hesitates on acceleration

- ☐ Worn, faulty or incorrectly-gapped spark plugs (Chapter 1).
- ☐ Vacuum leak at the carburettor, throttle body, inlet manifold or associated hoses (Chapter 4).
- ☐ Faulty carburettor (Chapter 4).
- ☐ Fuel injection system fault (Chapter 4).

Engine stalls

- ☐ Vacuum leak at the carburettor, throttle body, inlet manifold or associated hoses (Chapter 4).
- ☐ Fuel filter choked (Chapter 1).
- ☐ Fuel pump faulty, or delivery pressure low (Chapter 4).
- ☐ Fuel tank vent blocked, or fuel pipes restricted (Chapter 4).
- ☐ Faulty carburettor (Chapter 4).
- ☐ Fuel injection system fault (Chapter 4).

Engine lacks power

- ☐ Fuel filter choked (Chapter 1).
- ☐ Fuel pump faulty, or delivery pressure low (Chapter 4).
- ☐ Uneven or low cylinder compressions (Chapter 2A).
- ☐ Worn, faulty or incorrectly-gapped spark plugs (Chapter 1).
- ☐ Vacuum leak at the carburettor, throttle body, inlet manifold or associated hoses (Chapter 4).
- ☐ Faulty carburettor (Chapter 4).
- ☐ Fuel injection system fault (Chapter 4).
- ☐ Faulty turbocharger, where applicable (Chapter 4).
- ☐ Brakes binding (Chapters 1 and 9).
- ☐ Clutch slipping (Chapter 8).

Oil pressure warning light illuminated with engine running

- ☐ Low oil level, or incorrect oil grade (Chapter 1).
- ☐ Faulty oil pressure sensor (Chapter 2A).
- ☐ Worn engine bearings and/or oil pump (Chapter 2A or 2B).
- ☐ Excessively high engine operating temperature (Chapter 3).
- ☐ Oil pressure relief valve defective (Chapter 2A).
- ☐ Oil pick-up strainer clogged (Chapter 2B).

Note: *Low oil pressure in a high-mileage engine at tickover is not necessarily a cause for concern. Sudden pressure loss at speed is far more significant. In any event, check the gauge or warning light sender before condemning the engine.*

Engine runs-on after switching off

- ☐ Excessive carbon build-up in engine (Chapter 2A or 2B).
- ☐ Excessively high engine operating temperature (Chapter 3).

Engine backfires

- ☐ Vacuum leak at the carburettor, throttle body, inlet manifold or associated hoses (Chapter 4).
- ☐ Faulty carburettor (Chapter 4).
- ☐ Fuel injection system fault (Chapter 4).

Engine noises

Pre-ignition (pinking) or knocking during acceleration or under load

- ☐ Ignition timing incorrect/ignition system fault (Chapters 1 and 5).
- ☐ Incorrect grade of spark plug (Chapter 1).
- ☐ Incorrect grade of fuel (Chapter 1).
- ☐ Vacuum leak at carburettor, throttle body, inlet manifold or associated hoses (Chapter 4).
- ☐ Excessive carbon build-up in engine (Chapter 2A or 2B).
- ☐ Faulty carburettor (Chapter 4).
- ☐ Fuel injection system fault (Chapter 4).

Whistling or wheezing noises

- ☐ Leaking inlet manifold or throttle body gasket (Chapter 4).
- ☐ Leaking exhaust manifold gasket (Chapter 4).
- ☐ Leaking vacuum hose (Chapters 4 and 9).
- ☐ Blowing cylinder head gasket (Chapter 2A).

Tapping or rattling noises

- ☐ Worn valve gear or camshaft (Chapter 2A).
- ☐ Incorrect valve clearances (Chapter 1)
- ☐ Ancillary component fault (water pump, alternator, etc) (Chapters 3, 5, etc).

Knocking or thumping noises

- ☐ Worn big-end bearings (regular heavy knocking, perhaps less under load) (Chapter 2B).
- ☐ Worn main bearings (rumbling and knocking, perhaps worsening under load) (Chapter 2B).
- ☐ Piston slap (most noticeable when cold) (Chapter 2B).
- ☐ Ancillary component fault (water pump, alternator, etc) (Chapters 3, 5, etc).

2 Cooling system

Overheating

- ☐ Auxiliary drivebelt broken - or incorrectly adjusted (Chapter 1).
- ☐ Insufficient coolant in system (Chapter 1).
- ☐ Thermostat faulty (Chapter 3).
- ☐ Radiator core blocked, or grille restricted (Chapter 3).
- ☐ Electric cooling fan or thermostatic switch faulty (Chapter 3).
- ☐ Pressure cap faulty (Chapter 3).
- ☐ Ignition timing incorrect, or ignition system fault (Chapters 1 and 5).
- ☐ Inaccurate temperature gauge sender unit (Chapter 3).
- ☐ Airlock in cooling system (Chapter 1).

Overcooling

- ☐ Thermostat faulty (Chapter 3).
- ☐ Inaccurate temperature gauge sender unit (Chapter 3).

External coolant leakage

- ☐ Deteriorated or damaged hoses or hose clips (Chapter 1).
- ☐ Radiator core or heater matrix leaking (Chapter 3).
- ☐ Pressure cap faulty (Chapter 3).
- ☐ Water pump internal seal leaking (Chapter 3).
- ☐ Water pump gasket leaking (Chapter 3).
- ☐ Boiling due to overheating (Chapter 3).
- ☐ Core plug leaking (Chapter 2B).

Internal coolant leakage

- ☐ Leaking cylinder head gasket (Chapter 2A).
- ☐ Cracked cylinder head or cylinder block (Chapter 2A or 2B).

Corrosion

- ☐ Infrequent draining and flushing (Chapter 1).
- ☐ Incorrect coolant mixture or inappropriate coolant type (Chapter 1).

3 Fuel and exhaust systems

Excessive fuel consumption

- ☐ Air filter element dirty or clogged (Chapter 1).
- ☐ Faulty carburettor (Chapter 4).
- ☐ Fuel injection system fault (Chapter 4).
- ☐ Ignition timing incorrect or ignition system fault (Chapters 1 and 5).
- ☐ Brakes binding (Chapter 9).
- ☐ Tyres under-inflated (Chapter 1).

Fuel leakage and/or fuel odour

- ☐ Damaged fuel tank, pipes or connections (Chapters 1 and 4).

Excessive noise or fumes from exhaust system

- ☐ Leaking exhaust system or manifold joints (Chapters 1 and 4).
- ☐ Leaking, corroded or damaged silencers or pipe (Chapters 1 and 4).
- ☐ Broken mountings causing body or suspension contact (Chapter 4).

4 Clutch

Pedal travels to floor - no pressure or very little resistance

- ☐ Leak in clutch hydraulic system (Chapter 8).
- ☐ Faulty hydraulic master or slave cylinder (Chapter 8).
- ☐ Broken clutch release bearing (Chapter 8).
- ☐ Broken diaphragm spring in clutch pressure plate (Chapter 8).

Clutch fails to disengage (unable to select gears)

- ☐ Leak or air in clutch hydraulic system (Chapter 8).
- ☐ Faulty hydraulic master or slave cylinder (Chapter 8).
- ☐ Clutch disc sticking on splines (Chapter 8).
- ☐ Clutch disc sticking to flywheel or pressure plate (Chapter 8).
- ☐ Faulty pressure plate assembly (Chapter 8).
- ☐ Clutch release mechanism worn or incorrectly assembled (Chapter 8).

Clutch slips (engine speed increases, with no increase in vehicle speed)

- ☐ Clutch disc linings excessively worn (Chapter 8).
- ☐ Clutch disc linings contaminated with oil or grease (Chapter 8).
- ☐ Faulty pressure plate or weak diaphragm spring (Chapter 8).

Judder as clutch is engaged

- ☐ Clutch disc linings contaminated with oil or grease (Chapter 8).
- ☐ Clutch disc linings excessively worn (Chapter 8).
- ☐ Faulty or distorted pressure plate or diaphragm spring (Chapter 8).
- ☐ Worn or loose engine mountings (Chapter 2A).
- ☐ Clutch disc hub or shaft splines worn (Chapter 8).

Noise when depressing or releasing clutch pedal

- ☐ Worn clutch release bearing (Chapter 8).
- ☐ Worn or dry clutch pedal bushes (Chapter 8).
- ☐ Faulty pressure plate assembly (Chapter 8).
- ☐ Pressure plate diaphragm spring broken (Chapter 8).
- ☐ Broken clutch disc cushioning springs (Chapter 8).

5 Manual transmission

Noisy in neutral with engine running

- ☐ Primary gears and bearings worn (noise apparent with clutch pedal released, but not when depressed) (Chapter 7A).*
- ☐ Clutch release bearing worn (noise apparent with clutch pedal depressed, possibly less when released) (Chapter 8).

Noisy in one particular gear

- ☐ Worn, damaged or chipped gear teeth (Chapter 7A).*

Difficulty engaging gears

- ☐ Clutch fault (Chapter 8).
- ☐ Worn or damaged gear linkage (Chapter 7A).
- ☐ Incorrectly-adjusted gear linkage (Chapter 7A).
- ☐ Worn synchroniser units (Chapter 7A).*
- ☐ Seized spigot bearing in the flywheel (Chapter 2A).

Jumps out of gear

- ☐ Worn or damaged gear linkage (Chapter 7A).
- ☐ Incorrectly-adjusted gear linkage (Chapter 7A).
- ☐ Worn synchroniser units (Chapter 7A).*
- ☐ Worn selector forks (Chapter 7A).*

Vibration

- ☐ Lack of oil (Chapter 1).
- ☐ Worn bearings (Chapter 7A).*

Lubricant leaks

- ☐ Leaking oil seal (Chapter 7A).
- ☐ Leaking housing joint (Chapter 7A).*

Although the corrective action necessary to remedy the symptoms described is beyond the scope of the home mechanic, the above information should be helpful in isolating the cause of the condition, so that the owner can communicate clearly with a professional mechanic.

6 Automatic transmission

Note: *Due to the complexity of the automatic transmission, it is difficult for the home mechanic to properly diagnose and service this unit. For problems other than the following, the vehicle should be taken to a dealer service department or automatic transmission specialist.*

Fluid leakage

- [ ] Automatic transmission fluid is usually deep red in colour. Fluid leaks should not be confused with engine oil, which can easily be blown onto the transmission by air flow.
- [ ] To determine the source of a leak, first remove all built-up dirt and grime from the transmission housing and surrounding areas, using a degreasing agent or by steam-cleaning. Drive the vehicle at low speed, so that air flow will not blow the leak far from its source. Raise and support the vehicle, and determine where the leak is coming from. The following are common areas of leakage.
  - a) *Fluid pan (Chapter 7B).*
  - b) *Dipstick tube (Chapter 1).*
  - c) *Transmission-to-fluid cooler fluid pipes/unions (Chapter 7B).*

Transmission fluid brown, or has burned smell

- [ ] Transmission fluid level low, or fluid in need of renewal (Chapter 1).

General gear selection problems

- [ ] The most likely cause of gear selection problems is a faulty or poorly-adjusted gear selector mechanism. The following are common problems associated with a faulty selector mechanism.
  - a) *Engine starting in gears other than Park or Neutral.*
  - b) *Indicator on gear selector lever pointing to a gear other than the one actually being used.*
  - c) *Vehicle moves when in Park or Neutral.*
  - d) *Poor gear shift quality, or erratic gear changes.*
- [ ] Refer any problems to a Honda dealer, or an automatic transmission specialist.

Transmission will not downshift (kickdown) with accelerator pedal fully depressed

- [ ] Low transmission fluid level (Chapter 1).
- [ ] Incorrect selector cable adjustment (Chapter 7B).

Engine will not start in any gear, or starts in gears other than Park or Neutral

- [ ] Incorrect starter inhibitor switch adjustment - where applicable (Chapter 7B).
- [ ] Incorrect selector cable adjustment (Chapter 7B).

Transmission slips, shifts roughly, is noisy, or has no drive in forward or reverse gears

- [ ] There are many probable causes for the above problems, but the home mechanic should be concerned with only one possibility - fluid level. Before taking the vehicle to a dealer or transmission specialist, check the fluid level and condition of the fluid as described in Chapter 1. Correct the fluid level as necessary, or change the fluid and filter if needed. If the problem persists, professional help will be necessary.

7 Driveshafts

Clicking or knocking noise on turns (at slow speed on full-lock)

- [ ] Lack of constant velocity joint lubricant, possibly due to damaged gaiter (Chapter 8).
- [ ] Worn outer constant velocity joint (Chapter 8).

Vibration when accelerating or decelerating

- [ ] Worn inner constant velocity joint (Chapter 8).
- [ ] Bent or distorted driveshaft (Chapter 8).

8 Braking system

Note: *Before assuming that a brake problem exists, make sure that the tyres are in good condition and correctly inflated, that the front wheel alignment is correct, and that the vehicle is not loaded with weight in an unequal manner. Apart from checking the condition of all pipe and hose connections, any faults occurring on the anti-lock braking system should be referred to a Honda dealer for diagnosis.*

Vehicle pulls to one side under braking

- [ ] Worn, defective, damaged or contaminated front or rear brake pads/shoes on one side (Chapters 1 and 9).
- [ ] Seized or partially-seized front or rear brake caliper/wheel cylinder piston (Chapter 9).
- [ ] A mixture of brake pad/shoe lining materials fitted between sides (Chapter 9).
- [ ] Brake caliper mounting bolts loose (Chapter 9).
- [ ] Worn or damaged steering or suspension components (Chapters 1 and 10).

Noise (grinding or high-pitched squeal) when brakes applied

- [ ] Brake pad friction lining material worn down to metal backing (Chapters 1 and 9).
- [ ] Excessive corrosion of brake disc/drum - may be apparent after the vehicle has been standing for some time (Chapters 1 and 9).

Excessive brake pedal travel

- [ ] Faulty master cylinder (Chapter 9).
- [ ] Air in hydraulic system (Chapter 9).
- [ ] Faulty vacuum servo unit (Chapter 9).

Brake pedal feels spongy when depressed

- [ ] Air in hydraulic system (Chapter 9).
- [ ] Deteriorated flexible rubber brake hoses (Chapters 1 and 9).
- [ ] Master cylinder mountings loose (Chapter 9).
- [ ] Faulty master cylinder (Chapter 9).

8 Braking system (continued)

Excessive brake pedal effort required to stop vehicle
- ☐ Faulty vacuum servo unit (Chapter 9).
- ☐ Disconnected, damaged or insecure brake servo vacuum hose (Chapters 1 and 9).
- ☐ Primary or secondary hydraulic circuit failure (Chapter 9).
- ☐ Seized brake caliper/wheel cylinder piston(s) (Chapter 9).
- ☐ Brake pads/shoes incorrectly fitted (Chapter 9).
- ☐ Incorrect grade of brake pads/shoes fitted (Chapter 9).
- ☐ Brake pads/shoes contaminated (Chapter 9).

Judder felt through brake pedal or steering wheel when braking
- ☐ Excessive run-out or distortion of brake disc/drum (Chapter 9).
- ☐ Brake pad/shoe linings worn (Chapters 1 and 9).
- ☐ Brake caliper mounting bolts loose (Chapter 9).
- ☐ Wear in suspension or steering components or mountings (Chapters 1 and 10).

Brakes binding
- ☐ Seized brake caliper/wheel cylinder piston(s) (Chapter 9).
- ☐ Incorrectly-adjusted handbrake mechanism (Chapter 9).
- ☐ Faulty master cylinder (Chapter 9).

Rear wheels locking under normal braking
- ☐ Seized brake caliper/wheel cylinder piston(s) (Chapter 9).
- ☐ Faulty brake pressure regulator (Chapter 9).

9 Suspension and steering

Note: *Before diagnosing suspension or steering faults, be sure that the trouble is not due to incorrect tyre pressures, mixtures of tyre types, or binding brakes.*

Vehicle pulls to one side
- ☐ Defective tyre (Chapter 1).
- ☐ Excessive wear in suspension or steering components (Chapters 1 and 10).
- ☐ Incorrect front wheel alignment (Chapter 10).
- ☐ Accident damage to steering or suspension components (Chapters 1 and 10).

Wheel wobble and vibration
- ☐ Front roadwheels out of balance (vibration felt mainly through the steering wheel) (Chapter 10).
- ☐ Rear roadwheels out of balance (vibration felt throughout the vehicle) (Chapter 10).
- ☐ Roadwheels damaged or distorted (Chapter 10).
- ☐ Faulty or damaged tyre (Chapter 1).
- ☐ Worn steering or suspension joints, bushes or components (Chapters 1 and 10).
- ☐ Wheel bolts loose (Chapter 10).

Excessive pitching and/or rolling around corners, or during braking
- ☐ Defective shock absorbers (Chapters 1 and 10).
- ☐ Broken or weak coil spring and/or suspension component (Chapters 1 and 10).
- ☐ Worn or damaged anti-roll bar or mountings (Chapter 10).

Wandering or general instability
- ☐ Incorrect front wheel alignment (Chapter 10).
- ☐ Worn steering or suspension joints, bushes or components (Chapters 1 and 10).
- ☐ Roadwheels out of balance (Chapter 10).
- ☐ Faulty or damaged tyre (Chapter 1).
- ☐ Wheel bolts loose (Chapter 10).
- ☐ Defective shock absorbers (Chapters 1 and 10).

Excessively-stiff steering
- ☐ Lack of steering gear lubricant (Chapter 10).
- ☐ Seized track rod end balljoint or suspension balljoint (Chapters 1 and 10).
- ☐ Broken or incorrectly adjusted auxiliary drivebelt (Chapter 1).
- ☐ Incorrect front wheel alignment (Chapter 10).
- ☐ Steering rack or column bent or damaged (Chapter 10).

Excessive play in steering
- ☐ Worn steering column universal joint(s) (Chapter 10).
- ☐ Worn steering track rod end balljoints (Chapters 1 and 10).
- ☐ Worn rack-and-pinion steering gear (Chapter 10).
- ☐ Worn steering or suspension joints, bushes or components (Chapters 1 and 10).

Lack of power assistance
- ☐ Broken or incorrectly-adjusted auxiliary drivebelt (Chapter 1).
- ☐ Incorrect power steering fluid level (Chapter 1).
- ☐ Restriction in power steering fluid hoses (Chapter 1).
- ☐ Faulty power steering pump (Chapter 10).
- ☐ Faulty rack-and-pinion steering gear (Chapter 10).

Tyre wear excessive

Tyres worn on inside or outside edges
- ☐ Tyres under-inflated (wear on both edges) (Chapter 1).
- ☐ Incorrect camber or castor angles (wear on one edge only) (Chapter 10).
- ☐ Worn steering or suspension joints, bushes or components (Chapters 1 and 10).
- ☐ Excessively-hard cornering.
- ☐ Accident damage.

Tyre treads exhibit feathered edges
- ☐ Incorrect toe setting (Chapter 10).

Tyres worn in centre of tread
- ☐ Tyres over-inflated (Chapter 1).

Tyres worn on inside and outside edges
- ☐ Tyres under-inflated (Chapter 1).
- ☐ Worn shock absorbers (Chapters 1 and 10).

Tyres worn unevenly
- ☐ Tyres out of balance (Chapter 1).
- ☐ Excessive wheel or tyre run-out (Chapter 1).
- ☐ Worn shock absorbers (Chapters 1 and 10).
- ☐ Faulty tyre (Chapter 1).

10 Electrical system

Note: *For problems associated with the starting system, refer to the faults listed under "Engine" earlier.*

Battery will only hold a charge for a few days

- [ ] Battery defective internally (Chapter 5).
- [ ] Battery electrolyte level low - where applicable (Chapter 1).
- [ ] Battery terminal connections loose or corroded (Chapter 1).
- [ ] Auxiliary drivebelt worn - or incorrectly adjusted (Chapter 1).
- [ ] Alternator not charging at correct output (Chapter 5).
- [ ] Alternator or voltage regulator faulty (Chapter 5).
- [ ] Short-circuit causing continual battery drain (Chapters 5 and 12).

Ignition/no-charge warning light remains illuminated with engine running

- [ ] Auxiliary drivebelt broken, worn, or incorrectly adjusted (Chapter 1).
- [ ] Alternator brushes worn, sticking, or dirty (Chapter 5).
- [ ] Alternator brush springs weak or broken (Chapter 5).
- [ ] Internal fault in alternator or voltage regulator (Chapter 5).
- [ ] Disconnected or loose wiring in charging circuit (Chapter 5).

Ignition/no-charge warning light fails to come on

- [ ] Warning light bulb blown (Chapter 12).
- [ ] Disconnected or loose wiring in warning light circuit (Chapter 12).
- [ ] Alternator faulty (Chapter 5).

Lights inoperative

- [ ] Bulb blown (Chapter 12).
- [ ] Corrosion of bulb or bulbholder contacts (Chapter 12).
- [ ] Blown fuse (Chapter 12).
- [ ] Faulty relay (Chapter 12).
- [ ] Broken, loose, or disconnected wiring (Chapter 12).
- [ ] Faulty switch (Chapter 12).

Instrument readings inaccurate or erratic

Instrument readings increase with engine speed

- [ ] Faulty voltage regulator (Chapter 12).

Fuel or temperature gauges give no reading

- [ ] Faulty gauge sender unit (Chapters 3 and 4).
- [ ] Wiring open-circuit (Chapter 12).
- [ ] Faulty gauge (Chapter 12).

Fuel or temperature gauges give maximum reading

- [ ] Faulty gauge sender unit (Chapters 3 and 4).
- [ ] Wiring short-circuit (Chapter 12).
- [ ] Faulty gauge (Chapter 12).

Horn inoperative, or unsatisfactory in operation

Horn operates all the time

- [ ] Horn contacts bridged or horn push stuck down (Chapter 12).

Horn fails to operate

- [ ] Blown fuse (Chapter 12).
- [ ] Cable or cable connections loose or disconnected (Chapter 12).
- [ ] Faulty horn (Chapter 12).

Horn emits intermittent or unsatisfactory sound

- [ ] Cable connections loose (Chapter 12).
- [ ] Horn mountings loose (Chapter 12).
- [ ] Faulty horn (Chapter 12).

Windscreen/tailgate wipers inoperative, or unsatisfactory in operation

Wipers fail to operate, or operate very slowly

- [ ] Wiper blades stuck to screen, or linkage seized or binding (Chapters 1 and 12).

- [ ] Blown fuse (Chapter 12).
- [ ] Cable or cable connections loose or disconnected (Chapter 12).
- [ ] Faulty relay (Chapter 12).
- [ ] Faulty wiper motor (Chapter 12).

Wiper blades sweep over the wrong area of the glass

- [ ] Wiper arms incorrectly positioned on spindles (Chapter 1).
- [ ] Excessive wear of wiper linkage (Chapter 12).
- [ ] Wiper motor or linkage mountings loose or insecure (Chapter 12).

Wiper blades fail to clean the glass effectively

- [ ] Wiper blade rubbers worn or perished (Chapter 1).
- [ ] Wiper arm springs broken, or arm pivots seized (Chapter 12).
- [ ] Insufficient windscreen washer additive to adequately remove road film (Chapter 1).

Windscreen/tailgate washers inoperative, or unsatisfactory in operation

One or more washer jets inoperative

- [ ] Blocked washer jet (Chapter 1).
- [ ] Disconnected, kinked or restricted fluid hose (Chapter 12).
- [ ] Insufficient fluid in washer reservoir (Chapter 1).

Washer pump fails to operate

- [ ] Broken or disconnected wiring or connections (Chapter 12).
- [ ] Blown fuse (Chapter 12).
- [ ] Faulty washer switch (Chapter 12).
- [ ] Faulty washer pump (Chapter 12).

Washer pump runs for some time before fluid is emitted from jets

- [ ] Faulty one-way valve in fluid supply hose (Chapter 12).

Electric windows inoperative, or unsatisfactory in operation

Window glass will only move in one direction

- [ ] Faulty switch (Chapter 12).

Window glass slow to move

- [ ] Regulator seized or damaged, or in need of lubrication (Chapter 11).
- [ ] Door internal components or trim fouling regulator (Chapter 11).
- [ ] Faulty motor (Chapter 11).

Window glass fails to move

- [ ] Blown fuse (Chapter 12).
- [ ] Faulty relay (Chapter 12).
- [ ] Broken or disconnected wiring or connections (Chapter 12).
- [ ] Faulty motor (Chapter 11).

Central locking system inoperative, or unsatisfactory in operation

Complete system failure

- [ ] Blown fuse (Chapter 12).
- [ ] Faulty relay (Chapter 12).
- [ ] Broken or disconnected wiring or connections (Chapter 12).

Latch locks but will not unlock, or unlocks but won't lock

- [ ] Faulty switch (Chapter 12).
- [ ] Broken or disconnected latch operating rods or levers (Chapter 11).
- [ ] Faulty relay (Chapter 12).

One solenoid/motor fails to operate

- [ ] Broken or disconnected wiring or connections (Chapter 12).
- [ ] Faulty solenoid/motor (Chapter 11).
- [ ] Broken, binding or disconnected latch operating rods or levers (Chapter 11).
- [ ] Fault in door latch (Chapter 11).

A

ABS (Anti-lock brake system) A system, usually electronically controlled, that senses incipient wheel lockup during braking and relieves hydraulic pressure at wheels that are about to skid.

Air bag An inflatable bag hidden in the steering wheel (driver's side) or the dash or glovebox (passenger side). In a head-on collision, the bags inflate, preventing the driver and front passenger from being thrown forward into the steering wheel or windscreen.

Air cleaner A metal or plastic housing, containing a filter element, which removes dust and dirt from the air being drawn into the engine.

Air filter element The actual filter in an air cleaner system, usually manufactured from pleated paper and requiring renewal at regular intervals.

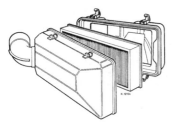

Air filter

Allen key A hexagonal wrench which fits into a recessed hexagonal hole.

Alligator clip A long-nosed spring-loaded metal clip with meshing teeth. Used to make temporary electrical connections.

Alternator A component in the electrical system which converts mechanical energy from a drivebelt into electrical energy to charge the battery and to operate the starting system, ignition system and electrical accessories.

Ampere (amp) A unit of measurement for the flow of electric current. One amp is the amount of current produced by one volt acting through a resistance of one ohm.

Anaerobic sealer A substance used to prevent bolts and screws from loosening. Anaerobic means that it does not require oxygen for activation. The Loctite brand is widely used.

Antifreeze A substance (usually ethylene glycol) mixed with water, and added to a vehicle's cooling system, to prevent freezing of the coolant in winter. Antifreeze also contains chemicals to inhibit corrosion and the formation of rust and other deposits that would tend to clog the radiator and coolant passages and reduce cooling efficiency.

Anti-seize compound A coating that reduces the risk of seizing on fasteners that are subjected to high temperatures, such as exhaust manifold bolts and nuts.

Asbestos A natural fibrous mineral with great heat resistance, commonly used in the composition of brake friction materials. Asbestos is a health hazard and the dust created by brake systems should never be inhaled or ingested.

Axle A shaft on which a wheel revolves, or which revolves with a wheel. Also, a solid beam that connects the two wheels at one end of the vehicle. An axle which also transmits power to the wheels is known as a live axle.

Axleshaft A single rotating shaft, on either side of the differential, which delivers power from the final drive assembly to the drive wheels. Also called a driveshaft or a halfshaft.

B

Ball bearing An anti-friction bearing consisting of a hardened inner and outer race with hardened steel balls between two races.

Bearing The curved surface on a shaft or in a bore, or the part assembled into either, that permits relative motion between them with minimum wear and friction.

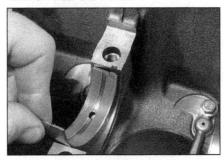

Bearing

Big-end bearing The bearing in the end of the connecting rod that's attached to the crankshaft.

Bleed nipple A valve on a brake wheel cylinder, caliper or other hydraulic component that is opened to purge the hydraulic system of air. Also called a bleed screw.

Brake bleeding Procedure for removing air from lines of a hydraulic brake system.

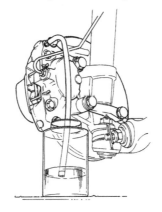

Brake bleeding

Brake disc The component of a disc brake that rotates with the wheels.

Brake drum The component of a drum brake that rotates with the wheels.

Brake linings The friction material which contacts the brake disc or drum to retard the vehicle's speed. The linings are bonded or riveted to the brake pads or shoes.

Brake pads The replaceable friction pads that pinch the brake disc when the brakes are applied. Brake pads consist of a friction material bonded or riveted to a rigid backing plate.

Brake shoe The crescent-shaped carrier to which the brake linings are mounted and which forces the lining against the rotating drum during braking.

Braking systems For more information on braking systems, consult the *Haynes Automotive Brake Manual*.

Breaker bar A long socket wrench handle providing greater leverage.

Bulkhead The insulated partition between the engine and the passenger compartment.

C

Caliper The non-rotating part of a disc-brake assembly that straddles the disc and carries the brake pads. The caliper also contains the hydraulic components that cause the pads to pinch the disc when the brakes are applied. A caliper is also a measuring tool that can be set to measure inside or outside dimensions of an object.

Camshaft A rotating shaft on which a series of cam lobes operate the valve mechanisms. The camshaft may be driven by gears, by sprockets and chain or by sprockets and a belt.

Canister A container in an evaporative emission control system; contains activated charcoal granules to trap vapours from the fuel system.

Canister

Carburettor A device which mixes fuel with air in the proper proportions to provide a desired power output from a spark ignition internal combustion engine.

Castellated Resembling the parapets along the top of a castle wall. For example, a castellated balljoint stud nut.

Castor In wheel alignment, the backward or forward tilt of the steering axis. Castor is positive when the steering axis is inclined rearward at the top.

Catalytic converter A silencer-like device in the exhaust system which converts certain pollutants in the exhaust gases into less harmful substances.

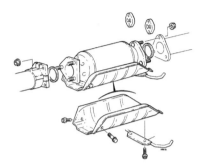

Catalytic converter

Circlip A ring-shaped clip used to prevent endwise movement of cylindrical parts and shafts. An internal circlip is installed in a groove in a housing; an external circlip fits into a groove on the outside of a cylindrical piece such as a shaft.

Clearance The amount of space between two parts. For example, between a piston and a cylinder, between a bearing and a journal, etc.

Coil spring A spiral of elastic steel found in various sizes throughout a vehicle, for example as a springing medium in the suspension and in the valve train.

Compression Reduction in volume, and increase in pressure and temperature, of a gas, caused by squeezing it into a smaller space.

Compression ratio The relationship between cylinder volume when the piston is at top dead centre and cylinder volume when the piston is at bottom dead centre.

Constant velocity (CV) joint A type of universal joint that cancels out vibrations caused by driving power being transmitted through an angle.

Core plug A disc or cup-shaped metal device inserted in a hole in a casting through which core was removed when the casting was formed. Also known as a freeze plug or expansion plug.

Crankcase The lower part of the engine block in which the crankshaft rotates.

Crankshaft The main rotating member, or shaft, running the length of the crankcase, with offset "throws" to which the connecting rods are attached.

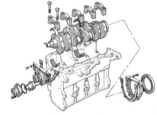

Crankshaft assembly

Crocodile clip See Alligator clip

D

Diagnostic code Code numbers obtained by accessing the diagnostic mode of an engine management computer. This code can be used to determine the area in the system where a malfunction may be located.

Disc brake A brake design incorporating a rotating disc onto which brake pads are squeezed. The resulting friction converts the energy of a moving vehicle into heat.

Double-overhead cam (DOHC) An engine that uses two overhead camshafts, usually one for the intake valves and one for the exhaust valves.

Drivebelt(s) The belt(s) used to drive accessories such as the alternator, water pump, power steering pump, air conditioning compressor, etc. off the crankshaft pulley.

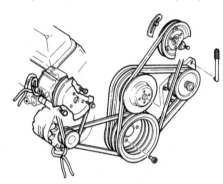

Accessory drivebelts

Driveshaft Any shaft used to transmit motion. Commonly used when referring to the axleshafts on a front wheel drive vehicle.

Drum brake A type of brake using a drum-shaped metal cylinder attached to the inner surface of the wheel. When the brake pedal is pressed, curved brake shoes with friction linings press against the inside of the drum to slow or stop the vehicle.

E

EGR valve A valve used to introduce exhaust gases into the intake air stream.

Electronic control unit (ECU) A computer which controls (for instance) ignition and fuel injection systems, or an anti-lock braking system. For more information refer to the *Haynes Automotive Electrical and Electronic Systems Manual*.

Electronic Fuel Injection (EFI) A computer controlled fuel system that distributes fuel through an injector located in each intake port of the engine.

Emergency brake A braking system, independent of the main hydraulic system, that can be used to slow or stop the vehicle if the primary brakes fail, or to hold the vehicle stationary even though the brake pedal isn't depressed. It usually consists of a hand lever that actuates either front or rear brakes mechanically through a series of cables and linkages. Also known as a handbrake or parking brake.

Endfloat The amount of lengthwise movement between two parts. As applied to a crankshaft, the distance that the crankshaft can move forward and back in the cylinder block.

Engine management system (EMS) A computer controlled system which manages the fuel injection and the ignition systems in an integrated fashion.

Exhaust manifold A part with several passages through which exhaust gases leave the engine combustion chambers and enter the exhaust pipe.

F

Fan clutch A viscous (fluid) drive coupling device which permits variable engine fan speeds in relation to engine speeds.

Feeler blade A thin strip or blade of hardened steel, ground to an exact thickness, used to check or measure clearances between parts.

Feeler blade

Firing order The order in which the engine cylinders fire, or deliver their power strokes, beginning with the number one cylinder.

Flywheel A heavy spinning wheel in which energy is absorbed and stored by means of momentum. On cars, the flywheel is attached to the crankshaft to smooth out firing impulses.

Free play The amount of travel before any action takes place. The "looseness" in a linkage, or an assembly of parts, between the initial application of force and actual movement. For example, the distance the brake pedal moves before the pistons in the master cylinder are actuated.

Fuse An electrical device which protects a circuit against accidental overload. The typical fuse contains a soft piece of metal which is calibrated to melt at a predetermined current flow (expressed as amps) and break the circuit.

Fusible link A circuit protection device consisting of a conductor surrounded by heat-resistant insulation. The conductor is smaller than the wire it protects, so it acts as the weakest link in the circuit. Unlike a blown fuse, a failed fusible link must frequently be cut from the wire for replacement.

G

Gap The distance the spark must travel in jumping from the centre electrode to the side electrode in a spark plug. Also refers to the spacing between the points in a contact breaker assembly in a conventional points-type ignition, or to the distance between the reluctor or rotor and the pickup coil in an electronic ignition.

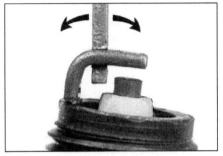

Adjusting spark plug gap

Gasket Any thin, soft material - usually cork, cardboard, asbestos or soft metal - installed between two metal surfaces to ensure a good seal. For instance, the cylinder head gasket seals the joint between the block and the cylinder head.

Gasket

Gauge An instrument panel display used to monitor engine conditions. A gauge with a movable pointer on a dial or a fixed scale is an analogue gauge. A gauge with a numerical readout is called a digital gauge.

H

Halfshaft A rotating shaft that transmits power from the final drive unit to a drive wheel, usually when referring to a live rear axle.

Harmonic balancer A device designed to reduce torsion or twisting vibration in the crankshaft. May be incorporated in the crankshaft pulley. Also known as a vibration damper.

Hone An abrasive tool for correcting small irregularities or differences in diameter in an engine cylinder, brake cylinder, etc.

Hydraulic tappet A tappet that utilises hydraulic pressure from the engine's lubrication system to maintain zero clearance (constant contact with both camshaft and valve stem). Automatically adjusts to variation in valve stem length. Hydraulic tappets also reduce valve noise.

I

Ignition timing The moment at which the spark plug fires, usually expressed in the number of crankshaft degrees before the piston reaches the top of its stroke.

Inlet manifold A tube or housing with passages through which flows the air-fuel mixture (carburettor vehicles and vehicles with throttle body injection) or air only (port fuel-injected vehicles) to the port openings in the cylinder head.

J

Jump start Starting the engine of a vehicle with a discharged or weak battery by attaching jump leads from the weak battery to a charged or helper battery.

L

Load Sensing Proportioning Valve (LSPV) A brake hydraulic system control valve that works like a proportioning valve, but also takes into consideration the amount of weight carried by the rear axle.

Locknut A nut used to lock an adjustment nut, or other threaded component, in place. For example, a locknut is employed to keep the adjusting nut on the rocker arm in position.

Lockwasher A form of washer designed to prevent an attaching nut from working loose.

M

MacPherson strut A type of front suspension system devised by Earle MacPherson at Ford of England. In its original form, a simple lateral link with the anti-roll bar creates the lower control arm. A long strut - an integral coil spring and shock absorber - is mounted between the body and the steering knuckle. Many modern so-called MacPherson strut systems use a conventional lower A-arm and don't rely on the anti-roll bar for location.

Multimeter An electrical test instrument with the capability to measure voltage, current and resistance.

N

NOx Oxides of Nitrogen. A common toxic pollutant emitted by petrol and diesel engines at higher temperatures.

O

Ohm The unit of electrical resistance. One volt applied to a resistance of one ohm will produce a current of one amp.

Ohmmeter An instrument for measuring electrical resistance.

O-ring A type of sealing ring made of a special rubber-like material; in use, the O-ring is compressed into a groove to provide the sealing action.

Overhead cam (ohc) engine An engine with the camshaft(s) located on top of the cylinder head(s).

Overhead valve (ohv) engine An engine with the valves located in the cylinder head, but with the camshaft located in the engine block.

Oxygen sensor A device installed in the engine exhaust manifold, which senses the oxygen content in the exhaust and converts this information into an electric current. Also called a Lambda sensor.

P

Phillips screw A type of screw head having a cross instead of a slot for a corresponding type of screwdriver.

Plastigage A thin strip of plastic thread, available in different sizes, used for measuring clearances. For example, a strip of Plastigage is laid across a bearing journal. The parts are assembled and dismantled; the width of the crushed strip indicates the clearance between journal and bearing.

Plastigage

Propeller shaft The long hollow tube with universal joints at both ends that carries power from the transmission to the differential on front-engined rear wheel drive vehicles.

Proportioning valve A hydraulic control valve which limits the amount of pressure to the rear brakes during panic stops to prevent wheel lock-up.

R

Rack-and-pinion steering A steering system with a pinion gear on the end of the steering shaft that mates with a rack (think of a geared wheel opened up and laid flat). When the steering wheel is turned, the pinion turns, moving the rack to the left or right. This movement is transmitted through the track rods to the steering arms at the wheels.

Radiator A liquid-to-air heat transfer device designed to reduce the temperature of the coolant in an internal combustion engine cooling system.

Refrigerant Any substance used as a heat transfer agent in an air-conditioning system. R-12 has been the principle refrigerant for many years; recently, however, manufacturers have begun using R-134a, a non-CFC substance that is considered less harmful to the ozone in the upper atmosphere.

Rocker arm A lever arm that rocks on a shaft or pivots on a stud. In an overhead valve engine, the rocker arm converts the upward movement of the pushrod into a downward movement to open a valve.

Rotor In a distributor, the rotating device inside the cap that connects the centre electrode and the outer terminals as it turns, distributing the high voltage from the coil secondary winding to the proper spark plug. Also, that part of an alternator which rotates inside the stator. Also, the rotating assembly of a turbocharger, including the compressor wheel, shaft and turbine wheel.

Runout The amount of wobble (in-and-out movement) of a gear or wheel as it's rotated. The amount a shaft rotates "out-of-true." The out-of-round condition of a rotating part.

S

Sealant A liquid or paste used to prevent leakage at a joint. Sometimes used in conjunction with a gasket.

Sealed beam lamp An older headlight design which integrates the reflector, lens and filaments into a hermetically-sealed one-piece unit. When a filament burns out or the lens cracks, the entire unit is simply replaced.

Serpentine drivebelt A single, long, wide accessory drivebelt that's used on some newer vehicles to drive all the accessories, instead of a series of smaller, shorter belts. Serpentine drivebelts are usually tensioned by an automatic tensioner.

Serpentine drivebelt

Shim Thin spacer, commonly used to adjust the clearance or relative positions between two parts. For example, shims inserted into or under bucket tappets control valve clearances. Clearance is adjusted by changing the thickness of the shim.

Slide hammer A special puller that screws into or hooks onto a component such as a shaft or bearing; a heavy sliding handle on the shaft bottoms against the end of the shaft to knock the component free.

Sprocket A tooth or projection on the periphery of a wheel, shaped to engage with a chain or drivebelt. Commonly used to refer to the sprocket wheel itself.

Starter inhibitor switch On vehicles with an automatic transmission, a switch that prevents starting if the vehicle is not in Neutral or Park.

Strut See MacPherson strut.

T

Tappet A cylindrical component which transmits motion from the cam to the valve stem, either directly or via a pushrod and rocker arm. Also called a cam follower.

Thermostat A heat-controlled valve that regulates the flow of coolant between the cylinder block and the radiator, so maintaining optimum engine operating temperature. A thermostat is also used in some air cleaners in which the temperature is regulated.

Thrust bearing The bearing in the clutch assembly that is moved in to the release levers by clutch pedal action to disengage the clutch. Also referred to as a release bearing.

Timing belt A toothed belt which drives the camshaft. Serious engine damage may result if it breaks in service.

Timing chain A chain which drives the camshaft.

Toe-in The amount the front wheels are closer together at the front than at the rear. On rear wheel drive vehicles, a slight amount of toe-in is usually specified to keep the front wheels running parallel on the road by offsetting other forces that tend to spread the wheels apart.

Toe-out The amount the front wheels are closer together at the rear than at the front. On front wheel drive vehicles, a slight amount of toe-out is usually specified.

Tools For full information on choosing and using tools, refer to the *Haynes Automotive Tools Manual*.

Tracer A stripe of a second colour applied to a wire insulator to distinguish that wire from another one with the same colour insulator.

Tune-up A process of accurate and careful adjustments and parts replacement to obtain the best possible engine performance.

Turbocharger A centrifugal device, driven by exhaust gases, that pressurises the intake air. Normally used to increase the power output from a given engine displacement, but can also be used primarily to reduce exhaust emissions (as on VW's "Umwelt" Diesel engine).

U

Universal joint or U-joint A double-pivoted connection for transmitting power from a driving to a driven shaft through an angle. A U-joint consists of two Y-shaped yokes and a cross-shaped member called the spider.

V

Valve A device through which the flow of liquid, gas, vacuum, or loose material in bulk may be started, stopped, or regulated by a movable part that opens, shuts, or partially obstructs one or more ports or passageways. A valve is also the movable part of such a device.

Valve clearance The clearance between the valve tip (the end of the valve stem) and the rocker arm or tappet. The valve clearance is measured when the valve is closed.

Vernier caliper A precision measuring instrument that measures inside and outside dimensions. Not quite as accurate as a micrometer, but more convenient.

Viscosity The thickness of a liquid or its resistance to flow.

Volt A unit for expressing electrical "pressure" in a circuit. One volt that will produce a current of one ampere through a resistance of one ohm.

W

Welding Various processes used to join metal items by heating the areas to be joined to a molten state and fusing them together. For more information refer to the *Haynes Automotive Welding Manual*.

Wiring diagram A drawing portraying the components and wires in a vehicle's electrical system, using standardised symbols. For more information refer to the *Haynes Automotive Electrical and Electronic Systems Manual*.

Note: *References throughout this index are in the form - "Chapter number" • "page number"*

Preserving Our Motoring Heritage

< *The Model J Duesenberg Derham Tourster. Only eight of these magnificent cars were ever built – this is the only example to be found outside the United States of America*

Almost every car you've ever loved, loathed or desired is gathered under one roof at the Haynes Motor Museum. Over 300 immaculately presented cars and motorbikes represent every aspect of our motoring heritage, from elegant reminders of bygone days, such as the superb Model J Duesenberg to curiosities like the bug-eyed BMW Isetta. There are also many old friends and flames. Perhaps you remember the 1959 Ford Popular that you did your courting in? The magnificent 'Red Collection' is a spectacle of classic sports cars including AC, Alfa Romeo, Austin Healey, Ferrari, Lamborghini, Maserati, MG, Riley, Porsche and Triumph.

A Perfect Day Out

Each and every vehicle at the Haynes Motor Museum has played its part in the history and culture of Motoring. Today, they make a wonderful spectacle and a great day out for all the family. Bring the kids, bring Mum and Dad, but above all bring your camera to capture those golden memories for ever. You will also find an impressive array of motoring memorabilia, a comfortable 70 seat video cinema and one of the most extensive transport book shops in Britain. The Pit Stop Cafe serves everything from a cup of tea to wholesome, home-made meals or, if you prefer, you can enjoy the large picnic area nestled in the beautiful rural surroundings of Somerset.

> *John Haynes O.B.E., Founder and Chairman of the museum at the wheel of a Haynes Light 12.*

< *Graham Hill's Lola Cosworth Formula 1 car next to a 1934 Riley Sports.*

The Museum is situated on the A359 Yeovil to Frome road at Sparkford, just off the A303 in Somerset. It is about 40 miles south of Bristol, and 25 minutes drive from the M5 intersection at Taunton.

Open 9.30am - 5.30pm (10.00am - 4.00pm Winter) 7 days a week, *except Christmas Day, Boxing Day and New Years Day*
Special rates available for schools, coach parties and outings Charitable Trust No. 292048